"Bril, Kell, and Rasche have edited a timely, insightful, and deeply thought-provoking volume on a topic that sits right at the frontier of our current knowledge: the interrelation of sustainable finance and technology. It fills an important void by focusing on the real-world implementation of urgently needed solutions to our most pressing sustainability challenges. This book, therefore, is an absolutely essential read for companies, executives, and investors who are genuinely interested in bringing about transformational ESG change in their organizations and indeed, within society at large."

Ioannis Ioannou, *London Business School*

"A great book and blueprint for our transition to a more sustainable future."

Rose Marcario, *former CEO Patagonia*

"As the founder Executive Director of the UN Global Compact, Georg Kell's unique insights have shaped the discourse in responsible business since the inception of the Global Compact in 2000. In this publication, Georg Kell and colleagues aptly capture the opportunities in innovative financing, technologies and accountability frameworks that raise the ambition for the private sector."

Sanda Ojiambo, *CEO and Executive Director, UN Global Compact*

"The climate and sustainability challenge is the toughest, and most important, one modern society needs to address. But what made society modern is the force of technology. Reconciling the urgency of one with the potential (and peril) of the other is a critical imperative. This anthology draws together key voices to help bridge that gap."

Azeem Azhar, *author,* Exponential

"Have you been wondering about ESG and how technology might be part of the solution? Then this might be a worthwhile read for you. My colleagues across asset management and academia have written the book with complementing chapters about futuristic views on technology impact, paired with how asset managers might integrate technology and digitalisation in the still virgin ESG analytic work. The book also raises important questions about the ESG implications on reverse globalisation and the impact on geopolitics – relevance underlined by the recent events in Ukraine."

Peter Branner, *Chief Investment Officer APG Asset Management*

Sustainability, Technology, and Finance

This book explores the swiftly emerging nexus between sustainability, finance, and technology.

Leading practitioners and academic thought leaders reflect on the ways in which technology and digitalization shape how sustainable finance professionals address environmental, social, and governance (ESG) issues. Together, the contributors identify three spheres in which technology shapes how investors make sense of such issues:

- ESG and technology: finance professionals need to know about how technological innovations, such as chemical recycling for plastics, in the real economy shape firms' ESG performance;
- ESG through technology: technological developments, such as AI and blockchain, can enable finance professionals to offer more fine-grained ESG analyses; and
- ESG as technology: the ESG agenda itself is influenced by technological developments that are not well understood by practitioners (e.g., data mining for Bitcoin creating significant emissions).

Using practically relevant examples and recent insights from people working in the field, the book explores the linkages between sustainability, technology, and finance in different contexts and shows how practitioners can accelerate needed change processes.

This book primarily addresses practitioners in companies and investment firms as well as students enrolled in executive education and MBA programs.

Herman Bril is Managing Director & Head of Responsible Investment at PSP Investments. He has 30 years of experience in international financial institutions across investment management, derivatives trading, treasury, and development finance.

Georg Kell is Chairman of Arabesque, a technology company that uses AI and big data to assess sustainability performance, and Chairman of the Volkswagen Sustainability Council. Georg founded the UN Global Compact, the world's largest corporate sustainability initiative. He also oversaw the launch of the PRI, PRME, and SSE.

Andreas Rasche is Professor of Business in Society at the Centre for Sustainability at Copenhagen Business School (CBS) and Associate Dean for the CBS Full-Time MBA program. He has authored more than 60 academic articles in top international journals and published various cases on topics related to ESG and corporate sustainability.

Sustainability, Technology, and Finance

Rethinking How Markets Integrate ESG

Edited by

Herman Bril,
Georg Kell, and
Andreas Rasche

Routledge
Taylor & Francis Group
LONDON AND NEW YORK

Cover image: Getty Images/metamorworks

First published 2023
by Routledge
4 Park Square, Milton Park, Abingdon, Oxon OX14 4RN

and by Routledge
605 Third Avenue, New York, NY 10158

Routledge is an imprint of the Taylor & Francis Group, an informa business

British Library Cataloguing-in-Publication Data
A catalogue record for this book is available from the British Library

Library of Congress Cataloging-in-Publication Data
Names: Bril, Herman, 1967– editor. | Kell, Georg, editor. | Rasche, Andreas, editor.
Title: Sustainability, technology and finance : rethinking how markets integrate ESG / edited by Herman Bril, Georg Kell, and Andreas Rasche.
Description: Milton Park, Abingdon, Oxon ; New York, NY : Routledge, 2023. | Includes bibliographical references and index.
Subjects: LCSH: Sustainable development. | Economic development. | Appropriate technology.
Classification: LCC HC79.E5 S86666 2023 (print) | LCC HC79.E5 (ebook) | DDC 338.9/27—dc23/eng/20220622
LC record available at https://lccn.loc.gov/2022025894
LC ebook record available at https://lccn.loc.gov/2022025895

ISBN: 978-1-032-20056-9 (hbk)
ISBN: 978-1-032-20054-5 (pbk)
ISBN: 978-1-003-26203-9 (ebk)

DOI: 10.4324/9781003262039

Typeset in Minion
by Apex CoVantage, LLC

Contents

Figures

Tables

Boxes

Contributors

Inna Amesheva is Director ESG Research and Regulatory Solutions, ESG Book GmbH. With a diverse background in sustainability and entrepreneurship, Inna had the opportunity to build and scale a number of sustainability-focused ventures throughout Europe and Asia. In her current role as ESG Research Director at ESG Book a leading technology and sustainable intelligence solutions firm, Inna heads the development of the company's ESG regulatory service offering, in light of the fast-evolving sustainability disclosure landscape. Inna volunteers her free time as a UNSDSN Youth Senior Advisor, fostering youth-led projects and developing digital ecosystems to deliver the Sustainable Development Goals (SDGs). She is passionate about environmental sustainability and enhancing economic opportunity for all. Inna holds a PhD in International Climate Law and Policy from Hong Kong University Law School and an LLB from the University of Birmingham Law School.

Madelyn Antoncic is a Senior Fellow, New York University Development Research Institute and Director, Sustainable Economic and Climate Development (SECDEV) Initiative. She is a Member of the Board and Risk Committee of ACWA Power, KSA, and of the Board of S&P Global Ratings; and serves on the Editorial boards of the Journal of Risk Management in Financial Institutions and the Journal of A.I., Robotics & Workplace Automation. She was Senior Advisor to UNCTAD on SDG reporting; is former World Bank VP and Treasurer; and former CEO of SASB. She is known for her leadership in financial innovation and implementation of national climate-related disaster risk reduction and mitigation structures to help countries mitigate and transfer to the markets climate-related disaster and other risks. She has held leadership roles in large complex global financial institutions for over 30 years, having begun her career as a Federal Reserve economist. She is widely published on ESG issues and is an internationally recognized expert on risk and ESG; a frequent speaker at various fora including at the UN General Assembly SDG Biz Forum Plenary; and the subject of graduate school case studies concerning the Great Financial Crisis. She is the recipient of numerous awards; was listed among the 100 Most Influential People in Finance; and among the top thought leaders helping shape accounting in 2020 and beyond. She holds a PhD in Economics, a minor in Finance from NYU and was an Alfred P Sloan Foundation Doctoral Fellow.

Nina Arquint was appointed Chief Risk Officer at Swiss Re Corporate Solutions, effective 1 July 2019, and Member of the Corporate Solutions Executive Committee with effect from 1 January 2020. She joined Swiss Re Corporate Solutions from the Group Risk Management, where she was Head, Group Qualitative Risk Management, reporting to the Group CRO. She had the group-wide responsibility for the identification and oversight of emerging, operational, political, regulatory, and sustainability risk as well as information security. Prior to joining Swiss Re, Nina Arquint was Head of the Strategic Services Division and Member of the Executive Board of the Swiss Financial Markets Supervisory Authority FINMA.

Andreas Berger joined Swiss Re in March 2019 as Chief Executive Officer Corporate Solutions and Member of the Group Executive Committee. He started his insurance career in 1995 at Gerling Group, followed by various leadership positions at Boston Consulting Group. He returned to Gerling in 2004, as Head of Commercial Business and International Programs and Affinity Business. When Allianz Global Corporate & Specialty SE (AGCS) was created in 2006, Andreas Berger became its Global Head of Market Management & Communication. He most recently held the position of Chief Regions & Market Officer (Central & Eastern Europe, Mediterranean, Africa and Asia) at AGCS.

Andrea Bonime-Blanc is Founder/CEO of GEC Risk Advisory, a strategic governance, ESG, ethics and cyber advisor to business, NGOs, and government. A former global executive at Bertelsmann, Verint, and PSEG, she serves on several boards/advisory boards (Crisp, WireX, Cyber Future Foundation, Greenward Partners, Ethical Intelligence); is Independent Ethics Advisor to the Financial Oversight and Management Board for Puerto Rico; and a life member of the Council on Foreign Relations. She is a sought-after global keynote speaker, a professor of Cyber Leadership, Risk Oversight and Resilience at NYU, and author of many articles and books including *Gloom to Boom: How Leaders Transform Risk into Resilience and Value* (Routledge 2020).

Herman Bril is Managing Director & Head of Responsible Investment at PSP Investments since July 2022. With 30 years of experience in international financial institutions in multiple countries, Bril possesses broad-level expertise encompassing asset management, pension funds, life insurance, investment banking, derivatives trading, and treasury operations. Herman was the CEO of Arabesque Asset Management after a five-year stint as CIO at the UN Pension Fund in New York, where he successfully developed and implemented the fund's sustainable investment strategy.

Herbert Diess was born in Munich in 1958, and studied automotive engineering and mechanical engineering in his hometown. With a Doctorate in Engineering, he moved from the Technical University of Munich to Robert Bosch AG in 1989, where he most recently worked as Technical Managing Director of the Treto plant in Spain. In 1996, he followed the call of BMW AG and took on various management tasks in production, development, and technology at the Munich carmaker. In 1999, he took over the management of the plant in Birmingham, England, and then in Oxford, before being appointed head of BMW Motorcycles in 2003. In 2008, he became Board Member for Purchasing and Supplier Network, and finally in 2012, Board Member for Technical Development at BMW AG. In 2015, the Supervisory Board of Volkswagen AG appointed Dr. Diess as a member of the Group Board of Management of Volkswagen AG and Chairman of the Volkswagen brand. He was Chairman of the Board of Management of Volkswagen AG from April 2018 until August 2022.

Dante A. Disparte is Chief Strategy Officer and Head of Global Policy for Circle. He is also Founder and Chairman of Risk Cooperative and a globally recognized leader in risk, technology, and resilience. He was a former member of the Federal Emergency Management Agency's National Advisory Council, serves on the World Economic Forum's Digital Currency Governance Consortium, and is a life member of the Council on Foreign Relations. He has authored hundreds of articles and papers and contributed to numerous books, including co-authoring the acclaimed treatise *Global Risk Agility and Decision Making* (Macmillan 2016).

Eduard van Gelderen is Senior Vice President and Chief Investment Officer at PSP, overseeing the Total Fund strategy, responsible investment strategies, sponsor relations, and a knowledge-driven innovation portfolio. He is the chair of the AIMA Global Investor Board. He holds an MBA from Erasmus University, is a CFA and FRM charter holder, and received specific training at Insead, NYU, Stanford University, and MIT. Prior to joining PSP, Eduard held several senior-level positions at world-class organizations, including

SMD at UC Investments, CEO of APG Asset Management, and Deputy CIO of ING Investment Management.

Elias Ghanem is Global Head of Capgemini's Financial Services Market Intelligence, leading its thought leadership initiatives, including the acclaimed World Reports series related to the future of banking and insurance. Previously, Elias launched Telr, an online payment gateway, elected the "2014 Startup of the Year" in the Middle East. Elias served at Visa as APAC Head of Visa Consulting and at PayPal as regional MD in Southeast Asia and India, and the Middle East. A seasoned professional with extensive banking and payments experience, Elias sits on boards of several high-growth start-ups in Washington, Singapore, Barcelona, Beirut, and Dubai.

Bjørn K. Haugland is Co-Founder and Chief Executive Officer of Skift Business Climate Leaders. Skift is a business-led climate initiative with a mission to accelerate the transition to a low-carbon economy and support the government in delivering on its national climate commitments by 2030. Skift build networks of CEOs to drive systems transformation across their industries, at speed. Haugland is today a board member of The Peace Research Institute Oslo (PRIO), WWF, Sporveien, and Kezzler. Also, he is Member of the Advisory Board for Centre for Responsible Leadership. He is Co-Founder of Zeabuz, a new service for urban, emission-free, autonomous ferries; and Terravera, a tech foundation to make sustainability a reality by giving anyone insights to support their everyday decisions. He is Member of The Norwegian Board of Technology (NBT), which advises the Norwegian Parliament and government on new technology. Also, he is Member of Norwegian Academy of Technological Sciences. Haugland has an MSc in Naval Architecture—Marine Structures and Hydrodynamics—from The Norwegian Institute of Technology in Trondheim, and he attended the "Strategic International Leadership" program at International Institute for Management Development (IMD) and "Leading Digital Transformation" (INSEAD).

Lars Jaeger is a Swiss–German author, entrepreneur, financial theorist, and alternative investment manager. He writes on the history and philosophy of science and technology (has completed his tenth book in 2022) and has in the past also been an author on hedge funds, quantitative investing, and risk management. In his widely read blog as well as other media, he frequently writes on issues concerning scientific developments, new technologies, and their meaning for society. Jaeger has for many years been an influential voice in the hedge fund industry on fostering developments toward more transparency, liquidity, and cost-efficiency. He is the founder and CEO of Alternative

Beta Partners AG and currently serves GAM as Head of Alternative Risk Premia. Prior to that, he was a partner of Partners Group, where he was responsible for the hedge fund business and initiated the alternative beta business. Lars Jaeger holds a Doctorate Degree in Theoretical Physics from the Max Planck Institute for the Physics of Complex Systems, Dresden, and a master's degree in Physics from the University of Bonn. He is a CFA charterholder and financial risk manager (FRM). He is based in Zurich.

Georg Kell is Chairman of Arabesque, a technology company that uses AI and big data to assess sustainability performance relevant for investment analysis and decision-making. Also, he is Co-Chair of the DWS ESG Advisory Board and Speaker of the Volkswagen Sustainability Council. Georg Kell is the founding Director of the United Nations Global Compact. During his career of almost three decades at the United Nations, working directly with former Secretary Generals Kofi Annan and Ban Ki-moon, he built the UN Global Compact and oversaw the launch of its sister initiatives, including the Principles for Responsible Investing (PRI) and the Sustainable Stock Exchanges (SSE).

Winston Ma, CFA is Managing Partner and Co-Founder of CloudTree Ventures and Adjunct Professor at the NYU School of Law on sovereign wealth fund (SWF) topics. He serves as the board chairman of Mountain & Co. I Acquisition Corp., a Nasdaq-listed SPAC company. He is former Managing Director and Head of the North America office at China Investment Corporation (CIC) and Author of *The Hunt for Tech Unicorns—How Sovereign Funds Are Reshaping Investment in the Digital Economy* (2020). Prior to that, Ma served as Deputy Head of Equity Capital Markets at Barclays Capital, Vice President at J.P. Morgan Investment Banking, and Corporate Lawyer at Davis Polk & Wardwell LLP. He was selected as 2013 Young Global Leader at the World Economic Forum (WEF) and in 2014, he received the NYU Distinguished Alumni Award.

Christof Mascher has held several leadership positions within Allianz insurance group over the past 30 years and is currently acting as an independent director and senior advisor. He joined Allianz Austria in 1989, and after several positions in information management, he served as CFO and COO of the company. In 2006, he moved to Allianz Germany as COO. From 2009 until his retirement in 2020, he served as global COO at Allianz SE responsible for information technology, operations, and digitalization. Christof Mascher holds a Doctorate in Law from the University of Innsbruck and a MA in Philosophy from the University of Vienna.

Ashby Monk is Executive Director at Stanford University's Center for Sustainable Development and Global Competitiveness. Named by *CIO Magazine* as one of the most influential academics in the institutional investing world, his work has appeared in *the Economist, the New York Times, the Wall Street Journal, Financial Times, Institutional Investor, Reuters*, and *Forbes*, among a variety of other media. He focuses on design and governance of institutional investment organizations and holds a Doctorate in Economic Geography from Oxford University, a master's degree in International Economics from the Universite de Paris I—Pantheon Sorbonne, and a bachelor's degree in Economics from Princeton University.

Luis Neves was born in Portugal. In 1975, he finished his university degree in history. In 1998, he started an international career in Switzerland, and developed an intensive activity at European and international levels. In May 2004, he joined the Corporate Sustainability and Citizenship Department from Deutsche Telekom. In 2008, he was assigned to the position of Vice President Corporate Responsibility and in January 2013, he was appointed Senior Vice President Group Climate Change and Sustainability Officer. In 2006, he was elected Chairman of GeSI. Under his leadership, GeSI became a globally recognized industry organization and a "thought industry leader" in the area of climate change. Luis has been holding positions in many international organizations and initiatives.

David Ouellet is SVP and Chief Technology and Data Officer at PSP Investments. In this capacity, he is focused on sustaining PSP's growth with effective tools and technologies that meet and exceed the future of technological trends, including digital innovation, data and analytic, cloud and artificial intelligence solutions. Previously, David was Vice President and Head, Strategic and Business Planning. Prior to joining PSP, David worked in Technology Consulting at KPMG for over ten years, two of which were in China. He holds a bachelor's degree in Commerce from McGill University and is a Chartered Professional Accountant.

Andreas Rasche is Professor of Business in Society at the Centre for Corporate Sustainability at Copenhagen Business School (CBS). He acts as Associate Dean for the CBS MBA program and is Visiting Professor at the Stockholm School of Economics. He has authored more than 50 academic articles in international top journals and published various cases on topics related to ESG and corporate sustainability. He has authored and edited numerous well-known books, such as *The United Nations Global Compact: Achievements, Trends, and Challenges* (Cambridge University Press) and *Building the Responsible Enterprise* (Stanford University Press). He is Associate Editor of *Business Ethics Quarterly* and joined Copenhagen Business School from Warwick Business School in 2012.

Dane Rook is Research Engineer at Stanford University's Center for Sustainable Development and Global Competitiveness. His work explores the intersection of machine intelligence and long-term investing. Previously, he was Researcher at Kensho (an AI-start-up acquired by S&P) and J.P. Morgan. He holds a doctorate from the University of Oxford (as a Clarendon Scholar), a master's degree from the University of Cambridge, and a bachelor's degree from the University of Michigan. Dr. Rook is an advisor to technology start-ups in the US and Europe.

Asgeir J. Sørensen obtained an MSc degree in Marine Technology in 1988 from NTNU, and PhD in Engineering Cybernetics from NTNU in 1993. In 1989–1992, Sørensen was employed at MARINTEK. In the years 1993–2002, Sørensen was employed in various positions in the ABB Group. In 2002, Sørensen become co-founder of the company, Marine Cybernetics AS, where he was acting as President and Chief Executive Officer (CEO) until June 2010. In 2012, 2015, and 2017, Sørensen became a co-founder of the companies Ecotone AS, Eelume AS, SESx Marine Technologies AS, and Zeabuz AS, respectively. Since 1999, Sørensen has held the position of Professor of Marine Control Systems at the Department of Marine Technology, NTNU. He is currently the key scientist and Director of the NTNU AMOS and VISTA CAROS.

Asoka Wöhrmann served as CEO and Chairman of the Managing Directors of DWS Group from November 2018 until June 2022. Before rejoining DWS in 2018 as CEO, Asoka was the Head of the Private Client business in Germany of the Private & Commercial Bank (PCB) of Deutsche Bank for three years. He had previously spent 17 years at DWS, working in various managerial functions, including serving as its global Chief Investment Officer. He also held leading positions within the Fixed Income, Multi Asset, Absolute Return and Currency divisions of the asset manager's fund platform. Asoka started his career as a portfolio manager in 1998. Before joining DWS, he was a post-graduate lecturer at the Technical University Vienna and the University of Magdeburg.

Foreword

by Lord Browne of Madingley

We have come a long way since shareholder value theory dominated the business world. This was the widely held belief that the duty of business leaders was to make as much profit as possible for shareholders and to look after the interests of other stakeholders only as much as the law required. Corporate social responsibility (CSR) was an early response to the widespread dissatisfaction, which emerged as a result of this endemic corporate disinterest for wider societal good. It was well intentioned, but it failed because it was detached from companies' core commercial activity. Real change was not delivered and the bond of trust between business and society was weakened as a consequence.

Environmental, Social, and Governance (ESG) is the modern-day successor of CSR, but it is not simply a rebrand of the old approach. It is fundamentally different because it is anchored in a company's performance. ESG frameworks are increasingly used around the world, and there are multiple providers of ratings—measures of how well a company is doing in attending to the environment, societal goals, and its own governance. The most effective frameworks feature hard-edged targets which are established independently and performance which is assessed independently, on a regular basis. Unlike CSR, when ESG is done well, companies communicate performance to stakeholders regularly and transparently, and corporate strategy is shaped as a result. The business world is coming to understand that positive progress on ESG measures leads to sustainable companies which perform sustainably.

Things are moving quickly and societal attitudes are changing. Sustainable finance has emerged as one of the most significant forces, redefining markets and encouraging positive ESG behaviors in all areas of society, particularly with regard to the environment and climate change. Governments have set net-zero targets and are coming under increasing pressure to set a carbon price which would provide the proper framework to stimulate sustainable investing at scale. Consumers are demanding information about the goods and services they consume and are driving significant changes to products and supply chains. Business leaders and corporate executives are rapidly seeing the benefits to be derived from supporting actual measurable actions within their companies such as science-based targets, against which they can track greenhouse gas reductions. Investors, for their part, are responding to pressure from shareholders and taking a more nuanced approach, avoiding simplistic actions such as divestment of high-carbon assets and taking more responsibility for the impact of their investments by applying pressure on corporate strategies and executive compensation to drive emissions down.

I am an engineer and I am a businessman. It is because of both that I am an optimist. Engineering sits at the interface between the lab and the market, and business is the engine of human progress. I have seen firsthand how breakthroughs in engineering and technology can change people's lives for the better, and I am a firm believer in the power of business to improve the human condition. This book begins by examining the role that technology has played in the history of human development and goes on to examine how humanity has channeled the power of technology and finance to change the world in which we live. Importantly, it then turns to the question of how these forces, which have brought about so much good, can be harnessed to bring about sustainability in all areas of human activity.

A variety of new technologies are being developed, which have the power to change the world for the better in the environmental, energy, life sciences, and agricultural spheres to name but a few. But when new technologies are used to integrate ESG considerations into investors' decision-making and the way a company operates on a day-to-day basis, systemic change is achieved. Exploring this idea, they make a distinction between ESG *and* technology, and ESG *as and through* technology—a phenomenon which will be recognizable to anyone currently engaged in corporate sustainability.

Building on their 2021 volume on sustainable finance and ESG, Bril, Kell, and Rasche now turn their attention to technology and its many interdependencies. In this volume, they delicately interweave the theoretical discussion about sustainability, finance, and technology with real-world examples and practitioner insights. I have long had a preoccupation with the real-world delivery of solutions to society's problems and this collection makes a very significant contribution to that endeavor.

Abbreviations

3DP	Three-Dimensional Printing
4IR	Fourth Industrial Revolution
AI	Artificial Intelligence
AOMS	Centre for Autonomous Marine Operations and Systems
APAC	Asia Pacific
API	Application Programming Interface
AR	Augmented Reality
AUD	Australian Dollar
AUM	Assets Under Management
AUV	Autonomous Underwater Vehicles
B2B2C	Business-to-Business-to-Consumer
BCI	Brain–Computer Interface
CAPM	Capital Asset Pricing Model
CBDC	Central Bank Digital Currencies
CCS	Carbon Capture Storage
CCUS	Carbon Capture Use and Storage
CDP	Carbon Disclosure Project
CDSB	Carbon Disclosure Standards Board
CEO	Chief Executive Officer
CFC	Chlorofluorocarbon
CO_2	Carbon Dioxide
COP	Conference of the Parties
CRISPR	Clustered Regularly Interspaced Short Palindromic Repeats
CSR	Corporate Sustainability Reports
CSRD	Corporate Sustainability Reporting Directive
D&O	Directors and Officers
DAO	Decentralized Autonomous Organizations

DARPA	Defense Advanced Research Projects Agency
DDOS	Distributed Denial of Service
DEI	Diversity, Equity, and Inclusiveness
DeFi	Decentralized Finance
DLT	Distributed Ledger Technology
DNA	Deoxyribonucleic Acid
DNSH	Do No Significant Harm
DTA	Digital Twin Aggregates
DTI	Digital Twin Instances
DwP	Digital with Purpose
D&O	Directors and Officers
EU	European Union
ESG	Environmental, Social, Governance
ESGT	Environmental, Social, Governance, Technology
ESMA	European Securities Market Authority
ESS	Energy Storage System
ETF	Exchange Traded Fund
GDP	Gross Domestic Product
GDPR	General Data Protection Regulation
GeSI	Global Enabling Sustainability Initiative
GFC	Great Financial Crisis
GHG	Greenhouse Gas
GPS	Global Positioning System
GRI	Global Reporting Initiative
GTAC	Global Thresholds & Allocations Council
HCFC	Hydrochlorofluorocarbon
HFC	Hydrofluorocarbon
HNWI	High Net-Worth-Individual
UHNWI	Ultra-High-Net-Worth-Individual
IABS	International Accounting Standards Board
ICT	Information and Communication Technology
IEA	International Energy Agency
IFRS	International Financial Reporting Standards
IIRC	International Integrated Reporting Council
ILO	International Labour Organisation
IMO	International Maritime Organization
IOSCO	International Organization of Security Commissioners
IoT	Internet of Things
IP	Intellectual Property
IPCC	Intergovernmental Panel on Climate Change
IRGC	International Risk Governance Center
ISSB	International Sustainability Standards Board

IT	Information Technology
ITU	International Telecommunication Union
IWAI	Impact Weighted Accounts Initiative
IRGC	International Risk Governance Center
KYC	Know Your Client
LOC	Labs on a Chip
ML	Machine Learning
MW	Megawatt
MWh	Megawatt Hour
NFRD	Non-Financial Reporting Directive
NGFS	Network for Greening the Financial System
NGO	Non-Governmental Organization
NLP	Natural Language Processing
NTNU	Norwegian University of Science and Technology
OECD	Organisation for Economic Co-operation and Development
OMS	Order Management System
PBoC	People's Bank of China
PMS	Portfolio Management System
PV	Photovoltaic
PRI	Principles for Responsible Investment
P&L	Profit and Loss
ROV	Remotely Operated Vehicles
RPA	Robotic Process Automation
R&D	Research and Development
SaaS	Software as a Service
SASB	Sustainability Accounting Standards Board
SDG	Sustainable Development Goals
SDI	Sustainable Development Investments
SEC	Securities and Exchange Commission
SFDR	Sustainable Finance Disclosure Regulation
SI	Sustainable Investing
SME	Small- and Medium-Sized Enterprise
SRTI	Ship Recycling Transparency Initiative
SWF	Sovereign Wealth Fund
TCFD	Task Force on Climate-Related Financial Disclosures
ToC	Theory of Change
TWh	Terawatt-Hours
UAV	Unmanned Aerial Vehicles
UN	United Nations
UNFCCC	United Nations Framework Convention on Climate Change
UEEE	Used Electronic and Electrical Equipment
USD	US Dollar

USV	Unmanned Surface Vehicles
VAT	Value Added Tax
VC	Venture Capital
VR	Virtual Reality
WFP	World Food Programme

1

Sustainable Finance and Technology

Making the Connection

Herman Bril, Georg Kell, and Andreas Rasche

INTRODUCTION

The last quarter of the twentieth century witnessed the transformational and intertwined rise of two forces: the information and communication technology (ICT) revolution and the financialization of the economy. Carlota Perez (2002: ix) demonstrated that

> very big changes in technology entailed not just the extraordinarily rapid growth of a few new industries, but also, over more prolonged period, the rejuvenation of many old industries, which found ways to use the new technology, influenced by the new industries, called the techno-economic paradigm.

Also, she pointed out that any transformation in technology could take place only through an interactive and accompanying process of social, political, and managerial change. As Schumpeter already pointed out in 1939, clusters of radical innovations are dependent on financial capital. The symbiosis between capital and technology was very clear in the dot-com bubble, a stock market bubble caused by excessive speculation in the late 1990s, a period of massive growth in the use and adoption of the Internet.

This human-powered complex system is the nature of capitalism and gives rise to the sequence of technological revolution, financial bubble, collapse, golden age, and political unrest. Progress (like evolution) is a painful, but necessary, process generating winners and losers, hence the need for a just transition. Another challenge, as Azhar (2021) remarks, is that the pace of

DOI: 10.4324/9781003262039-1

technological change is accelerating, and we have arrived in the exponential age transforming business, politics, and society. Azhar (2021) argues that

> our age is defined by the emergence of several new general-purpose technologies, each improving at an exponential rate. It starts with computing but also encompasses energy, biology, and manufacturing. The breadth of this change means that we have entered a wholly new era of human society and economic organization.

Human progress powered by the industrial (technological) revolution created unprecedented, however uneven, improvement of life globally. But this also created exponential pressure on the planet. Humans constitute the largest force of change on the planet, and they pushed us into a new geological epoch: the Anthropocene. The astoundingly stable Holocene for the last 10,000 years is over, and we are approaching Earth's tipping points pushing the boundaries of relevant Earth system processes (Gaffney & Rockström, 2021). We are facing systemic long-term climate risk, in the midst of rising geopolitical tensions and polarization within countries, a world battling with the COVID-19 pandemic, and the fastest technological change we ever witnessed, with global financial assets worth $400 trillion. *All of this implies that we must better understand how sustainability, technology, and finance play together, and this is what this book aims to do.*

Without doubt, environmental, social, and governance (ESG) investors face many challenges: they must better understand sustainability-related risks and opportunities; they need to deal with enormous volumes of ESG data (which in some cases is even conflicting); and they need to judge the potential of new innovations in the real economy. To cope with these challenges, investors have to increasingly "technologize" (Monk & Rook, 2020: 3) their operations—that is, they must rethink their relationship vis-à-vis existing and newly emerging technologies.

But such rethinking is easier said than done. In their recent book, *The Technologized Investor*, Ashby Monk and Dane Rook (2020) conclude that the relationship between finance and technology is usually not given sufficient attention so that "most Investors are failing to use advanced technologies" (p. 16). This edited volume was born out of the need to better understand how financial market participants as well as corporations in the "real" economy apply (digital) technologies. We do not aim to provide a conclusive mapping of the relationship between sustainability, finance, and technology. Rather, we want to offer "food for thought" about how this relationship has evolved (so far), the impact it has created on different types of actors, and the challenges that remain to be addressed. This book unpacks multiple facets of the link between sustainability, finance, and technology—ranging from reflections about how investors use evolving technologies to perspectives on how technology shapes the risks and opportunities that are connected to corporate sustainability.

Yet, we caution that just because we better understand how technology shapes the ESG universe does not imply that investors will automatically "technologize." Even when we better grasp how certain technologies can support work within the field of sustainable finance, there is still a need to reflect on how we can challenge established mindsets and outdated ideologies that shape our thinking. Investors, like most other professional people, talk mostly to their peers. Often, these conversations happen within existing communities of practice with little influence from the outside. This makes it more difficult to identify blind spots that may impede the uptake of new investment technologies.

TECHNOLOGY, DIGITALIZATION, AND DATA

Sustainability discussions increasingly refer to three terms: technology, digitalization, and data. In some cases, these terms are used interchangeably (e.g., technology and digitalization) while in other cases, it remains unclear what exactly is being talked about. It is therefore important to spend some time reflecting on these three terms and how they relate to each other.

What Is Technology?

Defining technology is tricky. The meaning of the term has changed throughout time (e.g., early uses were limited to technical education Mannix & Stratton, 2005); and there is no agreed-upon definition of what technology constitutes. Stiegler (1998: 17), for instance, defined technology broadly as "the pursuit of life by means other than life" which makes it difficult to distinguish the term from other concepts (e.g., a "good"). Thomas Hughes (2004: 2) famously said that defining technology "is as difficult as grasping the essence of politics." Rather than settling on one definition, we want to highlight two different understandings of technology.

The first understanding sees technology as an object. W. Brian Arthur (2009: 28) defined technology as "a means to fulfil a human purpose." This definition is still broad, but it categorizes technology as something that humans can make use of. In a similar vein, Read Bain (1937: 860) described technology as all "tools, machines, utensils, weapons, instruments, housing, clothing, communicating and transporting devices and the skills by which we produce and use them." Arthur (2009: 28) also allowed for another definition that comes closer to Bain's one: "technology as the entire *collection of devices and engineering practices available to a culture*" (emphasis in the original). These definitions highlight that technology is mostly about "things" (e.g., devices) and "practices" (e.g., routines). A second understanding of technology would view it less as an object but rather as the application of science (MacKenzie & Wajcman, 1999), such as when scientific methods and findings are applied in an industry setting.

Taken together, both perspectives give us a good understanding of what technology can be. Technology is surely not only about objects. As we know from our common knowledge, many technologies have emerged due to science being applied. However, technology also does not rest exclusively on scientific insights and whatever object is being produced is usually not just the product of science but must also fulfil other criteria (e.g., related to design, aesthetics, usability, and so on). For instance, using artificial intelligence (AI) to analyze ESG data cannot just rest on the application of scientific insights (e.g., which algorithms work best), but the results of the analysis also need to be accessible and understandable for the end user.

Digitalization and Data

Digitalization is about the application of digital technologies and therefore describes how social interactions are increasingly restructured through digital communication (Bloomberg, 2018). It therefore describes how we move from analog to digital operations and how this shapes our life. Although digitalization gained traction with the rise of the Internet, it is not a new phenomenon. In the 1950s, the first hard drives already allowed for some (limited) digitalization. However, the applicability and scalability were limited at the time—the first hard drives weighed over a ton and could store only 5MB (Flyverbom et al., 2019).

Arthur (2017) outlined three stages of the digital revolution. His argument is that digitalization "morphed" every 20 years or so. In the 1970s and 1980s, the first morph brought integrated circuit technology, which accelerated computing power and also miniaturized the latter. In the 1990s and 2000s, computers were increasingly linked with each other through the Internet. This shift allowed for some physical actions to be executed in a digital manner. The last morphing started in the 2010s and is still ongoing. It is based on the emergence of cheap sensor technology; sensors that are built into cars, watches, and homes. Due to these sensors, we have access to large volumes of data that infiltrate almost every aspect of personal and business life. Parallel advances in computing power and the creation of intelligent algorithms enable us to analyze and use this data.

Of course, data is essential for digitalization. Yet data has existed for a long time, and it is not dependent on the existence of computers. Scientists have collected and analyzed data for many centuries. The *OECD Glossary of*

Statistical Terms views data as the "physical representation of information in a manner suitable for communication, interpretation or processing by human beings or by automatic means" (OECD, 2006). In other words, data refers to pieces of information that can be collected, stored, and analyzed. ESG data is therefore about pieces of information that are used to judge the sustainability performance of an organization. Because this definition talks about "physical representation," it is important to acknowledge that data reflects facts or information in the real world (e.g., ESG data reflects real-world phenomena like emission levels). Some data also focuses on the "digital traces" that we leave behind whenever we navigate through the digital world. This is what scholars have called "datafication" (Cukier & Mayer-Schoenberger, 2013). Datafication implies that we turn specific situations and parts of our (analog) life into (digital) data—friendships become "likes" on social media platforms, and one's location is turned into GPS coordinates (Flyverbom et al., 2019).

In the ESG context, it is important to differentiate structured data from unstructured (or alternative) data. Structured data is typically very well organized, easy to search, and usually consists of defined data types with patterns (Taylor, 2021). Firms' sustainability reports contain for the most part structured data (e.g., data points related to resource use). By contrast, unstructured data is not organized via predefined models or categorization schemes, and patterns within the data are not easily recognizable. For instance, human-generated unstructured data would be data from social media platforms, while machine-generated unstructured data would be data from satellite images or sensor data. While patterns in such data are often not easily recognizable, new analytical techniques such as AI can help to detect patterns even in unstructured content. Unstructured data is increasingly relevant for ESG-related decision-making (Monk et al., 2021), as it allows to create novel insights beyond the self-reported corporate data.

HOW DO SUSTAINABILITY, FINANCE, AND TECHNOLOGY CONNECT?

While sustainability and finance are connected through the discourse on sustainable finance and ESG (Bril et al., 2021), it is less clear how ESG relates to technology. We suggest considering three different perspectives on the relationship between ESG and technology. Naturally, the three perspectives are based on analytical distinctions which overlap in practice. Figure 1.1 provides a summary of the three perspectives.

ESG and Technology

Technological changes and innovations are disrupting companies' business models and allow for sustainable business practices to move mainstream (e.g.,

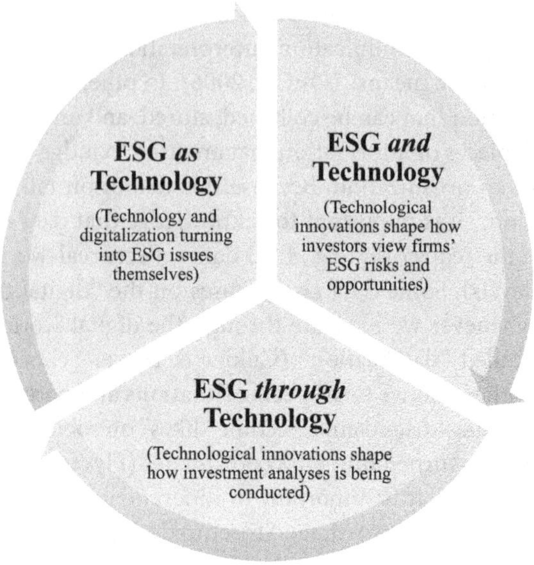

FIGURE 1.1 Three Perspectives on the Relationship Between ESG and Technology

new battery technologies enabling electric mobility). These changes have consequences for how investors value companies and how they view risks and opportunities in the context of sustainability. The "ESG and Technology" perspective looks at the many technological innovations in the economy and tries to understand how these innovations can impact the ESG performance of companies (Kell & Rasche, 2021).

ESG-minded investors need to develop basic knowledge of technologies like carbon capture, robotics, battery storage capacity, and hydrogen energy so that they can judge ESG-related opportunities and risks. The "ESG and Technology" perspective also provides a platform to discuss how technology and sustainability reshape entire industry dynamics. Consider, for instance, how new technological developments create so-called sector couplings between different industries, such as when energy-consuming sectors and energy-producing sectors are increasingly intertwined. The rise of electric mobility, for example, requires that the automotive industry is increasingly "electrified" (Appunn, 2018). Such dynamics unfold creative destruction processes that impact how investors assess companies.

There is, of course, no conclusive list of technological developments that an ESG investor should be aware of. Whether and how a technology is impacting a firm's ESG performance is influenced by many factors, including, but not limited to, the industry a company operates in, the company's size, its geographic location, and the regulatory environment it faces. Also, while some technologies are well known by now (e.g., increased battery storage driving decarbonization in some sectors), other technologies are just about to emerge. In 2021, the *World Economic Forum* (2021) listed self-fertilizing crops, on-demand drug manufacturing, energy through wireless signals, and 3D printed houses as some of the most promising emerging technologies that can help to address ESG challenges.

ESG through Technology

Sustainable finance itself has been exposed to massive changes due to digitalization. While a decade ago sustainable finance was mostly practiced through screens (excluding or including firms with low/high ESG performance), more recent innovations in AI and machine learning (ML) have opened up new possibilities for investors to integrate ESG criteria into portfolio construction. These new investment technologies evolve alongside the technological changes in society at large.

Monk and Rook (2020: 16–24) have outlined a short history of investment technology. They conclude that almost each major innovation in investment technology (e.g., double-entry bookkeeping and telegraph-enabled stock-tickers) is related to advances in one (or more) of three capabilities: (1) latency of data (i.e., the speed with which investment-related data can be communicated); (2) depth of data (i.e., the level of detail and complexity of investment analyses); and (3) resource efficiency (i.e., how efficient investors' organizational resources can be utilized). These three capabilities are interlinked and trade-offs exist. For instance, if investors find ways to obtain and analyze relevant data more swiftly, this can potentially come at the expense of analytical depth (Monk & Rook, 2020: 17). We therefore must debate advances in investment technology against this background. We need to see where new analytical techniques can help investors gain a competitive advantage and at which cost such an advantage may be created.

Recently, the role of AI and ML within ESG-related investment decisions has been much discussed (Selim, 2021). The starting point for such discussions is usually the recognition that "traditional" ESG data does not give investors a comprehensive perspective on companies' ESG performance. Some problems relate to the fact that most ESG data is self-reported and hence likely to be biased. Other problems occur when focusing on what rating agencies do with this data and the divergence of evaluations that is created due to raters using different methodologies (Berg, Koelbel, & Rigobon, 2020). Given these constraints, AI can be used to advance portfolio decision-making, especially in situations where investors want to include extra-financial information (e.g., news items, social media) into the analysis. We can think of AI delivering early "digital smoke signals" (Lohr,

2013)—that is, hidden risks and anomalies that would otherwise escape the attention of investors (Antoncic, 2020). Also, AI can be used by venture capital (VC) investors to make investment decisions. For instance, Antretter et al. (2020) trained an algorithm to make VC investment decisions. They found that the algorithm outperformed inexperienced VC investors while experienced investors fared much better.

Whatever their application, new technologies allow investors to supplement the use of structured data sources with analyses of vast amounts of unstructured data. Sentiment analysis algorithms, for instance, are increasingly used to study the tone that underlies a conversation. Using natural language processing (NLP), such algorithms can extract attitudes and other subjective information from texts. Sentiment analysis can be used to study a company's commitment to ESG, for example, when analyzing data from quarterly earnings calls (S&P Global, 2020). In the end, such applications can meaningfully supplement existing data sources and hence allow for a more fine-grained analysis of firms' ESG performance.

ESG as Technology

Technology and digitalization not only affect how ESG is practiced; they increasingly also constitute ESG issues themselves. For instance, consider the role of cybersecurity which can significantly undermine the stability of firms' operations and hence must be considered within governance-related discussions. Further, Bitcoin-related activities (to which some investors are exposed) have a negative carbon footprint and hence impact environmental performance. Some have called this emerging agenda Environmental, Social, Governance, Technology (ESGT) (Bonime-Blanc, 2020). ESGT is important because it emphasizes that some technological issues, which have significant consequences for a firm's level of sustainability, are not adequately captured by more traditional ESG thinking.

Adding the "T" to ESG does not just imply to find a new acronym or to promote a new framework (we already have enough acronyms and frameworks). Corporations must understand that many technological issues impact exactly those risks and opportunities that ESG analyses are trying to assess. In some contexts, technological issues can be treated as topics that need to be addressed on their own. In other contexts, technological issues will interact significantly with established E, S, and G topics. Consider, for instance, the role of cybersecurity. Through the COVID-19 pandemic working from home has become a new norm for large parts of the global workforce. This exposes firms to new cybersecurity risks, and it also throws up questions on the potential social impact of firms' cybersecurity measures (e.g., aligning such measures with human and labor rights). Further, a lack of adequate cybersecurity can impact client privacy in cases where potential sensitive and confidential information may be shared unduly (Nasdaq, 2020).

Beyond the Three Perspectives

The three perspectives do not exist in isolation (indicated by the arrows in Figure 1.1). Which technologies are used by investors depends on what kind of innovations are mainstreamed within the economy. Also, which ESGT issues become salient depends on the general trajectory of technological developments and their uptake by the finance community.

A possible fourth perspective on the relationship between ESG and technology would be to consider firms' own reporting practices and how these practices are shaped by technological innovations. Increasingly, firms can produce more granular sustainability data allowing them to zoom in on parts of their supply chain or regional operations (Amesheva, 2017). For instance, Patagonia's famous *Footprint Chronicles* allows the consumer to follow the ESG performance of the company's products along all stages of the value chain (including raw material sourcing). Without doubt, such fine-grained ESG data create higher levels of transparency and can support investment analysis (especially if such data is combined with technologically advanced investment methods). However, as this book is primarily concerned with the investor side of ESG, we do not further unpack this perspective within the forthcoming chapters.

ESG AND/AS/THROUGH TECHNOLOGY—MORE THAN JUST *TECHNÉ*

Whenever we reflect on technology and digitalization, we focus primarily on "the techné"—that is, the manifold techniques, mechanisms, practices, and devices that allow us to better govern ESG issues. For instance, synthesizing algorithms as well as powerful hardware are part of ESG's techné. What we usually forget is that the application of these new technologies has far-reaching consequences for how we understand ESG itself.

First, the techné that we apply within ESG changes the very way we understand knowledge (epistemes). Through the technologies that we use to analyze firms' ESG performance we establish truth claims. However, the nature of these claims differs depending on what kind of data and analytical tools we are using. Consider the example of big data. Whenever we analyze traditional data sources, we base truth claims on the hope that all the self-reported data reflects a firm's ESG performance (although we know that it is not perfect). Yet, whenever we use large volumes of unstructured data to gain ESG insights, we do not rely on this assumption. In fact, when we analyze large volumes of media stories or social media data, we can "afford" some inaccuracies (e.g., the inclusion of some less relevant stories; Flyverbom et al., 2017). Using big data sources implies that we can afford some inaccuracies in exchange for analyzing much larger volumes of real-time data to gain relevant ESG insights (see also Mayer-Schönberger & Cukier, 2013). This implies that we need to evaluate some of the novel insights gained through AI and ML based on different epistemic standards.

Second, the techné that is being applied influences what we can and cannot "see". Traditional technologies in the ESG field often rely on Excel sheets, which come with their own problems (e.g., tracing the latest version of a spreadsheet in a large organization; Monk & Rook, 2020: 22–24). With new technologies and analytical techniques come new ways of visualizing companies' ESG performance. For instance, multidimensional interactive visualization tools that rely on real-time data are increasingly used to translate large volumes of data into something that ESG practitioners can grasp. Visualizations are important tools; they may emphasize some ESG characteristics while they can also hide others. Hence, how and what is being visualized influences the way in which ESG is being conducted (e.g., the problems, risks, and opportunities that are being made visible to practitioners).

Finally, ESG's techné also influences the formation of professional identities. Often, the introduction of new investment technologies challenges established identity patterns. The success of implementing new technologies relies on having data-savvy managers and analysts who at least in some cases uphold different professional identities than "traditional" financial market actors. Implementing novel investment technologies into well-established organizational structures and cultures therefore implies to discuss how newly emerging patterns of professional identity can be aligned and integrated. In some cases, firms can also become too reliant on technologies. Consider the example of Google where Douglas Bowman—at the time Google's visual design leader—left the company in 2009 because he couldn't agree with a design philosophy "that lives or dies strictly by the sword of data" (Shankland, 2009). Integrating technology into organizations can create such identity battles, and financial market participants must take them into consideration if they want to put ESG investing on different technological pillars.

CORPORATE LEADERSHIP IN TIMES OF TECHNOLOGIZED ESG INVESTMENT

If ESG investment becomes more technologized, it is not only investors that need to change. Corporate leadership will be challenged as well. Most C-level executives know that their firm must change to effectively address ESG practices. However, too many businesses are following the crowd in only changing with ESG nurturing *transition management*. Yet, for firms to fully reap the advantages of technology and sustainable finance moving closer together, we need to look at how firms can change through ESG encouraging *transformational change*.

The Status Quo: ESG as Transition Management

As a response to the mainstreaming of ESG-related debates, many firms have developed neatly defined plans for corporate change. They have set aspirational goals and remodeled systems, processes, and organizational structures. Some companies developed low-carbon strategies based on product innovation. More than 2,300 firms have approved or are in the process of developing science-based targets for reducing their greenhouse gas emissions (as of Feb 2022). Yet, for too many companies, changing toward ESG has turned into an exercise that implies simply managing long checklists, like engineers optimizing the efficiency of a machine. We label this type of change "transitional"—it certainly alters what corporations are doing, but the change remains detached from the core of the corporation. Such a way of approaching ESG is unlikely to be successful when considering the rapid technological changes outlined in this book.

We believe that there are three reasons why transition-based change management is unlikely to deliver in the long run, both for the corporation and for the society at large.

(1) *Creating a Parallel ESG Organization:* Transition-based change rests on the work of formal sustainability or ESG departments, which are often isolated from other core functions of the corporation. Many firms have created "parallel" ESG organizations, which are structurally, process-wise, and mentally separated from the rest of the firm. No doubt, these departments do important work. For instance, they collect and analyze ESG data, manage partnerships, and function as a hub to coordinate actions. However, this type of parallel ESG organization causes high internal coordination costs, which slow down decision-making and confuse responsibilities. As a result, ESG remains poorly integrated into the core strategy and existing governance systems. In many firms, the VP of sustainability presents the firm's ESG report to the board of directors once a year. However, the board itself is not seen as the right place to systematically discuss the risks and opportunities related to managing ESG issues.

(2) *Neglecting System Dynamics*: Transitional change assumes that there is an end state of the change process (equilibrium) and that this end state is known. However, managing change processes, especially those

that include technological developments, that support corporate sustainability implies that you cannot determine your future destination in detail. Firms' ESG practices are shaping and are shaped by what analysts have called a volatile, uncertain, complex, and ambiguous (VUCA) context. Sustainability itself is not a stable end state. It is shaped by several interacting systems (e.g., the market system and various ecological systems) and constantly faces emergence, feedback loops, and disruptions. Businesses and financial institutions are nested within the broader complex adaptive systems of society and the natural environment. However, most companies ignore their embeddedness into such systems.

(3) *Over-focusing on Actions:* Transitional ESG change assumes that modifying actions is sufficient in creating lasting impact on sustainability-related challenges. However, actions do not occur in a vacuum. They are guided by people's beliefs and behaviors. Changing ESG therefore means, most of all, to challenge and change peoples' mindsets. Focusing on what mindset people have vis-à-vis ESG issues is critical because well-intended actions are often impeded by cognitive biases and strongly held values. For instance, ESG change can remain poorly coordinated within firms because leaders engage in groupthink and therefore favor solutions that promote internal consensus at the expense of creating necessary disruptions. Such groupthink can impede actions in times where technological solutions emerge swiftly.

Most companies adopt transition-based ESG change, in large part because they are merely following what others are doing. These companies have changed *with* ESG; they have followed the evolution of corporate sustainability and modified their systems, processes, and structures. The true challenge, however, is how companies can instill a new corporate purpose and resilience in the minds of people and to manage ESG-related change in a way that accounts for the disruptive, complex, and uncertain character of (technologized) sustainability challenges and solutions.

Toward Transformational ESG Change

Transformational ESG change does not occur overnight. It requires managers to reframe how ESG is understood and perceived within the company. We believe that three practices are particularly important to initiate and drive such change.

(1) *Embrace Internal Disruption*: Many firms fear disruptive changes when managing their ESG practices. Some disruptions occur naturally as unforeseen shocks (e.g., the COVID-19 pandemic), and firms often

struggle to adjust their ESG practices. One reason for such inertia is that few organizations are willing to allow for *internal* disruptions to happen—that is, disruptions that challenge executives' mindsets. But transformational ESG change rests on firms' willingness to be continuously challenged by outside stakeholders to create a sense of crisis within the organization. Consider the example of Volkswagen which set up an independent Sustainability Council in 2016, right after it was hit by the global emissions scandal. The Council, which has extensive rights to information and consultation, helped to significantly accelerate technology shifts toward e-mobility and acted as a disruptor to the company's understanding of ESG issues.

(2) *Rethink Leadership Capabilities*: Leaders must acknowledge that transformational ESG change is enabled by a broader set of capabilities, a clear purpose, and a culture of diversity and inclusion. If transformational change is about shifts in mindsets and accepting that there is no clearly defined end goal, leaders must learn to tolerate uncertainty and failure. Changing ESG practices and aligning them with swiftly emerging technological developments is to some extent a trial-and-error process in which solutions and problems emerge, a process that Cohen et al. (1972) described as the garbage can model early on. Such emergence requires leaders to think flexibly—that is, to gather new information strategically and not overemphasize the role of ESG benchmarks that are supplied by rating agencies. In particular, boards have to develop these coping capabilities as they often set the framework in which ESG develops. Promoting diversity (e.g., within the board) is key to develop such capabilities, because diverse teams are critical for promoting innovation, reducing groupthink, and enabling better decision-making.

(3) *Fully Integrate Technology Into ESG Thinking*: Transformational ESG change is based on a different attitude toward technology. So far, most firms have decoupled the discussion of technological change and corporate sustainability, at best seeing technology as something that contributes to risks and opportunities related to ESG issues. However, technological advances often provide the disruptions that require transformational ESG change and hence need to be considered in their own right. Take the example of COVID-19. Over the course of just a few months, the COVID-19 crisis has brought about years of change in the way companies across all sectors and regions do business. Companies have accelerated the digitization of their customer and supply chain interactions and of their internal operations, and the share of digital or digitally enabled products in their portfolios has dramatically increased. Such technological disruptions are intertwined with transformational

ESG change, in terms of both increased risk awareness and better recognition of opportunities for future growth.

While transitional change through ESG practices can contribute in some way to sustainable development, only transformational change will allow us to fully integrate technological developments into ESG management. It is therefore important to recognize that a discussion of technology and sustainable finance requires to also reflect on and challenge corporations and investors' deeply held values and beliefs.

CONTRIBUTIONS TO THIS BOOK

This book aims to be a resource for those interested in the emerging links between sustainability, finance, and technology. We have invited leading practitioners and academic thought leaders to share their views on which kind of links have emerged (or will emerge) and how these links impact companies as well as investors. While designing the book, we looked for a balance between: (a) contributions that come from the corporate world and those coming from an investor angle and (b) contributions that come from practitioners and those that were written by academic voices (plus those that manage to live in both worlds). We are convinced that by bringing together these different perspectives, we have produced a timely and relevant book that inspires and motivates.

The contributions cover a wide range of topics, starting with important fundamental reflections about how technology shapes human development (see the chapter by Lars Jaeger) and ranging to discussions of how technology has shaped companies' ESG practices (see the chapter by Herbert Diess) as well as investors' (see the chapter by Ashby Monk and Dane Rook). One contribution also looks at how technological issues themselves are turned into ESG issues (see the chapter by Andrea Bonime-Blanc and Dante A. Disparte). The contributors to this book do not claim to have all the answers—they aim to uncover unanswered questions when it comes to the complex relationship between sustainable finance and technology and, at the same time, also reflect on unquestioned answers that may impede progress in the field.

Finding the right balance between unquestioned answers and unanswered questions may be the key to advance the discussion of how sustainability, finance, and technology interact.

REFERENCES

Amesheva, I. (2017). *Five Technology Trends Defining the Future of Corporate Sustainability.* Available at: www.eco-business.com/opinion/five-technology-trends-defining-the-future-of-corporate-sustainability/ (Accessed: 13 January 2022).

Antoncic, M. (2020). Uncovering hidden signals for sustainable investing using Big Data: Artificial intelligence, machine learning and natural language processing. *Journal of Risk Management in Financial Institutions*, 13(2), 106–113.

Antretter, T., Blohm, I., Siren, C., Grichnik, D., Malmstrom, M., & Wincent, J. (2020). Do algorithms make better—and fairer—investments than angel investors? *Harvard Business Review Digital Articles*, 2–6.

Appunn, K. (2018). *Sector Coupling—Shaping an Integrated Renewable Energy System*. Available at: www.cleanenergywire.org/factsheets/sector-coupling-shaping-integrated-renewable-power-system (Accessed: 13 January 2022).

Arthur, W. B. (2009). *The Nature of Technology*. New York: Free Press.

Arthur, W. B. (2017). Where is technology taking the economy? *McKinsey Quarterly*, 4, 32–43.

Azhar, A. (2021). *The Exponential Age—How Accelerating Technology Is Transforming Business, Politics, Society*. New York: Diversion Books.

Bloomberg, D. (2018). *Digitization, Digitalization, and Digital Transformation: Confuse Them at Your Peril*. Available at: www.forbes.com/sites/jasonbloomberg/2018/04/29/digitization-digitalization-and-digital-transformation-confuse-them-at-your-peril/?sh=256a8fa2f2c7 (Accessed: 11 January 2022).

Bonime-Blanc, A. (2020). *Boom to Gloom: How Leaders Transform Risk Into Resilience and Value*. London: Routledge.

Cohen, M. D., March, J. G., & Olsen, J. P. (1972). A garbage can model of organizational choice. *Administrative Science Quarterly*, 17(1), 1–25.

Cukier, K., & Mayer-Schoenberger, V. (2013). The rise of big data. *Foreign Affairs*, 92(3), 27–40.

Flyverbom, M., Deibert, R., & Matten, D. (2019). The governance of digital technology, big data, and the internet: New roles and responsibilities for business. *Business and Society*, 58(1), 3–19.

Flyverbom, M., Madsen, A. K., & Rasche, A. (2017). Big data as governmentality in international development: Digital traces, algorithms, and altered visibilities. *The Information Society*, 33(1), 35–42.

Gaffney, O., & Rockstrom, J. (2021). *Breaking Boundaries—The Science of Our Planet*. London: Penguin Random House.

Hughes, T. P. (2004). *Human-Built World: How to Think About Technology and Culture*. Chicago, IL: University of Chicago Press.

Kell, G., & Rasche, A. (2021). Renewing markets from within: How businesses and the investment community can drive transformational change. In H. Bril, G. Kell, & A. Rasche (Eds.), *Sustainable Investing: A Path to a New Horizon*. London: Routledge, pp. 45–65.

Lohr, S. (2013). Searching bigdata for 'digital smoke signals'. *New York Times*, August 7. Available at: www.nytimes.com/2013/08/08/technology/development-groups-tap-big-data-to-direct-humanit arian-aid.html

MacKenzie, D. A., & Wajcman, J. (1999). *The Social Shaping of Technology* (2nd edition). Buckingham: Open University Press.

Mannix, L. H., & Stratton, J. A. (2005). *Mind and Hand: The Birth of MIT*. Cambridge, MA: MIT Press.

Monk, A., Prins, M., & Rook, D. (2021). Data defense in sustainable investing. In H. Bril, G. Kell, & A. Rasche (Eds.), *Sustainable Investing: A Path to a New Horizon*. London: Routledge, pp. 263–284.

Monk, A., & Rook, D. (2020). *The Technologized Investor*. Stanford, CA: Stanford University Press.

Nasdaq (2020). *2020 Sustainability Report*. Available at: www.nasdaq.com/docs/2021/06/16/2020_Sustainability_Report.pdf (Accessed: 17 January 2022).

Organization for Economic Co-operation and Development (OECD) (2006). *Data*. Available at: https://stats.oecd.org/glossary/detail.asp?ID=532 (Accessed: 12 January 2022).

Perez, C. (2002). *Technological Revolutions and Financial Capital*. Cheltenham: Edward Elgar.

Selim, O. (2021). ESG and AI. In H. Bril, G. Kell, & A. Rasche (Eds.), *Sustainable Investing: A Path to a New Horizon*. London: Routledge, pp. 227–243.

Shankland, S. (2009). *Google Designer Leaves, Blaming Data Centrism*. Available at: www.cnet.com/tech/services-and-software/google-designer-leaves-blaming-data-centrism/ (Accessed: 14 January 2022).

S&P Global (2020). *How Can AI Help ESG Investing?* Available at: www.spglobal.com/en/research-insights/articles/how-can-ai-help-esg-investing (Accessed: 14 January 2022).

Stiegler, B. (1998). *Technics and Time 1: The Fault of Epimetheus.* Stanford, CA: Stanford University Press.

Taylor, C. (2021). *Structured Versus Unstructured Data.* Available at: www.datamation.com/big-data/structured-vs-unstructured-data/ (Accessed: 13 January 2022).

World Economic Forum (2021). *Top 10 Emerging Technologies of 2021.* Available at: www.weforum.org/reports/top-10-emerging-technologies-of-2021 (Accessed: 13 January 2022).

PART I

ESG and Technology

2

History of Technology and Its Future in the Context of Human Development

Lars Jaeger

An astonishing contradiction characterises our time: more and more people are living a life of utmost comfort, almost total security and an unprecedented level of health into the old age. At the same time, most think the state of the world is bad and getting worse. You could say: heaven and hell exist in parallel for us; they interpenetrate in the here and now. Another paradox even lies on top of this contradiction: the same trigger is responsible for both scenarios—scientific and technological progress. It ensures that we now live in a society that has long surpassed all past hopes in terms of paradisiacal quality. But it is also the reason why we look to the future with the greatest concern.

The fact is that our world is changing faster and faster. In his 1932 novel *Brave New World*, Aldous Huxley describes a society in which people are sorted into different castes at birth by means of biotechnological manipulation. At the same time they have all their desires, cravings, and appetites immediately satisfied by permanent consumption, sex and the happiness drug soma. The novel will be familiar to most readers in its basic outlines. Less well known is the year in which Huxley sets his action. It is the year AD 2540, more than 600 years after the novel was published! Even the visionary Huxley could not have imagined that the real technological possibilities could not only reach this scenario after only one century but far eclipse it.

In his novel, Huxley describes that through technological development, man no longer only massively changes his environment and thus his living conditions but also himself. In fact, in the real world today, the human body and mind have by now become the object of optimisation. We are at a crossroads, whether we go into the future self-determined and even happier and

DOI: 10.4324/9781003262039-3

better off than today or whether sooner or later our body will be degraded to a machine by genetic and nanotechnologies and our mind will be permanently satisfied and at the same time conditioned by a kind of soma drug. More extremely stated: A "human crisis" decides on our future as human beings; it is more urgent, more revolutionary and more threatening than even climate catastrophe or overpopulation.

At the moment, the greed for returns of technology investors, the ideology of Silicon Valley transhumanists and, more generally, the capitalist logic of exploitation still seem to decide our future, degrading us to passive spectators or sufferers. If we do not want the new technologies to roll over us, each of us must participate in actively shaping our future in a positive way in the coming decades. This requires three things:

(1) Knowledge of what technological developments are all about;
(2) Motivation, courage and the willingness to get involved in shaping the future; and
(3) Intellectual, philosophical and spiritual guidelines.

THE PARADISE SCIENTIFIC TECHNOLOGIES DEVELOPED IN THE TWENTIETH CENTURY AND THE NIGHTMARES ABOUT THE FUTURES

Today, despite all our fears, in the developed countries we have a quality of life that has never been achieved before.

- We all have a secure roof over our heads, no one has to freeze or go hungry.
- The socially disadvantaged can rely on state benefits.
- Today, more people die from too much food than from too little, more are killed in accidents than in wars, and for the first time in human history, infectious diseases are less deadly than infirmities of old age.
- Thanks to minimally invasive surgical techniques, antibiotics and a balanced diet, most of us enjoy good health into (increasingly) old age.
- We have access to fresh drinking water and the most delicious culinary delights (our great-grandparents hardly ever saw a papaya or mango all their lives).
- We have a lot of free time, which we can fill with plenty of educational opportunities and the best entertainment.
- We benefit from the possibilities of almost unlimited mobility, travelling to exotic countries.
- Digital communication allows us to (immediately) exchange ideas with friends all over the world.

The list of amenities of modern life that make our existence so unbelievably comfortable and diverse compared to that of our ancestors could be continued at will. We live better than ever—and the best part is that we appreciate it all! Representative surveys show that people's subjective, individual satisfaction is stable at a high level. But how do a permanent sense of crisis and a feeling of well-being go together?

Both extremes of this strange balancing act have the same roots: scientific and technological progress.

- Science and technology have reduced human suffering more than any other tradition of mind (which is precisely what science is: an attempt to understand the world with the help of our minds). They enable us to live in unparalleled security, to enjoy the highest levels of health, enormous material wealth, a great sense of subjective satisfaction and a quality of life that our grandparents and all generations before could only dream of.
- At the same time, technological progress has brought us new problems such as environmental degradation, population explosion and nuclear threats. Many people envision a future in which everything we know is destroyed by technology or in which an Armageddon wipes out humanity as a whole.

We are dominated by a comfortable but blind faith in technology, we enjoy the luxury of cars, computer tomography and sewage disposal, trust in the functioning of smartphones, digital data communication and antibiotics, at the same time we fear and demonise technological progress.

What is new, however, is what we expect from technological change for the future. Until the nineteenth century, philosophers and literary figures of the Western world drew decidedly positive pictures of what lay ahead for mankind in their visions of the future. It all began in 1516, with Thomas More's *Utopia*. Utopia is a world in which all people (more precisely: all men) have equal rights. Working time is six hours a day, and there is free choice of occupation and unrestricted access to educational goods. Everyone receives what they need from the community. Such a society must have seemed like paradise to people 500 years ago. Thomas More's Land of Utopia became the eponym for the fictional future worlds that represented hopeful counter-designs to the dreary everyday life of the respective present.

It was not until the twentieth century that the picture changed, utopias became dystopias. The futures of the last hundred years predominantly describe unpleasant-to-apocalyptic worlds shaped by ecocide, murderous robots, totalitarian regimes and nuclear annihilation. George Orwell's *Nineteen Eighty-Four* (written in 1948) and Aldous Huxley's *Brave New World*, flagship novels about the future in the twentieth century, describe nightmare worlds brought about by despotic world dictatorships made possible solely by modern technologies. And Alfred Döblin wrote the novel *Mountains, Seas and Giants* even before *Berlin Alexanderplatz*, which appeared in 1924, and tells of a world divided into two large power blocs, in which the settlement of Greenland results in the melting of the ice masses.

The fact is that there are plenty of challenges that technical progress has brought us. Many technology sceptics thus believe that the only solution is to forego technological development. However, this logic forgets the other side of the coin: new technologies have always been excellent problem solvers. Hunger, diseases, the effects of extreme weather events and many other human plagues could be reduced to a fraction of the scale that was quite normal for previous generations. Harvard Professor Steven Pinker makes a fiery plea for science and enlightenment in his readable book *Enlightenment Now*. In Pinker's view, science and technology are the driving forces behind the positive developments of the past centuries—and will continue to be so in the future.

Today, there is even the prospect of eradicating hunger, disease and other sufferings altogether. If we do not allow the sciences to solve problems because we do not trust them, we deprive ourselves of the best tool for dealing with today's challenges. Even tasks like global warming, pollution and energy supply will only be solved with the help of new technologies. Most of us have long forgotten or never knew: 70 years ago, European and American cities already had a massive smog problem. People suffered from severe respiratory problems, the number of cancer cases had skyrocketed. In the 1950s, the air in the Ruhr area in Germany was thick enough to cut through; if white laundry was dried outside, it was grey in the evening (what we saw in East Germany until 1990). In April 1961, Chancellor candidate Willy Brandt said in a speech in the Bundestag in Bonn: "The sky over the Ruhr must become blue again!" And it did in fact become blue again. Another example from (West) Germany: even in the 1980s, bathing in the Rhine was life-threatening; fish were scarce in Germany's mightiest river at that time. Klaus Töpfer, then Minister of the Environment, jumped into the Rhine as part of a PR campaign in Bonn to promote clean rivers in Germany, albeit wearing full-body protection so as not to endanger his health. Today, children bathe in the same place and you can fish in the Rhine again. Long-lost fish species have returned.

The reason for these successes: new technologies, such as catalytic converters for industrial incinerators and later also for car exhaust gases, as well as wastewater treatment, have had the effect of drastically reducing smog, acid rain and toxic waste in the rivers. Work continues on this front: new energy, environmental and climate technologies are at the centre of global research programmes. Environmental activists often object that more economic growth inevitably leads to more climate-damaging energy consumption.

But it is precisely economic growth that generates the necessary financial resources as well as the technologies to counter climate-damaging pollution. Poor countries cannot afford environmental protection.

Even those problems that one would initially classify as "socially induced" crises, and which at first glance seem to have little connection to technologies, call for a scientific approach and the use of new technologies. For example, the enormous migration movements in the Middle East and in some African countries can probably only be reduced if the families can find a livelihood in their home countries. After all, it is mostly people without alternatives who listen to warmongers or make the perilous journey to safer countries. Technology can help them generate more agricultural yields, bring more transparency to political decision-making processes or enable higher education through digital media. Instead of preventing science from solving problems, we need to do a better job than before ensuring that it brings fewer problems into the world.

To summarize: while science and technology always create problems, they are also the best problem solvers—and this in recent years often faster than creating the probems.

THE DEVIL ON THE WALL

Resistance to technology is gaining momentum. Five reasons can be identified that make technological change so unpopular and ensure a pessimistic view of the future.

(1) *Perceived Straitjacket*: Technologies impose their beat and rhythm on us. This was first experienced by workers on the power looms of the eighteenth and nineteenth centuries. In the early twentieth century it was the assembly line for workers, and today, technical and mathematical optimisation processes create time constraints ("just-in-time" production and distribution) to which we must adhere. The result is a feeling of being at the mercy of others and lacking control over our lives.

(2) *Increasing Complexity*: We sense the vast processes that are changing the world but understand little of what is actually underlying this. This combination of intuitive sensing and not knowing or not understanding creates uncertainty.

(3) *Incomprehensible Speed*: The sheer speed of technological change and the associated speed of social change overwhelm us mentally and emotionally. Unlike in the past, scientific and technological breakthroughs are no longer a matter of decades; they now take place every quarter of a year. The complexity of scientific and technological developments is also increasing dramatically. We no longer see ourselves as shaping

societal changes but have trouble even reacting to the maddeningly fast and increasingly confusing transformations.

(4) *Confusing Diversity*: We are experiencing a multitude of dramatic changes at the same time. This is precisely what is historically new: in the last 250 years, people have been exposed to individual and thus manageable technological upheavals and their crisis-like effects. Today, the constant parallelism of innovations overwhelms most people.

(5) *Globality*: The consequences of technological development are no longer local. Problems in seemingly distant continents such as Africa and Asia show their effects directly here in Europe and North America. Many of the problems caused by technology are global: issues such as nuclear war, environmental destruction, overpopulation, climate catastrophe, artificial superintelligence and genetic manipulation affect and threaten humanity as a whole. Even questions of social justice, energy supply or nutrition can meaningfully be dealt with only on a global level.

Technological change threatens to overtake us, so it seems to many. Because it overwhelms us, we face it with negative feelings and a dystopian view of our future. The good news is that there are identifiable arguments underlying the views of dystopias, and by debunking it, we can find our way back to a positive view of the future and thus to an active role that we can take.

TECHNOLOGICAL CHANGES IN THE PAST

In earlier centuries, technological progress was rather one-dimensional. Since about 1650, that is, since the scientific revolution, individual fields of knowledge dominated the respective scientific thinking and technological development. Initially, and for about 150 years, this was mechanics, before at the end of the eighteenth-century combustion processes and thermodynamics moved to the centre, which found its technological culmination with the invention of steam and heat engines. Then came (in rather easy terms) the age of electricity, followed by chemistry, electromagnetism, atomic and quantum physics and genetics.

Part of this string-of-pearls effect is that for almost three centuries, with a few exceptions, the disciplines were strictly separated from each other. Physicists kept to themselves, chemists had their own metier, medical doctors were hardly considered scientists but rather craftsmen. All in all, the scientific landscape was still quite manageable, so that it was possible for polymaths such as Kant and Goethe to be at the height of their times in numerous fields of natural research, in addition to their philosophical and literary work.

In the later part of the twentieth century, the picture changed dramatically. In the individual disciplines, knowledge grew at an unprecedented rate. Even more revolutionary was that knowledge and methods were now being applied across fields, and completely new areas of science were emerging. Here some examples:

- Chemists and physicists jointly developed the applications of quantum physics;
- Biologists and chemists worked together on the fundamentals of molecular genetics;
- Physicists and biologists began to study living systems with physical methods (which by now has gone far beyond John von Neumann's and Alan Turing's first modern methods from the early 1950s);
- Physicists and mathematicians laid the foundation for modern information theory;
- Biologists, chemists, physicists and neuroscientists developed an ever deeper understanding of the materialistic processes in our brain and thus many mental processes inside us.

The number of research fields developed by leaps and bounds, and they all exchanged more and more ideas with each other ranging from new quantum technologies to optimisation algorithms, from nanochemistry to reproductive genetics, from artificial intelligence to robotics, from atomic physics in imaging techniques to brain and consciousness research. Countless fields of science are today closely intertwined in a very complex way; together they form a perfect breeding ground for the emergence of new key technologies.

And something is also happening on the timeline: scientific and technological progress is racing ahead at an increasingly insane pace, so fast that we can no longer keep up with our perception. While there is much discussion about future technologies, few anticipate how much they will shake us up. "We tend to overestimate the impact of technologies in the short term and underestimate them in the long term," as American researcher and Stanford Professor Roy Amara put it. For example, hardly anyone is aware that already today,

- new genetic engineering methods can specifically manipulate eye colour, body size and perhaps soon intelligence of humans;
- robots the size of viruses, so-called nanobots, are used in living organisms, for example, to fight cancer cells or to administer targeted medication;
- medicine allows paraplegics to walk again;
- robots are controlled solely with the help of thoughts;
- in animal experiments, brains are interconnected so that they act as a single thinking organ;

- living bacteria are produced 100 per cent artificially;
- meat is printed out in 3D printers;
- so-called quantum computers are being constructed whose computing power is so immense that they will revolutionise the development of medicines as well as intelligence services, finance and chemical research.

Life in 1995 was not so different from life in 1970—haircuts and other fashions had changed and there was more prosperity overall. But if you go about the same period of time, a quarter of a century, from 1995 to the present, you end up in a completely different world. The present has hardly anything in common with 1995—it has not been a time of "normal" technological change. Who can imagine a world today without the internet, email, music without CDs, digital TV, satellite navigation or minimally invasive surgery? More and more new innovations are leading us into new dimensions of mastering nature and shaping life that seemed unimaginable just a few years before. The speed of technological change is increasing dramatically, and the desire of scientists to understand the world has long since turned into a will to shape it.

TECHNOLOGICAL DISRUPTION: FIVE KEY TECHNOLOGIES

For some years now, something completely new has been added: the appropriation by humans of the nature surrounding us, which has characterised our cultural and technological history for millennia, has in recent years been joined by a second project: the genetic, biological, medical, neurological and consciousness-technological reshaping and redesigning of our physical as well as mental predispositions and abilities—in other words, of ourselves.

The list of key technologies that massively influence our lives is getting longer and longer, more and more fascinating as well as frightening. Five of them will be presented here, because they have what it takes to change the individual human being but also human civilisation and the human condition itself.

Key technology 1: genetic engineering for designer babies

Almost unnoticed by the public, a powerful new technology was discovered in 2012 that allows genetic engineers direct access to individual genes and their targeted manipulation. Since then, it has become the most important tool in genetic engineering. Its name will soon be as well known as DNA or AIDS: "CRISPR." CRISPR stands for "Clustered Regularly Interspaced Short Palindromic Repeats" and describes sections of repeated DNA in the genome of many bacteria. In 2012, the bioscientists Emmanuelle Charpentier and Jennifer Doudna discovered that a combination of CRISPR and other enzymes, so-called Cas ("CRISPR-associated") proteins, can be used to target and manipulate specific DNA targets in vitro. They received (one can argue too late) the Nobel Prize for it in 2020.

The specific CRISPR–Cas9 complex enables extraordinarily precise, rapid and cost-effective intervention in the genetic material of living organisms. The technology is already being used to modify the genetic material of plants. In animals and humans, genetic technologists are still in the early stages, but they are working flat out on radical new applications. The potential of CRISPR is immense, including the chance to manipulate humans. In May 2015, the scientific journal *Nature* asked the question: "Where in the world could the first CRISPR baby be born?" Looking at the respective legal situation, the answer at the time was: Japan, China, India, or Argentina. In November 2018, the race was decided: a previously unknown Chinese scientist announced that he had created the first genetically edited humans. He had altered their genome to make them immune to HIV for life. It had not taken more than a moderately equipped laboratory and basic knowledge of genetic engineering. With CRISPR children, we have finally arrived at the age of human experimentation and designer babies.

And the possibilities of CRISPR technology are far from exhausted. In February 2019, an article appeared in *Nature* introducing a new enzyme complex that functions very similarly to Cas9, but is about 40% smaller. CasX, as the new complex has been christened, could prove particularly powerful for use in humans, as the human immune system should accept it more easily. On the other hand, there is the horror scenario of specific human characteristics, not least intelligence or external attractiveness, being altered with the help of CRISPR.

- Could genetically optimised humans soon be cognitively and physically superior to "normal humans"?
- What happens if CRISPR is added to the arsenal of biological warfare?
- Can we allow the technology to be applied to human egg and sperm cells? Because then not only one individual will be altered but also all future offspring from here onwards.

CRISPR is indeed the most important biotechnological breakthrough of this century so far. Philosophers, theologians and ethicists are already discussing the power and dangers of the new method.

Key technology 2: with AI to superintelligence

The surprising victory of the computer AlphaGo over the Go world champion Lee Sedol in March 2016 showed a broad public how far the learning algorithms of artificial intelligence (AI) have already come. For AlphaGo is not just a fast computer. It consists of an unimaginably large number of learning—one is tempted to say living—neuronal connections that directly mimic the learning and thinking processes of the human brain.

Somewhat less in the public eye was a new version of AlphaGo just 18 months later: in 100 games it played against the world's best chess computer up to that time. These had been fed with data from millions of historical chess games and thus the centuries-old experience of chess-playing humans; its computing power was 70 million positions per second. AlphaGo won 28 times and drew 72 games—in other words, it did not lose a single time. The amazing thing was: AlphaGo had only been fed the rules of the board game four (!) hours earlier, and it could also "only" evaluate 80,000 positions per second. Four hours were enough to turn it from a beginner into the unbeatable, best chess machine in the world! In this short time, it played against itself and optimised its neuronal connections; it had to learn openings or game strategies by itself. The new AphaGo also learnt to play Go in no time at all: this more powerful, self-learning version also beat its predecessor, which had been fed with historical games, 100:0 in a hundred games after four hours of learning to play against itself!

The learning and optimisation processes underlying today's AI (so-called deep learning) enable a massive increase in machine intelligence across the board: future computers will no longer be able to cope exclusively with the specific purpose for which they were designed, for example, playing chess or searching databases, but will be able to be used in far more diverse areas. Sooner or later, AI will be superior to human intelligence in most, perhaps even all, cognitive matters. Incidentally, this also applies to areas that most people today still regard as unchallengeable domains of human ability: intuition, creativity and grasping other people's emotions. The latter in particular, so-called affective computing, will probably already be a standard capability of AI systems in the next few years. The effects are potentially very positive, for example, when it comes to caring for people or in therapeutic treatments when it is important to react appropriately to the emotions of the other person. However, very threatening scenarios are also conceivable, for example, machines recognising our emotions and manipulating them, and doing so significantly more effectively than by cognitive means. For example, former Google employee and Silicon Valley expert Tristan Harris reports that the company YouTube already has digital simulations of almost two billion people and their online behaviour based on the viewing habits of its users. With them, the company optimises its AI algorithms to determine which videos will keep individuals on the platform the longest and then recommend them to them. "Silicon Valley is hacking into our brains," Harris says. Since then, the situation has only worsened considering how TikTok and other apps have gained attraction.

AI will soon be able to read us much better than we can read ourselves by analysing what is probably the most everyday form of our communication: speech. For example, the German company Precire Technologies developed software that can create a very accurate personality profile of a person based only on that person's voice. To do this, the AI experts had trained neural networks on voice data together with the psychological profiles of about 5,000 test persons. And this was very successful: companies are already using this software in job application processes. It doesn't take much imagination to imagine what a powerful tool this software is in the hands of totalitarian systems to perfect their surveillance.

One path to an AI that is fundamentally and in everything superior to humans could ultimately also lead via quantum computers, which provide a whole new order of magnitude of computing capacity necessary for complex neural networks. The hyperintelligent computers, in turn, would advance science even faster and in turn create more artificial systems that would then be even more intelligent. Such a feedback loop would ensure that humans would quickly no longer be able to keep up intellectually with these rapid technological advances. AI experts speak of "superintelligence" in this context.

As early as 1993, the mathematician and computer pioneer Vernor Vinge published the prediction that "within 30 years we will have the technological means to create superhuman intelligence." We are well on our way to fulfilling this prediction for the year 2023. We should be concerned by Vinge's sentence immediately following: "A little later, the era of humans will be over."

Already today, developments in the field of AI threaten dramatic social and political shifts and upheavals with the potential for massive social crises. High-ranking economists are already warning of great social inequality between a few winners and many losers in a "winner takes it all" economy of the digital world. A large number of people are threatened with loss of jobs and social significance. And not only in the lower wage segment: academics such as doctors, lawyers and teachers will also be affected. In as little as 25 years, up to 50% of today's professions could have become superfluous. In the future, social inequality will no longer result from the exploitation of people but simply from the social insignificance of many occupational groups.

In addition, the country with the most developed AI will most likely become the dominant economic and military power. At the moment, it looks like two countries are fighting for global supremacy based on this technology: the USA and China, which has caught up strongly in the last five years and is poised to leap to first place. The Europeans and others have long been left behind in these races and relegated to being extras.

Key technology 3: improving our minds with neuro-enhancement

The more we learn about the genetic, chemical and neurological backgrounds of feelings such as trust, compassion, forbearance, generosity, love and faith, the more we will be able to use this knowledge to manipulate ourselves and others. In the last 20 years, knowledge about our brain has multiplied. The more deeply neuroscientists understand its functioning and the processes of our decision-making, the more precisely they can influence how we feel, think and experience.

- Today, mental illnesses are already alleviated by the introduction of neurotransmitters, but our performance can also be manipulated in this way—keyword: "brain doping."
- Direct stimulation of the corresponding areas in our brain by neuro-electrical impulses also changes or controls mood, attention, memory, self-control, willpower, comprehension, sexual desire and much more.
- Scientists are working on microchips that can be implanted in the brain, where they can permanently improve our state of mind, raise our sense of well-being, increase intelligence, memory and concentration or even provide lasting bliss. They thus go beyond the soma drug from Huxley's *Brave New World.*
- Brain researchers are already making brains and machines interact. Using brain–computer interfaces (BCIs), for example, they are transferring content from a person's brain to a machine so that the machine in turn assists the person with various tasks. This technology will probably be used first in video games to make them even more experiential with the help of artificial sensory impressions projected directly into the brain.
- It is even conceivable to bring different human brains into direct contact with each other via neurointerfaces and thus connect several brains to form a collective consciousness.

Direct access to the neuronal structures in our brain enables the targeted manipulation of emotions and intellectual performance as well as the connection of human brain and machine.

These interventions have a significant impact on our perception. How we see ourselves and our environment has been solely dependent on stimuli from the external world throughout human history. Light waves reach our eye, sound waves our ear, smells our nose. New technologies of consciousness, on the other hand, no longer need "real" reality at all. By playing virtual realities (VR) to our brain, our perception can be reshaped almost at will.

An important philosophical insight from our experiences with VR so far is that the human mental self-image (the philosopher Thomas Metzinger calls this the "phenomenal self-model") is anything but stable and can be manipulated relatively easily. Incidentally, experiences with hallucinogenic drugs also lead to this insight. The insights of recent consciousness research go even further: our entire inner model of ourselves is of a virtual nature and thus also the reality that our sensory impressions create for us. So it is hardly surprising that with suitable set-ups we can very easily identify with an artificial body image instead of our biological body, with a so-called avatar.

By intervening directly in the functional layers of our self-model, VR and other neurotechnologies could soon give rise to entirely new states of consciousness. Virtual embodiments outside our biological body make fascinating applications conceivable in which our self-model is coupled to artificial sensory and action organs. The first approaches to controlling all kinds of robots and other machines directly with our minds using an avatar and recording brain activity already exist.

Key technology 4: using digital algorithms and big data to control our lives

In 2018 alone, humans and machines produced as much data as in the entire history of mankind. Collecting and sharing this data are no longer limited to computers and smartphones. Keyword "smart home": our smartphone is directly connected to the heating and all the everyday appliances in our home. Also popular is the idea of so-called wearables, which are items of clothing into which various sensors are directly incorporated and connected to apps that permanently measure our pulse and other body values. It no longer needs a computer at all. The objects of our everyday life regulate their needs among themselves in the "Internet of Things." This is made possible by ultra-fast mobile internet: in 2020, 5G was switched on, enabling breathtaking speeds of up to 10 gigabits per second.

Sounds great: how easy the "Internet of Things" makes our lives! But there is a catch. The data we leave behind everywhere, like bacteria after a sneezing fit, is collected, processed with ever more powerful algorithms and ever smarter AI and used for ever more comprehensive purposes. From them, our behaviours, preferences and character traits can be specifically read out and the patterns of our lives calculated.

For example, banks still make the decision whether to grant a loan today on the basis of key figures such as debt records, income, collateral, and so on. But already there are algorithms that leave this decision to an AI that determines our creditworthiness based on our digital profile on the internet. Then it could be that you do not get a loan because you spend too much money on video games. Or someone has to pay more for their health insurance because they do not exercise enough. Big data makes it possible for decisions to be made about us that we no longer have any say in.

Companies like Google, Microsoft, Facebook and Apple, as well as the state, are collecting data about us without our knowledge, sometimes in places and from devices that are "completely unsuspicious" like TVs or Xbox consoles. In a world of total connectivity, our privacy will disappear by algorithms and big data. Already, today, companies like Facebook earn tens of billions of dollars with personalised digital advertising. In the US, companies already keep a "customer lifetime value" for each of their customers. Using dozens, hundreds, even thousands of personal data, algorithms calculate how much each individual buyer is likely to earn them over their entire "customer life." With the appropriate software for face and image recognition and a dense network of cameras, the creation of movement profiles of individual people in real time is no longer a problem. So, soon, we will hardly be able to do anything without someone finding out about it. As Eric Schmidt, the head of Google, put it, "If there's something you don't want anyone to know about, maybe you shouldn't do it anyway." Here, hard-core profit interests are underpinned with moral religious pretensions.

Key technology 5: cheating death

In the last 150 years, human life expectancy has doubled. And at 2.5 years per decade, it continues to increase. So the question is: will we be able to live as long as we want? In fact, most of today's genetic researchers assume that ageing processes can be stopped or even reversed at the cellular level. Genetic manipulation could make a primal human dream come true: the eternal fountain of youth.

Animal cells, for example, those of the nematode *Caenorhabditis elegans*, can already be completely reprogrammed through targeted editing, that is, changing, rewriting or deleting individual parts of the DNA strand. For example, a worm whose gene that forms an enzyme called SGK-1 has been switched off lives 60 percent longer than its non-manipulated conspecifics. Why should a similar approach not be possible with human cells?

Another approach to achieving immortality is to grow whole organs outside the body using stem cells. As soon as existing organs lose their functionality, the replacement organs could be implanted into the respective body. This is precisely the goal of the "3D Organ Engineering Initiative" at Harvard University, which has already achieved amazing success: in 2019, it reported the cultivation of an artificial kidney.

Stem cell therapies are another powerful tool from the toolbox of modern biotechnology available for the purpose of disease prevention and life extension. Stem cells are cells that have not yet differentiated into special cell types such as muscle, skin or fat cells. They can be used to produce any tissue (in the case of embryonic stem cells) or even specific tissue types (in the case of adult stem cells). In 2011, it was even possible to grow human heart tissue from stem cells. In the same year, significant visual improvements were achieved in the USA with stem cell therapies in patients suffering from retinal disease. Even the cure of serious diseases such as Parkinson's, diabetes or paraplegia is within reach through the use of stem cells.

RESHAPING THE HUMAN BEING

The five key technologies listed show that we are on the threshold of a revolution in the very nature of being human. In the last 250 years, man has profoundly changed his environment and living conditions through science and technology, and in many cases, we still have a lot of trouble adjusting to and coping with these changes. Yet, the biological and psycho-spiritual foundation of our being has remained largely untouched. But now, for the first time in history, man himself is becoming the object of technological developments. In the dynamics of progress, we are at a point where biotechnology, genetic engineering, quantum technology and neurotechnology are transforming the human being and human civilisation in a hitherto unimaginable way and decisively changing our image of ourselves and of human beings as well as the rules of our lives and coexistence. So what awaits us is not just another industrial revolution, of which there have already been a few, but we must prepare ourselves for a first *revolutionem humanam*, a revolution of being human in itself, an "inversion" of what makes us human in our innermost being and what we define ourselves as.

The focus of our attention is on the specific "crises" (economic and financial crises, political crises, refugee crises, etc.) and the long-term meta-crises (ecological crises, demographic crisis, cultural crises, etc.). Indeed, they are threatening and dangerous. But we have also seen that we are capable of countering difficulties like these through technological, political, social and economic development. In all likelihood, this will continue to be the case in the future. The real crisis, however, is only glimpsed by us: the transformation of the human being. This is a crisis in its true sense. For the coming years will decide in which direction humanity will continue to develop.

How could this real crisis be overcome? How could we resolve the conflicts that a genetic and neurobiological reconstruction of the human being would entail? In order not to be overrun by progress, we need to find answers to many individual questions. Here are just a few of them:

- What consequences should AI, big data and complete electronic data surveillance have on our society—and which not?
- How do we avoid becoming definitively "digitally demented" with increasing digital networking and thus becoming manipulated zombies without a will of their own?

- What does it mean for a person's identity if he or she is the result of genetic optimisation?
- What about his autonomy when he or she can connect directly with other brains—and others with his or hers?
- Who bears responsibility when avatars controlled by a person's thoughts act in the real world?
- Is a person still an individual if they can no longer distinguish between real and downloaded memories?
- What does it mean for our self-esteem when the work performance of a large part of society has become redundant?
- Do we want to achieve lasting happiness by manipulating our neurotransmitters?
- What does it mean for our coexistence when we can cure every conceivable disease and people live much longer than today?

The rapid progress of science raises the question of which of the technological design options we should implement. Science cannot give us the answer, only we can. The following nine key technologies do not directly fuel the human crisis, but each one equally represents a huge potential for change in our society and is indirectly relevant to the human crisis. So they are equally fascinating and incendiary—it is up to us to decide whether we apply them for our general benefit or whether they become a danger to the majority of people.

Key technology 6: the immeasurable computing power of the quantum computer

The most influential physical theory of the twentieth century was without doubt quantum theory. It made semiconductor and laser technologies possible. Without it, there would be no microchips, no computers, no mobile phones, no satellite navigation, no microwave ovens, no nuclear technology, no imaging procedures in medicine and many other technologies that have become a matter of course in our everyday lives. It is estimated that today between a quarter and half of the gross national product of industrialised nations is based directly or indirectly on inventions with a quantum theoretical basis.

Yet quantum physics has by no means exhausted its technological potential. One exciting future technology is a completely new computer that directly uses the quantum properties of subatomic particles for data storage and processing. Instead of processing bit by bit like classical computers, such a quantum computer computes in parallel on numerous quantum states, so-called *quantum bits*. This enables a computing speed that is thousands to millions of times faster than that of conventional computers. This would open up completely new possibilities for the calculation of complex problems such as:

- the construction of synthetic molecular compounds and solids that can be used, for example, as active ingredients in pharmaceuticals, as efficient catalysts for chemical reactions or as tools with completely new material properties;
- the optimisation of traffic flows;
- the further development of AI.

For a long time, 50 qubits were considered the magic limit: above this size, the superiority of quantum computers over the most powerful conventional computers becomes noticeable. In this context, Google speaks of quantum supremacy. In spring 2019, systems from IBM, Google, Alibaba and co. scratched at precisely this mark. If they manage the 50 qubits, this would be a literal "quantum leap."

Key technology 7: building at the atomic level with nanotechnology

Next to the quantum computer, the most groundbreaking vision of future quantum technologies is the construction of ultra-small machines that can perform work at the level of atoms. Such nanomachines could assemble individual atoms as if according to a building-block principle and thus synthetically produce every chemically possible (i.e., energetically stable) compound. They could even produce or replicate themselves. Nature has long since shown us that this is possible: DNA is nothing other than a self-replicating nanomachine that is capable of producing the most amazing structures—just think of the multiform synthesis of proteins.

In fact, researchers are already succeeding in specifically manipulating structures on an atomic scale and even producing basic building blocks for nanomachines: rolling nano-wheels, nano-gears that turn along a jagged edge of atoms, propellers, hinges, grippers, switches and much more. Small motors and vehicles can already be developed—and they are all about one ten-thousandth of a millimetre in size. A great future is predicted for nanomachines, especially in medicine. They could, for example, be inserted into the human body with the task of independently searching for cancer cells and destroying them. The second generation of quantum technologies will change our lives at least as much as the first generation with computers, lasers, atomic energy and imaging techniques in medicine.

Key technology 8: smart factories and the Internet of Things

We have already become accustomed to numerous digital everyday helpers, from the app that informs us in real time about train delays, to the electronic measurement of the steps we have walked, to Tinder, which shows contemporaries in the immediate vicinity who are ready to mate. We also already know about the refrigerator that automatically orders more groceries. But what about an umbrella that flashes when it starts to rain and thus attracts the attention of those who want to leave the house, or a wallet that becomes increasingly difficult to open the lower the credit balance on the credit card.

These helpers are also no longer a problem technologically. With increasing computing capacity, faster networking through ultra-fast mobile internet and ever more intelligent data processing, the development of such "smart things" will continue rapidly. To achieve what we want, we no longer need to use a computer either; everyday things will take care of this among themselves without our direct intervention.

The objects of our everyday life are networked in the Internet of Things. They are increasingly taking away the annoying things of everyday life and making our lives more pleasant—and ourselves more dependent. Since 2012, more machines, toys, alarms, etc., are connected to the internet than there are people on Earth. By 2020, there were almost ten times as many.

Key technology 9: 3D printers—everything instantly available

Not only everyday objects communicate with each other. Increasingly, manufacturing technology, goods production and logistics are also being automated; machines and workpieces are networked in the production process via the internet; and products can therefore be called up and produced immediately. The 3D printer brings industrial manufacturing processes into the living room at home. The basic principle of 3D printing is simple: any three-dimensional objects are built up layer by layer under digital control. From entire houses that are "printed" within 24 hours to medicines that are assembled atom by atom. With the right software and materials, any desired product can be produced easily and very cheaply.

Our economy is still characterised by competition for limited goods. But it is foreseeable that with 3D printing technology we will have almost unlimited resources of goods. Some economists already see it as the spark for the next industrial and social revolution. 3D printers will fundamentally change our economy because material goods will no longer be limited resources—they will be directly and cheaply available to everyone.

Key technology 10: food from the lab instead of the field

For as long as man has existed, he has gathered or hunted his food or produced it in the barn and on the field. Even the use of the most modern agricultural methods and genetic engineering has not changed this. But in the future, a large part of our food will be produced artificially. 3D printing also plays a major role in this development. With it, any material can be assembled from a "handful" of atoms—including edibles. And exactly that is announced to be revealed within the next months now:

- The Israeli company Redefine Meat has already planned the market launch of its patented 3D printing technology for meat substitutes, which is to explicitly replicate the texture, taste and appearance of beef (interestingly, among its investors is Germany's largest poultry farmer, the PHW group, which, among others, represents the Wiesenhof brand).
- The company UPSIDE Foods (formerly known as Memphis Meats), originating from the USA, announced that in 2021 it will launch chicken-type food as the first cell-cultured meat-like product.
- In 2018, the company byFlow had already established the first 3D-printed restaurant in cooperation with 3-star chef Jan Smink in the Dutch city of Wolvega. However, their food 3D printer is mainly aimed at products in the bakery industry. It works with refillable cartridges containing any pastry food to create customised dishes.
- Meanwhile, other suppliers have also established themselves in 3D printing for meat edibles. Besides UPSIDE Foods and Redefine Meat, probably best known are Novameat in Spain and Aleph Farms, also in Israel. These two have also declared 2021 as a breakthrough year for their products.

Key technology 11: trust through decentralised data

Economics is based on trust. Trust that the banknote can really be exchanged for the equivalent value printed on it, that the share in the securities account corresponds to a value in the real world, that the entry in the land register actually guarantees ownership of the house, etc. Institutions such as banks, stock exchanges, notaries and other state institutions provide legal security. But all these "agents of trust" are fallible. Money can lose its value, banks can go bankrupt, stock exchanges can crash, and states can defraud their citizens through corruption.

A new technology makes it possible to bypass these intermediaries for business transactions: the blockchain. It eliminates the need for intermediaries between buyers and sellers and for money as a central and state-controlled entity. Blockchains manage economic processes in decentrally managed networks (so-called peer-to-peer networks): a large group of people who do not know each other (and do not even have to trust each other) keep a record of what belongs to whom and what is true. This means a much more reliable basis for trust than previous institutions.

Specifically, blockchains are electronically stored blocks ("journals") that—hence the name—are linked together in a chain and stored on many computers at once for anyone to see. The ownership of money (e.g., Bitcoins) or basic values corresponds to the possession of a cryptological key that represents the respective credit. The authority that guarantees the security of the transaction is no longer an institution but the community of all participants. They all possess the information that Mr Müller is the owner of the house in the centre of Zurich. Because only he possesses the correct key. If someone wanted to manipulate this information, a majority of the participants would have to agree to the change (which is practically impossible if the number of participants is sufficiently high). Blockchains would therefore make, for example, the land register as we know it superfluous.

The potential applications of blockchains go far beyond monetary transactions. More generally, they enable the recording and preservation of "truths" that cannot be centrally manipulated by a corrupt state or other private interests, since they must always be confirmed decentrally by a majority. Participants in a blockchain are thus secure in their assets. They can transact without the need for an intermediary bank or centrally regulated currencies. Truths are also safe from manipulation.

Key technology 12: new energy technologies

One of the physicists' promises of salvation for our future energy supply is nuclear fusion. Unlike conventional nuclear power plants, where heavy atomic nuclei are split (leaving radioactive waste), here two light atomic nuclei fuse. This process also produces radioactive waste but to a much lesser extent and with much shorter decay times. Nuclear fusion is the most important form of energy generation in our universe. Our Sun also generates its almost infinite energy output in this way.

In fact, plasma physicists hope that in the future, by means of the same processes as inside the Sun, almost any amount of cheap, clean and environmentally friendly energy will be available on Earth. The experimental reactor "Iter" in Cadarache, France, built by an international consortium, is expected to produce initial results from 2030. However, a significant net electricity output is not expected until 2040 at the earliest.

The technological possibilities for generating energy from the Sun, water, wind, biomass and geothermal energy are also making enormous progress in terms of efficiency and effectiveness. For example, thousands of scientists and engineers are working on increasing the efficiency of solar cells. Today, solar panels have an efficiency of around 20%; conceivable are panels that make 75% or even 90% of the incident solar energy available. But even more futuristic ideas already exist. Engineers are thinking, for example, about capturing solar energy by satellite and directing it to earth. Will this enable us to stop climate change? On the other hand, there is the question: what will a society look like in which energy consumption hardly causes any costs, is clean and climate-neutral?

Key technology 13: biosensors and nanorobots in our bodies

Whereas in the past analysis devices the size of suitcases or cupboards were needed in laboratories, today tiny (nano-)biomarker systems are used—every pregnancy test and every alcohol tube into which a car driver has to blow is an example of this miniaturisation. Biomarkers need only extremely small amounts of liquid to cause colour reactions through chemical processes. Biosensors can also work electronically: there are already microprocessor chips, the so-called labs-on-a-chip (LOC), which can determine a diagnosis for numerous disease symptoms in a few minutes. One particularly active area of LOC research involves the diagnosis and treatment of HIV infection. There are 40 million people living with HIV in the world, about 90% of whom have never been tested for the disease, and only 1.3 million are receiving antiretroviral treatment. HIV LOCs could make a decisive contribution to improving global health.

However, nano-particles do not only take over the analysis, they already transport drugs in the human body to the diseased tissue with pinpoint accuracy, so that pathogens or mutated cells are attacked with active substances. However, the future promises of medicine are even more exciting. Here are some of them.

- Ultra-small nanorobots that constantly move through our bodies looking for pathogens;
- Automatic, every-morning nano-checks while brushing our teeth, using biomarkers that indicate serious diseases in their early stages;
- Replacement of defective body parts with implants made of corresponding nanoparticles.

The possibilities of the medicine of the future are to those of today in a similar relationship as today's medicine is to medieval medicine. Molecule-sized machines replace surgery and become part of our bodies. They move through the bloodstream to diseased organs and release drugs there or perform surgical procedures directly.

Key technology 14: synthetic life—when man plays god

In addition to gene optimisation, life extension, crop breeding and stem cell therapy, genetic engineering opens up yet another exciting possibility of intervention in creation: the creation of completely artificial life, tailor-made for specific purposes. Life from scratch is what genetic researchers call this new field of research in biology.

In spring 2010, gene pioneer Craig Venter announced that his team had succeeded in building an artificial genome in the laboratory and implanting it in a cell of the bacterium *Mycoplasma capricolum* that had previously been stripped of its natural DNA. The artificial bacterium was not only viable, it could even reproduce! This was followed, in March 2014, by the news that the team led by biologist Jef Boeke had succeeded in completely reconstructing one of the 16 chromosomes of baker's yeast (*Saccharomyces cerevisiae*) in the test tube and with some desirable modifications. Yeasts are so-called eukaryotes. Their genetic material is much more extensive and complicated than that of the bacteria and viruses in Venter's studies. Humans are also eukaryotes; basically, the jump from the bacterial genome to the baker's yeast genome is greater than that from the baker's yeast genome to the human genome. So the first steps towards artificially producing more complex life forms have been taken. Boeke and his team have by now achieved the critical milestone of the completion of synthesis of the first functional eukaryotic chromosome in yeast.

Gene pioneers like Venter and Boeke are already talking about a new era in biology in which synthetic life forms are produced for industrial or medical purposes, for example. Artificially produced bacteria, for example, could break down oil spills on the world's oceans and decompose plastic, and CO_2-"eating" microbes from the lab could even stop climate change. The new discipline of synthetic biology will be able to create life forms that have never existed on our planet before and that can be used for very specific purposes.

THE COMBINATION MAKES IT

All these key technologies will revolutionise our lives in the future. In mutual interaction, they even develop a much more dramatic potency. Here are a few examples.

- The combination of AI, robotics and virtual reality will dramatically change the self-image of humans and their abilities—far more than religions or the Enlightenment have done so far.
- The computational power of quantum computers is expected to be used to make the learning and optimisation algorithms of artificial neural networks orders of magnitude faster and more efficient. This would dramatically speed up the development of AI.
- Today, genetic engineers use a database of many millions of individual genes to simulate how they would have to be combined to obtain synthetic creatures with desired characteristics. Ever-improving AI or quantum computers could vastly speed up the identification of useful gene sequences.
- The combination of genetic engineering, AI and data analysis enables personalised medicine, tailored to the individual patient, which diagnoses and acts far more efficiently than conventional examinations and

treatments. This lead the US cardiologist and geneticist Eric Topol to claim that "artificial intelligence represents the greatest transformation of medicine in history."

- The neural optimisation algorithms of AI have also long since found their way into drug research. The goal of a new discipline called "computational biotechnology" is to create designer molecules with specific properties, such as high efficacy in drugs. In particular, this involves the design of specific, very complex protein structures. It is precisely these very complicated structures and patterns that AI algorithms are getting better at finding.
- AI algorithms and inorganic chemistry are also a promising team: huge databases are searched for possible crystal structures with promising properties.
- When quantum 3D printers and nanotechnology come together, matter—for example, from a handful of dust—can be arranged in a targeted way (even atom by atom, if necessary) and shaped into almost any form and function. A next stage would be to integrate a nano-3D printer into the materials themselves. Then the objects could renew or reproduce themselves automatically as needed.
- The combination of genetic engineering, stem cell research and nanotechnology will increase our physical and mental well-being as well as our life expectancy to previously unimagined dimensions. A concrete vision of medical scientists is that many small nanorobots, biomarkers, DNA chips and other telemedical devices will move permanently in our bodies, preventively examining our bodily functions, detecting pathogens, gene mutations and dangerous deposits in the bloodstream, fighting viruses, inhibiting inflammation, removing cysts and cellular adhesions and preventing strokes by opening blocked arteries.
- Digital technologies like AI and blockchain can reshuffle the cards of the global economy. Most bankers, lawyers and notaries would have to look for a new profession.

THE COMBINATION OF KEY TECHNOLOGIES POTENTIATES THEIR IMPACT—BOTH THEIR BENEFITS AND THEIR DANGERS

Now we know how immense the opportunities and challenges are that await us in shaping our future. Next, let us look at how we can overcome our propensity to manipulate so that we develop all of the aforementioned technologies to our best advantage.

It is not companies but democratically elected parliaments that must decide how we live in the future. The state is not meant as an all-powerful "saviour" but as an executive organ of the wishes of committed citizens who, through pressure, achieve that politicians pass ever better laws. Corresponding rules must also function globally. This is shown by the three technology areas examined in more detail here.

(1) Big data, AI and our privacy
(2) CRISPR and genetic engineering
(3) Neuro-enhancement and consciousness technologies

Big data, AI and our privacy

As late as 1983, there was fierce opposition to the planned census in the Federal Republic of Germany. It involved 36 questions about the housing situation, the people living in the household and their income. "Privacy is sacred," they said. The Federal Constitutional Court ruled in favour of the plaintiffs and stopped the project. Only one generation later, we carelessly hand over the supermarket chain's bonus card with every purchase, surf the internet without a care in the world, Google and shop, email and chat, use every app without hesitation and thus give many times more insight into our private lives than the state wanted to know about us 35 years ago. If we also wear digital wearables in the future and a more powerful AI is able to detect ever finer patterns in our behaviour, we will no longer have any secrets from Google and Co. If we do not take countermeasures, their algorithms will manipulate and control us ever more uninhibitedly.

In Europe, this development has brought legislators on the scene, albeit very late and still too timidly. With the General Data Protection Regulation (GDPR) of May 2018, personal data protection became valid law. In the USA, by contrast, data protection is not regulated by law at all; even an independent data protection supervisory authority is lacking. But the topic is being discussed. Among other things, this is ensured by events like the data protection scandals surrounding Facebook and Cambridge Analytica, as well as recurring data thefts, such as at Yahoo at the end of 2017, as well as political interventions such as the GDPR, which has also made people think in the USA. The state of California introduced its own data protection law in mid-2018, which is partly based on the European GDPR.

In China, by contrast, "personal data protection" is not even being discussed. The free access of the Chinese internet companies Baidu and Tencent to the personal data of their customers is an important competitive advantage for them in the global competition for leadership in AI. For the Chinese government, they are also a gift: with the help of AI and big data, they are massively expanding their control over citizens, such as through the so-called *Citizen's Score*.

At the political level, the effort to develop global standards seems to be at an impasse. But the experts are putting on the pressure. For example, the EU Commission recently set up an expert group that addressed the public in December 2018 with a paper titled "Ethical Foundations for Trustworthy AI", which even explicitly asked for input. This explicitly talks about the fact that we need an anthropocentric approach to shape the development of AI in such a way that

- the individual human being, his dignity and freedom are protected;
- democracy, law and order and civil rights are upheld; and
- equality, protection of minorities and solidarity are promoted.

To achieve what the authors call "trustworthy AI," the paper identifies a wide range of measures at both technical and non-technical levels. The basic guidelines for any AI technology must be:

1. do good to people;
2. not to cause human suffering;
3. promote human autonomy;
4. apply the principle of fairness; and
5. achieve transparency and traceability in all effects.

These are (albeit still very tender) beginnings of such an important societal discussion on the issues of future technology design, in this case AI. How autocratic countries like China will develop in terms of data protection is hard to foresee today. However, human rights groups there have already realised that a new and extremely important field of activity has opened up for them.

CRISPR and gene technology

In questions of the application of new genetic engineering possibilities, different standards seem to prevail worldwide. In Western democracies, clear laws prohibit gene editing on human embryos. Concerns about any form of eugenics are generally very high here. This is different in China, where there is a much more open attitude towards genetic engineering on humans.

Nevertheless, Chinese government representatives immediately condemned the birth of the first CRISPR baby reported in November 2018, and publicly pilloried the person responsible, Jiankui He. So there are definitely incentives for Chinese scientists and the Chinese government to behave according to certain ethical norms. China does not want to be seen by the international community as a rogue state without conscience, and Chinese scientists fear for their international reputation. Thanks to He's experiments, an international, public discussion about the use of CRISPR is finally taking place.

What has eluded the public until now: there have already been CRISPR experiments on human embryos in the USA, too. In July 2017, a team of researchers, led by the controversial biologist Shoukhrat Mitalipov in Portland, Oregon, had attempted to create genetically modified human embryos using CRISPR. They were able to show that defective genes that cause hereditary diseases can be corrected safely and efficiently with the help of CRISPR. Still, the US National Academy of Sciences draws a red line. "Genome editing to improve traits or abilities beyond ordinary health raises concerns about whether the benefits outweigh the risks, and about fairness if available only to some individuals," said Alta Charo, Co-chair of the National Academy of Sciences' study committee. But these vague words also show that there is still a need for a much more active discussion in society about how to shape future genetic engineering. Just as leading CRISPR experts did in spring 2015, when they published the appeal that genetic engineering options must be limited.

The discussion is far from over but has so far been able to prevent the worst excesses. The question is: do CRISPR treatments on humans have to be banned worldwide to prevent human breeding? But we must also ask ourselves whether it is ethically justifiable not to use the genetic engineering possibilities to prevent serious hereditary diseases. The discussion and legal regulation of biotechnologies are a must. Scientists, politicians, entrepreneurs, doctors but also those who are affected by hereditary diseases must face this challenge.

Neuro-enhancement and technologies of consciousness

Developments towards "virtual embodiment" also raise massive ethical questions. What about the responsibility of our actions in virtual space? What about our autonomy when we connect with avatars? How can we control that these avatars do not act on the basis of our unconscious impulses?

As in the ethical debates on AI and CRISPR, the question of possible military applications is of particular importance in relation to consciousness technologies and brain–computer interfaces. With the use of American drones in Pakistan or Somalia, we have experienced (and are still experiencing) the first beginnings of warfare through avatars. There is no way around an international moratorium here. However, VR technologies could also help us to achieve an increase in our empathic abilities in addition to an increase in our biological, neurological and cognitive potential, for example, by feeling completely into other beings by means of a virtual embodiment.

LAST WORDS

We face the mammoth task of deciding for all key technologies which applications will benefit humanity as a whole and which will harm it. In order to make these decisions, we have to ask and answer philosophical, ethical and spiritual questions. If you are a young person today and are thinking about which professions will be significant in the future and will not be taken over by intelligent machines, you will find what you are looking for in philosophy, anthropology or theology. Government agencies and also companies like Google and Myriad Genetics will be desperate for experts in these fields, in addition to well-trained programmers and technicians.

A particularly future-proof career choice is thus: Philosopher.

3

ESG—A Transformational Journey for Asset Management, Industries, Technology, and Society*

Asoka Wöhrmann

GREEN INDUSTRIALIZATION: A NEW ERA OF INDUSTRIALIZATION

More and more, society, politics, and businesses are accepting their responsibility for a thriving and worthwhile future for the generations to come. The transformation that accompanies this collective reality cannot be overstated. One of the most important phases in the development of modern humanity was the Industrial Revolution of the nineteenth century. It made the world what it is today, for better or for worse. It has created more prosperity for more people and made modern societies in a globalized world possible. But it has also initiated the climate changes that we must combat today: we are at the beginning of a green industrialization. It is the next industrial revolution. And there is no alternative to it. It is about nothing less than the climate-neutral preservation of what the Industrial Revolution of the nineteenth century once laid the foundation for: prosperity and progress for more people than ever before. As a logical consequence, this green industrialization will represent the greatest economic and social transformation in 150 years.

The resulting, in some cases fundamental, change of business models will be heavily influenced by technological change. On the one hand, technology plays an equally important role in finding solutions to ESG issues, and on the other hand, when it comes to analysis, information plays an important role in enabling more accurate data and analysis across all businesses.

* This book chapter was finalized in May 2022

DOI: 10.4324/9781003262039-4

It is easy to note that one of the major challenges, besides the cultural and technological innovation required, is the entire sphere of ESG-related data, starting with disclosure, ideally supported by standardized frameworks, time reference, over data sources and assessment.

This green industrialization requires reliable data in order to properly assess risk factors and steer capital to the most compelling opportunities in the E, S, and G spectrum, and most urgently toward climate mitigation and adaptation. To achieve this, a radical overhaul in corporate reporting and in the way we use data as it relates to sustainability must occur. The asset management industry can not only play a major role in analyzing and processing ESG information to make proper investment decisions but also use the role in capital markets to advocate and support the further evolvement of global disclosure frameworks. The goal must be to achieve more consistency, comparability, and more transparency in the assessment of E-, S-, and G-related information in a globally consistent manner, eventually providing a truly holistic picture of future investment opportunities. On this basis, institutional and retail investors alike can make a valuable contribution to the green industrialization transformation.

Understanding the need for an increase in the volume and diversity of sustainability data

The world has enjoyed unprecedented prosperity over the past 100 years when measured in terms of wealth and life expectancy. However, these achievements have come at a cost since according to the Dasgupta Review the stock of natural capital, such as forests, fisheries, agricultural land, and minerals, has fallen by 40% on a per capita basis since 1992 (Dasgupta, 2021).

Investors around the world are therefore demanding to know how their capital is used and the impact their capital is having on the world. What holds us back is that we are still stuck in a world of corporate reporting more reflective of the 1970s than the twenty-first century. However, a new industrial revolution has arrived, fueled by technologies encompassing digitalization, artificial intelligence (AI), automation, biotechnology, fintech, and clean technologies, which offers the opportunity to address major environmental challenges, such as climate change, biodiversity loss, and social inequality, as well as deliver economic prosperity. In addition, technology will be instrumental in altering our current linear economic model of "Take-Make-Waste" to a circular one which delivers growth in a more sustainable manner.

The Business and Sustainable Development Commission (BSDC) has identified growth and investment opportunities around the United Nations Sustainable Development Goals (SDGs) which have become an important template for sustainability-themed investing. The BSDC estimates the SDGs

Climate Parameter	Manifestation	1.5°C heating	2.0°C heating	2.0°C impact
Extreme Heat	Global population exposed to severe heat at least once every five years	14%	37%	2.6x worse
Sea-Ice-Free Arctic	Number of ice-free summers	At least 1 every 100 years	At least 1 every 10 years	10x worse
Sea Level Rise	Amount of sea level rise by 2100	0.40 meters	0.46 meters	0.06 meters
Permafrost	Amount of Arctic permafrost that will thaw	4.8 mn km^2	6.6 mn km^2	38% worse
Crop Yields	Reduction in maize harvests in tropics	3%	7%	2.3x worse
Fisheries	Decline in marine fisheries	1.5 mn tonnes	3 mn tonnes	2x worse

FIGURE 3.1 Half a Degree of Warming Makes a Big Difference

(Source: DWS Research Institute, World Resources Institute (September 16, 2021), "Ambitious Climate Action by G20 Countries Can Limit Global Warming to 1.7 Degrees Celsius." Forecasts are based on assumptions, estimates, opinions, and assumptions or analyses and may prove inaccurate or incorrect.)

could be a key driver of economic growth and unlock opportunities worth up to US$12 trillion per annum by 2030, or more than a tenth of global output. In addition, almost 400 million jobs could be created across the food and agriculture, cities, energy, and materials and health and well-being sectors (BSDC, 2017).

One of the most urgent tasks on the SDG agenda is addressing climate change, which has also become the primary focus of policy making and investors' attention. However, assessments from the Intergovernmental Panel on Climate Change (IPCC, 2021) and Climate Action Tracker (2021) provide grim reading. They show that even our current worst estimates are proving too optimistic, we have already warmed by 1.2°C since pre-industrial levels, and we are on a path to 2.7°C. This holds extreme risks since the cost of inaction to contain temperature within 1.5°C threatens us on multiple fronts (see Figure 3.1). In addition, global financial losses attributable to extreme weather events continue to spiral upwards. Thankfully, technology provides a promising route to address these issues, help secure a more credible path toward Net Zero, and deliver sustainable economic growth.

Moving beyond climate to encompass broader sustainability issues

Two months before the WHO declared COVID-19 a pandemic, a global survey released by Edelman at Davos, in January 2020, found that 56% of people believed that capitalism, as it exists today, does more harm than good in the world (Edelman, 2020). The survey moreover found that trust in companies can be strengthened if these entities contribute to communities, deal fairly with suppliers, pay a decent wage, and partner with external organizations and governments on key issues.

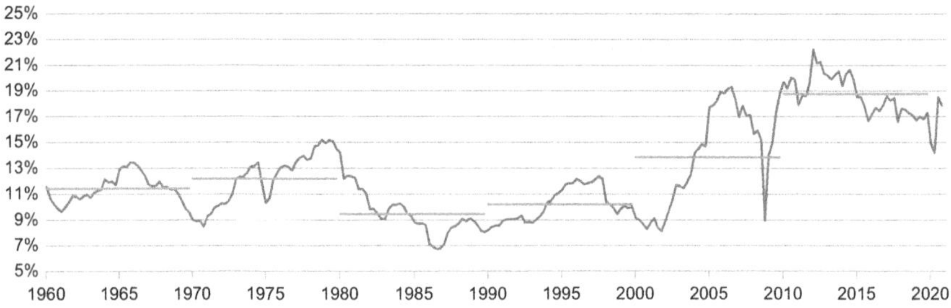

FIGURE 3.2 US Corporate Business Profits After Tax Divided By Employee Compensation

(Source: Board of Governors of the Federal Reserve System: Z.1 Financial Accounts of the United States, DWS Investment GmbH as of March 2021.)

The COVID-19 pandemic has led to even greater investor attention on the financial materiality of social factors, an area of the ESG investing landscape that has often been overshadowed by the responsibilities of integrating the multiple dimensions of climate risk. But social risk has become more acute in recent years since when it comes to globalization, digitalization, and the associated productivity gains, these have been increasingly accruing to the owners of capital rather than labor (see Figure 3.2). In the coming years, the transition to a low-carbon economy also threatens workers and communities across multiple sectors such as mining, manufacturing, and agriculture, which is also focusing investor attention on social protection.

The challenge has been the lack of progress in well-defined social metrics, for example, in the area of human rights and product safety. However, progress in this area is taking place. An example of legislation focused on social issues can be seen in Germany and the Supply Chain Act, which will come into force in January 2023. To ensure compliance with minimum social standards, companies will have to have a risk profile for each supplier and report annually on potential risks in their supply chain as well as the countermeasures they have put in place with noncompliance resulting in potentially large fines. At EU level, the development of a social taxonomy to complement the bloc's environmental classification system is providing a taxonomy which provides the relevant social metrics around employee, consumer, and community rights and protection.

Technology fuels transformation

What can be viewed today is akin to a sixth innovation wave focused on the technologies of the green industrialization. Indications suggest that this innovation wave could be even more powerful in terms of its speed and the extent of disruption. As in previous innovation waves, which began with mechanization and the age of steam in the eighteenth–nineteenth centuries to biotech and information technology at the end of the twentieth century, this green innovation wave will render many old business models obsolete. Asset managers have an important role to play in this transformation through their corporate engagement strategies. These strategies have become increasingly focused on sustainability issues and even more toward specific outcomes of sustainability measures.

Technology will be central to a Net Zero pathway

To achieve Net Zero will require action on multiple fronts. It will necessitate the deployment of technologies to help decarbonize key sectors. Most important will be the energy, transportation, and food systems which represent a significant share of global greenhouse gas emissions.

What is also required is scaling effective technologies to capture existing carbon from the atmosphere. Even with our best efforts to reduce them, there will still be some emissions in activities which simply do not have an alternative production process such as in the cement, steel, and chemical sectors. Net Zero is consequently a state in which emissions that simply cannot be eliminated are compensated by absorption and removal of greenhouse gases from the atmosphere. It is the absorption and removal of GHGs or Carbon Capture, Use, and Storage (CCUS), which will likely be almost indispensable to achieve Net Zero. The deployment of CCUS technologies will require much higher carbon prices. This is why the green industrialization needs policy frameworks to support them.

But decarbonizing and the deployment of technologies to capture existing carbon from the atmosphere will still not be enough when it comes to building a credible Net Zero climate strategy. These efforts must be supplemented by steps to protect and restore our land, forests, and oceans, given the role these ecosystems play in carbon reduction and removal. Our seas, for example, are being damaged by acidification due to rising temperatures, plastic, and chemical pollution, overfishing, whaling, seabed mining, resource exploitation, and coastal habitat destruction. While public policy has a central role to play in conferring legal protection to these ecosystems, technology will help accelerate this green transformation.

Analysis conducted by Project Drawdown (2020) has revealed some interesting individual- and nature-related actions which can deliver powerful climate-friendly solutions. Table 3.1 shows the top ten actions individually and by sector when it comes to reducing and removing carbon emissions from the atmosphere.

TABLE 3.1
Nature-Related Actions Are Vital, Both Individually and Collectively

Top individual actions for reducing and removing carbon emissions	Gigatons CO_2e reduced or sequestered (2020–2050)—1.5°C scenario	Top sectors for reducing and removing carbon emissions	Total gigatons CO_{2e} reduced/ or sequestered (2020 -2050)—1.5°C scenario
Onshore wind turbines	147.72	**Food, agriculture, land, and oceans**	**766.31**
Utility-scale solar photovoltaics	119.13	**Renewable electricity**	**392.31**
Refrigerant management and alternative refrigerants	108.28	**Buildings**	**254.73**
Reduced food waste	101.71	**Transport**	**97.46**
Plant-rich diets	91.72	**Health and education**	**85.42**
Health and education	85.42		
Tropical forest restoration	85.14		
Improved clean cookstoves	72.65		
Distributed solar photovoltaics	68.64		
Silvopasture (integrating trees into livestock pastures)	**42.31**		

(Source: DWS analysis of Project Drawdown 2021, www.drawdown.org/solutions/table-of-solutions.)

Wind turbines (1st) and photovoltaics (2nd) are widely recognized climate solutions, but we are still a long way to recognize that a sustainable future can be achieved through addressing food waste (4th), changing our diets (5th), health and education (6th). It may be surprising to see refrigeration (3rd) as being among the most important routes to address climate change.

In the past, every refrigerator and air-conditioning unit used to contain chemical refrigerants to absorb and release heat. Chlorofluorocarbons (CFCs) and hydrochlorofluorocarbons (HCFCs) are harmful for the ozone layer and were replaced by hydrofluorocarbons (HFCs). While this replacement was great for the ozone layer, it was terrible for the climate as their "warming" impact on climate is between 1,000 and 9,000 times greater than CO_2. The good news is that society is beginning to address this issue. It is estimated that by 2028, natural refrigerants, ammonia, and propane will be used instead, and HFCs will be completely phased out. However, since refrigeration and air-conditioning units typically have long life-spans, early adoption of these "cleaner" units needs to be encouraged.

The path to Net Zero requires working on multiple fronts, which in turn requires time and resources. Therefore, there is a need to shift from "single solution" thinking toward a more holistic approach, where the links between climate and our economic and social activities are incorporated by all stakeholder actions, whether it relates to investment, legislation, policy making, reporting, or data collection.

Some examples of how technological innovation is permeating across all sectors

Technologies are successfully being deployed to address major environmental and social challenges across all areas of our economy. To illustrate how technologies can facilitate the Net Zero trajectory, DWS examined the agricultural, building, and marine sectors which, according to estimates from Hannah Ritchie and Max Roser in Our World in Data (2020), together accounted for approximately 40% of global greenhouse gas emissions.

(1) Agricultural sector: Techniques are being deployed to help cope with the increasing demands on the food sector from global population growth, rising incomes, and climate change. Such solutions include recycling wastewater, rainwater harvesting, drip irrigation technology, precision planting and hybrid seeds, improved infrastructure and pipes, as well as introducing desalination facilities. Technologies can also help to deliver more site-specific weather intelligence and disease probability mapping, which can enable a more optimal crop production process. This, in turn, can ensure fertilizers and pesticides are used more efficiently and so reduce the ecological footprint of farming. In addition, lab-grown meat from cultured cells could cut the environmental costs of producing meat and reduce the unethical treatment of farm animals.
(2) Building sector: Accelerating the retrofitting of buildings can support the economic recovery, cut emissions, and improve energy security. In addition, technologies like smart metering are improving the energy and water efficiency of buildings, and initiatives which improve the insulation and ventilation of our building stock can have positive impacts on air quality, reducing respiratory and cardiovascular diseases and allergies.
(3) Marine sector: Outdated technologies and working practices continue to prevail across marine industries. "SeaTech" is a term used to refer to marine industry applications of big data, blockchain, biotech, and the Internet of Things (IoT) technologies. There is potential for technology developments to help advance the sustainable oceans agenda.

For instance, underwater sensors, robots, and cameras will reveal sea creatures to catch and avoid, changing ocean conditions, and goings-on in farmed fish pens.

Consistent reporting and disclosure lay the ground for sound investment decisions

With all the changes being spurred by technology, and prompting fundamental corporate transformation, we are moreover facing the considerable challenge of capturing and assessing the data that reflect these changes. In addition to the actual change, we have another challenge: how can we ensure the information is accurate, comparable across sectors, and, even more importantly, that the information we receive from different sources provide a holistic picture of the current and future ESG footprint of a firm?

Assessing the other side of transformation

Effectively addressing these sustainability challenges requires a significant upgrade in corporate reporting and disclosure. What exists today satisfies an old notion that the sole responsibility of companies is to increase profits, as expressed in Milton Friedman's famous 1970 op-ed in the *New York Times*.

Antiquated reporting frameworks are therefore no longer fit for purpose since, today, investors around the world are demanding increasing disclosure about how their capital is used and the impact their capital is having on the world. Despite these demands, investors face significant challenges in several aspects of ESG data management: the availability of standardized and globally comparable data as well as the generation and availability of forward-looking sustainability information.

What exists currently can be best described as reporting overload with an array of frameworks. However, change is afoot as the standard setters like the Sustainability Accounting Standards Board (SASB), the International Integrated Reporting Council (IIRC), the Global Reporting Initiative (GRI), the Carbon Disclosure Project (CDP), and the Carbon Disclosure Standards Board (CDSB) are working together to create a comprehensive corporate reporting system while the Big Four accountancy firms, in consultation with the World Economic Forum's International Business Council, are working to "mainstream" ESG reporting. The International Financial Reporting Standards (IFRS) Foundation is developing a global set of comparable and consistent sustainability reporting standards governed by the new International Sustainability Standards Board (ISSB). The formation of the ISSB is an important milestone in the evolution of sustainable reporting standards for corporates and the financial industry alike. Globally consistent sustainability disclosure frameworks will serve asset managers as a crucial basis for risk and opportunity analyses of E, S, and G criteria in their fiduciary investment decisions.

This greater focus on sustainability reporting is not only welcome but also crucial, since ESG investing without a global standard will be marred with conflicts of interests and will ultimately fail investors' desire to put capital to work to address humanity's sustainability challenges.

From our standpoint, such reporting frameworks clearly need to go beyond climate and beyond environmental aspects to capture the broader planetary issues such as biodiversity loss as well as extend into the social and inequality arenas. There is also an increasingly common understanding that useful and relevant reporting must ultimately focus on double materiality, that is, how the world affects companies as well as how companies affect the world. This approach also needs to be science-based to ensure maximum credibility. Combined, these will help to facilitate and provide a more comprehensive picture of the changes happening and construct a reliable decision base for investors supporting the transformation needed.

It cannot be overstated that the ability to support sustainable transformation by targeted investments requires an overhaul and dynamic approach to disclosure and reporting frameworks. It will require new ways of how investors engage with investee firms and how respective progress can be tracked and reported. Policy makers, corporations, asset managers, and data providers all need to play their role by transforming the way they operate individually and by applying new technologies collectively.

ENGAGE, SUPPORT, ADVOCATE—THE ROLE OF ASSET MANAGERS

As fiduciary investors for clients, who are increasingly demanding sustainable actions in their investments, asset managers are in a good position to facilitate the green industrial transformation. Academic literature underlines that asset managers can have substantial sustainable impact on the economy by evoking positive ESG change in investee firms via shareholder engagement (see, e.g., Barko et al., 2021; Dimson et al., 2015; Semenova & Hassel, 2019). There are key areas by which asset managers can actively support the shift to a low-carbon economy with the goal to ultimately achieve Net Zero within sustainable capital markets: portfolio company engagement and client engagement, interaction with accounting standard boards, and public advocacy with governments.

Engagement as a key driver of change and improved disclosure

As a fiduciary asset manager, we see ourselves as active owners, which means working in dialogue with the companies in which we invest to ensure they actively address ESG factors and set a clear path to Net Zero.

In my experience active ownership is an integral part of investment processes. Our active ownership is designed to be guided by the concept of double materiality: it is not just environmental and social impacts on the company that can be material but also impacts of a company on the climate and society—or any other dimension of sustainability.

As outlined earlier, investment decisions need to be based on reliable data, with the comprehensiveness of ESG information still in development to answer the needs for better comparability and more forward-looking information. It is important to note that assessments do not have to be consistent, as differing views open up investment opportunities. This is particularly the case for forward-looking information or assessments.

It takes constant reviews and evolution of the engagement approach to ensure the right focus in stakeholder dialogue, so that change can be supported and information can be appropriately captured. These engagement efforts tend to be time-intensive and require continued one-to-one interactions based on existing sustainability data, among other points. Academic evidence (see earlier) has demonstrated the merits in such engagements not only for achieving financial performance but also for potentially beneficial sustainability outcomes.

There is value in targeted and focused engagement, so that ambitious but realistic targets can be set and constantly monitored. As a first step, disclosure on key performance indicators (such as exposure to certain sustainability risks or identified adverse sustainability impacts in line with the guidance of double materiality) is key, which in turn enables you to conduct a qualitative assessment on responsiveness and progress made. In case engagement efforts yield further insights on achieving sustainability outcomes (e.g., measured by contribution to the SDGs) or mitigating adverse impacts, there is the opportunity to complement quantitative assessments of ESG data with qualitative engagement insights.

Such an enhanced engagement approach requires increasingly comprehensive and quality-assured data as the basis of analyses and demands on companies. The focus of future data on sustainability criteria must be on timeliness and comparability, rather than consistency, of assessments in order to make new engagement concepts effective. Active ownership and engagement are not restricted to equity investments which entitle fiduciaries to vote on their clients' behalf and to engage with firms. Engagement also includes corporate bond holdings and even includes non-issuers such as credit rating agencies, index providers, or stock exchanges.

The future of engagement principles is focused on sustainability outcomes

I am convinced there is a major shift toward the impact of stakeholders in engagement, being one aspect of the tectonic shift from shareholder-focused goals to sustainable ESG targets. Institutional investors increasingly want to positively impact the sustainable performance of their investee firms by addressing ESG issues during shareholder engagements.

I believe the future of engagement is no longer about leading discussions with investees for the purpose of purely gathering information but to focus on predefined targets to achieve impact and progress in ESG matters in a reasonable time frame. Such future picture assessments in turn become an integral part of the investment decisions, in particular for long-term investors targeting sustainable returns.

Making engagement strategies a powerful tool for greater transformation and measurable change requires novel technologies in data processing. Data sources are becoming increasingly sophisticated in order to provide investors with tools needed to make more informed decisions. These range from combining alternative data with traditional sources to add another dimension, using Artificial Intelligence (AI) to pick up and collate qualitative data from multiple sources as well as digitalizing engagement platforms.

Public advocacy to evolve reporting and disclosure

The path to more sustainability in our economies can be reached only if public and private stakeholders work together and create a regulatory framework that is transparent, robust, and credible. This framework is evolving, and asset managers need to use their experience and market insights to enter discussions with policy makers.

There are two main motivations for asset managers to lead such discussions: first, they are dependent on evolving rules for sustainability reporting which provide tangible, standardized data on investee companies and which enable them to provide useful information to investors and clients when it comes to their roles as a reporting entity. Second, I strongly believe in the effect of engagement to support the economy's transformation toward more sustainability.

Asset managers also play an important role in the progression of frameworks for responsible investing. On the one hand, large investors must evolve their own processes and tools. On the other hand, they also can and need to use their position for clear public advocacy and disclosure actions.

Along with the evolution of engagement concepts comes the requirement of reliable, consistent, and comparable information on a global scale as a prerequisite. The need for a global and consistent corporate disclosure and reporting system must be answered in due course, and it must be based on the principle of double materiality. Asset managers should welcome the decision for the consolidated new body for reporting standards ISSB, and I am pleased to see that Frankfurt hosts the lead office for this new ISSB. I expect this body to aggregate the already advanced work of established initiatives and expect timely and binding new frameworks. A necessary step that will be highly appreciated by many market participants, not only in the finance but also in the corporate arena.

As a second focus of advocacy efforts and to further support the effectiveness of engagement activities besides engagement principles, I would argue for a legal framework that makes it easier to follow an engagement approach, for example, by reviewing rules on "acting in concert" if asset owners vote together at an annual general meeting to bring in more ambitious ESG strategies in a company. In their second Sustainable Finance Strategy published in July 2021, the European Commission acknowledges this issue and asks supervisory agencies to look into it. Urgent legal clarification that investors' common engaging for more sustainable governance in an investee company should not count as "acting in concert" is therefore needed.

Asset managers must also pursue their own transformation. This includes setting Net Zero targets on a scientific basis—using the latest climate and energy models that provide guidance on necessary decarbonization pathways. There are many voluntary initiatives and public–private projects for this, for example, the Net Zero Asset Manager Initiative. Engagement therefore also applies to the exchange with other companies in the financial sector as well as with political and supervisory authorities.

While the private sector can innovate, at-scale adoption of change requires a clear path by policy makers as the main drivers of change.

THE MEASUREMENT OF ESG FOOTPRINTS, RISKS, AND OPPORTUNITIES

Materiality has been a guiding principle in financial accounting for a long time. The concept of double materiality as introduced in the context of the EU sustainability disclosure regulation takes this a step further. Now disclosure from any firm is meant to address what sustainability issues affect their business and adds the new question about their own impact on people and the environment. The goal of any ESG-related data assessment, as with any standard financial assessment, must be to measure risks and opportunities, to eventually create a better understanding of future sustainability impacts.

Mitigating subjectivity and finding a balanced view

Any investor is dependent on information on the sustainability profile of an asset: how well is the company placed concerning business opportunities arising from sustainability? What are the sustainability risks? What impact does the company's business have—by either behavior or products—on the sustainability for the direct environment and our planet as a whole?

One approach to that challenge is to subscribe to external expert knowledge by sourcing quantitative and qualitative data on sustainability, be it from commercial vendors or trusted NGO sources. There are multiple ESG data vendors and NGOs, but there is no gold standard yet. While one vendor may excel or set standards for the passive ESG index Exchange Traded Fund (ETF) business, another may set the standards for actively managed funds. There are also single NGOs setting the standards for Net Zero path alignment for companies or assessing political and personal freedoms of sovereign states. Asset managers should always act as fiduciary to their clients and always act in their best interest. In the context of ESG evaluations, this requires to consider multiple sources for ESG data to generate a view that is as comprehensive as possible to come to a sound assessment.

The challenge of subjectivity in any data assessment and thus also in sustainability matters will never go away even in an evolved world of full disclosure. This is because seemingly objective data, for example—reported carbon emissions—need to be valued against certain criteria. For example, does the company excel or lag behind with these emissions compared to peers? Is the company on track with their Net Zero plans with these emissions? What impact would future regulatory carbon pricing have on the business model?

The multi-data source approach mitigates the subjectivity challenge to a large extent, but it leaves the questions of how to best aggregate data from different sources and how to evaluate consensus or non-consensus. Non-consensus means that one source puts the emphasis on an item another source has not put a focus on. As long as there is some consensus—maybe not between all sources but between a majority of sources—there is value in that assessment. A range of educated opinions should be considered when generating an ESG signal. What always works is aggregation of information, which means the aggregation of the information contained in the data, not the aggregation of the data itself.

Fiduciary investors need to look at a relative, not an absolute scale: who are the true leaders, the true laggards in the respective field? What is needed is a trustworthy consensual leader or laggard mark?

The concepts described here produce reliable ESG signals to measure sustainability risks and opportunities when based on data from trusted multiple sources. This is the interface to the use of modern software and data management techniques.

OUTLOOK: ESG INVESTING AND INDUSTRY 4.0 TECHNOLOGIES

Purposeful ESG investing is of the highest relevance to finance the green industrialization and further a smooth and speedy transition, as outlined at the beginning of this chapter. In general, Industry 4.0 technologies influence ESG investing in two ways: first, they change a company's ESG footprint. While the usage of Industry 4.0 technologies remains the ultimate decision of the investee company, asset managers can engage with the company to consider ESG aspects when transitioning to Industry 4.0 technologies. Second, Industry 4.0 technologies can increase ESG data availability and quality.

In the following, this second aspect will be focused on. In particular, two influential technologies and their impact on ESG investing, namely AI and blockchain, are outlined.

ESG investing and AI

Recent achievements in data proliferation, computing power, and AI algorithms have created much technological progress in AI. While certain AI ESG use cases already deliver useful insights, AI will become increasingly important in ESG investing.

Responsible ESG investing must consider views from multiple stakeholders such as the company itself, its employees and clients, NGOs, and regulatory institutions. Multiple ESG data sources need to be taken into account to complement and verify company-disclosed ESG data. ESG data sources are hence diverse: besides data expressly generated to report on a company's ESG status (traditional ESG data), data originally generated for other purposes (alternative ESG data) must be considered. Examples for alternative ESG data include newspaper and social media data, satellite images, patent data, and data from IoT sensors. The frequent availability of alternative ESG data, often in real time, allows to consider detailed multiple stakeholder views. AI technologies are often needed to derive useful ESG information from these multiple and diverse data sources.

ESG data quantity from these multiple data sources is growing at an exponential pace. It is estimated that up to 80% of (the ESG) data available comes in unstructured format, as for example, text and pictures that can only to a limited extent be analyzed with conventional software. AI technologies can help to tackle these two issues: they can sift vast amounts of traditional and alternative ESG data and can succeed in turning unstructured data into structured information, which can then be used and assessed for sound ESG-integrated investment decisions or as a base for engagement activities.

These advantages are set off by some drawbacks. Comprehensiveness of data is partly devalued by noisy and sometimes poor-quality data. For example, when looking at social media data, younger employees might be overrepresented on professional networking sites such as LinkedIn, which might devalue ESG diversity insight drawn from this source.

To explore the use of new technologies in practice, I will now look at two exemplary ESG AI use cases, namely ESG sentiment analysis and patent data analysis.

Use case example 1: ESG sentiment analysis

Sentiment analysis is an AI use case already in frequent use. It scans, for example, the tonality of news data discussing ESG topics such as ESG-specific controversies. In that case, it yields a negative sentiment signal that alerts the investment professional to review the ESG activities of the company. Sentiment analysis has its limitations, though, as the AI tool might not always be able to decode subtle wording and decipher cultural language differences.

Sentiment analysis primarily combines the two powerful AI technologies of Natural Language Processing (NLP) and Machine Learning (ML).

NLP models can process and generate human language. Building an NLP application for sentiment analysis can draw on already existing open-source NLP applications, such as Google's powerful state-of-the-art model BERT, which is also used to interpret Google queries. However, domain-specific training of the NLP is needed to understand specific finance and ESG taxonomy. The domain-specific training heavily influences the reliability of the obtained sentiment signals, as it reflects opinions on controversial ESG topics. For example, the domain training could define the usage of nuclear energy as satisfying environmental ESG requirements because of its low carbon emissions and consequently assign a positive sentiment. On the contrary, it could create a negative sentiment if the usage of nuclear energy is evaluated as violating those requirements due to nuclear waste, for example. This demonstrates that contrary to common belief, AI models reflect human opinions (and biases) and are not inherently objective.

Domain training is nowadays primarily obtained by using the AI technology of supervised ML, which is a prevailing AI method. Supervised ML requires manually labeling massive amounts of training data, making economies of scale indispensable. During an initial training phase, the program autonomously determines algorithmic rules from the labeled training data. In the following production phase, new data is analyzed by applying these rules. As the rules remain largely unknown by humans, the ensuing ML algorithm is to a high degree opaque, which may entail continuing unwanted practices from the past. For example, rules may be derived from labeled data reflecting discriminatory traditions. ML's intrinsic opaqueness contradicts the transparency required by ESG investing and poses significant risk. The new field of explainable AI tries to remedy the opaqueness obstacle but is only at its beginning.

Thus, AI ESG sentiment analysis is characterized by specific advantages and disadvantages. Portfolio managers can profit from continuous signal availability around the clock and use the signals as alert for further analysis. As a drawback, intrinsic technicalities as controversial sentiment assignment or ML opaqueness limit signal usability. Thus, sentiment analysis seems good for complementing existing ESG scores and as a warning system but may need human supervision. In addition, emerging ESG concerns such as biodiversity may be in danger of underrepresentation, as the algorithms are trained on labeled data from the past and thus emerging topics may be underrepresented in the training data. This brief explanation already demonstrates that before using such applications, a thorough examination of the application benefits must take place, as well as detailed and continuous training of users in the case of an implementation.

Use case example 2: ESG patent data analysis

AI can also help to analyze patent data. The data is openly accessible from patent offices worldwide, which furthers global ESG investment. The data indicates a company's strategic research and development investments and informs from what kind of technologies and innovations the firm wants to benefit from in the future. As patent applications require considerable resources, patenting proves a certain commitment to the patented technologies, which corroborates the prediction.

Analyzing patent data may yield surprising insight: in a 2020 study of the National Bureau of Economic Research, the authors found that "oil, gas, and energy producing firms—firms with lower ESG scores, and who are often explicitly excluded from ESG funds' investment universe—are key innovators in the United States' green patent landscape" (Cohen et al., 2020: 2). The findings question the ESG investment strategy of mere exclusion that does not take forward-looking ESG information into account.

Two obstacles obstruct uncovering patent data information valuable for ESG investment. First, the data is unstructured, requiring AI techniques like NLP and ML, as discussed earlier. Second, assessing the "greenness" of patented technologies needs technical expertise and may sometimes be subject to difference of opinion. Human expertise and decision-making are needed. All in all, it is nontrivial to assess a company's relative ESG patent portfolio strength as compared to its competitors. Going forward, a hybrid human-machine approach seems best suited to tackle the difficulties and assess the valuable information contained in patent data.

To sum up, AI can substantially support ESG investment decisions by increasing ESG data availability and accuracy and thus contribute to ease the breakthrough of green industrialization. It has unique strengths and impresses with recently achieved major breakthroughs, mainly in NLP and ML, that will play a considerable role in ESG data generation in the future.

But AI is no silver bullet: its intrinsic limitations need to be taken into account. The AI industry itself may earn only mediocre ESG scores: AI opaqueness disguises (involuntary) discriminating AI algorithms. Further, the AI industry naturally tends to oligopolistic structures due to very high initial costs but then massive economies of scale. Several AI characteristics like high energy consumption, data privacy problems, or a lacking diversification of AI workforce conflict with ESG criteria.

While AI will increasingly become relevant to manage the massive amounts of ESG-relevant data from multiple sources, human judgment and domain knowledge cannot be discarded: humans must weigh the reliability of AI-derived ESG data.

ESG investing and blockchain

Blockchain is a specification of the Distributed Ledger Technology (DLT). DLTs store their database records on distributed peer-to-peer networks. DLT participants can trust in the information stored on the DLT because technical anti-fraud mechanisms like data replication on independent network nodes and consensus algorithms for transactions prevent hampering. Thus, control is distributed among a group of validators. Participants must neither confide in each other nor in a trustworthy intermediary nor a central authority. Accordingly, DLT exchanges trust in humans or organizations for trust in technology. Blockchain as a specification uses DLT to chronologically record transactions on blocks that are immutably chained together by cryptography.

Let's take a look at two exemplary ESG blockchain use cases, namely supply chain transparency and tokenization.

Use case example 1: blockchain to obtain supply chain transparency

Blockchains allow for comfortable and secure cross-company data exchange. The technology can be used to establish a trustworthy data ledger across the value chain of supply chain processes. In the timestamped data ledger, post hoc alterations are excluded, which additionally protects against fraud. The supply chain becomes more transparent, and ESG auditing can rely on a cleaner data lineage. For example, in a supply chain for electric car batteries, the raw material cobalt is often obtained by child labor. Such "tainted Cobalt" can leak into the global supply chain as outlined in a *Financial Times* article by H. Sanderson (2019). Ethical cobalt sourcing could be confirmed by validating the cobalt origin via blockchain. Smart contracts and related Industry 4.0 technologies like IoT devices can help to automatize supply chain processes and obtain better real-time supply chain transparency across the whole value chain.

But increased supply chain transparency does not guarantee uniform ESG auditing. Humans must decide to what extent a company's ESG impact shall be measured. For example, in carbon measurement it is important to define the scope of emissions to be measured. The Greenhouse Gas Protocol, a widely used standard to measure greenhouse gas emissions, defines three scopes for greenhouse gas emissions. Scope 1 measures emissions a company directly emits. Scope 2 also takes into account emissions caused by the energy used by the firm, while scope 3 considers all emissions along the whole upstream and downstream value chain of the company. Thus, blockchain can help to obtain more transparent supply chains, humans must evaluate the data and decide which scope of emissions has to be applied in order to obtain a reliable ESG rating of a company, for example.

Use case example 2: tokenization influencing ESG aspects

Assets may, in future, be increasingly tokenized via blockchains and not exclusively be issued traditionally. Tokenization, that is, the digital representation of value on a blockchain, will increase the efficiency of the issuance, trading, and post-trading processes. Boston Consulting Group estimated in 2020 that tokenized assets could "become the biggest financial asset class . . . by the end of the decade" (Burchardi et al., 2020: 1).

ESG investing must consider if tokenization changes the ESG assessment of an asset. At the moment, for many blockchains one important changing factor is the blockchain's energy consumption. Currently, Ethereum is the most common blockchain used for tokenization projects. In October 2021, one single on-chain Ethereum transaction used as much energy as an average US household consumes in six days (Digiconomist, 2022). If Ethereum implements the *proof of stake* consensus algorithm in 2022, the energy consumption will decrease massively.

Besides energy consumption, tokenization might impact other ESG factors. Tokenization increases transparency, which might increase or decrease ESG scores. While transparency lessens privacy, it also increases an asset's ESG data availability and data quality (e.g., for tokenized green bonds). Besides energy consumption and transparency effects, the higher efficiency of tokenized assets can lead to democratization of certain asset classes, especially alternatives or maybe even new asset classes such as collectibles (e.g., art or cars).

A prominent example for the complex consequences of asset tokenization is cryptocurrencies, which have a mixed ESG assessment. Important advantages include cryptocurrencies' transparent governance in the blockchain and the potential of cryptocurrencies to increase financial inclusion. Only two months after El Salvador added Bitcoin as an official legal tender, more citizens owned Bitcoin wallets than bank accounts according to Forbes (2021). In addition, in future, cross-border payment could become more affordable, though at the moment transaction costs for Bitcoin are considerable, as the technology lacks sufficient scalability. These important advantages are set off by undesired side effects, especially the high energy consumption. The University of Cambridge estimates that in May 2021, Bitcoin's weekly energy consumption exceeded the entire annual energy consumption of the Netherlands (The Economist, 2021). Bitcoin's high energy consumption is characteristic for blockchains using a certain technological setup (*proof of work* consensus algorithm). Because of the high energy consumption, the blockchain Ethereum has announced to switch to another consensus algorithm (*proof of stake*) which will reduce energy consumption by more than 99% (Fairley, 2019). Besides energy consumption problems, enforcement of anti-money laundering and know-your-client (KYC) regulations may be an issue in anonymous public blockchains.

To sum up, similar to any technology, blockchain mixes specific drawbacks and benefits. The current energy thirst of cryptocurrencies aggravates our urgent climate crisis though future technological innovations as a change from proof of work to proof of stake might remedy this problem. On the positive side, blockchain technology has considerable potential to help smoothen the transition to a green industrialization as, for example, outlined in the ESG supply chain use case earlier. The United Nations (2021) point out that blockchain might play an important role in the future for more sustainable development because of its promise for more transparency.

In this chapter, I asked how Industry 4.0 technologies influence ESG investing. For two prominent technologies, AI and blockchain, I outlined two use cases each. Both technologies can enhance the availability and reliability of ESG data but come with considerable intrinsic challenges such as AI's opaqueness and blockchain's considerable energy consumption.

CONCLUSION

All in all, the green industrialization represents the biggest change and challenge for society, corporates, states, technology, and our entire planet. It takes an unseen level of unbiased efforts, progressive thinking, and collaboration across sectors and initiatives to successfully master this change for the future of all, including the disadvantaged.

Yet, it is still a journey. We might need to adjust milestones on this path, but we cannot alter the direction. Asset managers must help move ESG investing from risk management alone to a more balanced approach of risk management and identifying new opportunities. Ultimately, this is about making transformational change possible by considering the entire spectrum of E, S, and G.

If policy makers pave the way and all stakeholders collectively and step by step evolve frameworks and commit to providing more transparency, consistency, and forward-looking perspectives, sustainability investing will become the new normal with no place to hide.

REFERENCES

Barko, T., Cremers, M., & Renneboog, L. (2021). Shareholder engagement on environmental, social, and governance performance. *Journal of Business Ethics*, https://doi.org/10.1007/s10551-021-04850-z (forthcoming, Online First)

Burchardi, K., Rogg, J., & Dethier, H. (2020). *Navigating the Digital Asset Ecosystem* (BCG Boston Consulting Group). Available at: https://image-src.bcg.com/Images/BCG-Navigating-the-Digital-Asset-Ecosystem-May-2020_tcm9-249683.pdf (Accessed: 11 February 2022).

Business & Sustainable Development Commission (BSDC) (2017). *Better Business Better World.* Available at: https://sustainabledevelopment.un.org/content/documents/2399BetterBusinessBetterWorld.pdf (Accessed: 11 February 2022).

Climate Action Tracker (2021). *The CAT Thermometer*. Available at: https://climateactiontracker.org/global/cat-thermometer/ (Accessed: 11 February 2022).

Cohen, L., Gurun Umit, G., & Nguyen Quoc, H. (2020). *The ESG-Innovation Disconnect: Evidence From Green Patenting.* National Bureau of Economic Research. Available at: www.nber.org/papers/w27990 (Accessed: 11 February 2022).

Dasgupta, P. (2021). *The Economics of Diversity: The Dasgupta Review*. Available at: https://assets.publishing.service.gov.uk/government/uploads/system/uploads/attachment_data/file/962785/The_Economics_of_Biodiversity_The_Dasgupta_Review_Full_Report.pdf (Accessed: 11 February 2022).

Digiconomist (2022). *Ethereum Energy Consumption Index*. Available at: https://digiconomist.net/ethereum-energy-consumption/ (Accessed: 11 February 2022).

Dimson, E., Karakas, O., & Li, X. (2015). Active ownership. *Review of Financial Studies*, 28(12), 3225–3268.

Edelman (2020). *Edelman Trust Barometer*. Available at: www.edelman.com/trustbarometer (Accessed: 11 February 2022).

Fairley, P. (2019). *Ethereum Plans to Cut Its Absurd Energy Consumption by 99 Percent*. Available at: https://spectrum.ieee.org/ethereum-plans-to-cut-its-absurd-energy-consumption-by-99-percent (Accessed: 11 February 2022).

Forbes (2021). *In El Salvador More People Have Bitcoin Wallets Than Traditional Bank Accounts*. Available at: www.forbes.com/sites/theapothecary/2021/10/07/in-el-salvador-more-people-have-bitcoin-wallets-than-traditional-bank-accounts/ (Accessed: 11 February 2022).

Intergovernmental Panel on Climate Change (IPCC) (2021). *Climate Change: Widespread, Rapid and Intensifying*. Available at: www.ipcc.ch/2021/08/09/ar6-wg1-20210809-pr/ (Accessed: 11 February 2022).

Project Drawdown (2020). *Table of Solutions*. Available at: https://drawdown.org/solutions/table-of-solutions (Accessed: 11 February 2022).

Ritchie, H., & Roser, M. (2020). *CO_2 and Greenhouse Gas Emissions*. Available at: https://ourworldindata.org/co2-and-other-greenhouse-gas (Accessed: 11 February 2022).

Sanderson, H. (2019). Congo, child labour and your electric car. *Financial Times*. Available at: www.ft.com/content/c6909812-9ce4-11e9-9c06-a4640c9feebb (Accessed: 11 February 2022).

Semenova, N., & Hassel, L. G. (2019). Private engagement by Nordic institutional investors on environmental, social, and governance risks in global companies. *Corporate Governance: An International Review*, 27(2), 144–161.

The Economist (2021). *As the Price of Bitcoin Has Climbed So Has Its Environmental Cost*. Available at: www.economist.com/graphic-detail/2021/05/14/as-the-price-of-bitcoin-has-climbed-so-has-its-environmental-cost (Accessed: 11 February 2022).

United Nations (2021). *Sustainability Solution or Climate Calamity the Dangers and Promise of Cryptocurrency Technology*. Available at: www.un.org/sustainabledevelopment/blog/2021/06/sustainability-solution-or-climate-calamity-the-dangers-and-promise-of-cryptocurrency-technology/ (Accessed: 11 February 2022).

4

How Can Corporate Leverage Tech and Sustainability through Collaboration?

Digital with Purpose—Current Practices and Trends

Luis Neves

INTRODUCTION

In the midst of the Fourth Industrial Revolution (4IR), where we are seeing rapid digital transformation and the blurring of the physical, virtual, and digital spheres, the world continues to face challenges that grow more complex every day. Be it: climate change, inequality, cybersecurity, geopolitical conflicts, economic instability, or the metaverse—governments and businesses alike are struggling to catch up to an ever-evolving environment.

Introduced by the United Nations (2015) as a "a blueprint to achieve a better and more sustainable future for all people and the world by 2030," the UN Sustainable Development Goals (SDGs) represent the next stage of global targets, which require all of us to do better and aim higher for a fairer and greener world. Although an initiative of the UN and mainly a pledge for member states, the SDGs are also a framework for organizations of all shapes and sizes—schools, third-sector entities, businesses, and citizens, among others.

The growing importance of sustainability in today's world means corporates can no longer afford to miss out on understanding their environmental, social, and governance (ESG) impact. By embedding sustainability within one's corporate strategy, organizations are better positioned not only in terms of making long-term investments but also in cutting out inefficiencies across the board. In an age where resources are scarce and amassing waste

DOI: 10.4324/9781003262039-5

becomes the norm, we see, in addition to existing technologies, new innovative solutions and tools being developed that can enable businesses to do more responsibly and effectively.

This chapter touches on the specific digital technologies which can enable organizations to meet their SDG ambitions, as well as the principles that must go hand in hand with the deployment of these solutions. Additionally, understanding that digital technologies also come with negative impacts, the chapter identifies the externalities that may arise, which must be immediately addressed and mitigated.

Citing the key findings of the seminal report "Digital with Purpose" (DwP) and its accompanying movement, the chapter aims to challenge businesses in the information and communication technology (ICT) sector, small and medium enterprises (SMEs), and large, non-digital business organizations that are at the forefront of the 4IR to commit to Four Universal Commitments and take a path toward being purpose driven through digital technologies. Dubbed a movement of leaders, the DwP movement presents a path for organizations that are ready to drive the sustainability and digital agendas toward 2030 for a better world. The movement is a race to the top, recognizing that competition is healthy, drives innovation and best practice, and can help companies to achieve their goals quicker together. The DwP framework was developed as "the Tool" to help business on its way to achieve the "sky," a better world for all by 2030.

THE DIGITAL TECHNOLOGIES THAT CRITICALLY INFLUENCE THE WORLD

As digital technologies continue to penetrate every facet of society, there is an urgent need for a deeper understanding of how technology will impact progress toward sustainable development. After all, in order for the bold commitments outlined in the 2030 Agenda to be delivered, all actors and stakeholders must work together toward a common purpose so we can address the problems that we are facing today. Be it hunger, poverty, inequality, climate change, privacy and security, ethical values, digital inclusion, or economic growth, digital technologies are a vital enabler to accelerate on current efforts being made and take us to new heights and achieve our goals.

In the DwP report published by the Global Enabling Sustainability Initiative (GeSI) and Deloitte (2019), seven digital technologies are identified as the most impactful tools to help meet the SDGs. An understanding of the key technologies and their significance in today's world is critical for organizations and professionals to successfully address ESG issues of tomorrow. The following is an overview of the technologies highlighted in the report.

Digital access

Digital access is the transfer of information and data from A to B. It not only facilitates the delivery of digital products and services across the world in a matter of seconds, but it also empowers people to take part in today's economies and societies.

The delivery of digital access can be provided by a range of technologies: satellite reception, mobile communications, and the Internet—which then need to be transmitted through a hardware device, such as a laptop or mobile phone. These moving parts require telecommunications infrastructure providers, handset manufacturers, and mobile network operators to extend access and enhance connectivity.

In practice, digital access and greater data capacity of mobile networks allow organizations and individuals to interact online, as well as take part in the digital marketplace without being restricted by distance. Against the backdrop of a global pandemic, it is through digital access that governments, international organizations, and agencies can share information, raise awareness, and map out data around COVID-19.

Fast Internet

Fast Internet refers to the different types of connections that facilitate the volume and frequency of data exchanges, which include next-generation networks such as 4G and 5G.

As highlighted by Ofcom (2021), the UK's Office of Communications, next-gen networks have rapidly developed over the years, allowing for greater utility through faster speeds. If 2G made it possible for mobile phones to make calls and send text messages, 3G allows one to effectively access the Internet, while 4G provides these services at 5–7 times the speed and accommodate greater capacity for activities such as gaming, video streaming, and virtual meetings, among others.

Following previous generations, 5G offers even greater speed and capacity that can facilitate the connection of multiple devices at the same time. Additionally, the latency reduction (the delay between user action and when the response is received) opens the door for the deployment of new technologies. With interactions, transactions, and exchanges of data rapidly increasing, 5G is well positioned to deliver on the enabling potential of the subsequent technologies.

Cloud

Cloud technologies allow on-demand access to shared resources such as networks, servers, storage, applications, data, and services. They enable individuals and large organizations alike the ability to operate in digital ecosystems in a pay-as-you-go model. Cloud solutions allow greater efficiency in terms of costs and deployment as opposed to purchasing and maintaining physical data centers and servers.

All the other technologies on this list utilize cloud technology in some way and is used by many types of organizations globally. Be it for health sciences, education, or consumer services, cloud technology is a great driver of the digital transformation that we are seeing today and will only continue to streamline processes across sectors.

Internet of Things (IoT)

IoT are the suite of technologies that allow the connection of physical objects to the Internet and facilitates communication through sensors or software. The IoT platform makes it possible for connected objects like smartphones, appliances, wearable fitness devices, and even cars to send and/or receive information and function as designed; this connection is usually coupled with a user interface that translates the data into an easily understandable form.

For the most part, IoT technologies are mainly deployed in consumer products, environmental and utility management, as well as in the manufacturing industry. In the vision of a so-called smart city or smart future, society would rely on IoT to enable a transformative change for all—making things more efficient and solutions more effective through the analytics generated to enhance decision-making. For this vision to be realized, manufacturers and software providers would need to work together to develop the sensors that will allow the collection of vast swaths of information and manage the interoperability of devices. Additionally, the telecommunications sector must step in to host these network technologies that facilitate the transmission of information, while platform and cloud providers translate the information into a secure user interface.

Cognitive technology

Cognitive technology refers to machine learning (ML) and artificial intelligence (AI), the application of advanced analytics to develop useful insight. According to IBM (2021), ML looks at how data and algorithms can be used to imitate the way human beings learn with the aim of greater accuracy as more information is collected. AI, on the other hand, is the analysis of data to perform tasks, help with decision-making, and undertake tasks that would have required "human intelligence."

It is through these statistics, algorithms, and analyses that streaming platforms such as Netflix and Amazon are able to process the information gathered from your previous purchases or views and then turn them into recommendations for you to buy more and consume more content.

Cognitive technologies have great potential in replacing humans in judgment and decision-making processes such as in robotics or robotic process automation (RPA), which are machines that are programmed to perform tasks as seen in car manufacturing facilities that combine hardware and parts.

Digital reality

Deloitte (2018) defines digital reality as the large spectrum of technologies that "enable simulation of reality in various ways." The digital reality ecosystem includes:

- Augmented Reality (AR)—adds digitally created content into the user's real-world environment;
- Virtual Reality (VR)—creates a fully digital environment that replaces the user's real-world environment;
- Mixed Reality—a combination of digital content in the real world that allows both environments to interact;
- 360° Video—provides a new perspective for users by being able to view one's environment in all directions;
- Immersive Experience—creates a multisensory digital experience that is delivered by the aforementioned technologies.

Digital reality will be a strong driver in enabling the Future of Work while augmented reality can provide hands-on, realistic training for workers to sharpen skills in a safe and more engaging environment—an option for those in the manufacturing, industrial, and health care sectors.

Blockchain

Blockchain is a digital distributed, decentralized ledger technology that allows for the management of shared ledgers across a network. The ledger is organized into blocks of data linked into a chain with other blocks of data—hence blockchain—with each new transaction recorded, adding to the ledger. Blockchain technology is difficult to change and hack as the ledger's security only gets more secure as blocks continue to be added to the chain, requiring hackers to corrupt every single block across all the distributed versions.

Blockchain can be used to store data and digital records, allowing access to only a handful of users with the key to access the information. Also, it allows for the use of smart contracts, which require codes to execute actions based on instructions that have been validated by all the parties involved. With all the excitement around this technology, there is a great potential for

Digital Access: connectivity between people and of people to the internet via telecommunications infrastructure (fixed or mobile), devices (handheld devices and computers) and software.

Fast Internet: next generation connectivity that provides speed, capacity and reliability at fundamentally higher levels including high speed fixed broadband, 4G and 5G.

Cloud: the provision of highly scalable, advanced IT capabilities as hosted services. Typically, on-demand and pay-as-you-go and including an ever-widening breadth of capabilities including infrastructure, network, storage, computing power, applications and data.

IoT (Internet of Things): the suite of technologies enabling the connection of physical objects to the internet, and enabling communication from, and to, the object about the object's condition, position and surroundings.

Cognitive: the application of advanced analytics, machine learning (ML) and artificial intelligence (AI) approaches to big data to develop insight.

Digital Reality: virtual digital worlds or systems (Virtual Reality), or mixed virtual and physical worlds (Augmented Reality).

Blockchain: digital, distributed ledgers of transactions maintained on multiple computer systems controlled by different entities and accessible by all participants without the need for intermediaries enhancing accuracy, verifiability and security.

FIGURE 4.1 Digital Technologies

(Source: GeSI and Deloitte.)

blockchain to be used in securing remittances, direct payments, contracts, and personal identification storage to access services as seen in the system deployed by the United Nations World Food Programme (WFP) for refugees to access aid (WFP, 2021).

In addition to identifying the digital technologies that will affect the world in different ways (see Figure 4.1 for a summary), what is important is to explore how these technologies deliver on the goals toward a more sustainable future. The DwP report presents a new framework that lays out four impact functions:

(1) Connect and communicate: In its most basic form, technology can help transmit data and therefore enables connections between people,

transmit information across the Internet, and improve the efficiency of markets locally and globally.

(2) Monitor and track: Digital technologies allow us to monitor and track the human and natural environments—be it populations, people, or activities, real-time and wide-reaching observation of the world is important to help us intervene and take action where necessary.

(3) Analyze, optimize, and predict: With the power of digital technologies, we are able to collate, process, manipulate, and interpret large volumes of data across different sources. In addition, the latest technologies can help us make better informed decisions through analytics and predict future outcomes, enabling rapid innovation and development.

(4) Augment and autonomate: Today's technologies allow us to simulate the world to create a bridge between the physical and the digital, empowering humans to interact and observe the environment in engaging ways. With this bridge, we are then able to create autonomous systems or to "autonomate."

THE NEGATIVE EXTERNALITIES TO UNDERSTAND AND THE DIRECT IMPACTS OF THE ICT SECTOR

Digital technologies can and are already driving progress toward the SDGs, but to adequately support the level of digital transformation that can bring about impactful change, one must address the negative externalities that may arise.

Three categories of implications and negative externalities have been identified.

- Intended externalities—occurs when technologies are deployed to achieve an intended outcome that is deliberately malicious or harmful;
- Consequential externalities—unavoidable impacts that come from the use of technologies;
- Unintended consequences—occur due to a combination of qualities that are inherent to the use of technology and/or preexisting social structures.

The following are some of the most vital negative externalities that must be mitigated, with ethical and control structures put in place.

Greenhouse gas (GHG) emissions

More and more in recent years, digital technologies typically drive economic growth, which lead to greater consumption, extraction of resources, and emissions that affect the biosphere. To meet the Paris Agreement commitments, the ICT sector must strongly reflect on how it can manage its 800 Mt CO_2

energy usage (GeSI & Deloitte, 2019), estimated to increase by 11% at 900 Mt CO_2 by 2030. If things continue with the current business-as-usual trajectory, the ICT sector will make up 1.7% of global GHG emissions by 2030.

Cryptocurrency mining is the practice of gathering cryptocurrency after successfully solving equations using computers and is enabled by blockchain. The greater the capacity and speed of a computer to solve these equations, the more electricity is consumed. To put it in perspective, a recent study argues that Bitcoin's electricity consumption, at 121.36 terawatt-hours (TWh) a year, is greater than that of Argentina's at 121 TWh (Cambridge Bitcoin Electricity Consumption Index, 2022).

Electronic waste (e-waste)

E-waste is a negative externality that results from widespread uptake and deployment of digital technologies and will continue to contribute to the degradation of the biosphere unless urgent action is taken. E-waste can enter waterways and ecosystems, causing an increase in toxin levels that will impact marine and terrestrial life.

E-waste contains valuable materials that are extracted through burning and incubating in acids, among other methods. In countries where informal or improper recycling of e-waste takes place, residents have more elevated levels of metals in their system, harmful toxins and pollutants are released in the air, and workers are exposed to harmful working conditions with little to no safety training.

For example, a paper in the *International Journal of Environmental Research and Public Health* (Lebbie et al., 2021) reveals how e-waste burning and dismantling activities pose a serious threat to children's health in African countries, where informal and unsafe e-waste management are commonplace. With the growing demand for electronic devices, the import of used electronic and electrical equipment (UEEE), from countries such as Germany, the UK, Belgium, and the Netherlands, is a large market in Africa. UEEE are often "shipped legally under the pretense that it is usable or can be repaired," but the reality is that more than half of the UEEE imported are discarded as they are beyond repair—thus a major contributor to the e-waste problem in the region.

Digital divide

Digital technologies democratize information and provide access to markets on a global scale, but it can also exacerbate inequality for reasons such as a lack of infrastructure, poor digital skills, or affordability of services among others.

According to the International Telecommunication Union (ITU) (ITU, 2018), a little over 51% of the global population, or four billion people, use the Internet. However, what is critical to note is the distribution between developed and developing countries; in 2018, almost 81% of the population in the developed world are using the Internet, while in developing countries this is only at 45%. Bridging the digital divide means extending connectivity to some of the world's least developed countries to bring about a digital transformation that benefits all and leaves no one behind.

Digital trust and responsibility

Coupled with the digital divide and what must go hand in hand with it is digital trust and responsibility. Developing relevant internet content, strengthening regulatory frameworks, and promoting trust can help ensure that improved access leads to wider use. In recent years, we have been seeing an increasing number of cases which present the consequences of poor cybersecurity practices and the irresponsible/unethical use of technology when things are left unchecked. Recent examples include:

- Ransomware attacks costing multimillion dollar schemes—these involve the theft and encryption of data and demanding large sums of money for the key;
- Social media platforms such as Facebook and Twitter and their role in inciting violence, spreading misinformation, and attempts in undermining democratic processes;
- Instagram and its harmful impacts on mental health, especially for younger users;
- Cryptocurrency as the currency of choice for money laundering and organized crime.

Today's world reveals a more challenging virtual space where technology owners, designers, and users alike must work together to safeguard safety online and offline.

DIGITAL WITH PURPOSE—A MOVEMENT OF LEADERS

It is without a doubt that digital technologies do have a role to play in the achievement of the SDGs and Paris Agreement commitments. They can play a critical role in creating a truly sustainable world. For this to fully materialize, a drastic change in the development and deployment of digital technology is needed. With organizations and businesses facing increasing amounts of pressure from stakeholders globally, articulating and demonstrating how their activities impact society and our biosphere must be the norm.

Against this backdrop, coupled with the responsible use of the aforementioned technologies is a need for a shared ambition within the ICT sector and stakeholder groups toward a purpose-driven agenda—an agenda driven by a new leadership with vision that understands the contribution that their company can make to the greater good. An organization's purpose must therefore be shaped by the SDGs and accelerated by technology.

To embrace this opportunity and achieve such an impact through digital technologies is precisely the goal of GeSI's DwP movement. We have built a community of experts to navigate a best-in-class approach, working with the giants of the ICT sector and the global supply chain to catalyze collective action and deployment of new technologies. DwP is an ambitious movement of leaders joining forces in a race to deliver against the Paris Agreement and SDGs by 2030, who believe in a world where technology, innovation, and collaboration can transform the fortunes of our planet.

The movement is not about repackaging existing efforts or restating previously declared intentions or promises—it is a race to the top and driven by measurable action. Members share an ambition to create business value through radically accelerating the enabling power of digital technology for the SDGs while minimizing negative externalities that may arise.

To effectively tackle the health of our planet and inequality across society, it will take a big team effort. No one business or industry can do it alone. To meet the change needed and catalyze collective action among corporates, the DwP movement launched by GeSI is centered around Four Universal Commitments that make up the DwP performance framework, which I will explain in more detail in the following sections.

(1) Recommit to the 2030 Agenda
(2) Define a role and specific contribution to the SDGs
(3) Embrace the principles of transparency and collaboration
(4) Harness the potential of digital technologies to support these commitments

Recommit to the 2030 Agenda

The 2030 Agenda for Sustainable Development is the common language in which governments, organizations, and businesses worldwide speak—one must take advantage of the foundations already set for the Agenda and take ownership about what these goals mean to one's activities. For many, the SDGs remain poorly understood and leaders must make efforts to educate and fully integrate the ambition of the Agenda into daily life by making public statements in support of the SDGs, as well as weaving these statements into internal and external communications.

An example of this work in practice is that of the world-leading global technology services provider, NTT Ltd. and declaring its intention to be a "Business Avenger" by cementing its commitment to the SDGs by 2030. Additionally, in November 2021, NTT announced a series of commitments to reduce emissions and take an active role in contributing to a more connected, sustainable future for all, citing important stakeholders demanding for businesses to be more purpose-led. The efforts include empowering its employees to volunteer and support initiatives that support the SDGs, as well as diversity among its executive teams. Finally, NTT Ltd. announced a more concerted effort to working with an ecosystem of stakeholders to accelerate its intended impact goals cementing a public commitment with key targets.

Define a role and specific contribution to the SDGs

From individuals to organizations, we all have a role to play in achieving the SDGs—whether it be as consumers, citizens, or businesses, action can take many shapes and forms. However, organizations have a particular responsibility and capacity to direct the power of their core operations to galvanize action toward progress on a larger scale.

Organizations must be clear on their role in achieving the SDGs and how it is woven into their business models—this must then be communicated to stakeholders along with an articulation as to how a commitment to the SDGs will ensure long-term success, open the doors to opportunities, and mitigate risks.

It is essential to run a materiality analysis to understand which SDGs are most relevant to the organization and stakeholders, looking at aspirations and the negative externalities. Results from these exercises will provide the necessary guidance to building a road map that embraces the SDGs and science-based targets to reduce GHG emissions.

We see an example of this articulation in the 2020 Verizon ESG Report (Verizon, 2021), where the American network operator identified the priority goals and targets which mostly aligned to its core business purpose, highlighting SDGs:

- 4: Quality Education
- 7: Affordable and Clean Energy
- 8: Decent Work and Economic Growth
- 9: Industry, Innovation and Infrastructure
- 13: Climate Action
- 15: Life on Land
- 16: Peace, Justice and Strong Institutions

Articulation and reiterating one's commitment to the SDGs through evidence-based analysis will prove to be the main differentiator between the businesses of yesterday and the leaders of tomorrow.

Embrace the principles of transparency and collaboration

Any organization that fails to be transparent risks its ability to accelerate progress, manage activities, and address shortcomings. Embracing the 2030 Agenda means taking notes from the third sector and mapping out a theory of change (ToC); this means identifying the main outcomes to be achieved, recognizing the preconditions to help meet those goals, and the possible challenges one may face along the way through evidence-based research.

In addition to this, building partnerships that can enhance efforts toward the SDGs is critical to success. The world is becoming more interconnected every day, and one cannot achieve these ambitious goals without knowledge sharing and working with other businesses, nonprofit and nongovernmental organizations, as well as global, national, and local entities for deeper capacity-building.

The UN Global Compact (2021) is the world's largest corporate responsibility initiative. The Global Compact works to encourage organizations to align with its ten principles which focus on "human rights, labour, environment and anti-corruption," as well as "take strategic actions to advance broader societal goals"—this includes the SDGs. With over 12,000 signatories in more than 160 countries, the Global Compact boasts active participation across many sectors of all sizes.

Embracing a community of learning and development, the Global Compact engages with its participating companies through its Academy program, which includes e-learning courses and virtual sessions among resources.

Harness the potential of digital technologies to support these commitments

DwP reiterates how organizations have an opportunity to accelerate on its progress against the SDGs through the responsible deployment of digital technologies to:

(1) Provide a systemic understanding required for impact transparency;
(2) Provide proper management information to make informed decisions;
(3) Catalyze impact through innovation, core operations, and products/services;
(4) Facilitate cross-sector collaboration.

While utilizing technology to enable digital transformation is a step forward, what one should strive for is purpose-led transformation *powered* by digital.

With these Four Universal Commitments in mind, DwP identifies the ICT sector as a key driver to achieving these goals. As the sector continues to grow and the use of digital technologies expanding globally, companies have a particular obligation and opportunity to maximize their contribution. The following are some recommendations:

(1) Lead on the universal commitments;
(2) Operate responsibly by addressing key ESG challenges and be transparent about your common purpose;
(3) Call out areas of greatest risk and opportunity by working together with associations and trade organizations to explore where the greatest contribution can be made through core products and services;
(4) Seek to decouple growth from environmental degradation, especially as the world continues to consume massive volumes of data and energy, including e-waste;
(5) Lead on cybersecurity and ethics by safeguarding the rights of users and implementing strong codes of conduct that will lead toward good practices;
(6) Enable the development and deployment of technologies in countries where ICT has yet to fully mature by partnering with governments and other third-sector entities, ensuring a strong commitment to "leave no one behind."

By aiming for a purpose-led transformation through digital, empowered by the Four Universal Commitments and driven by ambitious leadership and will, an organization can find itself better positioned and prepared for the future.

THE DIGITAL WITH PURPOSE FRAMEWORK—A TOOL TO DRIVE POSITIVE IMPACT

With the Universal Commitments as the foundation, to ensure the aforementioned commitments are implemented, GeSI developed "the DwP Framework." This unique framework provides a rigorous and robust process for corporates to articulate their ambitions for SDG impact and track their progress through impact measurement in three different pillars.

- *Purpose:* The Purpose pillar scores a company's overall commitment to the SDGs and impact transparency. DWP companies commit to becoming a purpose-led business, connecting their intended core business model to their desired impact on the SDGs, working to maximize their positive contribution and minimize their negative externalities.

- *Responsible business metrics:* Cover the concept of "digital impact themes": climate action, circular economy, supply chain, digital inclusion, privacy, trust, and responsibility, which represent the priority areas in which a company deploys technology to deliver their ambitions articulated in the Purpose Pledge (GeSI, 2021). They reflect how a business acts in a responsible manner in: (1) its own operations, (2) its interactions with its suppliers, and (3) the design, delivery, and end-of-life management of its products and services.
- *Digitally enabled solutions:* Framed by the SDGs, this set of metrics reflects how a business adds to its mainstream products and services to deliver innovative and additional solutions that allow its customers to improve the sustainability of their own operations. They cover the areas of health and well-being, education, climate, natural capital, and human rights.

All metrics were designed with an ambition toward making a real, measurable, credible, and transparent impact by 2030. Therefore, the so-called race to the top. Hence as well the competitive dynamic of the framework. Best practice will help less mature companies to evolve faster in their journey,

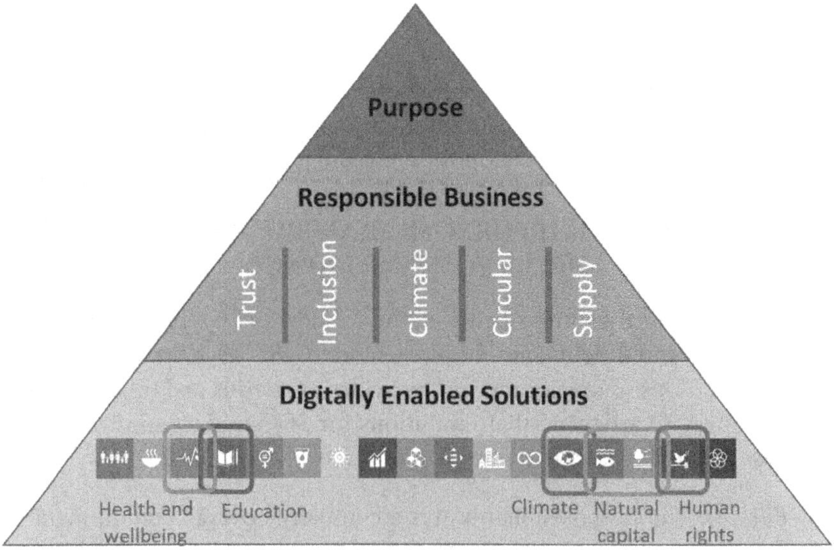

FIGURE 4.2 Digital With Purpose Framework

(Source: GeSI.)

opening themselves for additional opportunities which will impact their customer base and the collective desired impact.

To ensure a clear understanding of the "race to the top" concept as well as its competitive dynamics to drive business value through sustainability and innovative solutions, the ambition of the DwP metrics framework is made transparent to all corporates as follows.

Purpose

To be in the top decile for Purpose (i.e., scoring at least 90/100) a DwP company in 2030 would need to:

(1) Have a clearly articulated purpose that links core business activity to intended impact on SDG themes, and, beneath purpose, clearly call out the enabling impact themes, most material to their core business and stakeholder groups, that they seek to contribute toward through the development of digital solutions;
(2) Evidence that digital solutions that deliver the enabling impact themes have contributed to 500%+ of business revenue growth over the past five years;
(3) Evidence that digital solutions that deliver the enabling impact themes have been developed through a range of strategic interventions, including access to research and development, professional resources, and direct investment;
(4) Regularly measure and report on the impact of their solutions against the enabling impact themes (e.g., impacts in terms of SDG-linked benefit delivered, not just reach or number of users);
(5) Have a robust purpose governance system, with oversight sitting at board level and progress against enabling impact themes tied to management and employee reward.

Climate

To be in the top decile of DwP performance, a DwP company in 2030 would need to:

(1) Be exemplary in TCFD reporting;
(2) Have a 1.5°C aligned SBT;
(3) Have a Net Zero target for scope 1, 2, and 3 of 2035, or earlier;
(4) Have offset 50% of its residual emissions with carbon sinking credits and 50% with carbon non-sinking credits;
(5) Be purchasing >95% high-quality renewable electricity.

Circular economy

To be in the top decile (i.e., scoring at least 90/100), a DwP company in 2030 would need to:

(1) Be exemplary and publicly transparent in circularity aspirations and reporting (Aspire);
(2) Have a company strategy aligning innovation, people skills, operations, and external engagement with the latest in circularity principles and practices (Shape);
(3) Be a top 10% performer in circular products, services, and business models (against global benchmark)[1] (Deliver);
(4) Be a top 10% performer in circular plant, property, and equipment (against global benchmark) (Deliver);
(5) Be a top 10% performer in circular energy and water if applicable (against global benchmark) (Deliver).

Supply chain

To be in the top decile (i.e., scoring at least 90/100), a DwP company in 2030 would need to:

(1) Demonstrate a measurable and proactive increase in spend with suppliers who have an exemplary focus on sustainability;
(2) Establish a program to improve supplier workforce living wages;
(3) Actively eliminate medium- and/or high-risk indicators for labor management/worker rights for all evaluated suppliers by 2030;
(4) Have zero tolerance for incidents of child or forced labor for evaluated suppliers;
(5) Actively eliminate medium- and/or high-risk indicators for health and safety for evaluated suppliers by 2030.

Digital trust and responsibility

To be in the top decile (i.e., scoring at least 90/100), a DwP company in 2030 would need to ensure:

(1) Protection of customer data is integral to the development of products and systems;
(2) Users have genuine choice and control that puts them in charge of how their data is collected, used, and stored;
(3) Company publicly advocates against restrictions that hinder freedom of expression;

(4) Company stops the sale of technology products and services that undermine human rights and remedies negative impacts upon users;
(5) Stakeholders regularly collaborate to review human rights impact of a company's products and services;
(6) Company sets revenue and social impact targets to provide technology that helps protect human rights, privacy, and security.

Digital inclusion

To be in the top decile (i.e., scoring at least 90/100), a DwP company in 2030 would need to:

(1) Help people benefit from the competent use of ICT and digital technologies regardless of their gender, age, ethnicity, ability, disability, skills, language, sexual orientation, wealth, and geographical location;
(2) Demonstrate state of the art accessibility in delivered digital services and technology;
(3) Promote a diverse environment within companies and their suppliers' workforce and leave no one behind;
(4) Promote access to services for disabled people and tackle low accessibility rates in disadvantaged areas;
(5) Set minimum standards to work toward achieving widespread ICT literacy.

Digitally enabled solutions

To be in the top decile (i.e., scoring at least 90/100), a DwP company in 2030 would need to be:

(1) Actively addressing three SDG-related enabling themes;
(2) Working collaboratively across digital and customer sectors and with topic experts and NGOs;
(3) Supporting innovation and development to be establishing new applications;
(4) To be quantifying and reporting on the environmental and social benefits derived from solutions delivered;
(5) To be quantifying and reporting on the revenue derived from solutions delivered.

Another unique component of the DwP framework relates to the respect of key fundamental principles. The metrics are marked in the framework as "red flags" and they are in line with the Four Universal Commitments subscribed by the companies' CEOs in the "Pledge." Violation of such principles will lead, on first step, to giving companies the opportunity to resolve the matter within a reasonable albeit short period of time or, in case of non-compliance, to the exclusion and consequent loss of the certification in case it had been already awarded.

An overall DwP score will be calculated for each participating company, using weighted scoring against the framework criteria, providing a measure to which participants can take action on and overcome barriers to drive progress to achieve the SDGs. Companies are required to evolve in the framework overtime. Once data is verified, members will receive a DwP score and be awarded a rating and a certificate they can share publicly.

Figure 4.3 represents the schematic diagram for illustration purposes only.

It is relevant to stress that there is no similar ESG framework in the marketplace. The ESG market is scattered, and there is no consistent approach to ensure consistent reporting about a company's performance. On the other side, there is a proliferation of ESG standards in the marketplace, which either are old and no longer respond to the technology and business dynamics or else they are not performance driven and therefore instead of leading to progress, innovation, and business value, they represent a burden for companies. Finally, almost if not all, ESG standards are problem driven. There is no framework that awards innovation and enabling solutions leading to real positive impact.

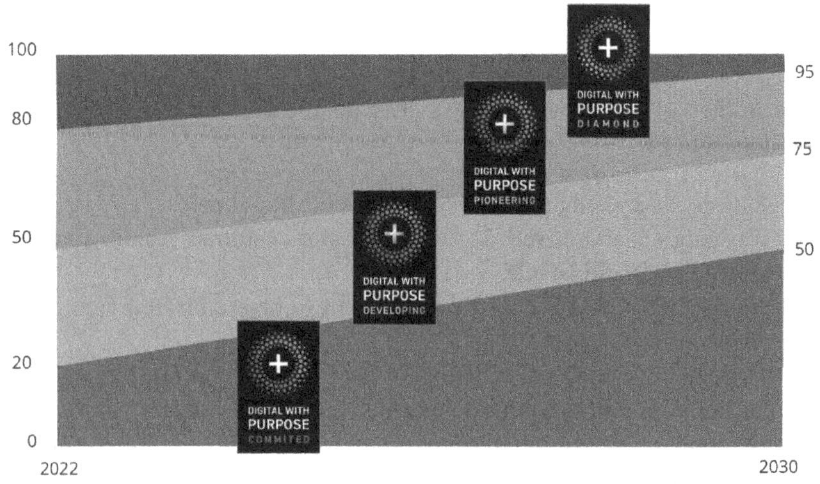

FIGURE 4.3 Digital With Purpose Certification Process

(Source: GeSI.)

The DwP framework is therefore a new, modern, business-driven, positive, credible, and ambitious transformative platform to establish a new direction for the ESG market, therefore breaking with traditional, conservative, and old-fashioned ESG approaches, which have proven not being providing the necessary dynamics to address the critical challenges we are confronted with, as it combines in a single place:

(1) All ESG elements, purpose, responsible business, and the opportunity dimension in a common and combined manner, designed not only to mitigate and address risk but also to encourage companies to drive through sustainability performance and competitive approach business value which responds to the fundamental challenges the world is confronted with;
(2) By aggregating combined and verified data from a single industry allows to measure and report transparently real collective impact providing investors and stakeholders with more reliable information for investment decisions;
(3) Because it was designed with an ambition toward 2030, will drive competition and accelerate reversal of negative trends while accelerating the positive;
(4) It is a framework driven by *real action* and NOT *by empty and repetitive "promises"*;
(5) It gives the overall performance and contribution to the society, in all its dimensions, of a given corporation.

CONCLUSION

The SDGs provide a comprehensive road map for change, a common agenda that we need in order to adequately address the challenges affecting society and our planet. Businesses and organizations alike must recognize that these commitments and what they aim to achieve are no longer a "nice-to-have" but a requirement for long-term success. The DwP report and its accompanying movement and framework are the answer to the challenges placed in front of us. We all know that the world has been living on "lip service," an array of promises that, if all realized, we would probably not have any reasons to worry about. This needs to change. And fast.

As the Intergovernmental Panel on Climate Change's (IPCC's) sixth Assessment Report found, we are not on the path that we had initially laid out from the Paris Agreement, and if further intervention is not made and made fast, the 1.5°C scenario could be out of our grasp within a few years (IPCC, 2021).

Inequality between people and regions continues to widen as explained by United Nations poverty expert Olivier De Schutter that the "top 10 per cent of people living in 38 [OECD] countries control 52 per cent of total net wealth, while the bottom 60 percent own just over 12 percent, condemning the poor to a lifetime of poverty."

These are just some of the issues that our society and planet are facing and they are indeed daunting, but we have the tools to address them in a targeted, responsible, and collaborative manner. All we need is the determination to turn previously stated commitments into impactful action. We need businesses to take the lead and those who talk the talk must also walk the walk.

The DwP movement is open to companies that are determined to take on the challenge and share an ambition to create business value through radically accelerating the enabling power of digital technology for the SDGs while minimizing negative externalities that may arise.

With a growing interest around ESG, stronger political will, especially around sustainability and climate action, as well as added support from key stakeholders, the next stage of the movement is for the private sector to step up and adhere to the Four Universal Commitments. By driving the agenda forward and taking these necessary steps with great purpose in mind, we will see a clearer path for a more sustainable future and put our planet back on track.

NOTE

1 The global benchmark will be provided by the Circulytics framework and is inherent in that scoring system.

REFERENCES

Cambridge Bitcoin Consumption Index (2022). *Bitcoin Network Power Demand*. Available at: https:// ccaf.io/cbeci/index (Accessed: 2 August 2022).

Deloitte (2018). *Digital Reality: Technical Primer*. Available at: https://www2.deloitte.com/us/en/ insights/topics/emerging-technologies/digital-reality-technical-primer.html (Accessed: 10 October 2021).

GeSI (2021). *Digital With Purpose Pledge*. Available at: https://documentcloud.adobe.com/ link/track?uri=urn:aaid:scds:US:4f8989de-f647-4ebd-93b4-ac03229e6a24 (Accessed: 19 October 2021).

GeSI and Deloitte (2019). *Digital With Purpose: Delivering a SMARTer 2030*. Available at: https:// digitalwithpurpose.gesi.org/ (Accessed: 5 October 2021).

IBM (2021). *What Is Machine Learning*. Available at: www.ibm.com/cloud/learn/machine-learning (Accessed: 10 October 2021).

Intergovernmental Panel on Climate Change (IPCC) (2021). *Assessment Report 6*. Available at: www. ipcc.ch/report/ar6/wg1/ (Accessed: 29 October 2021).

International Telecommunication Union (ITU) (2018). *Statistics*. Available at: www.itu.int/en/ ITU-D/Statistics/Pages/stat/default.aspx (Accessed: 5 October 2021).

Lebbie, T. S., Moyebi, O. D., Asante, K. A., Fobil, J., Brune-Drisse, M. N., Suk, W. A., Sly, P. D., Gorman, J., & Carpenter, D. O. (2021). E-waste in Africa: A serious threat to the health of children. *International Journal of Environmental Research and Public Health*, 18, 8488. https://doi. org/10.3390/ijerph18168488

Ofcom (2021). *What Is 4G?* Available at: www.ofcom.org.uk/phones-telecoms-and-internet/advice-for-consumers/advice/what-is-4g (Accessed: 6 October 2021).

UN Global Compact (2021). *What Is the Global Compact?* Available at: www.unglobalcompact.org/what-is-gc (Accessed: 29 October 2021).

United Nations (2015). *Take Action for the Sustainable Development Goals.* Available at: www.un.org/sustainabledevelopment/sustainable-development-goals/. (Accessed: 29 October 2021).

Verizon (2021). *Verizon 2020 ESG Report.* Available at: www.verizon.com/about/sites/default/files/esg-report/2020/Verizon_2020_ESG_Report.pdf. (Accessed: 20 October 2021).

World Food Programme (WFP) (2021). *Building Blocks* (2021). Available at: https://innovation.wfp.org/project/building-blocks. (Accessed: 18 October 2021).

5

Decarbonization as a Chance

Herbert Diess

"Climate protection through innovation" has turned into a fashionable buzzword lately. But what does it actually mean? I was the CEO of the Volkswagen Group until August 2022, one of the largest carmakers in the world, which is going through the greatest transformation in its history—turning itself from a manufacturer and wholesaler of cars into a mobility company geared to operate millions of connected and self-driving battery-electric vehicles around the world. To transform a company like this with more than 670,000 people and 120 production sites around the world, it needs a clearly orchestrated innovation strategy spanning various sectors and covering the entire value chain. To transform an economy to zero emissions through innovation, we need the same.

The Volkswagen Group's core product is the automobile—one of the greatest innovations in human history. A modern car is full of intelligent solutions from generations of smart minds. But the most fascinating thing about a car is the integration of all these ideas, the wide variety of highly complex components in a small space. A good car is always more than the sum of its parts. A good car is created when everything from the software to the chassis, the powertrain, the body, and many other components work together in an ideal way.

I am convinced that the same basic principle applies to climate protection. The actions we take have to fit together. We have to take a cross-industry approach. For example, we need intensive cooperation between the energy industry and the automotive industry. We need close coordination between industry and science, and we need a partnership between the private and the

DOI: 10.4324/9781003262039-6

public sectors. I believe in climate protection that is based on facts, delivers results, and that is logically integrated.

The facts have never been clearer. Over the past 150 years, our knowledge of the state of our planet has increased enormously. We have built global networks and technologies of communication, trade, and environmental observations. We know that we as humans are the central cause of global warming and that it is challenging our very survival on this planet.

The results of the recent climate conference in Glasgow confirm that massive environmental changes are taking place; they also show that, due to the complex interactions, individual technical improvements alone will not be enough to master the intensifying climate challenges.

So far, the human actions simply have not been consistent enough; there is much more that could be done to combat climate change. Many technical concepts are ready for use. Political action and the power to shape change are indispensable.

THE RESPONSIBILITY OF THE VOLKSWAGEN GROUP AND THE TRANSPORTATION SECTOR

About 16 percent of global CO_2 emissions can be attributed to the transportation sector (see Figure 5.1). This mainly comes from burning nearly two-thirds of the world's oil consumption. In addition to passenger transportation—primarily individual transport—the transportation sector also includes freight transport, shipping, and air traffic. The Volkswagen Group and its brands are a major market player.

We sell ten million cars each year; with the acquisition of Navistar, we are the world's second-largest truck manufacturer; and 80 percent of ocean-going vessels run on engines from MAN Energy Solutions.

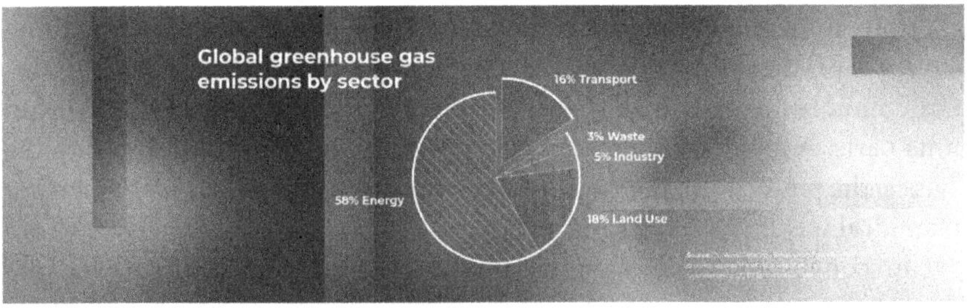

FIGURE 5.1 Global Greenhouse Gas Emissions by Sector

(Source: Volkswagen Group and OurWorldInData.org—research and data to make progress against the world's largest problems. Licenced under CC-BY by the author Hannah Ritchie.)

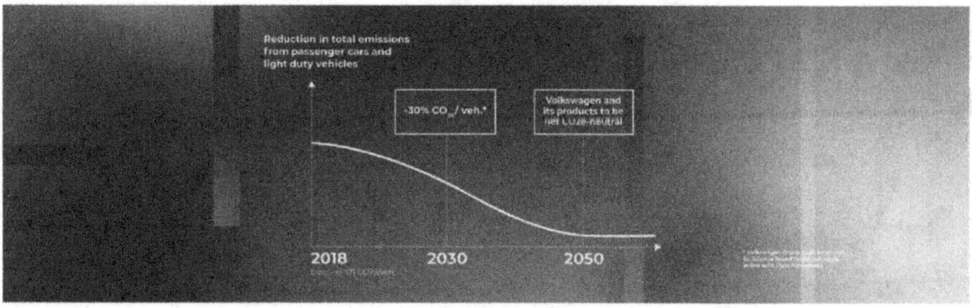

FIGURE 5.2 Reduction in Total Emissions from Passenger Cars and Light Duty Vehicles

(Source: Volkswagen Group.) * Volkswagen Group goals approved by Science-Based Targets initiative in line with Paris Agreement

The transportation sector must be decarbonized quickly without harming the global economy. For us, it is especially important that individual mobility, the ability to move around by car, will be preserved for people and remain affordable for many.

Mobility is a basic human need. It is a fundamental right in a free society. The restrictions imposed by the pandemic in particular have shown how important this basic need is for all of us.

The Volkswagen Group has the responsibility to reduce CO_2 emissions in all our fields of activity as quickly as possible. We are convinced that mankind can stop the anthropogenic climate change and achieve the 1.5 degree target.

We are electrifying passenger cars and, step by step, commercial vehicles. And we are beginning to convert our marine diesel engines from MAN ES to liquefied natural gas. A precursor for the later use of synthetic fuels from wind and solar energy.

We will reduce the CO_2 emissions of our passenger car and light commercial vehicle fleet by 30 percent per vehicle over their entire life cycles by 2030 (see Figure 5.2), compared with 2018. A reduction of around 14 tons from around 47 tons per vehicle; in particular, through the electrification of our vehicle fleets. In 2030, nearly 70 percent of our cars sold in Europe will be electric.

ENERGY TRANSITION IS KEY

But even an ID.3 today still has a CO_2 footprint of 27 tons in the European energy mix throughout its life cycle (see Figure 5.3).

This is made up as follows:

In production and the supply chain, we have already cut emissions from 14.4 tons to 13.7 tons by switching our plants and battery cell production to green electricity.

FIGURE 5.3 CO_2 Footprint of an ID.3
(Source: Volkswagen Group.)

The 13.7 tons of CO_2 consist of battery cells: 3.8 tons, other parts of the supply chain: 8.8 tons, in-house production, and logistics: 1.1 tons.

Use and maintenance: 13.3 tons. In other words, half of the footprint. This can be reduced to nearly zero by charging with green electricity.

In most of the European countries like Norway, Sweden, and Switzerland, the ID.3 is already driving with green energy.

The prerequisite for decarbonizing the transport sector is the availability of green electricity from the Sun and wind.

Energy generation and distribution must be the top priority. Let me give you an example of the effect: our power plant in Wolfsburg generates electricity for the plant and district heat for the city of Wolfsburg.

We are currently converting it from coal to gas. That will save 1.5 million tons of CO_2 per year, equivalent to the annual emissions of 870,000 cars. It is also cost-effective at just €14 per ton! That's just roughly 20 percent of the price of CO_2 certificates in the EU ETS in early 2022. But the dependence on gas remains.

The solution: MAN Energy Solutions is already working on an innovative technology to replace district heating from fossil-fuel power plants. A heat pump plant with sector coupling is being piloted in Esbjerg (see Figure 5.4).

With an overall heating capacity of 50 MW, the plant will supply around 100,000 inhabitants with approximately 235,000 MWh of heat per year. This will save 100,000 tons of CO_2 annually—equivalent to the CO_2 emissions of 55,000 cars.

The heat pump generates climate-neutral heating energy from renewable energy sources—with high efficiency: the electrical energy input generates three to four times as much heat energy.

Heat pumps will be the best solution for decarbonizing all applications where heat below 100 degrees is needed and which today still use fossil fuels.

Costs for decarbonization can be high and vary from sector to sector. It will be particularly difficult and expensive in those areas that cannot be electrified: high-temperature processes, steel, cement, chemicals, aviation, and shipping.

FIGURE 5.4 Esbjerg Heat Pump
(Source: Volkswagen Group.)

FIGURE 5.5 Carbon Capturing
(Source: Volkswagen Group.)

The unavoidable remaining emissions, which we don't have any technical or economic solutions for yet, will have to be removed from the atmosphere to reach the 1.5 degree climate target.

Carbon capturing (see Figure 5.5) to remove the CO_2 is feasible, but not yet on scale and it is still very expensive. Our estimations are that at scale it could cost about US$100 per ton, also very much depending on the availability of cheap renewable energy.

THE FINANCIAL BUSINESS CASE ACCELERATES THE CHANGE

Many other technologies needed for decarbonization are ready for use now. For some of them, it is just a matter of industrialization and then scaling. The VW Group has set up a venture capital fund with an initial volume of €300 million to invest in a number of decarbonization projects and innovative start-ups.

Analysts from Goldman Sachs estimate that in their 1.5 degree scenario a cumulative US$56 trillion will be invested in green infrastructure by 2032—that makes it the largest area of growth.

More and more industries are recognizing the opportunities, and even sophisticated investors like Bill Gates are financing major sustainability projects. The financial business case is accelerating the change.

Progress in decarbonization today varies widely across economies. Germany's emissions total 8.4 tons of CO_2 per capita per year, China emits 7 tons per capita, and the US 16 tons. Sweden switched very fast to carbon-free energy production and implemented a CO_2 price of €100, which led to a shift in consumer preferences. The CO_2 emissions amount to only 4.2 tons per capita, without compromising its standard of living. And despite those measures it's one of the fastest growing economies in Europe.

Let's assume that we can use the measures outlined to reduce the CO_2 footprint in an industrialized country like Germany from around 8.4 tons to 3–4 tons in the medium term: to reach climate neutrality the cost would amount to €300 to €400 a year for capturing roughly €1 per day for every inhabitant. A small amount compared to the horrible scenarios that experts forecast if we don't act. In less industrialized countries, the amount is many times lower.

Mind you, many solutions for reducing CO_2 are already cheaper today than the old fossil methods that we are used to.

Solar or wind power is in some regions already cheaper than coal power. Electric heat pumps reach amortization after only a few years and from then on are cheaper than heating with fossil fuels.

Electric cars are cheaper to run than combustion engine cars, electric city buses make public transport cheaper than using diesel or hybrid buses.

Decarbonization will make many things more affordable, not more expensive.

Subsidies in worldwide fossil technologies are still estimated to be much higher than investments in renewable energies (see Figure 5.6). Coal subsidies, reduced taxes on diesel, tax-free kerosene, air travel with a reduced VAT rate are slowing the transition into renewables. Hesitant political reforms in

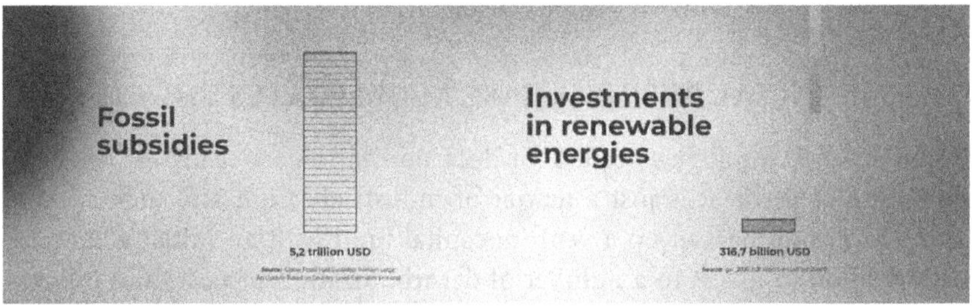

FIGURE 5.6 Fossil Fuel Subsidies Versus Investments in Renewable Energies

(Source: Volkswagen Group, IMF report "Global Fossil Fuel Subsidies Remain Large," Ren21 "Global Status Report 2020".)

the subsidy scheme are delaying the economic transition that would already be possible today.

Reducing CO_2 is possible without sacrificing our standard of living. We can continue to fly on vacation—it may be a little more expensive. We can still eat meat—maybe a little less—it's healthier anyway. We are still mobile—with CO_2-free electric cars and airplanes with synthetic fuels.

Entire ecosystems can become climate-neutral as some worldwide projects will demonstrate. One is our European blueprint Astypalea, a Greek island where we are installing a fully electric transportation network based on green energy.

What's true on Astypalea is true elsewhere: more and more people are switching to modern means of transportation. The new car is losing many of its negative qualities—it's becoming cleaner, safer, and more comfortable.

BETTER UTILIZATION OF CARS ACCELERATES THE CHANGE

Another big lever to reduce CO_2 emissions is better utilization. Today, a car used for private or business purposes is one of the world's worst-utilized assets: driven for only about one hour a day on average, it is parked the rest of the time, which in turn leads to major expenses for infrastructure such as parking spaces.

What's more, it prolongs the lifecycle of those vehicles. The result: less environmentally friendly, more outdated technologies are used for too long. Better utilization accelerates the change!

In the future, electric robotaxis will drive around the whole day to transport more people than today on one trip. This leads to a highly efficient use with fewer cars and fewer parking spaces in the cities.

Car sharing can double the utilization to approximately two hours a day—a major improvement in utilization and reduction of parking spaces that are needed.

FIGURE 5.7 Volkswagen Electric Vehicles

(Source: Volkswagen Group.)

A significant improvement can be achieved by combining usage, which means to use the same car for sharing, rental, and subscription. This would once again double the usage time of cars.

With rental cars mainly being used on weekends and car sharing being used Mondays through Fridays, utilization can be maximized. The technological game changer will be your virtual key on your smartphone, which gives you easy, 24/7 access to a large car fleet. A multipurpose use of the fleets with one key can potentially increase the utilization of the cars up to three or four times compared to today.

CLIMATE PROTECTION AND QUALITY OF LIFE ARE NO OPPOSITES

There is plenty of reason to be optimistic. A future of mobility in better harmony with nature and the environment is possible. It will be more sustainable, more comfortable, and much safer. The technologies are becoming available fast. Soon it will be a matter of scaling them up quickly and removing obstacles to expansion.

This requires a willingness to change and joint action among policy makers, industry, and society to build the infrastructures. Instruments such as CO_2 pricing foster processes to the buildup of renewable energies.

Climate protection and quality of life are not opposites. Climate protection is cheaper than adapting to climate change and brings sustainable benefits for the quality of life.

To safeguard individual mobility, we have to decarbonize the transportation sector through electrification with green energy, fast cross-sector work, and alignment is necessary. That is why we founded the CEO Alliance (see Figure 5.8). Together with European companies such as ABB, E.ON, Enel, Iberdrola, SAP, or Schneider Electric, we support and advise the European

FIGURE 5.8 CEO Alliance

(Source: Volkswagen Group.)

Commission on the implementation of the Green Deal. We are sharing ideas and experiences, working across industries on specific projects that contribute to climate goals. And we know: we can tackle climate change much more effectively when we work together rather than individually.

Our generation—which is now at the levers of power and can drive change—has the responsibility to enable future generations to live on this planet in peace and social and economic security.

The goal must be to limit human-driven climate change while maintaining or improving the quality of life for all people globally. If we work together with a consistent strategy, we can do it.

6

Ocean Technology as a Growing Space in Which to Reimagine Business

The Role of Start-Ups*

Bjørn K. Haugland† and Asgeir J. Sørensen‡

INTRODUCTION

Norway plays an important international role as one of the main actors in the blue economy. More than ever, a holistic and sustainable approach is needed to address *global challenges*, *value creation*, and *knowledge-based management* of the northern regions and oceans. We are heading into the United Nations Decade (2021–2030) of Ocean Science for Sustainable Development—*The Science We Need for the Ocean We Want* (Intergovernmental Oceanographic Commission, 2019). A common act between the stakeholders across the value chain to create a demand and delivery enables ocean technology as a growing space in which to reimagine business, where the role of start-ups may play an instrumental role to create needed disruptions in terms of both novel solutions and speed in implementation. This chapter is a further elaboration of earlier published materials by the authors in Wassman et al. (2021).

The objective of this chapter is to demonstrate how thorough knowledge, wisdom, and courage combined with political leadership are needed to solve the global challenges and avoiding promising solutions thought to be a *part-of-the-solution* instead becomes *part-of-the-problem*. A holistic and

* The work is sponsored by the Research Council of Norway through the Centre of Excellence funding scheme, NTNU AMOS project number 223254.

† Skift, Business Climate Leaders, www.skiftnorge.no/en/, Oslo, Norway, e-mail: bjorn@skiftnorge.no

‡ NTNU AMOS, www.ntnu.edu/amos/, Centre for Autonomous Marine Operations and Systems, Department of Marine Technology, Norwegian University of Science and Technology (NTNU), Trondheim, Norway, e-mail: asgeir.sorensen@ntnu.no

DOI: 10.4324/9781003262039-7

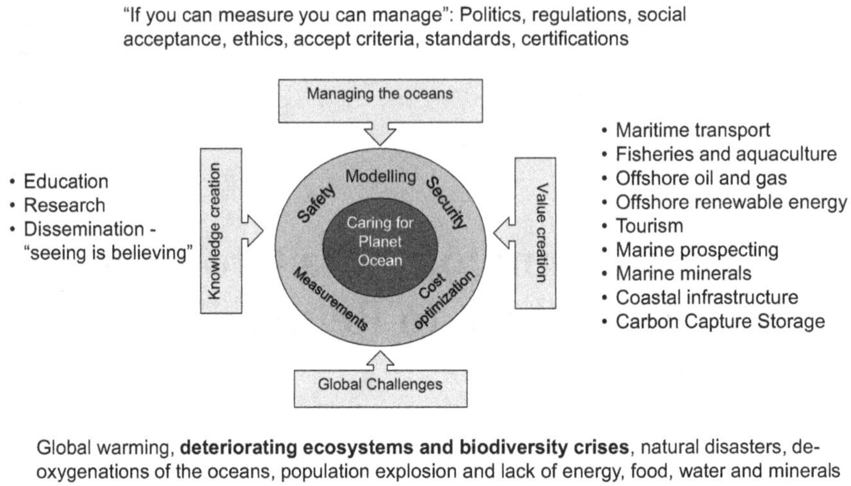

FIGURE 6.1 Sustainable Value Creation Requires a Holistic Approach

sustainable perspective of the blue economy (see Figure 6.1) that sweeps all stakeholders, including policy makers, is needed to achieve both the impact and the implementation at the speed we require. The changes that take place in northern and Arctic regions and seas increase in speed and extend and are strongly interconnected to activity on land and coastal areas around the globe. The oceans are connecting and belonging to all of us, and we are in a hurry to understand and take proper actions. We must create incentives for *demand* and *deliver* across the entire value chain stimulating the stakeholders from a think tank to an executional do-tank to develop competence, knowledge, innovations, and new start-ups subject to:

- *global challenges* related to climate change, lack of energy, minerals and food, acidification and pollution of the oceans, biodiversity crisis, natural disasters, and the need for green logistics;
- *value creati*on (products, services etc.) in terms of fisheries, aquaculture, maritime transport, oil and gas exploitation, offshore renewable energy, marine minerals, tourism, coastal and urbanization infrastructure;
- *governance and knowledge-based management* of the oceans, coastal areas, and the Arctic; and
- *enabling technology* such as information and communication technology (ICT), material technology, biotechnology, autonomy, big data cybernetics, nanotechnology, and interdisciplinarity.

When it comes to preserving and developing human health and well-being in the short- and long-term for the generations to come, we face a few dilemmas.

Increasing occurrences of extreme weather, accelerated melting of ice on land and sea, rising sea levels, pollution, and global diseases should indeed motivate us to develop toward more sound and sustainable human activities. The cost of overlooking this fact will simply be too high in both economical and humanitarian terms. Indeed, it is our belief that knowledge and competence can contribute to technology innovations and policy in two ways. To create changes fast enough in the desired direction, technology innovations may be implemented as a transformative process while others may be more disruptive. Start-ups supported by academia, industrial and financial partners are often the most effective way to go disruptive and fast as no strings are attached to legacy products and services. Successful implementation relies on political leadership that enforces incentives and regulations. Fortunately, also long-term responsible industry actors and investors that are looking beyond the next quarterly economic reporting have similar interests. It does not need to be a contradiction between value creation and sound knowledge-based governance. For instance, for the fisheries and aquaculture industry it is obvious that a healthy ocean is not only good but a precondition for business. Being proactive for existing industry and start-ups, we may regard the 17 United Nations (UN) Sustainable Development Goals (SDGs) as the largest and most systematic market study of the world, providing possibilities for economic growth and a better future. Knowledge and competence will be instrumental for the development of technology and services contributing to improved solutions.

Decades of systematic ocean science research using ships, landers, and buoys, and lately advanced marine robotics and sensors have told us how extensive and vulnerable the ecosystems are in the High North and Arctic Ocean. Even during the winter and polar night season, the marine ecosystems are fully functional and active. Threats to these ecosystems span from discharge of toxic substances, inflow of warm water, and the intrusion of invasive species from the South. During the polar night, we have studied how sensitive the behavior of zooplankton and fish are to artificial light pollution (e.g., ships, settlements). The light climate influences the hunting and escape strategies of many species such that they easily become disturbed by artificial light several kilometers away from the source as well as tenfolds of meter into the depth. The same behavior using large ships emitting light may also be an error source in quantification of marine resources for research and management purposes during the night and winter season (polar night).

We may claim that the advection pump of warm Atlantic water into the Arctic Ocean and the corresponding outflow of cold Arctic water, both taking place in the Fram Strait between Greenland and Svalbard, are of crucial importance for life in the northeastern Northern Atlantic and the Arctic Ocean. Any changes in these water fluxes do not directly affect only the local climate but have ramification all over the Northern Hemisphere. In simple terms, we can regard the Fram Strait as an oceanographic and biological "war zone" between the South and the North. Today's climate change moves this war zone further North, with possible devastating effects on the Arctic sea life including sea birds.

As in the ancient times of the ice age, the pressure by human exploitation of resources on the Arctic regions literally follows the ice edge. This applies today for also whaling, fisheries, shipping, tourism, mining, oil, and gas, defined as the blue economy.

THE BLUE ECONOMY

The Norwegian economy is dominated by the blue economy (see Figure 6.2). Common factors for the blue economy are that the activities are taking place in the oceans, and that they are both local and global in their presence and trade. Concerning a more accessible new Arctic Ocean, we may foresee a global race for securing access to potential valuable fisheries, hydrocarbons, and mineral resources. In addition, less multi-year sea ice will open new Arctic shipping routes. Hence, the level of human activities and possible environmental impact are expected to increase in a vulnerable environment where our knowledge is still rather limited.

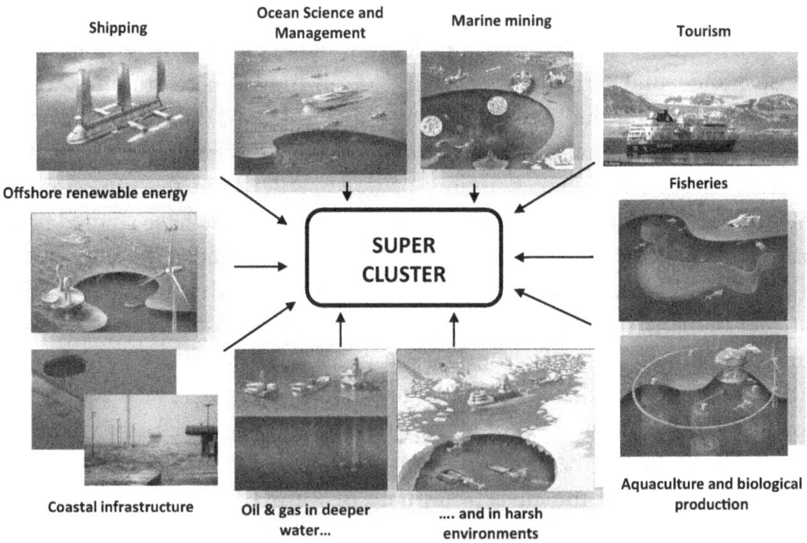

FIGURE 6.2 The Blue Economy
(Source: *courtesy*: NTNU AMOS/Stenberg.)

Offshore oil and gas, maritime industry, and fishery and aquaculture are the three largest sectors of the Norwegian blue economy. They are all of great importance for Norwegian well-being, providing an important contribution to the world in the supply of energy, transportation, and food. Emerging business areas are offshore renewables (primarily offshore wind), tourism, and marine mining. Benefiting from ocean science and bioprospecting (the process of discovery and commercialization of new products based on biological resources), we may also see huge potentials in new marine species, bacteria, molecules, etc. to produce new pharmaceutical substances.

Reduced emission footprint in oil and gas

National oil and gas activities mostly take place in three areas—the North, Norwegian, and the Barents Seas. Defining the border line for the sea ice edge in the Norwegian Arctic regions restricting how far north oil and gas activities on the Norwegian continental shelf can take place has been vivid. Oil and gas activities in the High North are not only of concern in Norway. There are also large terrestrial and offshore activities in Russia, Canada, and the USA. Exploitation of hydrocarbons is not sustainable. Carbon capture storage (CCS) in ground reservoirs and other capturing methods in the ocean (e.g., kelp and micro algae production) may be methods to reduce the problem. The work to replace polluting energy sources such as coals and heavy oil with cleaner sources using renewables is intensified. Regardless of how the energy transition will happen, the 50 years of experience and knowledge gained from designing and operating offshore oil and gas installations and conducting marine operations in harsh environments will be instrumental in developing offshore renewables.

Toward zero-carbon shipping

Maritime transport is probably the most environmentally friendly method to transport large amounts of goods and humans to secure primary logistics needs. However, shipping is still in global terms a severe single source for greenhouse gasses, black carbon, and unintentionally causing the spread of invasive species with ballast waters and hull fouling. The UN International Maritime Organization (IMO) has therefore enforced a plan to reduce emissions in international shipping in total by 50% in 2050, compared to the 2008 level. A reduction of up to 50% may not look ambitious. However, it will indeed create changes in organization of logistic chains and motivate new ship concepts with hybrid power plants using greener fuel mixtures, batteries, hydrogen, ammonia, etc. Reducing ship speed and selecting unmanned autonomous ships will represent possible solutions. A driver for rapid transition toward zero-carbon shipping may be to enforce even stricter requirements for reduced emission in all maritime activities. This may be regulated by authorities using, for example, a tax on emission and creating a commercial *demand* and *delivery* mechanism from customer to producer through the entire supply chain. The combination of regulators and financial institutions is a significant driver for the transition. License to operate and financial security are closely interconnected. For the various shipping segments from deep sea shipping, regional shipping, domestic shipping, short sea shipping, and urban transportation, it is evident that new commercial positions are to be taken, and we see a race for innovations and investments in new technology, services, and infrastructure. The response in the market is seen in, for example, the form of innovation and spin-outs, where:

- owners and logistic suppliers of goods to be transported commit to using zero-carbon shipping fuels (ref. Amazon and Ikea);
- partnerships between established and new actors developing a demand for knowledge, solutions, global infrastructure, and distribution systems supporting green fuel types on ships (e.g., the Mærsk Mc-Kinney Møller Center for Zero Carbon Shipping);[1]
- existing and new actors set up and develop production and distributions systems for green fuel types, batteries, and charging systems;
- novel logistics and ship concepts are developed for the various shipping segments.

The more capital-intensive innovations are often handled by the established enterprises, which may enter into joint ventures with other companies or investors developing solutions for batteries and new fuel types (e.g., Aker,[2] Yara),[3] while the smaller start-ups seek more disruptive and less capital-intensive opportunities for autonomous urban ferries (e.g., Zeabuz)[4] and energy-efficient high-speed craft using air cavity to reduce resistance (e.g., SES-x Marine Technologies).[5]

Toward offshore aquaculture

Coastal aquaculture is currently struggling with ectoparasites and harmful algae blooms. In addition, the environmental impact of aquaculture is of concern in many fjords. Offshore aquaculture in more exposed areas has become the next step for growth in this business. It is likely that the activity level will move northwards and to areas with better access to natural supply of food for farmed fish, such as the dominant zooplankton species *Calanus finmarchicus*.

Toward offshore wind

When it comes to climate, biodiversity, and short-term profit, we obviously face several policy and economic dilemmas and possible conflicts of interest. For instance, more costly offshore wind turbines may have less negative impact on biodiversity than developing cheaper wind turbine parks on untouched land. However, going offshore may potentially increase spatial area conflicts with fisheries. In economic terms, we may ask how to evaluate and price limited resources such as land and terrestrial ecosystems when setting up cost balance sheets for new energy projects. Similarly, shortage of minerals, unless we increase our mining activities, may challenge further growth of green alternatives such as solar energy and batteries for energy storage in, for example, cars and ships.

Electrifying remote settlements and ports

The settlements on Svalbard are today dependent on hydrocarbon-driven power plants for production of electricity (local coal and transported diesel). It is really a contradiction that one of the most environmentally sensitive areas in Norway is not supplied with greener and more renewable energy. We may turn this contradiction to an opportunity where Svalbard and other remote areas can be a destination for developing and testing hybrid power plants combining solar and wind-driven energy production with energy storage and possible production of green fuel types such as ammonia becoming a green port for ships as well. The use of hydrocarbons is then limited to a minimum. Smart hybrid power plants that work autonomously without large transmission networks may be a natural next step powering societies and ships on a global scale with greener energy with less impact on climate and biodiversity. Why not start at remote areas such as Svalbard and then use this experience for further export of knowledge, products, and services on a global scale for remote areas.

Climate adaptation of coastal infrastructure

Climate adaptation as well as novel concepts for the crossing of fjords and bays are increasingly important for the coastal economies. Most of the world population lives in urban settlements close to the sea. We can hardly comprehend the cost of adapting these cities and land areas to increasing sea level of only a few decimeters due to melting of land fast ice. Global and local infrastructure enterprises must look for innovative solutions for damage reduction.

ENABLING TECHNOLOGY

As we have seen, we face challenges and enjoy opportunities where technology and its use play important roles for human activities and corresponding impact on life and environment. There are many drivers for technology developments such as market needs, exploration needs (and dreams) accessing new and maybe extreme environments, as well as policy-driven rules and regulations. Game-changing technology is often provided through so-called enabling technologies. Enabling technology may be defined in different manners. Here, it is technology that can be applied to drive radical and thorough changes of public and industry inventions and innovations. For instance, drivers for technology developments for improved mapping and monitoring of the oceans in the High North including the Arctic Ocean may be improved operability, access to remote and harsh environments (deep water, under ice, extreme coldness, etc.), long distance with limited ability to communicate, demand for improved coverage, and higher resolution of data in spatial and temporal scales, reduced cost, improved safety, and so on.

In this context, we may categorize the following as enabling technologies with relevance for the ocean technology.

- ICT
- Nanotechnology
- Biotechnology
- Material technology
- Big data cybernetics and data analytics
- Autonomous systems

Combined with fundamental knowledge fields such as mathematics, physics, chemistry, biology, computer science, and engineering and by integrating disciplines and technologies, we may be in the position to conduct research and innovations based on disruptive, game-changing technology. What lies in front of us may be beyond imagination. Examples could be to develop technology inspired by nature that is far more efficient and effective than today's solutions, for example, applying multi-scale and distributed systems for sensing and actuation: micro-to-macro (see Figures 6.3 and 6.4).

START-UPS—DOING THE RIGHT THING RIGHT

In order to meet the grand challenges, long-term and focused efforts are needed. Being heavily involved in one of the most successful research institutions in Norway—the Centre of Excellence scheme—we will exemplify how research is chasing impact and where enabling technologies and interdisciplinary knowledge will help us toward a better future. Probably, even more

FIGURE 6.3 Disruptive Innovations Beyond Imagination from Micro to Macro Scales (Source: courtesy: NTNU AMOS/Stenberg.)

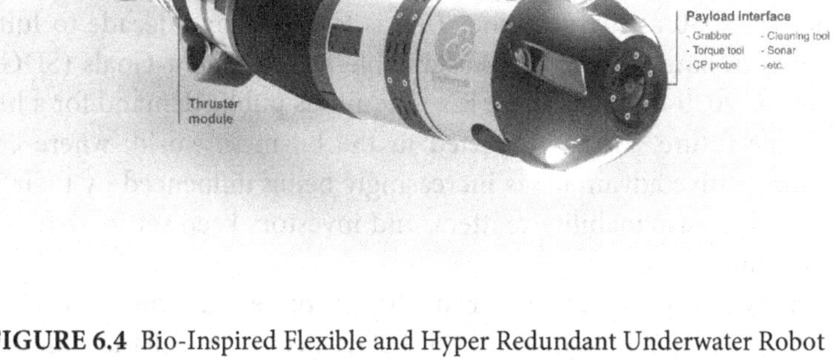

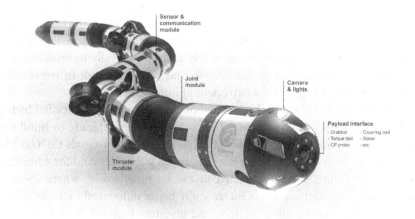

FIGURE 6.4 Bio-Inspired Flexible and Hyper Redundant Underwater Robot (Source: courtesy: Eelume.)

important is research-based education with training of the next-generation engineers, scientists, and decision-makers having a holistic and sustainable mindset. In addition, when relevant we should drive innovation which here means new methods, products, or processes that are valuable and applied. Important factors for innovation success are the authorization and mission given to the research team—or simply—*the license to create*. At NTNU AMOS[3] innovation processes are done systematically in cooperation with the partners NTNU, Equinor, SINTEF, DNV, Research Council of Norway, and other industry collaborators. The innovation arenas are existing industry companies, public agencies, universities and research institutes, and start-up companies. Up to now eight new companies are founded because of research-driven innovation well-tuned with technology trends, market needs, and global challenges. Sustainability has become a vital part of innovation processes and enterprises' bottom line in terms of reputation and license to operate. In the following, we will present two examples in this context where start-ups play a role for the ocean technology.

Example 1: how to measure ESG

The world needs rapid transformation toward a sustainable future—and a definition of what that future entails. Fake news, misleading information, and greenwashing create a constant struggle for politicians, businesses, and consumers. Everyone is tasked with making their own definition of what sustainability is, and what it is not. We simply cannot continue in this direction. Someone must take responsibility to confront the madness—before it is too late.

The world as we know it is at great risk. Unsustainable global practices continuously harm the Earth and its ecosystems, and four of the planetary boundaries for sustainable development have already been exceeded because of human activity. A failure to act swiftly and purposefully to breach out of business-as-usual and adopt sustainable practices will result in irreversible environmental changes to the detriment of human well-being.

The clock is ticking, and the international community spearheaded by the UN has set 2030 as the deadline. That is less than one decade to fulfill the ambitions outlined in the UN Sustainable Development Goals (SDGs) put forth in the 2030 Agenda. There is a ubiquitous public demand for a healthy, sustainable future. This is reflected in the business world, where companies' competitive advantage is increasingly being influenced by their ability to respond to sustainability matters, and investors keep setting stricter ESG requirements.

At the same time, fake news, profit-driven studies, superficial sustainability campaigns, and greenwashing clutter the market. Within all that clutter, there is still no objective or generally accepted way to represent sustainability, let alone in a comparable manner. Existing reporting standards remain disconnected, voluntary to use, and subjectively tailorable, rendering companies' reported sustainability impacts highly unreliable and noncomparable. As we enter this decade of action, we do so without the required tools to collaborate, document, and measure our progress toward the SDGs and sustainability at large. We are stuck in a thick fog, and there is no verified, transparent way to assess sustainability.

How can we reach our sustainability goals without a way to measure our success?

We cannot.

That is the gap the start-up foundation TERRAVERA™ strives to fill.

The vision of TERRAVERA™ is to enable technology and global collaboration in harmonious combination with innovative thinking and courage to define and measure true sustainability and by that enable everyone to make the right decisions.

A global scientific consensus is targeted through: *Representing reality through an open digital infrastructure, where data and models of value chains, businesses, and products and services give insights on true sustainability.*

TERRAVERA™ aims to realize the vision and fulfill the purpose by creating a digital platform where academics, experts, research institutions, and partners can collaborate on defining true sustainability measurement. The platform will facilitate cooperative development of complex and interconnected sustainability models that are rooted in scientific evidence. TERRAVERA™ seeks to fuel further innovation by creating a massive global movement and by making our technology readily available for anyone to use.

We acknowledge that the TERRAVERA™ vision is beyond ambitious and that what they are trying to achieve is so monumental that no one has ever come close to realizing it. That is why TERRAVERA™ aims to create an open, global platform for uniting knowledge and facilitating transparent sustainability measurement across all industries. But just like Rome was not built in a day, defining and measuring true sustainability will take years of hard, dedicated, interdisciplinary, and collaborative work to achieve.

To get the boulder rolling, TERRAVERA™ has started developing a digital infrastructure that will act as the epicenter of all sustainability assessments. At the core of this infrastructure lies a set of tools (within a digital platform) that can be utilized to model reality and evaluate sustainability in a transparent way. Researchers and field matter experts in academia, qualified contributors, and leading research institutions collaborate to define interconnected models that are implemented using the platform toolkit. All efforts toward such model development are carried out independently and without any conflicts of interest, for the sole purpose of contributing to defining and measuring true sustainability.

TERRAVREA™ strives to make the technology accessible and easy to use for everyone to gain sustainability insights and make more informed decisions based on these. The ultimate aspiration of TERRAVERA™ is to empower people to act based on facts and thus drive the world toward a more sustainable allocation of our scarce resources.

A digital infrastructure for collaboration: *providing digital infrastructure that allows humans and machines to work together to establish insights and represent sustainability in one number.*

Technically, TERRAVERA's digital infrastructure can be categorized as Platform as a service (PaaS), where the users are responsible for their own applications and data, although we do provide some applications as well. The platform itself is also capable of retrieving and aggregating data securely, all through one unified portal. All internal and external communication with the TERRAVERA™ platform happens through an application programming interface (API), which allows for the development of a digital ecosystem surrounding the platform. This means that you are free to develop and connect your own applications to the platform as you wish, for instance, your ERP or procurement system. TERRAVERA™ is also developing tools on top of the same infrastructure, currently including TerraLight, TerraCalc, and TerraPortal. In addition to independently developed models for sustainability, the platform supports integration of established frameworks such as the EU Taxonomy.

Example 2: technology for mapping and monitoring

Enabling technologies such as ICT, autonomy and microelectromechanical (MEMS) systems provide new possibilities for the development of sensors, sensor-carrying platforms (Figures 6.3 and 6.4), connectivity, and big data analytics. The sensor-carrying platforms operating from space to ocean space are (Berge et al., 2020):

- Underwater—landers and buoys, remotely operated vehicles (ROVs), autonomous underwater vehicles (AUVs), gliders, and profilers.
- Sea surface—ships and unmanned surface vehicles (USVs).
- Air and space—satellites, unmanned aerial vehicles (UAVs), and airplanes.

Low-cost small satellites and in particular *nano* (1–10 kg) and *micro* satellites (10–100 kg) carrying customized payload sensors and communication devices have opened for a step change for remote sensing and communication in polar orbits at altitude of 450–500 kilometers with about 3–6 hours for each passing. Swarms of satellites will provide a significantly improved spatial and temporal coverage. NTNU has decided to launch two small satellites as a pilot: one for hyperspectral imaging of ocean colors and one for supporting Arctic communication.

Environmental mapping and monitoring may be carried out by single platforms, swarms of platforms, or a combination of several types denoted as *heterogeneous sensor-carrying platforms*. Each platform and sensor has various capabilities in terms of spatial and temporal resolution and coverage as seen in Figure 6.5. By combining them, we face a paradigm shift in terms of capabilities that may be 100–1,000 times higher than the state-of-the-art technology only some years ago. The entailed increase in data harvesting does also create new challenges in handling big data sets. To take full benefit of the data and develop efficient adaptive strategies for sampling and measurements for the sensor-carrying platforms, refinement of models, and co-simulation with numerical simulation models of the oceanography and ecosystems is essential.

From a High North and Arctic perspective, the environment can be characterized as remote and harsh for scientific operations and even more demanding during the polar night due to the darkness and extreme coldness.

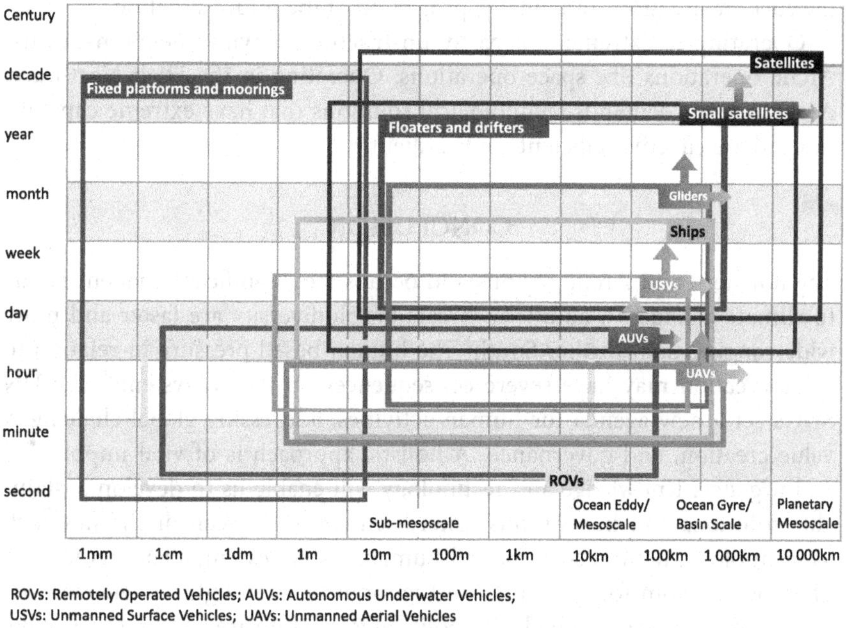

FIGURE 6.5 Spatial and Temporal Resolution and Coverage of Different Platforms

(Source: Redrawn from Berge et al., 2020.)

Recent campaigns have also taught us the importance of light sensitivity on marine life and the effect of possible light pollution from ships. Use of robots as sensor-carrying platforms gives a far more precise picture of the ecosystem. Enabling technology and proper operational procedures may be the only way to reveal the processes in the Arctic Ocean. The spatial scale is enormous with large variability in the seasons and over the years. This clearly also tells us the importance of prolonged presence and the potential for improved autonomous sensor-carrying platforms that can process the data onboard for improved real-time planning and replanning of the operations. Being successful in the design and operation of autonomous platforms, this clearly shows us the importance for multidisciplinary teams with an innovation mindset. Several start-ups have contributed to disruptive innovations.

Risk management is crucial for successful operation avoiding collisions, loss of vehicles, etc. This applies for the environment and operation of the sensor-carrying platform itself. As the autonomy level increases, more of the risk assessment and corresponding response must be done by the robotic platform itself. Improved sensors for situation awareness and more automated analysis of the sensor data locally enable the sensor-carrying platforms to cooperate, optimize, and replan the mission. Situation awareness is here defined as, perception of the elements in the environment; comprehension of the current situation; and, finally, projection of the future situation.

Operating in extreme and partly unstructured environments makes the Arctic operations like space operations. Operating in the High North and Arctic regions demands technological solutions that have extreme capabilities and are effective, efficient, and resilient.

CONCLUSION

The northern and Arctic regions and oceans face significant challenges due to climate change. In addition, threats on biodiversity are faster and more wide-ranging than further South. The human-based pressure in relation to value creation may have severe consequences on the ecosystems. The UN SDGs set a new agenda for human activities, addressing global challenges, value creation, and governance. A holistic approach is of vital importance and urgency. Knowledge and technology will enable us to develop sustainable solutions and innovations. Interdisciplinary between disciplines such as technology, natural science, and humanities are essential success factors. There is no room for arrogance and ignorance. Thorough knowledge, wisdom, and courage combined with political leadership are needed to solve the global challenges and avoiding promising solutions thought to be a *part-of-the-solution* instead becomes *part-of-the-problem*.

Ocean technology is a growing space in which to reimagine business.

NOTES

1 Mærsk Mc-Kinney Møller Center for Zero Carbon Shipping: www.zerocarbonshipping.com
2 Aker: www.akerasa.com
3 Yara Marine Technologies: https://yaramarine.com
4 Zeabuz: https://zeabuz.com
5 SES-X Marine Technologies: https://sesxmarinetechnologies.com

REFERENCES

Berge, J., G. Johnsen, J., & Cohen, H. (2020). *Polar Night Marine Ecology—Life and Light in the Dead of Night. Advances in Polar Biology*. Cham: Springer Nature.

Intergovernmental Oceanographic Commission (2019). *The Science We Need for the Ocean We Want: The United Nations Decade of Ocean Science for Sustainable Development (2021–2030)*. Available at: https://unesdoc.unesco.org/ark:/48223/pf0000265198

Wassman, P. (edited) with Auad, G., Babin, M., Balton, A. A., Carmack, E. C., Corell, R. W. et al. (2021). *Whither the Arctic Ocean? Research, Knowledge Needs and Development en Route to the New Arctic*. Bilbao: Fundacion BBV.

PART II

ESG as and through Technology

7

Mitigating the Risks and Nurturing the Opportunities

Data and Tech Vital in Tackling Companies' ESG Challenges*

Nina Arquint** and Andreas Berger†

OUR FOCUS AND APPROACH TO THE SUBJECT

This chapter discusses and highlights the way in which the Swiss Re Group and its commercial insurance arm, Swiss Re Corporate Solutions, leverage their risk management knowledge, data analytics capability, and technological expertise to address the sustainability challenges facing the corporate world. Broadly speaking, the content will be structured in the following way:
It leads in with the Ausnet case study, *Mitigating bushfire risk in Australia*, which illustrates one of the numerous ways Swiss Re and Swiss Re Corporate Solutions use knowledge, data and tech to nurture companies' sustainability opportunities. This is followed by a description of Swiss Re Group's and Swiss Re Corporate Solutions' approach to risk. This entails not only risk transfer but also the data-driven insights they provide customers in this context of sustainability.

The subsequent section deals with physical risk driven by climate change and natural disasters. Also, it examines subsets of physical risk, including transition and liability risk. The main body of the chapter summarizes some of the concrete ways the Group and Corporate Solutions employ data and tech to come to grips with sustainability and ESG-related risks on customers' behalf. The concluding section provides a synopsis of Swiss Re's sustainability

* This chapter was finalized in November 2021 and hence does not take into account recent geopolitical and socioeconomic developments.

** Chief Risk Officer, Swiss Re Corporate Solutions.

† Chief Executive Officer, Swiss Re Corporate Solutions.

DOI: 10.4324/9781003262039-9

approach and a reminder of how climate change will be felt across all business functions.

MITIGATING BUSHFIRE RISK IN AUSTRALIA

The relationship with Ausnet demonstrates one of the numerous ways Swiss Re Corporate Solutions uses knowledge, data, and tech to nurture companies' sustainability opportunities.

Australian energy company, Ausnet Services, approached Swiss Re Corporate Solutions in 2019, to better understand the impact of climate risk on bushfire perils, bushfire risk management practices, and potential solutions.

AusNet Services operates electricity networks in some of the most bushfire-prone regions in Australia. Devastating bushfires are a regular occurrence in many parts of the country, the most destructive of which occurred following a heatwave in southeastern Australia in 2010. According to Swiss Re's publication, "Sovereign Insurance—Creating financial resilience against the growing burden of natural disasters," this catastrophe resulted in 2,029 houses being lost, 173 fatalities, and losses in excess of AUD one billion (Swiss Re, 2018). See Figure 7.1.

Because effectively mitigating operational and financial risks is fundamental to business operation, Ausnet commissioned Swiss Re for its

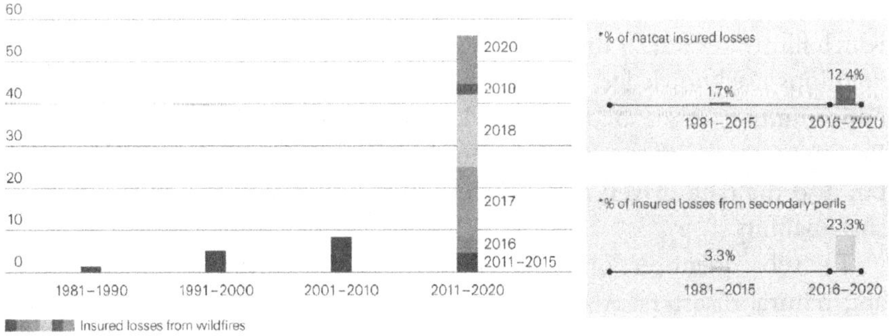

FIGURE 7.1 Global Insured Losses From Wildfire, in US$ Billion at 2020 Prices

(Source: Swiss Re Institute.)

Note: New scientific evidence points to a lengthening of average fire seasons. This gives reason to believe that climate change is likely a significant factor in the growing scale of wildfire-related losses in different regions of the world, including in regions where fires have historically happened only rarely. However, it is not the only contributor. Also important is the parallel development of socioeconomic trends such as rapidly growing exposure in areas adjacent or within undeveloped natural areas and suboptimal fire management strategies that may have led to an increasing availability of natural biomass fuels.

expertise on the impact of climate risk on bushfire perils and bushfire risk in Australia. Also, they wanted to benefit from our knowledge of fire management practices in California and potential financial solutions for managing that risk.

The customer concluded that the analysis carried out on climate drivers for southeast Australia and innovative financial solutions were particularly insightful. It highlighted, they said, new ways existing data could be brought together to generate leading indicators of bushfire risk in southeast Australia and how data could be used to create new financial risk instruments. Our insights will help ensure AusNet Services has avenues to maintain effective and low-cost financial risk mitigation as insurance markets tighten around the world.

Bushfire mitigation strategies are particularly challenging for utilities operators. There is no "one size fits all" approach to improving grid infrastructure to prevent wildfires. Instead, key strategies are to learn quickly from loss experience and prioritize improvements which will have the greatest impact on risk exposure at the lowest cost.

Compared to human operation, embracing Internet-of-Things (IoT) technology such as sensors, automatic fault detection, drone inspections, and other means may provide robust reactions to failure events and improved outcomes at lower long-term costs.

Potential solutions can take the form of physical and financial solutions—as well as pre- and post-event financing options. Pre-event financing options include Parametric Drought Insurance, where fast disbursements of payouts during or immediately prior to the bushfire season can lead to far-improved economic outcomes compared to indemnification of destroyed assets.

This relationship with Ausnet demonstrates one of the numerous ways Swiss Re Corporate Solutions uses knowledge, data, and tech to nurture companies' sustainability opportunities. Moreover, it shows how Swiss Re Corporate Solutions can benefit not only from the Group's over 150 years of accumulated risk management expertise but also from its significant capacity and appetite for risk.

SWISS RE MAKES THE WORLD MORE RESILIENT

The role of new technology, specifically data and analytics capabilities, will further our ability to offer services and risk insights that help our customers and partners make better, data-driven business decisions.

What does sustainability risk mean in the context of Swiss Re Corporate Solutions' business strategy and approach to its customers? The concept of sustainability, or sustainable development, broadly equates with responsible investment and business practices, as defined by the United Nations Sustainable Development Goals (SDGs). The principles underlying such practices are grouped under the headings, Environmental, Social, and Governance (ESG). For Swiss Re and Swiss Re Corporate Solutions—and for all socially responsible corporates—the concept of sustainability has two significant, interlinked implications. First, for business strategy: Swiss Re's goal is to help strengthen world resilience. It does this by addressing the protection gap, that is the difference between economic and insured losses, to help the world rebuild, renew, and move forward. Today, 75% of risks—from natural catastrophes and climate change, to aging populations and cybercrime—remain uninsured (Swiss Re, 2022a). And second, the concept embraces an overarching, ethics-based understanding of how societies can—and should—make progress.

At the heart of Swiss Re's strategy are its clients and partners. Working with them to insure against large losses through risk transfer will continue to be the most essential part of the group's strategy. Our research, solutions, and tools will enable an improved understanding of future risks and opportunities. Through strong tech partnerships, we create platforms to process, transfer, and distribute risks—including access to capital markets, B2B2C products, and new ecosystems.

Crucial role of strong risk management discipline

Swiss Re's concerted effort to adhere to ESG principles would be impossible without strong risk management discipline. The latter helps ensure Swiss Re's profitability and sustainable growth, making the company more resilient so that it can honor the promises it makes to its clients. Its independent, broad, and long-term perspective to risk-taking protects Swiss Re's reputation and financial strength, steering away from destabilizing risks and helping clients take on those risks that are worth taking. It has a strong interest in supporting clients, not only to mitigate negative risks but also to leverage the upside opportunities that sustainability risks generate. One crucial requisite in this context is its unrelenting effort to fully understand the new, sustainability-related risks that clients could be embarking on. And these risks very often arise when clients enter new fields that involve new products and new technology.

One of the major tasks Swiss Re's risk experts address is ensuring sustainable and responsible practices by identifying, mitigating, and eliminating potential ESG risks inherent in our business transactions and investments. This task also includes defining which business falls outside our risk appetite.

In this connection, we use ESG data as part of our qualitative risk assessment in the Directors and Officers (D&O) Insurance sector. The challenges in this field are twofold: first, ESG rating methodologies are not standardized and still in development. And second, there are still significant limitations in respect to the availability of ESG data. Currently, we have such data only on 40–45% of companies in our D&O book. So these facts beg the question whether claims correlate with a company's ESG rating. For example, if a company scores well in terms of its governance, then the likelihood of it attracting D&O claims is, or should be, correspondingly less. That being said, it is not always straightforward to find such correlations, and this sometimes makes it difficult to use data analytics in the search for effective solutions to sustainability challenges. The industry still has to dig deeper. Accurately assessing how much of a company's activity is actually aligned to ESG principles will depend on mastering the measurability challenge.

SUSTAINABILITY RISKS CAN COME IN MANY GUISES—PHYSICAL, TRANSITIONAL, AS WELL AS THOSE RELATED TO SUPPLY CHAINS AND LIABILITY

As argued by Swiss Re, climate change manifests in more frequent and more severe weather extremes (Swiss Re, 2021a). Taken together with rapid urban development and accumulation of wealth in disaster-prone areas, secondary perils, such as winter storms, hail, floods, or wildfires, lead to ever-higher catastrophe losses.

Physical and natural catastrophe damage in the wake of climate change

In August 2021, Swiss Re estimated that deep winter freeze, hailstorms, and wildfires contributed to insured natural catastrophe ("nat cat") losses of US$40 billion in the first half of 2021. This is above the previous ten-year average of US$33 billion and the second highest on record for a first half-year after 2011, when major earthquakes in Japan and New Zealand pushed the six-month total to US$104 billion. Man-made disasters triggered another estimated US$2 billion of insured losses in the first half of this year, lower than usual and likely reflecting remaining COVID-19 restrictions (Swiss Re, 2021b).

The effects of climate change are manifesting in warmer temperatures, rising sea levels, more erratic rainfall patterns, and greater weather extremes. Taken together with rapid urban development and accumulation of wealth in disaster-prone areas, secondary perils, such as winter storms, hail, floods, or wildfires, lead to ever higher catastrophe losses. See Figure 7.2.

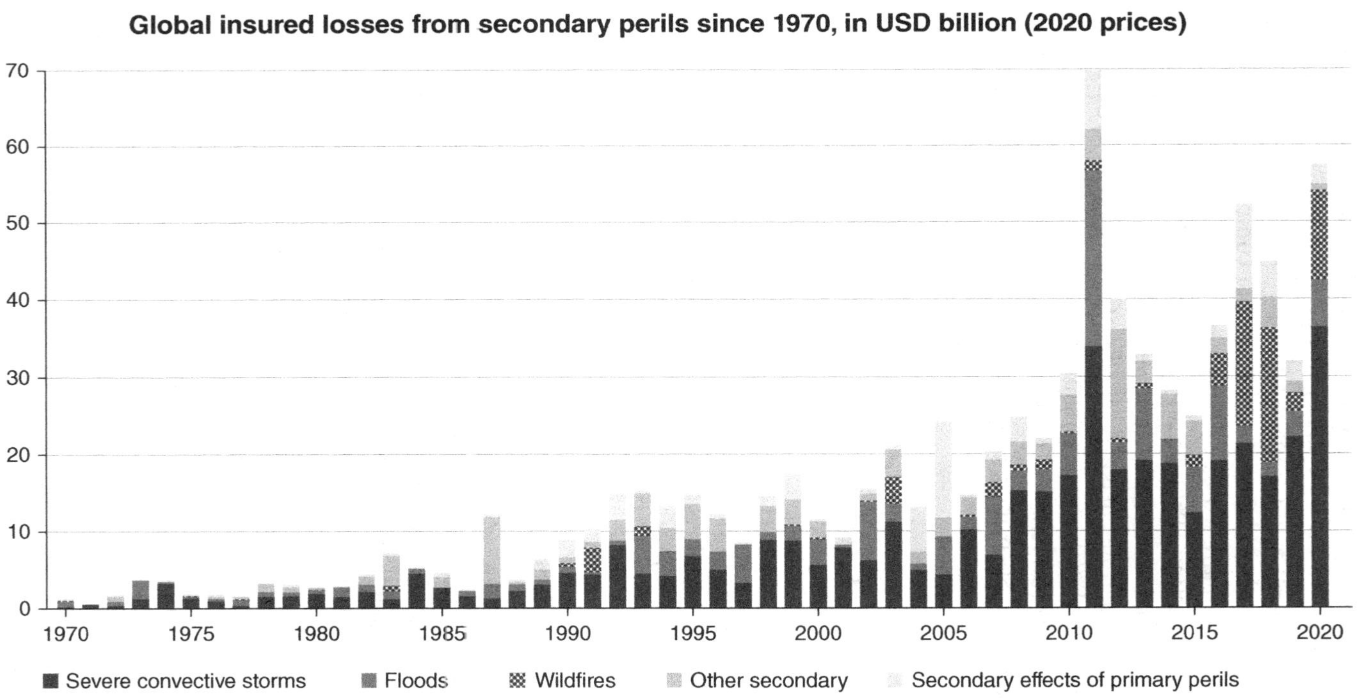

FIGURE 7.2 Insured Losses from Secondary Perils Have Been Growing Steadily

(Source: Swiss Re Institute.)

Note: Among them, losses from severe convective storms represent the biggest component. However, in recent years, losses from wildfires have been growing fastest.

Further losses at the time of writing have underscored the growing risks of these perils, exposing ever larger communities to extreme climate events. For example, winter storm Uri reached the loss magnitude that peak perils such as hurricanes can wreak (Business Insurance, 2021). Swiss Re experts concluded that the insurance industry needs to upscale its risk assessment capabilities for these less-monitored perils to maintain and expand its contribution to financial resilience.

Crucial mitigating role of re/insurance

Such losses throw into stark relief the severe impact climate change-induced physical risk can have. Economies in south and southeast Asia are most vulnerable to the physical risks associated with climate change. These countries have the most to gain if the world is able to rein in temperature increases. Many advanced economies in the Northern Hemisphere are less vulnerable, being both less exposed to adverse developments in weather patterns associated with climate change and better resourced to cope. These are the conclusions reached by the Swiss Re Institute's "Economics of Climate Change" publication from 2021 (Swiss Re Institute, 2021a).

Physical risks from sustainable infrastructure?

Against the backdrop of climate change impact, increasing urbanization and development in high-risk areas (such as along coastlines and flood plains) result in more property standing in harm's way. For companies and economies, this mandates working with insurers to help offset the risks. More focus needs to be given to resilient infrastructure that is able to withstand the physical stresses that it could face.

Take green roofs: these comprise specific vegetation designed and installed on a series of components, including moisture retention material, a drainage system, a root barrier, and a protective layer for both the insulation and the underlying roof surface. With increased urbanization, they are becoming a major trend. They offer many advantages to building owners and occupiers, the general public, and the environment. These include better insulation, reduced power consumption, stormwater retention, improved air quality, and a biodiverse environment offering aesthetic diversity.

However, green roofs may introduce property considerations and concerns that owners and occupiers should properly address when reviewing their property and business risks. These potential downsides include water leakage damage, susceptibility to collapse, and damage from natural hazards (Swiss Re Corporate Solutions, 2020a).

According to Swiss Re's 2020 SONAR publication, there could be a further potential downside to the "green" building trend. Current building requirements are being continually amended to minimize the impact of the built environment on the planet, which means cutting emissions and energy usage. However, the lack of long-term experience with new and more sustainable building materials also poses new challenges for insurance underwriters and indeed the general public (Swiss Re Institute, 2020).

Further risks associated with renewable energy sources are fires on roof-mounted photovoltaic (PV) systems and lithium-ion technologies

Although rare, when fires on roof-mounted PV systems happen, a combination of electrical hazards, combustible components, and limited access can result in significant losses. One fundamental, early stage precaution building owners should take is the design of their PV installation to establish good principles of loss prevention. Actions taken at the design stage influence the overall performance over the life of the system and its fire resilience (Swiss Re Corporate Solutions, 2020b).

Energy storage systems (ESS) using lithium-ion technologies enable on-site storage of electrical power for future sale or consumption and reduce or eliminate the need for fossil fuels. Economic advantages include a stored supply of power that can be used on demand, to reduce time-of-use rates and demand charges, or during power outages. However, ESS using these technologies introduce fire and explosion hazards that building owners and occupiers should be aware of when considering this sustainable power source (Swiss Re Corporate Solution, 2021a).

Transition risks

From a business perspective, Swiss Re Cooperate Solutions is wholly dedicated to nurturing companies' sustainability opportunities, even though this is not always an easy task. Helping corporates on the journey to "net zero" emissions is an example. The transition risk involved in moving away from fossil fuels is highly complex, since the challenges vary according to company and industry. Indeed, many stakeholders in the process are still trying to get their heads around what transition risk actually means for their portfolios in terms of possible divestment or restructuring. See Figure 7.3.

To deepen its understanding of this issue, the Swiss Re Institute partnered with the International Risk Governance Center (IRGC) to publish a paper analyzing low-carbon transition risk. The report says that in the context of climate change policy, "transition" has come to refer to the changes required to meet the goal of limiting global temperature increases to well below 2°C, and ideally to 1.5°C, above pre-industrial levels. The energy system is central to this goal: at the heart of the transition is the need to reduce CO_2 and other

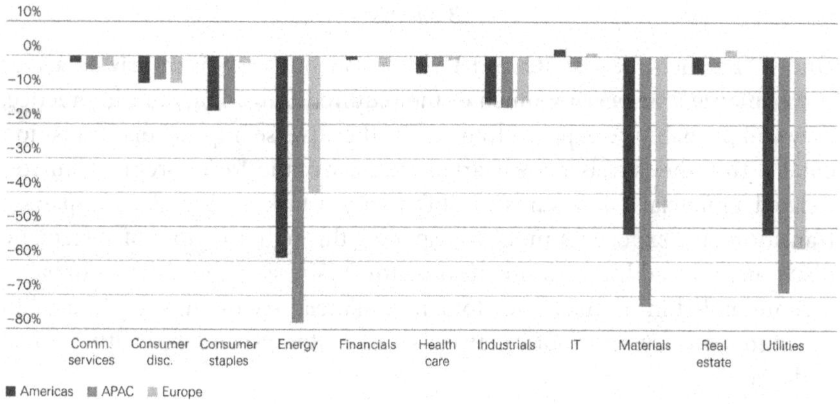

FIGURE 7.3 Transition Risk

(Source: Blackrock Carbon Tax Impact Model, Swiss Re Institute.)

Note: Based on modelling by Blackrock, we find that earnings in the utilities, materials, and energy sectors would be most impacted by immediate imposition of a US$100 per metric ton global carbon tax. By region, the revenue-weighted earnings impact would be roughly—20% in Asia Pacific (APAC) and about—-15% in the Americas and Europe.)

greenhouse gas emissions by shifting from fossil fuels to low-carbon energy sources, notably renewables. The report also points out that a successful transition will necessarily be a highly complex process, entailing very substantial changes across myriad aspects of national and international life. Moreover, dealing with transition risk means being prepared to take decisions in the face of complexity, uncertainty, ambiguity, and possibly also emergency (EPFL, 2020).

Among the types of transition risks the report lists are those related to economy, business, and energy.

Economy

Under the heading "Economy," the report broadly notes that low-carbon transition will also involve significant macroeconomic risks and not just in financial markets. It cites one forecast predicting that a complete transition away from fossil fuels could wipe out not just the market valuations of fossil fuel producers but also between 0.6% and 8.2% of overall productive capital stock in the economies studied. On the other hand, prudent, well-managed handling of the transition away from fossil fuels should generate advantages such as significant investment in low-carbon infrastructure, plant and machinery, with potential spillover benefits from a period of intense innovation.

Business

Under "Business," Swiss Re and IGRC point out that since private sector companies will be bearing much of the required transition work in practice, they will probably be exposed to many of the adverse impacts that transition entails. This, they say, is at the heart of the work of the Task Force on Climate-Related Financial Disclosures (TCFD), whose task is to make companies' transition risk exposures more transparent through a regime of systematic disclosures. In addition to financial sector businesses, these disclosures are recommended in particular for four nonfinancial sectors mostly exposed to transition: energy; transport; materials and buildings; and agriculture, food, and forestry.

Energy

Looking at "Energy," the report notes that should the transition away from the global energy system's reliance on fossil fuels be poorly planned and/or implemented, the result is likely to be interruptions in energy supply, for example, due to loss of flexibility and resilience or to imbalances between supply and demand, if fossil fuel plants are hurriedly taken offline. Technical risks to the energy system include potential failures in facilities such as wind power plants or cybersecurity vulnerabilities in smart energy grids or virtual power stations. In addition, renewable sources of energy are more prone to interruption than fossil fuels.

Supply chain risks

Comprehensive protection starts with companies truly understanding their supply chains—both upstream and downstream—to keep their businesses running in the face of natural catastrophes.

Events such as the grounding of container ship Ever Given in March 2021, and supply shortages during the global pandemic, have highlighted the interconnectivity between organizations in different parts of the world and the stress put on global supply chains in times of uncertainty. At the time of writing, many businesses, with some justification, are viewing supply chain disruption principally as a consequence of demand resurgence following the relaxation of pandemic-related restrictions.

A longer-term threat to supply chain resilience could, however, emanate from extreme weather events related to climate change. For example, the 2021 wildfires in California shut down rail lines and trucking routes, causing significant breaks in supply chains, disrupting business up and down the chain. This event is unlikely to be an anomaly. Since we live, build, and work in the areas most at risk to climate change—cities and towns along coasts, rivers, or adjacent to forests—people and assets will continue to be in harm's way.

Climate change is poised to have a lasting negative impact on our economy. The Economics of Climate Change, a recent publication from the Swiss Re Institute, found that if the Paris Climate Agreement and 2050 net-zero emissions targets are not met, the world economy could shrink by 10% in the next 30 years after large productivity and income losses (Swiss Re, 2021c).

Comprehensive protection starts with companies truly understanding their supply chains—both upstream and downstream—to keep their businesses running in the face of natural catastrophes. Even organizations that are adept at managing and mitigating climate risk in relation to their own operations may overlook climate risk further down their supply chain. For instance, when assessing a key supplier for a long-term purchase agreement, it becomes crucial to understand how resilient potential partners—and their suppliers—are to extreme weather events, in both the short and long terms.

It is not enough for companies to know who their vendors are, they need to also know where they are—and where their vendors' vendors are. Then, when companies meet with a Risk Engineering Services professional for a risk assessment, they can explore the details about their locations as well as the locations involved in sourcing all of the materials involved in production. Planning and mitigation can go a long way in making their supply chains—and ultimately their business—more resilient (Swiss Re Corporate Solutions, 2021b).

Supply chain transparency and modern slavery

Increasingly complex global supply chains create more risks, including those stemming from pandemics, business interruption, weather-driven shocks, cyber, and climate change. In addition, companies could face reputational damage, shareholder lawsuits, and personal liability of their management, especially if they fail to safeguard social standards along the supply chain or adhere to associated regulations.

Now more than ever, there is a rising demand for transparency at every step of the chain—and not just to satisfy regulators. Consumers increasingly expect to know the source of their products and expect companies to adhere to ethical and environmental standards.

The demand for supply chain transparency is closely tied to an ongoing humanitarian challenge: the International Labour Organisation (ILO) estimates that around 16 of the 40 million people trapped in modern slavery globally are exploited in the private sector such as domestic work, construction, or agriculture (ILO, 2022). Bills, such as the Supply Chain Law in

Germany, or the Modern Slavery Act in the UK, put additional pressure on companies to assume responsibility for ethical practices along their supply chains. These regulations could increase litigation risks associated with modern slavery. Identification of exploitation could potentially lead to liability claims, in particular with respect to director and officer covers. This raises the need for corporate risk managers to have a much more focused approach to supply chain management (Swiss Re Institute, 2021b).

Liability risks

From a liability perspective, underwriting will have to focus more on ESG risks in the evaluation and selection of companies to be insured. Liability insurers may be more reluctant to accept companies with poor ESG performance and increased liability exposure.

A one-dimensional view of climate change and natural catastrophes—one that focuses only on property risk—fails to comprehend the genuine relevance of ESG for the insurance industry. Indeed, we may be underestimating the implications for the liability landscape, from product safety to human rights considerations.

The changing liability risk landscape

Pressure is intensifying to meet the Paris Agreement and COP26 commitments as well as the SDGs. Consequently, expectations around corporate purpose targets are now high, from both shareholders and policy makers. ESG-compliant investing is already a huge market, and it will only get bigger in the future.

The EU Taxonomy Regulation, intended to promote private investment in green and sustainable projects—thus making a significant contribution to the European Green Deal—affects the entire financial sector and all companies required to report on corporate social responsibility in their management reports.

The economic implications and associated liability potential of ESG issues are enormous. Some recent examples include the 2018 Urgenda decision made by the Dutch Supreme Court. This obliged the country's government to reduce CO_2 emissions by at least 25% by the end of 2020 compared to 1990. The decision successfully invoked the European Convention of Human Rights to achieve state adherence to the Paris Agreement-defined climate goals.

Moreover, it is not just about climate. In France, the 150 largest companies are required to ensure that their suppliers do not violate human rights. The Netherlands will introduce a similar law in 2022.

An uptick in climate change litigation

According to a report published by the Geneva Association, *Climate Change Litigation—Insights into the Evolving Global Landscape*, global uncertainty and crises are a driver of litigation cases. Along with the seemingly unabated risk of pandemics, climate change presents an existential threat to global sustainability (The Geneva Association, 2021).

It points out that since the Paris Accords, climate litigation has grown in scope and become more widespread geographically. Moreover, the signs are that the number of cases being brought against corporates—and not just governments—is increasing. Among the reasons cited by the Association for this development are increased physical and transition risk, growing awareness of the climate crisis, and stronger climate commitments from governments, corporates, and investors. The implications of COVID-19 for economic recovery and climate-related actions are an additional factor.

From a liability perspective, underwriting will have to focus more on ESG risks in the evaluation and selection of companies to be insured. Liability insurers may be more reluctant to accept companies with poor ESG performance and increased liability exposure. In addition to underwriting considerations, there may also be reputational considerations. The use of ESG ratings could be very helpful in the medium term. It should be possible to see correlations between the quality of the ESG rating and the risk quality.

Insurers can bring their traditional technology and industry expertise to bear, along with digital data collection and algorithm-supported analysis. In the future, for example, risk and liability potentials relating to the supply chain could be permanently monitored in real-time processes.

HOW SWISS RE LEVERAGES DATA AND TECH TO GET TO GRIPS WITH SUSTAINABILITY RISK—SOLUTIONS AND EXPERTISE

Data is instrumental in tackling the challenges posed by climate change and more precisely physical climate risk.

To underwrite risks, re/insurers must understand them profoundly. This requires detailed knowledge and underlying data surrounding almost all aspects of the environment and human activities: construction, geography, climatology, geology, demography, health, and finance, to name just a few. On top of that, technological advances are transforming our industry's ability to analyze and mitigate risks. This enables it to support its customers as well as local and national governments through the development and implementation of climate adaptation policies and preventive measures.

Next, data is already allowing our industry to develop solutions that reduce the impact of climate change (Swiss Re, 2020a). For example, detailed flood mapping data combined with big data and advanced modeling capabilities allow the specific exposure of an individual property to flood risk to be calculated. This enables more specific pricing strategies that, combined with rebates for climate-proofing, can "nudge" owners and local governments into building more resilient housing stock.

And as Swiss Re CEO Christian Mumenthaler has pointed out, big data and cloud computing enable new insurance models that were formerly not possible due to lack of real-time connectivity and access to vast amounts of data (Swiss Re, 2021d). One such new model is parametric insurance, where indicators for natural disasters and weather events are currently the main triggers. However, with correctly chosen and curated data, other triggers can also be identified. Instead of wind speeds or rainfall to protect farmers from crop failure, new parametric insurance can be linked to indices that are not weather-related. For example, Swiss Re has now developed coverage for the loss of a tourist destination's attraction due to terrorism or travel disruption, using hotel occupancy or flight delays as triggers for payout. In this way, more currently uninsurable risks can also be covered.

All that being said, there is one important caveat we should not forget in this context: again, as Christian Mumenthaler has observed, the ongoing technology-based shift of re/insurers from "detect and repair" to "predict and prevent" will bring great progress in dealing with risks before an event. The new approaches to prevention must not forget, however, that certain risks are considered uninsurable. This is not to say that helping to mitigate an uninsurable risk is not worth at least as much to the industry as covering it financially. Nevertheless, we must accept that digitalization cannot overcome all currently uninsurable risks, but with it we can take an important step toward societal resilience and reducing the protection gap.

Another related example is COVID-19. As re/insurers, we have a unique opportunity—if not an obligation—to build greater resilience against future pandemics and other systemic risks. However, the re/insurance industry alone cannot cover a risk that hits many countries and areas of life simultaneously. Public–private partnerships are the only solution for future pandemic preparedness. Swiss Re is working with many countries to initiate such schemes and we are encouraged by early progress in this regard.

The following case studies seek to illustrate why we think data is essential to tackle the challenges posed by climate change and, more precisely, physical climate risk. The examples provide an overview of what we mean.

Climate risk solutions for corporates

Uniquely, Swiss Re's climate risk solutions capability leverages the same risk knowledge Swiss Re uses to base its own underwriting positions. In other words, the insights that it shares with its customers are the very same that impact its own profit and loss (P&L) statement.

Swiss Re believes that physical climate risk assessment is a natural starting point in broader climate engagement and forms an integral part of broader risk management. Such assessment enables companies to quantify the impact of physical climate risk on portfolios which are particularly exposed to the consequences of climatic changes now, as well as in the future.

Leveraging global climate model outputs and using a defensible, transparent methodology, Swiss Re uses climate risk scores to identify a portfolio's exposure to climate change risks beyond today. Its climate risk score framework combines forward-looking climate model data for precipitation and sea level rise with Swiss Re's current global flood and storm surge data to create a high-resolution assessment of physical climate risk.

This approach is at the heart of its climate risk solutions for corporates. With this service, customers can moreover benefit from "deep dives" into identified climate hotspots to obtain explicit loss costs.

Companies increasingly appreciate that a focus on sustainability means safeguarding long-term business interests, as well as being able to answer to stakeholders, investors, customers, and regulators. Climate risk is the defining challenge of our time, and assessing physical climate risk is an important first step toward better understanding its impacts now and in the future. (See also the earlier section "Mitigating bushfire risk in Australia.")

The uniqueness of Swiss Re's climate risk solutions capability is that the same risk knowledge Swiss Re uses to base its own underwriting positions on, that is, insights that impact its own P&L, is the very same it shares with its customers. Swiss Re's experts tailor the company's proprietary methodology and industry research to customers' needs (Swiss Re Corporate Solutions, 2021c).

PULSE—the engine behind international programs

Swiss Re Corporate Solutions' PULSE platform allows customers to review their policies, track premium payments, submit loss notifications, monitor claims, and track progress of a risk movement.

Swiss Re Corporate Solutions' PULSE platform is at the heart of its international programs' capability. PULSE enables commercial customers and their brokers to manage their insurance program from one secure place. It combines several aspects of customers' insurance programs onto one easy-to-use portal giving them access to real-time information. This knowledge allows them to review their policies, track premium payments, submit loss notifications, monitor claim, and track progress of a risk movement.

In a nutshell, PULSE can support customers in five key ways:

- As a centralized and integrated platform, it streamlines and automates the insurance process, generating substantial efficiency gains for the customer.

- It optimizes the handling of exposure and risk information. This ensures clear and regularly updated information, with increased accuracy. Customers can be consequently confident of reliable and compliant coverage.
- Also, it delivers real-time information in a standardized and user-friendly interface, enabling customers to track the progress of their quotes, policies, and cash movements for invoicing and claims.
- Furthermore, since the PULSE platform captures all relevant insurance program details, it enables a single comprehensive view for the customer.
- Lastly, the products and services to which it provides access gives stakeholders the tools to best manage their risks. Swiss Re's proprietary geo risk tool CatNet® is also embedded in the platform. It is designed to provide swift overviews and assessments of natural hazard exposures worldwide. It assesses the risk by combining hazard, loss, exposure, and the customer's insurance information with selected background maps and satellite imagery (Swiss Re, 2022b).

FLOAT—enhancing flood risk assessment

Events like Hurricane Harvey in 2017, where a large portion of flooded locations was outside a marked flood zone, show a gap between current flood zoning and the actual loss experience.

The flood assessment tool, FLOAT, is a way to assess and manage a location's flood risk using drones to capture location-specific elevation data. The collected dataset is transformed into a realistic visualization of the location, including a precise interactive simulation that shows potential vulnerabilities.

Solutions like FLOAT become more relevant each year as the economic cost of flood continuously increases. Heightened by climate change, extreme weather events such as torrential rainfall and severe storms are making the situation worse. Events like Hurricane Harvey in 2017, where a large portion of flooded locations was outside a marked flood zone, show a gap between current flood zoning and the actual loss experience.

When companies are not adequately protected against flood risks, they are far less able to bounce back and recover from a disaster. On the other hand, many companies have solid flood protection strategies in place and are resilient and prepared, suffering only minimal interruption to their operations after a flood event.

In addition, Swiss Re partners with their customers to help them foster internal risk awareness and business justification for flood protection measures. Moreover, the combination with other Swiss Re Corporate Solutions services such as PULSE allows a holistic risk management approach. Where available, Swiss Re overlays the digital dataset with historic information or predictable flood levels as well (Swiss Re Corporate Solutions, 2022a).

Parametric insurance covers—innovative index-based insurance solutions

When disaster strikes, companies need liquidity; a parametric solution ensures a fast payment process. Businesses receive the capital and liquidity they need to recover from a disaster more quickly when a parametrically measurable claims event occurs.

Buying traditional indemnity-based insurance to protect against physical climate risks is not always efficient. That's why Swiss Re Corporate Solutions has designed parametric protection with simple trigger and payout mechanisms. Such solutions use a customized formula so that once a predefined threshold is reached, payouts are triggered within days of the covered event. This is possible since the payout is based on an index—a measurable figure that correlates with the potential loss. Companies with parametrically measurable event coverage, in many cases associated with physical climate risk, receive a predefined payout based on the agreed measure, such as wind speed, at their location.

Parametric products can easily be distributed and sold through digital channels. Swiss Re has created an IT platform to fully leverage this kind of insurance. This platform ensures full speed and transparency by automating the entire insurance process from quoting to payout.

Working together with classical and alternative data providers, Swiss Re can create sophisticated indexes to cover companies' needs. These can include emergency cash relief in case of an earthquake and sophisticated multi-trigger non-damage business interruption products for corporates in case of hurricanes or floods (Swiss Re, 2020b).

The following two parametric solutions illustrate how data and technology are employed to cope with risks associated with natural perils and catastrophes.

FLOW—parametric water-level insurance

FLOW is designed to address situations such as the extreme dry spell in Central Europe during the summer of 2018. This weather-related challenge left the water levels of many rivers at record lows. Companies that rely on these rivers for shipping goods were faced with higher costs and decreased production volumes.

FLOW is an index-based water-level insurance, customized for companies with revenues and costs exposed to rivers' high or low water levels in

Europe. Swiss Re Corporate Solutions' experts structure an index formula which references to measured water levels at defined river gauges. The customized index approximates the company's water-level exposure regarding revenues and costs as close to the reality as possible. Each FLOW contract is tailor-made to the individual water-level exposure of the company. The payout is a fixed amount, for example, per day the index remains beyond the defined threshold value. The payout amounts are determined by factors such as loss of revenue due to business interruption, increased cost of operation, and extra expenses to mitigate the situation or to establish alternatives (Swiss Re Corporate Solutions, 2022b).

STORM—an index-based insurance solution that enables faster recovery following a tropical cyclone

Using wind speed at the insured's location(s), STORM is designed to closely mirror companies' experience during a tropical cyclone.

Companies exposed to tropical cyclone risk often face financial hardships in the aftermath of a hurricane, including insurance coverage gaps, such as peril-specific sublimits, deductibles, and exclusions, revenue disruption, and emergency response expenditures. Swiss Re Corporate Solutions' parametric STORM solution can complement a traditional program or offer stand-alone coverage for uninsurable or underinsured physical and financial exposures, helping companies get back on their feet more quickly.

Based on wind speed at the insured's location(s), STORM is designed to closely mirror companies' experience during a tropical cyclone. For example, within a day after a hurricane makes landfall, we receive high-resolution wind data, providing wind speed information for every point on the map. We determine the highest sustained wind speed during the hurricane at the policyholder's location(s). The policy pays out based on this wind speed, closely reflecting what the insured's location(s) experienced during the hurricane. We team up with the leading tropical cyclone wind speed data providers worldwide (Swiss Re Corporate Solutions, 2022c).

Constant evolution

It should, of course, be borne in mind that increasingly sophisticated parametric solutions did not just "fall from heaven" but are rather one dynamic consequence of the ongoing evolution of insurance modeling in general and Nat Cat modeling in particular.

According to Swiss Re's 2021 SONAR publication, scientific understanding of how microclimates and weather can shape potential losses is improving. Such knowledge can be incorporated as forward-looking risk assessment components in insurance modeling. As an example, systematic indices and heat maps for local, industry, and sector situations are enabling improved risk scenario analysis. Applications for such future-oriented scenario assessments include mappings of the economic resilience of countries, estimations of climate change effects, say on health, and on biodiversity and ecosystem services (Swiss Re Institute, 2021c).

THE SHIP RECYCLING TRANSPARENCY INITIATIVE

By collaborating with the Ship Recycling Transparency Initiative's (SRTI) network of forward-thinking businesses, Swiss Re Corporate Solutions wants to support the industry in understanding how to better track ship owners' scrapping activities not in keeping with ESG guidelines.

Swiss Re Corporate Solutions has signed up to the SRTI. In doing so, Swiss Re Corporate Solutions joins a growing list of organizations across the shipping value chain who are calling for greater transparency and responsible ship recycling. It is a telling example of how data sharing among companies can generate a stronger awareness of sustainable business practices.

The SRTI aims to use transparency to accelerate a voluntary market-driven approach to responsible ship recycling practices. Shipowners share information in relation to a set of disclosure criteria developed by industry stakeholders. By publicly disclosing their ship recycling policies, practices, and progress through the SRTI, the platform enables cargo owners, financial stakeholders, and others to use the data to inform their decision-making and reward good practice through the market.

By collaborating with SRTI's network of forward-thinking businesses, Swiss Re Corporate Solutions wants to support the industry in understanding how to better track shipowners' scrapping activities not in keeping with ESG guidelines, that is, not respecting standard environmental protocols and violating human rights. Signing up to the SRTI is part of Swiss Re Corporate Solutions' goals to help protect corporates' sustainability opportunities, share sustainability risk knowledge, and lead by example (Swiss Re Corporate Solutions, 2021d).

DELIVERING RISK INSIGHTS TO CORPORATE CUSTOMERS

Insurers such as Swiss Re Corporate Solutions have a wealth of risk insight services which wait to be unlocked for the benefit of corporate customers. The value of these services goes beyond transferring risks and also covers supply chain management and sustainability reporting.

One example of such a service is providing more transparency of the risks embedded in the structure of customers' supply and production chains. The idea is to develop a digital twin to deliver repeatable risk insights at multiple nodes of a supply chain. The data and insights could cover topics such as:

- marine cargo analysis, which would help customers understand risks in the logistics chain, in respect, for example, to pharma shipments;
- evaluation of location exposure (e.g., of a warehouse) to different Nat Cat perils; and
- business interruption risks, which entail a digital twin to model dependencies among suppliers and distributors as well as simulate and manage potential interruptions.

In a similar way, Swiss Re Corporate Solutions is helping companies advance their sustainability reporting, in respect to how they can better access data on their CO_2 footprint. This entails linking up with other data providers in the ESG domain.

Swiss Re Corporate Solutions adds value by bringing together data that would otherwise remain fragmented. This service is especially relevant to achieve enhanced supply chain transparency, an increasingly urgent task given regulatory scrutiny and demands from customers' retail customers.

CONCLUSION—SWISS RE'S APPROACH TO SUSTAINABILITY RISKS

In essence, this is about de-risking companies' investments into sustainable technology, providing risk management services that go beyond risk transfer products and actually doing what we say in respect to how we run our business.

Our group sustainability strategy is a long-term value driver, embedded throughout our re/insurance value chain. At its core, it involves managing and monitoring risks and opportunities associated with ESG issues. Sustainable re/insurance covers all our business activities, from the liability to the asset side of our balance sheet, our own operations, and dialogue with our stakeholders.

In our core business, it aims to develop innovative solutions, improve business, and investment performance on a risk-adjusted basis and thus to contribute to environmental, social, and economic sustainability (Swiss Re, 2020c).

Reflecting Swiss Re Group's approach to sustainability, Corporate Solutions has developed a strategic sustainability framework that focuses on three themes. These are, first, protecting customers' sustainability opportunities. This involves de-risking their investments into sustainable technology and providing them with the associated risk expertise. The second theme revolves around the provision of risk management services that go beyond risk transfer products to help customers actually understand their sustainability risks. And third, our sustainability framework is an expression of our own efforts to run our business in a sustainable way.

A REMINDER

Climate change-related risks affect everyone, but preparation now is key to limiting the cost further down the line and ensuring businesses and economies continue to thrive.

The impact of climate change will be felt across all societies, economies, and business functions. Grappling with such a widespread risk, and fully understanding its potential impact in an evolving landscape, requires a granular understanding of both customers' businesses and our own. We can achieve this through more and better data, from internal and external sources alike.

Putting in place better data harvesting measures, and the algorithms and technology to make use of them, is among the most important concrete actions businesses can take right now to better prepare themselves for the fallout from climate change. Using this information, companies can help mitigate the risk and upskill employees to ensure they are fully prepared for the impact across all parts of the business. Working with insurers and risk partners will help transfer any residual risk.

REFERENCES

Business Insurance (2021). *Insured Cat Losses $42B in First Half: Swiss Re.* Available at: www.businessinsurance.com/article/20210812/NEWS06/912343842/Insured-cat-losses-$42B-in-first-half-Swiss-Re (Accessed: 11 January 2022).

EPFL (2020). *Low-carbon Transition Risk.* Available at: www.epfl.ch/research/domains/irgc/spotlight-on-risk-series/low-carbon-transition-risk/ (Accessed: 11 January 2022).

International Labour Organization (ILO) (2022). *Forced Labour, Modern Slavery and Human Trafficking.* Available at: www.ilo.org/global/topics/forced-labour/lang--en/index.htm (Accessed: 11 January 2022).

Swiss Re (2018). *Sovereign Insurance—Creating Financial Resilience Against the Growing Burden of Natural Disasters.* Available at: www.swissre.com/dam/jcr:377df78e-9c98-478f-9d7b-18a692471586/Swiss%20Re_Sovereign%20insurance_Africa.pdf (Accessed: 11 January 2022).

Swiss Re (2020a). *Weathering the Storm: Climate Lessons for Climate Resilience.* Available at: www.swissre.com/risk-knowledge/risk-perspectives-blog/weathering-storm-crisis-lessons-for-climate-resilience.html (Accessed: 11 January 2022).

Swiss Re (2020b). *Grow Your Business by Boosting Consumers' Financial Resilience With Parametric Insurance.* Available at: www.swissre.com/reinsurance/property-and-casualty/solutions/parametric-solutions/grow-business-by-boosting-consumers-financial-resilience-parametric-insurance.html (Accessed: 11 January 2022).

Swiss Re (2020c). *Swiss Re Sustainability Report 2020.* Available at: https://reports.swissre.com/sustainability-report/2020/ (Accessed: 11 January 2022).

Swiss Re (2021a). *Extreme Weather in a Changing Climate: How Can We Be More Resilient?* Available at: www.swissre.com/risk-knowledge/mitigating-climate-risk/extreme-weather-climate-change.html (Accessed: 11 January 2022).

Swiss Re (2021b). *Severe Weather Events Drive Global Insured Catastrophe Losses of USD 42 Billion in First Half of 2021, Swiss Re Institute Estimates.* Available at: www.swissre.com/news-release/Severe-weather-events-drive-global-insured-catastrophe-losses-of-USD-42-billion-in-first-half-of-2021-Swiss-Re-Institute-estimates/c2a6e1c8-cd8f-4592-94cb-bc3c58ba2e4d; www.swissre.com/risk-knowledge/mitigating-climate-risk/extreme-weather-climate-change.html (Accessed: 11 January 2022).

Swiss Re (2021c). *The Economics of Climate Change: No Action Not an Option.* Available at: www.swissre.com/dam/jcr:e73ee7c3-7f83-4c17-a2b8-8ef23a8d3312/swiss-re-institute-expertise-publication-economics-of-climate-change.pdf (Accessed: 11 January 2022).

Swiss Re (2021d). *How We Can Overcome Uninsurability with Data.* Available at: www.swissre.com/risk-knowledge/risk-perspectives-blog/how-we-can-overcome-uninsurability-with-data.html (Accessed: 11 January 2022).

Swiss Re (2022a). *Our Approach.* Available at: www.swissre.com/about-us/our-approach.html (Accessed: 11 January 2022).

Swiss Re (2022b). *CatNet®.* Available at: www.swissre.com/reinsurance/property-and-casualty/solutions/property-specialty-solutions/catnet.html (Accessed: 11 January 2022).

Swiss Re Corporate Solutions (2020a). *Sustainability Series: Green Roofs.* Available at: Sustainability Series: Green Roofs | Swiss Re (Accessed: 11 January 2022).

Swiss Re Corporate Solutions (2020b). *Roof-Mounted Photovoltaic Systems.* Available at: https://corporatesolutions.swissre.com/insights/knowledge/roof-mounted-photovoltaic-systems-fire-risks.html (Accessed: 11 January 2022).

Swiss Re Corporate Solutions (2021a). *Sustainability Series: Energy Storage Systems Using Lithium-Ion Technologies.* Available at: https://corporatesolutions.swissre.com/insights/knowledge/energy-storage-systems-using-lithium-ion-technologies.html?r (Accessed: 11 January 2022).

Swiss Re Corporate Solutions (2021b). *Forewarned Is Forearmed: How Data Can Help Improve Supply Chain Transparency.* Available at: https://corporatesolutions.swissre.com/insights/knowledge/forewarned-is-forearmed-supply-chain-transparency.html (Accessed: 11 January 2022).

Swiss Re Corporate Solutions (2021c). *Climate Risk Solutions for Corporates.* Available at: https://corporatesolutions.swissre.com/insurance-solutions/sustainability/climate-risk-solutions-for-corporates.html (Accessed: 11 January 2022).

Swiss Re Corporate Solutions (2021d). *Swiss Re Corporate Solutions Signs Up to the Ship Recycling Transparency Initiative.* Available at: https://corporatesolutions.swissre.com/insights/news/Swiss-Re-Corporate-Solutions-signs-up-to-the-Ship-Recycling-Transparency-Initiative.html (Accessed: 11 January 2022).

Swiss Re Corporate Solutions (2022a). *FLOAT—Taking Flood Risk Assessment to the Next Level.* Available at: https://corporatesolutions.swissre.com/innovative-risk-solutions/weather-solutions/float.html (Accessed: 11 January 2022).

Swiss Re Corporate Solutions (2022b). *FLOW—Parametric Water-level Insurance.* Available at: https://corporatesolutions.swissre.com/innovative-risk-solutions/weather-solutions/flow.html (Accessed: 11 January 2022).

Swiss Re Corporate Solutions (2022c). *STORM—An Index-Based Insurance Solution That Helps You Recover Faster after a Tropical Cyclone.* Available at: https://corporatesolutions.swissre.com/innovative-risk-solutions/parametric-solutions/storm.html (Accessed: 11 January 2022).

Swiss Re Institute (2020). *Swiss Re SONAR—New Emerging Risk Insights.* Available at: www.swissre.com/institute/research/sonar/sonar2020.html (Accessed: 11 January 2022).

Swiss Re Institute (2021a). *The Economics of Climate Change.* Available at: www.swissre.com/institute/research/topics-and-risk-dialogues/climate-and-natural-catastrophe-risk/expertise-publication-economics-of-climate-change.html (Accessed: 11 January 2022).

Swiss Re Institute (2021b). *Modern Slavery—Pressure on Supply Chains.* Available at: www.swissre.com/institute/research/sonar/sonar2021/modern-slavery.html (Accessed: 11 January 2022).

Swiss Re Institute (2021c). *Swiss Re SONAR—New Emerging Risk Insights. What's Next in Insurance Modelling.* Available at: www.swissre.com/dam/jcr:5a8d21b6-3dff-4178-9f10-525850e7b3db/ (Accessed: 11 January 2022).

The Geneva Association (2021). *Climate Change Litigation—Insights Into the Evolving Global Landscape.* Available at: www.genevaassociation.org/sites/default/files/research-topics-document-type/pdf_public/climate_litigation_04-07-2021.pdf (Accessed: 11 January 2022).

8

Resilience as an Analytical Filter for ESG Data

Ashby Monk and Dane Rook

INTRODUCTION

The recent years have witnessed a meteoric rise in the consideration of environmental, social, and governance (ESG) factors in investment decision-making.[1] To help investors address ESG issues in their portfolios, a massive support infrastructure has emerged, which includes ESG ratings agencies, new ESG investment products, ESG research providers, and ESG consultants.[2] Despite this mushrooming ecosystem, actual ESG analysis (what might be thought of as the translation of ESG issues into financial risks) has yet to become part of mainstream investment practice. How might ESG analysis be made mainstream—just another "given" of investing?

Our answer is: *decrease the degree to which investors depend on the ESG ecosystem that has cropped up around them* (i.e., reduce the need for ESG intermediaries, by developing new modes of analysis that can translate the language of ESG into the lingua franca of finance). ESG intermediaries are chiefly focused on selling investors incomplete links in the investment chain—links that often do not fit cleanly with investors' current methods of portfolio construction, risk management systems, technology sets, or focal metrics. Instead, investors need comprehensive solutions for analyzing and acting on ESG factors, not piecemeal inputs to their processes and portfolios. We believe that these comprehensive solutions are most likely to come from investors themselves working directly with ESG datasets. We are not suggesting that investors forgo ESG intermediaries entirely: our proposal is simply that investors should pare back their reliance on ESG intermediaries

DOI: 10.4324/9781003262039-10

and become more comfortable in "getting their own hands dirty" with ESG data and analysis.[3]

Our suggestion of ESG disintermediation is drawn from years of direct conversations with investors (through both formal research interviews and informal discussion) about the role of ESG within the scope of their work. Throughout these interactions, we have encountered—and continue to encounter—the concern that ESG investing requires specialist skills that a typical investment professional lacks and cannot easily obtain. This concern seems to be underpinned by a (generally false) impression that ESG proficiency necessitates deep expertise, such as an advanced degree in climate science, environmental studies, law, or sociology. As a result, many investors defer to third parties to handle ESG components of their investment processes. In doing so, those investors become diners, rather than chefs who eat their own cooking—even though being a diner entails paying more for and knowing less about one's meals than the chef (and possibly going hungry if the restaurant closes or a reservation is unavailable!).

Metaphors aside, ESG will likely stay relegated to second-class citizenship—and remain poorly integrated with most investors' "core" processes—unless more investors gain proficiency in doing ESG analysis themselves. Such proficiency will require more than mere fluency in ESG terminology; also, it will demand that investors gain experience in making concrete assumptions about how ESG factors affect investment outcomes and subsequently testing those assumptions against data (which includes both ESG data and conventional financial data).

This iterative process of using data to inform assumptions, and then testing/refining those assumptions against more data, is at the heart of modern investment practice. Yet these iterative cycles are too rare when they concern ESG assumptions and ESG data: they tend to be outsourced to third parties (e.g., consultants, ratings agencies, or ESG fund managers) or performed by only a very small fraction of individuals within investors' own organizations (e.g., ESG units that are often under-resourced and segregated from the rest of the organization). In our view, excessive outsourcing and over-confinement of ESG analysis are restricting the mainstreaming of ESG in investing and unnecessarily so.

What is perpetuating this avoidance of ESG analysis by typical investors? Our work with dozens of leading investment organizations across the globe implicates two main culprits: (1) the explosive proliferation of ESG data and (2) difficulty in integrating ESG data with conventional metrics and models of risk and investment returns. Specifically:[4]

- **Proliferation.** The volume and diversity of ESG datasets has ballooned in recent years, but these datasets vary in their quality (e.g., accuracy, structure) and how well they capture investment-relevant information. This proliferation—which continues to accelerate—makes vetting ESG datasets a challenge: even for those datasets that are easily accessible to investors, determining which of them are best to use poses a significant difficulty. Third-party aggregation of ESG datasets (e.g., in the form of summary ESG ratings for companies) and shared metrics (i.e., use of a limited, standard set of metrics to judge ESG performance) have been suggested as potential solutions, but both of these suggestions are problematic (as we will discuss in the next section).

- **Integration.** Investors face fundamental difficulties in integrating the use of ESG analysis into their standard processes for risk and portfolio management—in part because typical ESG analysis is *issues-based* whereas most risk and portfolio analysis is *scenario-based*—that is, available techniques for analyzing ESG mostly focus on the stand-alone value of specific issues as they relate to a company's point-in-time valuation (e.g., how emissions reductions, promoting gender equality, and ethical sourcing of raw materials affect its stock price *in general*); while, in practice, the risk analyses used by investors tend to focus on how various factors impact portfolio dynamics during specific *scenarios*. These scenarios tend to concentrate on short-term downside events (e.g., market crashes) that unfold over intervals too short for the influence of ESG factors to be immediately apparent, at least when traditional risk analyses are used.

To summarise: *problems with proliferation and integration of ESG datasets have made it hard for investors to filter and analyze ESG data*, so they outsource much of this filtering and analysis to third parties. We believe that this overreliance on outsourcing is preventing investors from more fully embracing ESG in their investment practices and strategies.

We expect technology can play a role in alleviating investors' excessive reliance on ESG intermediaries—but only a partial role. Investors also need improved conceptual frameworks and tools with which to filter and analyze ESG datasets. The Resilience paradigm can help fulfill that need.[5]

Recently (in Rook et al., 2021), we introduced the notion of Resilience as a company's capabilities to *detect*, *absorb*, *recover*, and *learn* from shocks: large-scale events that disrupt the status quo, originate from outside the organization itself, and whose direct effects are felt over short timescales (although their indirect, derivative impacts may persist for long stretches of time thereafter).[6] Put simply, a company's Resilience is its capacity to position itself to best "bounce back" from a shock, by adapting or transforming in response to that shock.[7] Assessments of how ESG factors affect a company's Resilience offer investors a new lens through which to view ESG data—one that could underpin a new approach to filtering and analyzing ESG datasets. The heart of our logic is as follows.

(1) It is usually easier to assess the *value* of a company's ESG characteristics in specific cases than in general; and examination of specific cases is fundamental to how most investors analyze risk.
(2) ESG factors can play significant roles not only in how a company absorbs the initial impacts of a shock but also in how it recovers from the shock, especially if recovery involves significant adaptation or transformation by the company.
(3) By focusing on specific, portfolio-relevant shocks, investors can better filter for particular ESG datasets that are pertinent to that shock (in terms of hypothesized ESG characteristics that may help companies better absorb that shock and recover from it) and analyze the sensitivity of shock absorption and recovery to different levels of ESG performance (based on the filtered datasets).
(4) Analyzing specific, portfolio-relevant shocks can help investors to understand how to align their ESG practices with their current approaches and tools for managing risk.

We are not the first ones to propose analyzing ESG's value in mitigating the impact of shocks on companies—especially if shocks are assumed to take the form of natural disasters, corporate scandals, or supply chain disruptions. But existing proposals tend to focus only on ESG's role in how companies absorb the initial and direct impacts of shocks whereas Resilience assessment expands this focus to include understanding how ESG helps companies recover over longer horizons. Focusing only on absorption (and not recovery) can distort the influence that ESG has on companies' multi-horizon riskiness and performance and can easily undervalue ESG factors. Furthermore, our proposed Resilience assessment emphasizes not only how ESG helps companies recover from some pre-shock state (e.g., stock price, revenue level) but also whether it helps them adapt, or even transform, due to being stimulated by a shock—for example, whether an oil shortage prompts a delivery company to switch to an all-electric vehicle fleet.[8] Shock-induced transformations are clearly a type of innovation and one which has a tight link to ESG factors. As we elaborate in later sections, a company's ESG resources can strongly influence how well it can innovate and transform itself after a shock (just as a company's innovativeness can drive ongoing improvements to its ESG performance).[9] This relation between ESG, shocks, and innovation is not highlighted in previous studies of how ESG affects a company's ability to handle shocks.

Of course, shocks are not the only scenarios that are relevant to investors, nor are they the only channel by which ESG factors affect investment risk and return. Nonetheless, the mode of Resilience assessment that we are proposing is a principled approach that is capable of yielding deep insights into the connection between ESG and asset value. It is a mode of analysis that could be a starting point for many investors to become more committed to fully integrating ESG analysis into their wider investment processes rather than continuing to relegate ESG factors to ancillary considerations—ones that investors often depend on third parties to assess for them.

The rest of this chapter traces the following course. In the second section, we discuss some obstacles to the mainstreaming of ESG data that are extensions of the proliferation and integration problems. That discussion points to the need for new methods that investors can use to identify and analyze ESG datasets. We present the Resilience approach to doing so in the third section and give examples of its application. The fourth section briefly discusses some technologies that could beneficially complement Resilience analysis by making it more scalable, efficient, and insightful for investors. The last section concludes by suggesting some next steps in extending Resilience analysis.

We note here that this chapter deals with only "demand-side" solutions to ESG data problems—that is, it does not seek to remedy problems with ESG datasets themselves but rather how investors can use those datasets, given their present flaws. We moreover abstain from proposing any new metrics that investors might use to monitor and analyze either ESG variables or Resilience. Such proposals are beyond the scope of this chapter but are forthcoming in future work.

Also, we note that the value of Resilience analysis to investors is more than hypothetical: we know of at least three major investment organizations that have built significant capabilities around Resilience analysis and are experiencing significant benefits to having done so—including helping them to better navigate the COVID-19 pandemic. In Rook et al. (2021), we present a case study of one such organization (Manulife Investment Management). Our work with the other two organizations remains ongoing and must remain confidential until its conclusion; nonetheless, we can attest to the usefulness of Resilience analysis in practice, not just in theory.

OBSTACLES TO MAINSTREAMING ESG DATA

In this section, we briefly cover some of the main obstacles to the mainstreaming of ESG data that stem from properties of ESG datasets themselves (as well as how they currently tend to be used). These obstacles are all subproblems of *proliferation* and *integration*, which were described in the previous section. Clarification of these subproblems will help underscore the need for new approaches (such as Resilience analysis) that investors can use for filtering and analyzing ESG datasets. We note that some of these concerns—especially as relate to the quality and materiality of ESG datasets—have been raised elsewhere. For those concerns, we highlight problems that have not been well covered by the existing literature. Other concerns, such as the absence of innovation variables in ESG datasets, do not seem to be raised in earlier studies.

Quality

For some time, problems of quality have been recognized as a by-product of ESG data's rapid proliferation. In specific, the growing volume and variety of ESG datasets makes it increasingly challenging for investors to efficiently determine the quality of those datasets in any principled way. Efficiency here has two dimensions: efficiency in (1) deciding which datasets to assess for quality and (2) appraising the quality of any one dataset.

The "quality" of an ESG dataset has conventionally been taken as (some combination of) that dataset's accuracy, coverage (i.e., the percentage of a given industry, time frame, etc. that it covers, without missing data), and consistency (i.e., the degree to which the dataset agrees with other datasets). While these three elements of quality are undoubtedly desirable, we argue that this threefold depiction of quality is incomplete (as we discuss later). But even if one adopts this restricted definition of quality, it is evident that quality varies greatly among ESG datasets. This variability of data quality carries numerous costs for investors. Given the expansiveness of ESG, investors may need to acquire (i.e., purchase or gather) many ESG datasets, and such acquisitions are wasteful when the datasets are of poor quality. Likewise, it takes time to vet ESG datasets, and time spent vetting a poor-quality dataset is time that could have been spent on vetting ones of higher quality.

This combination of costliness in ensuring dataset quality and the variability in quality may increase the likelihood of herd behavior, whereby investors gravitate to ESG datasets that are already popular, on the assumption that these datasets will have been sufficiently vetted by other investors. There is one limited respect in which this herding might be beneficial: by lowering the implied cost of a popular dataset (by allowing some investors to get a free ride on the vetting efforts of others), some investors who might otherwise not have used ESG data might be enticed to do so. But, overall, any herding behavior regarding ESG datasets is likely to have implications that are more negative than positive, namely: since no one dataset can cover all ESG issues, herding will tend to restrict the ESG variables that investors attend to (possibly leading to the exclusion of highly relevant variables); and there are no guarantees that investors will herd on high-quality datasets (they may therefore make their investment decisions on data of suboptimal quality, which is likely to erode the overall value they perceive in considering ESG factors in investing). We expect that the propensity to herd on ESG datasets will only increase as the number and diversity of such datasets grows.

There is another problem that resides in the potential for herding: the quality of a dataset depends partly on context. That is, any given dataset may be "high-quality" if used to answer some investment questions but low-quality for answering others (we do not see quality as an intrinsic property of datasets—apart from accuracy, which is one of the few intrinsic elements of quality). This problem is not fully apparent if one restricts judgments of quality to accuracy, coverage, and consistency. A more encompassing perspective on quality is needed.

In Monk et al. (2019), we proposed a set of criteria for investors to judge the quality of datasets in a context-dependent way. These criteria are:

- *Reliability*: accuracy, precision, and verifiability of the data
- *Granularity*: detailed scale of the data (e.g., municipal versus national)
- *Freshness*: age/recency of the data
- *Comprehensiveness*: fraction of the relevant domain covered (e.g., households)
- *Actionability*: degree to which meaningful decisions can be made from the data
- *Scarcity*: extent or ease of availability of the data to other investors

We think that these criteria are fully applicable in assessing the quality of ESG datasets. Yet, which of these criteria matter most will vary across analyses. In the next section, we discuss how the Resilience approach to ESG analysis can shed light on the relative importance of each of these elements of quality for a given situation.

Materiality

The materiality of ESG factors to portfolio performance is one of the most contested topics in all of investing. Disputes over ESG's materiality often center on the divergent findings of empirical studies: some studies find that a company's ESG behavior and resources significantly improve its investment performance while other studies find that ESG factors exert negative or negligible influence on investment returns. This divergence in findings has caused many investors to exclude ESG factors from their analyses. Yet, a number of meta-studies (i.e., studies of the studies themselves) find evidence that this divergence may be overstated, and that it is substantially driven by the variability (in quality and focus) of the ESG datasets used in each.[10] Thus, the ESG materiality problem may be partly due to the mass proliferation of ESG data.

There is, however, another potential distortion of materiality that comes from researchers taking an overly blunt view of ESG's role in driving investment returns. Specifically, it makes intuitive sense that even *ESG factors that genuinely are material may not be material across all situations*—that is, they may exert significant effects on investment returns only in particular contexts. For example, ESG factors may matter less in periods of "normal" market activity than in periods of market turmoil; or (germane to this chapter), they may matter more for a company's recovery from specific types of shocks than its absorption of their immediate impacts. However, most empirical studies of ESG's influence on investment returns fail to account for this possibility of *situational materiality*.[11] Most commonly, they examine passive portfolios that do not change in composition during the time frame of study or else change according to simplistic rules (e.g., changes in relative market capitalizations). Yet, few investors are as completely passive as those studies imply, and the assumption of unrealistic passivity therefore runs the risk of understating the value of ESG factors to investors.[12]

Situational materiality aside, many investors now recognize that not all ESG factors are material for all companies: different industries, and companies within those industries, exhibit different sensitivities to individual ESG factors. However, identification of which ESG factors are material for which companies can be a source of confusion and disagreement, for both investors and companies themselves. Various approaches have been proposed to address this issue. The most prominent among them are *shared metrics* and *aggregate ratings*.

The shared metrics approach derives from groups of companies and investors attempting to collectively define which ESG factors are material for which industries and then suggesting standardized metrics that capture those factors. Although admirable and valuable, these efforts are inherently incomplete.[13] In general, they try to identify the ESG factors that are *most* material to an industry: they do not attempt to identify all material factors, and biases may therefore influence the factors they do identify and recommend. It should be noted that companies in particular have a self-interest in conveying a "good image" regarding their ESG activities and resources, and the shared metrics that groups of companies propose as material may therefore be selected to cast themselves in the most positive light (tantamount to greenwashing). Investor groups would seem to have less motivation for biased proposals of shared metrics. But neither investors nor companies can overcome the fact that materiality is uneven across companies. It is almost impossible to come up with a fixed list of ESG factors for an industry that both (1) includes all ESG factors that are truly material to every company in the industry and (2) excludes factors that are immaterial for at least some companies. The cutoff point for which ESG factors are considered "most" material to the industry is therefore inescapably arbitrary (to some degree). Selecting ESG datasets based solely on shared metrics can be a starting point for analysis, but it is far from a full solution.

Compared to shared metrics, *aggregate ratings* aspire to be more comprehensive in what ESG factors they consider.[14] These ratings usually take the form of ESG "scores" assigned to individual companies by ratings agencies (usually agencies that are for-profit entities). Mostly, these agencies produce a single score for each company, which is supposed to encapsulate its overall performance on ESG (although some agencies do produce additional subscores, e.g., by assigning separate ratings to each company's environmental, social, and governance activities). By accepting such scores, investors essentially delegate the job of determining materiality to ratings agencies. This delegation is problematic in numerous ways, many of which have been subjected to extensive study. Some of these exposed problems include the facts that:

- ESG scores assigned to companies often vary drastically across rating agencies.[15]
- Scores tend to be only useful for relative ranking of ESG performance; in general, they do not provide meaningful information about degrees of difference between companies (for instance, the difference between a score of 9 and a score of 7 may not be the same as that between a 7 and a 5).
- Aggregate scores tend not to be reliable inputs into models of investment return.
- There is generally a significant degree of subjectivity involved in rating agencies' assessments, and the rationale behind the subjective elements in ratings is often not visible to inspection by users of the scores (further, few ratings agencies are fully transparent on their methodologies, even with respect to the aspects of their scores that are objectively derived).

In essence, using aggregate ESG scores from ratings agencies resolves neither the proliferation nor the integration problems that investors face when attempting to use ESG datasets. Furthermore, if part of the purpose of using ESG data is to obtain a more granular picture of a company's activities (i.e., more granular than what is available from standard financial data), is it not somewhat wasteful to discard that granularity by packaging it into a summary score? As we will see, the Resilience approach to analysis has no need for this reductionism.

Potentials and Innovation

By and large, ESG datasets contain only "level" data (e.g., a company's level of carbon emissions over the last 12 months or some measure of the diversity of its leadership). Rarely are data on potentials for improvement explicitly included—for example, even though a company may have a positive amount of carbon emissions, it might be possible for the company to reduce those emissions *below* zero, such that it profitably is "carbon-negative." Hence, an implied baseline of zero emissions may be inappropriate. Yet it is rare for appropriate baselines for ESG variables to be explicitly included in ESG datasets, and such datasets therefore give investors a warped view of companies' potentials for improvement. And these potentials matter to the extent that it is possible for companies to translate them into future performance. These ESG potentials have analogues in conventional financial data—for example, the potential market size for a company's product or identifiable minimums for the costs of its inputs to production. Those financial analogues are some of the most valuable financial data that investors can obtain; the same would likely be true of ESG potentials, if they were readily available.

Nevertheless, potentials (whether related to ESG or conventional financial variables) are only hypothetical unless a company has enough resources to achieve them. In many cases, these resources relate to a company's capacity for innovation. Strangely, few ESG datasets capture the innovation resources of companies (at least those that are applicable to their ESG performance), despite innovation and continued improvement in ESG performance being related. It is true that some ESG variables can be interpreted as reflecting a company's prospects for ESG innovation (e.g., the diversity of its leadership team and its creativity may be positively correlated). But for the most part, a company's resources for ESG innovation may be very challenging to discern from a given ESG dataset. This is unfortunate, as ESG innovation may well be a key bridge between a company's ESG performance and its investment performance, as we will soon discuss.

RESILIENCE: SELECTIVE OVERVIEW AND RELATION WITH ESG DATA

Shocks are fundamental to our conception of Resilience, in part because they are a major force in financial markets. The largest (usually downward) moves in asset prices tend to be in reaction to shocks, and they can destroy many years' worth of price appreciation in just hours (or less).[16] In brief: an asset's Resilience is its ability to respond to shocks, both ex ante and ex post.

Absorption, Recovery, and ESG

Prior to a shock occurring, a company might *detect* that it is likely and respond accordingly. If the shock occurs, the company's response can be separated into three parts: *absorption* of the shock, *recovery* from the shock, and *learning* from the shock.[17] The four response components—detection, absorption, recovery, and learning—form the basis of our DARLing framework for analyzing Resilience, in terms of a company's resources and abilities related to each response component for a given type of shock.

One key feature of the DARLing framework is its temporal underpinnings—in particular, those related to absorption and recovery. Absorption tends to occur within a relatively short span of time after a shock hits whereas recovery often stretches over a longer horizon. Absorption may take place over the course of days, yet recovery can take months or years. Resilience, as measured by the DARLing framework, is therefore a multi-horizon property of companies and assets (which, as we will discuss shortly, has important implications for ESG analysis).

While the *timing* of shocks may be difficult to anticipate, the *nature* of shocks themselves is often foreseeable (e.g., a public reaction against a company's mistreatment of workers can be envisioned, even when the exact event that incites that reaction is difficult to predict). How well a company absorbs and recovers from those shocks can be just as foreseeable and tends to be a product of a company's operational setup, reputation, leadership, financial position, and culture—all of which are crosscut by ESG. Together, these elements play a significant role in determining the speed and extent to which a company absorbs and recovers from a shock (in terms of returning to a pre-shock level of normal operations or else transitioning to some "new normal"). Importantly, more Resilient companies should (all else equal) be able to exert greater control over how they absorb and recover from shocks, as compared to less Resilient companies. Hence, the absorption and recovery profiles of companies that are more Resilient may be more important to model than those of their non-Resilient counterparts.

Modeling shock absorption is a standard part of risk analysis for most investors, and it manifests itself in various commonplace risk measures, such as drawdowns and value-at-risk. But recovery modeling is less standardized and is often not (properly) factored into assessments of the riskiness of assets. This is perhaps due to the different characteristic timescales that are typically involved with absorption and recovery. However, separately considering the two gives a distorted view on risk. For example, on the day of some shock, the stock price of Company A drops 25% and Company B's stock drops 10%; three months later the stock of Company A has recovered to its pre-shock level whereas B's stock remains at 90% of its pre-shock price. Many conventional risk measures would consider Company A to be riskier than B because its stock is more volatile, even though A recovered to its pre-shock level and B did not. Yet, if the recovery in A's stock was highly likely, and B's non-recovery also highly likely, can it still be said that A is riskier than B? B appears better able to *absorb* the shock than A, but A recovers more readily than B—so it could be claimed that A is more Resilient than B (and therefore less risky). Many conventional risk measures miss this aspect of A's behavior, in part because they tend to focus on short timescales and so would concentrate more on the immediate impact of the shock (i.e., absorption). What is important to note here is that recovery and absorption are separable, even though they are often positively correlated.

Although both absorption and recovery are important (as are detection of and learning from shocks), there is an aspect of recovery that fundamentally distinguishes it from absorption, and that is the notion of trajectory. One might say that a company has "recovered" from a shock once it returns to its pre-shock performance level (in terms of stock price, profitability, or some other measurement over time). But recovery need not entail a return to the same trajectory that the company was following prior to the shock: while a company that simply returns to its normal levels and modes of operation might be said to have recovered, recovery can also take the form of achieving a "new normal" through *transformation* (e.g., after an oil-price shock, a company may make a switch to consuming only renewable energy). We believe that companies that are more able to undergo such transformations during recovery are more Resilient than those that can only return to normal.

Relatedly, we believe that companies with strong ESG performance are generally better positioned to undergo such post-shock transformations than poor performers are. This is due to the fact that many ESG resources can serve as fuel for transformation. For instance:

- High diversity in a company's leadership can broaden its perspective in the wake of a crisis, which may facilitate more creative and open-minded "pivots" in strategy and operations. High diversity, equity, and inclusiveness (DEI) in a company's workforce can also foster confidence in the company's long-term fairness, thus improving trust in its leadership and their willingness to innovate.
- A small environmental footprint can decrease dependence on specific physical inputs to production (in terms of natural resources), which will in general increase the ease with which a company can shift to new modes of production (whether through new products or processes).
- Strong governance (e.g., transparency measures, aligned compensation policies, thorough oversight of management by boards of directors) can help ensure that transformations are well planned and executed, with the appropriate time horizons kept in clear focus.

This capacity for transformation overlaps heavily with a company's innovativeness. Although it may not be true that strong ESG performance is required for a company to be innovative, we do expect that *companies must be innovative if they are to continually improve their ESG activities.* It is for this reason that the most useful ESG datasets should capture some aspects of companies' abilities to innovate, which will bear on their future ESG performance.

Even when companies do not undergo major transformations during post-shock recovery, strong ESG capabilities and resources can boost how effectively they absorb and recover from shocks, especially if the shocks themselves are connected with ESG issues (e.g., natural resource scarcity, climate change, human rights).[18] ESG and Resilience are therefore likely to be tightly coupled, and it makes sense to test them jointly.

Testing Resilience

It is vital to recognize that Resilience is a conditional property: it is incomplete to say that something is Resilient without specifying the types of shocks to which it is Resilient (something is Resilient *to* something else and rarely Resilient in a universal, unqualified sense). Testing for Resilience thus entails testing absorption and recovery behavior under particular shock *scenarios* and the extent to which ESG factors drive those behaviors.[19] For example, an investor might test:

- A crash in debt markets: and explore how workplace conditions affect Resilience of banks (e.g., in terms of employee retention and productivity). Or the bursting of a technology bubble and investigate how worker treatment by tech companies affects those companies' Resilience (again, in terms of employee retention and productivity).
- A data breach: and explore how a company's standing on shareholder rights affects how well it absorbs and recovers from the fallout of exposing its client data.
- A warning by a regulator that some ingredients to a company's products have negative long-term health effects: and explore how diversity in the company's leadership team and board influences its Resilience.
- A global shortage of a particular rare-earth element: and explore how a mining company's environmental practices and treatment of local populations affect its ability to navigate that shortage.

As might be guessed from these examples, Resilience analysis has the potential to reveal some nuanced relationships between ESG factors and investment/company performance. Yet, how might the analysis itself proceed? At a high level, Resilience analysis of ESG factors could resemble the following recipe:

Step 1. Choose a shock that is believed to be consequential for an investor's portfolio. That shock may be natural (e.g., a flood), economic (a sudden spike in unemployment), social (eruption of an equality or other human rights protest), something specific to a company's reputation (exposure of worker mistreatment), or any other shock that the investor might feel is worth investigating.

Step 2. Choose relevant companies that might be affected by the shock from Step 1. These may be companies with stocks, bonds, or options already owned by the investor or companies that the investor is considering owning.

Step 3. Identify ESG practices and resources for the companies from Step 2 that may help them to absorb and recover from the shock identified in Step 1.

Step 4. Identify and examine ESG datasets that are specifically applicable to the ESG practices and resources identified in Step 3.

Step 5. Using the data from Step 4, model how the specific ESG resources (from Step 3) of companies from Step 2 respond to the shock from Step 1, in terms of how well they initially respond to the shock (i.e., absorb it), as well as their long-term recovery from that shock. The investigated responses should be translated into investment-relevant variables, such as revenues, profitability, market share, stock price, credit rating, and so on.

Step 6. Investigate how changes to the levels of ESG resources (as compared to those identified in the data from Step 4) might alter the outcomes from Step 5. That is, use simulation to perform sensitivity analysis by assessing alternative paths to recovery.

This approach to Resilience assessment hinges on three activities: dataset search, simulation, and sensitivity analysis. In the next section, we discuss some technologies that could make Resilience assessment highly scalable and efficient for investors. But first, it is important to draw attention to what this approach (even without technological assistance) can enable.

What Investors Can Gain from Resilience Analysis

One should understand that the purpose of this type of Resilience analysis is not to value ESG resources and activities in general but rather to illuminate the context-specific relevance of ESG factors for companies of interest *under the condition of the shock*. What might this achieve for investors?

- It can help investors pinpoint which ESG factors are likely to be most material for a given company in handling a given shock. Pinpointing this materiality can assist investors in identifying which specific ESG factors they need to best understand. In most cases, it is easier for investors to gain specific understanding than general understanding—for example, by focused learning or engaging with consultants, who have sharp expertise in a particular area (rather than more general, but less insightful, knowledge).

- It can help investors to better understand what specific data and information they may be lacking, which can streamline searches for more relevant and higher-quality ESG datasets.
- It can help investors build clearer bridges between companies' ESG performances and the performance of investment portfolios. Because the outputs of this type of Resilience analysis are investment-relevant variables (i.e., ones that are directly usable for risk assessment and portfolio decisions), and are scenario-based, they might be readily integrated with investors' usual processes, for example, risk management.

The use of specific shock scenarios is key for how Resilience can become an analytical filter for selecting and examining ESG data: for a given shock, a relevant, high-quality ESG dataset is one that enables an investor to gain sharp visibility on how a company may absorb and recover from a specific shock. Relevance and quality are then functions of the shocks that are explored; and the shocks that an investor chooses to explore should be those which the investor expects to be most consequential for the companies it is studying. This helps address the proliferation problem of ESG datasets (in testing Resilience to a shock, investors need verify only the quality of datasets that are pertinent to the shock), so long as investors are efficiently able to search among ESG datasets. We look at technological solutions to that concern in the next section.

Use of Resilience to specific shocks for analytically filtering ESG datasets can alleviate some of the other aforementioned problems as well. In terms of integration with conventional risk analysis, most investors are familiar with scenario-driven risk management (and it is a core part of their standard processes). Scenarios are predicated on assumptions about how events will unfold, as are the simulated responses to those events by companies and portfolios. ESG data can thereby enter analysis through assumptions: the value of particular ESG activities and resources *under that scenario* can then be triangulated through sensitivity analysis. For example, imagine that a certain segment of consumers states that it will boycott companies that do not have diverse leadership teams. The sudden emergence of this sort of boycott movement (say, fueled by social media) could be an ESG shock scenario. An investor might model a company's Resilience under this scenario using assumptions, for example: (1) what percentage of the company's revenues come from the consumer segment that is launching the boycott (and what additional revenues may be lost from others being sympathetic to that segment); (2) what composition(s) for the leadership would count as diverse (and therefore escape the boycott); (3) what amount of time and money it would take for the company to reach those compositions. The sensitivity of scenario outcomes (in terms of how well the company in question can absorb and recover from the diversity shock) to these assumptions would then provide indicative values for: the materiality of leadership diversity to the company; the relevance and quality of ESG datasets on leadership diversity (depending on the assumptions of what constitutes a "diverse" leadership team); and Resilience of the company to diversity shocks. The threshold-based setup (i.e., assuming that there is some cutoff point at which a leadership team would be considered diverse) is somewhat simplistic and only one of a large range of possible setups that could drive scenario-based Resilience analyses. Nonetheless, it is a useful starting point for a broad class of ESG shocks and forges a clear link between risk and ESG factors, in terms of performance outcomes.

A concern could be raised that Resilience analysis may be burdensome for investors and that they would be better off turning to third parties to perform it for them. Our counterargument to such a concern is that, with the aid of technology, investors may be able to perform Resilience analysis at least as efficiently as many third parties and could gain a number of benefits in doing so themselves. These include cost-effectiveness, speed of turnaround, and the ability to conduct highly individualized, bespoke analysis (rather than having to rely on more generic analysis that third parties might perform to cater to a broad clientele). Additionally, investors who are able to conduct Resilience analyses themselves might cultivate comparative advantages in performing such analysis for specific types of company, shock, or ESG factor—and consequently turn that comparative advantage into outperforming investment portfolios.

TECHNOLOGIES FOR RESILIENCE ANALYSIS

Hypothetically, an investor could perform the type of analysis we have described previously without the aid of technology (other than that of a simple spreadsheet, if the datasets concerned were not too large). Yet doing so would be too restrictive, in terms of: the amount of time required for each analysis; limitations to the amount of data that can be used; and sophistication of analysis that can be performed. Use of suitable technologies could significantly help the scalability, efficiency, and richness of Resilience analysis that might be performed. In this brief section, we cover some of the technologies that we view as most beneficial to Resilience analysis.

Dataset Search

Perhaps, the most obvious way in which technology could assist Resilience analysis is through *dataset search*. By helping investors formulate hypotheses about relevant ESG factors in the context of specific shocks, Resilience analysis essentially shrinks the universe of ESG datasets that an investor must search to find appropriate datasets (i.e., by reducing it to only those datasets that bear on the relevant ESG factors identified by the hypotheses).

Various search tools could accelerate that filtering of datasets, as well as an investor's ability to access those relevant datasets that remain after filtering. For example, many platforms that provide ESG data (whether in the form of proprietary datasets or those sourced from other parties) offer search capabilities that are able to filter datasets based on user-specified properties, such as particular ESG topics. These platforms include those that are already familiar to most investors (such as Bloomberg, FactSet, S&P, and Nasdaq) along with platforms that specialize in alternative data (such as Neudata or Quandl).[20] Likewise, numerous search tools exist to help investors identify ESG datasets across the Internet (such as Google's Dataset Search utility, which returns only datasets, rather than other types of content).

Although these platforms and tools go far in making searches for ESG datasets more efficient, there are several clear improvements that could be made that would benefit investors, and these involve *semantic search* and *metadata*. Regarding semantic search: a key problem with "conventional" search is that it relies explicitly and exclusively on the search terms that a user provides. Semantic search, on the other hand, uses techniques that attempt to return results not only for what the searcher is explicitly seeking (based on their search query) but also for related searches. For example, if an investor searches for emissions datasets by entering the query "carbon emissions," a semantic search tool might return results for that query as well as for "greenhouse gas emissions" (or at least suggest that additional query). Semantic search may assist investors in finding pertinent ESG datasets by including search criteria that the investor might not have initially thought to include, and it could therefore potentially help enrich the inputs for analysis.

Better metadata (data about properties of datasets themselves) could also improve how investors search for ESG datasets. Many of the search platforms we mentioned earlier do include some forms of metadata that can be used to filter datasets, including the date ranges included in the dataset and listing of the variables included in the dataset. Other forms of metadata (which are not commonly included at present) would also benefit investors, such as those related to the criteria listed in the second section (e.g., listing the granularity and comprehensiveness of datasets).

Dataset Preprocessing

At present, many of the ESG datasets that are available to investors exist in forms that are not immediately amenable to analysis: they require some data operations (removal or handling of missing values, rescaling, normalization, etc.) that can consume nonnegligible amounts of an analyst's time. This preparation problem is familiar in data science, where *preprocessing* tools (e.g., data pipelines) are frequently used to automate some of the data preparation steps. Use of such tools could boost the scalability and speed of Resilience analysis by allowing more time to be spent on the analysis itself.

Models of Nonlinearity and Uncertainty

In modeling how ESG factors affect a company's responsivity to a shock, it should be apparent that such responses (whether as absorption or recovery) may be nonlinear, that is, the relationships between the level of some ESG variable and the company's post-shock performance may not be strictly ones that can be represented by linear functions. Analyzing nonlinear functions is in general more complicated than linear analysis, and investors could benefit from technologies that help them work with nonlinearities. In some cases, the specific form of a nonlinear relation may be apparent upfront (in terms of a cleanly identifiable functional form), but in other cases, it may need to be "learned" empirically. In the latter case, various machine learning algorithms can be applicable, as they are capable of representing complicated, highly nonlinear functions that exist in datasets (and may not be identifiable by other modes of analysis).

Regardless of whether models of companies' responsivities to shocks are derived from assumed functional forms or empirically from data, there may exist some residual uncertainty about those functional forms—that is, more than one form may be plausible. In such cases, it can be more appropriate to "blend" plausible forms rather than selecting among them. Alternatively, it can be sometimes beneficial to run analyses for each of the plausible forms separately. Various tools exist (mostly from the realms of data science and machine learning) to help deal with these forms of functional uncertainty (whether through automatically blending functional models or automating the rerunning of analyses for each of a given number of potential models). Use of such tools could help investors explore the sensitivity of outcomes from Resilience analysis to uncertainty about the models used to perform it.

Simulation and Sensitivity Analysis

Resilience analysis involves exploring the response behavior of a company to a shock over the course of time, as it absorbs and recovers from the shock (or not). This can be achieved through a variety of simulation methods. But, for the sake of scalability and efficiency, it is desirable for the manual effort required to set up and execute a simulation to be minimized. For very basic simulations, this can often be achieved in a conventional spreadsheet (especially when "macros" are used). Yet, for more intricate simulations (e.g., those with many variables that interact in complicated ways), other tools become necessary. Many financial institutions nowadays have access to more advanced simulation technologies (other than spreadsheets), although these do not always include the capability to model the "inner workings" of companies and how they relate to investment performance. That is, the simulators may represent company performance via some simple output variable (e.g., earnings) and connect this to stock price performance. However, Resilience analysis may frequently require examining some of the internal reactions of companies to shocks—for example, how a shock affects a company's labor costs, and then how that cost impact "flows through" to summary variables, such as earnings. Simulation technologies that readily allow modeling of both the internal and external dynamics of companies could therefore be highly useful for Resilience analysis.

Apart from simulation of investment outcomes from shocks, another key to Resilience analysis is exposing the sensitivity of such outcomes to changes in a company's ESG behavior and resources. That is, an essential aim of Resilience analysis is to help determine how much a particular ESG factor is *responsible* for how well a company absorbs or recovers from the effects of a shock. Being able to measure these ESG sensitivities can provide valuable insight about the relative materiality of various ESG behaviors and resources to a company's shock response. Some simulation platforms have tools for sensitivity analysis built in or at least produce outputs that are easily amenable to such analysis. Various mathematical and digital toolkits exist that could aid investors in conducting sensitivity analyses, and we expect that these will become crucial for quantitative studies of Resilience.

SUMMARY AND FUTURE DIRECTIONS

In this chapter, we have raised the issue of excessive intermediation in ESG investing. Our central assertion is that investors should develop more internal familiarity and capability in ESG analysis and that their present barriers to doing so come mainly from the proliferation of ESG datasets and the difficulty in integrating that data with their standard analytical processes. Resilience analysis, which looks at the response of companies to specific shock scenarios, represents a framework that investors might use to overcome these problems of proliferation and integration, as well as help investors gain deeper insight into the materiality of ESG factors to their portfolios.

The Resilience framework is young, and various aspects of its practical implementation require further definition and development. Perhaps, foremost among these is the design of metrics that directly captures Resilience, both as it pertains to ESG factors and otherwise. Such metrics may further strengthen the functional bridge between ESG variables and investment returns and help abbreviate and pithily communicate some elements of the style of Resilience analysis that we have proposed here. Another useful step for practical implementation of Resilience analysis would be the design of a comprehensive technological architecture (e.g., a digital platform) to streamline the use of Resilience analysis by investors. We intend to be involved in the nurture of both new metrics and technologies for Resilience in the coming years.

NOTES

1 Although "ESG" is typically defined (as it is here) as an adjectival acronym, it is often used as both an adjective (e.g., "ESG factors") and a stand-alone noun. We partake in this colloquial flexibility in this chapter.

2 By "investors," we are chiefly referring to investment organizations. In specific, we have institutional investment organizations in mind—such as public pension funds, endowments, and sovereign wealth funds (in addition to family offices).

3 Given the nature of the subject, it may be more apropos to say "getting their own hands clean."

4 We elaborate on these problems of proliferation and integration in the second section.

5 We view the connection between Resilience analysis and technology as symbiotic: an investor's adoption of one can help improve its use of the other.

6 Shocks need not always be "downside" events (though they typically are).

7 This property of bouncing back from shocks makes our notion of Resilience more aligned with concepts of Resilience in nonfinancial fields, such as engineering and ecology. Recently, some financial institutions have begun touting the importance of "resilience," but their (mis)usage of the term is more appropriately understood as *robustness*: they talk about assets that avoid changing in the face of shocks. The capacity for change (in terms of adaptation or transformation as a response to shocks) is fundamental to resilience (as other disciplines define it), and so we capitalize our concept of "Resilience" to differentiate it from how the term "resilience" is coming to be used in financial practice. We discuss the importance of distinguishing between Resilience and robustness in the third section (but for a more complete treatment, see Rook et al., 2021).

8 The Resilience approach does not eliminate the need for specialist ESG knowledge in investing. What it does is help to more precisely expose what specific information is needed to adequately understand particular relationships between ESG and performance—and specific information is almost always easier to obtain than general knowledge. Investors are familiar with this process of identifying specific information they lack and finding ways of acquiring it, either by internal learning or securing it externally (e.g., from specialized expert consultants or research providers; the case of investment in the pharmaceutical industry is analogous here). Our main point is: specialized information is often far easier to obtain than general knowledge; the approach we are advocating can help in more accurately determining what specialized information is needed.

9 We find it strange that *innovation* is not considered a standard ESG variable, as innovativeness and performance on environmental, social, and governance activities should be highly correlated. Relatedly, ongoing improvement in ESG activities by a company will almost certainly require the company to innovate (at some point in the future).

10 See, for example, Bohn et al. (2021), Christensen et al. (2021), Kotsantonis and Serafeim (2019), Kramer et al. (2020), Orsagh (2019), and references therein.

11 Situational materiality is distinct from notions of "dynamic materiality." We do not pursue a detailed discussion of the differences here but simply note they are not equivalent.

12 For example, if a specific ESG factor is found to accelerate the recovery of companies following a market-wide shock, then savvy investors might adjust their portfolios to increase the weight on companies for which that factor is most pronounced. Strategies such as this receive relatively little attention in the existing research literature.

13 See Peirce (2021).
14 See Walter (2019) for a recent critique of the ESG ratings industry.
15 See, for example, Christensen et al. (2021), Kramer et al. (2020).
16 Resilience applies equally to both systemic shocks and idiosyncratic shocks.
17 We think of absorption as the "immediate" impact of a shock on a company. Absorption is analogous to how much deformation a car goes in the event of a crash whereas recovery would be how repairable the deformation is. A nuance of this distinction is that higher absorptive capacity does not (on its own) necessarily lead to higher Resilience. Modern automobiles contain many more plastic parts than their predecessors. Those plastic components undergo damage much more readily than their metal counterparts (i.e., metal components can generally absorb larger shocks without being significantly damaged) but are cheaper to replace. Modern cars are thus more Resilient (and safer) than earlier cars.
18 ESG activities may also improve a company's ability to detect and learn from shocks, but we suspect these abilities are less helped by ESG factors than absorption and recovery are.
19 A "test" might amount to examining historical values, performing thought experiments ("war-gaming"), or building structured simulations with parameter estimates, among many other modes of analysis.
20 Following from Monk et al. (2019), we take "alternative data" (alt-data) as data that is "unconventional" (at least historically) for financial analysis. Examples of alt-data include satellite imagery, textual data taken from social media platforms, or the comments sections of websites, online reviews, and geolocation data (though these are a very meager sampling of the diversity and expansiveness of alt-data types).

REFERENCES

Bohn, J., Goldberg, L., & Ulucam, S. (2021). Transparency and best practices are essential for ESG investing. *CDAR Working Paper*. Available at: https://cdar.berkeley.edu/sites/default/files/bohn-esg.pdf (Accessed: 6 January 2022).

Christensen, D., Serafeim, G., & Sikochi, A. (2021). *Why Is Corporate Virtue in the Eye of the Beholder? The Case of ESG Ratings*. Available at: https://papers.ssrn.com/sol3/papers.cfm?abstract_id=3793804 (Accessed: 6 January 2022).

Kotsantonis, S., & Serafeim, G. (2019). Four things no one will tell you about ESG data. *Journal of Applied Corporate Finance*, 31(2), 50–58.

Kramer, M., Jais, N., Sullivan, E., Wendel, C., Rodriguez, K. Papa, C., Napoli, C., & Forti, F. (2020). One agency's A+ is another's "laggard"—and neither links to financial performance. *Institutional Investor*. Available at: www.institutionalinvestor.com/article/b1n706z8lqfscs/Where-ESG-Ratings-Fail-The-Case-for-New-Metrics (Accessed: 6 January 2022).

Monk, A., Prins, M., & Rook, D. (2019). Rethinking alternative data in institutional investment. *Journal of Financial Data Science*, 1(1), 14–31.

Orsagh, M. (2019). ESG analysis: Is judgment more important than data? *Principles for Responsible Investment Blog*, October 30. Available at: www.unpri.org/pri-blog/esg-analysis-is-judgement-more-important-than-data/5050.article (Accessed: 6 January 2022).

Peirce, H. (2021). Rethinking global ESG metrics. *Statement of the US Securities and Exchange Commission*, April 14. Available at: www.sec.gov/news/public-statement/rethinking-global-esg-metrics (Accessed: 6 January 2022).

Rook, D., In, S.-Y., & Monk, A. (2021). *The Resilience Manifesto: Integrating ESG and Risk Management, in Investment Portfolios and Organizations*. Available at: https://papers.ssrn.com/sol3/papers.cfm?abstract_id=3942909 (Accessed: 6 January 2022).

Walter, I. (2019). *Sense and Nonsense in ESG Investing*. Available at: https://papers.ssrn.com/sol3/papers.cfm?abstract_id=3480878 (Accessed: 6 January 2022).

9

Technology-Supported Investment Management

Eduard van Gelderen* and David Ouellet†

INTRODUCTION

How difficult is investing really? At a first glance, one is likely to conclude that it must be very difficult. There is a lot of volatility, many nomenclatures and acronyms are used, and only the best educated people seem to find their way around in the investment industry. And yet, in the long run there is a direct relationship between economic growth and the return in financial markets. Hence, provided the investment horizon is long enough, positive economic growth will translate into positive returns on financial assets. An old Dutch expression talks about "trommelpapier", meaning that you just store your financial assets, and the passing of time will do the rest. Obviously, the reality is less simple. Time horizons and investment objectives differ per type of investor, leading to different risk appetites and investment strategies. A buy opportunity for one investor can be a perfect sell opportunity for another investor; it doesn't necessarily mean they fundamentally disagree nor that they behave irrationally. As said, economic growth and financial returns are inextricably linked long term, but they do not run in parallel in the short and medium terms. Financial markets are forward-looking, and a positive economic outlook translates into positive market trends. If the actual economic growth falls short of that outlook or the outlook was simply too optimistic, markets will correct. In fact, markets could very well correct too much due to an overreaction on being wrong the first time. Fiscal and monetary policies

* Eduard van Gelderen is Chief Investment Officer at PSP Investments.
† David Ouellet is Chief Technology and Data Officer at PSP Investments.

DOI: 10.4324/9781003262039-11

by governments and central banks could decouple the real economy and financial markets too. Over the last two decades, we've witnessed exactly that. Monetary easing, stimulus packages, and quantitative easing have led to a stellar performance in capital markets. The resulting low-risk premiums and high valuations are not necessarily a reflection of the state of the economy going forward. With the impact of COVID-19 still there, the frictions in the supply chain and inflation looming around the corner, not many will argue there is as little risk as the risk premiums suggest. Some market participants argue that the risk premiums are low, because quantitative easing has placed a floor in the market; it's a free put option. Still, the divergence is simply not sustainable. The problem of how to normalize the relationship between the real economy and the financial markets isn't getting easier to solve after all these years of divergence. In fact, it's quite the opposite: it is a very uncomfortable feeling that most of the relationships and theories we've learned in business school and used as guidance in our investment decision-making are simply not working anymore.

Technology has always been part of the investment management world. Yet, we would argue that with the recent developments and innovations, technology has become as important as human capital to deliver the investment performance we're aiming for. Technology has an impact on many aspects of running an investment management organization. It is never an objective by itself; it serves a purpose and supports a strategy. McKinsey's approach provides a helpful competitive framework in this respect as in their view, a company can be truly successful only when it excels in (at least) one of the following three business models: customer intimacy, operational efficiency, or product innovation. Customer intimacy implies that client servicing and client solutions are what drives the business model. Application Programming Interface (API) is a good example of how technology can support this model. Information about the client's portfolio is directly accessible, the client receives advice on its investment portfolio and can trade securities via his/her mobile phone instantly. Operational efficiency means that the company is the lowest cost provider. Technology, such as cloud and open source solutions, is the driver of this model by supporting scale and efficient portfolio management and execution. In contrast to customer intimacy, standardization of the end product is a key feature. Passive investments or index-tracking are typical examples of this business model. Product leadership is all about innovation. The premise is that by launching new products, new demand will be created. This model does not necessarily look at disruptive innovation alone. Incremental innovation is equally important as capital markets change constantly and investment strategies need to adapt to new realities (Lo, 2004). In this case, technology focuses on providing the right data and analytical tools to improve decision-making and to evaluate new investment strategies.

A portfolio management system (PMS) in the broadest sense of the word (not just a record keeping system) is at the core of this model. This chapter will deal with technology from a product leadership perspective.

The aim of this chapter is to describe how to deal with the rapidly changing investment environment and the important role technology and knowledge management are going to play in the next decade. It takes the form of a case study as many examples relate to PSP Investments.[1] The first section will set the stage by providing an overview of the role technology has played over the years. Although relatively new, it will include a view on big data and artificial intelligence (AI) too. Moreover, this section will provide two case studies on how PSP Investments is using new techniques to assess and select private equity managers and to determine emerging risks in the portfolio. The next section will describe knowledge management as an approach to come to better investment decisions and how technology supports this management approach. This section also dives into the current discussions on responsible investments and climate change. Although news items on climate change and carbon emission show up in the media every single day, and new "green transition" initiatives and products are launched frequently, current knowledge of the topic is rather fragile and based on a nascent science. The chapter ends with a summary. The ambition is to convince the reader that technology and human capital are the two interwoven drivers of a successful and agile investment management organization.

THE TECHNOLOGIZED INVESTOR[2]

Starting in the early nineties as a financial analyst at an investment bank in Amsterdam, the job was to analyze listed companies and provide buy or sell recommendations. The technology supporting this task was a spreadsheet. Data was gathered from Reuters, annual reports, the stock exchange, and a variety of providers of macro- and sector data. The spreadsheets were set up to be able to follow the year-by-year changes in the corporate's financial data and to make predictions about what would happen to the company and its future share price. Spreadsheets could simply reflect the corporate balance sheet and profit-and-loss account, but more sophisticated analysts made sure that the spreadsheets included relationships between the different financial statements as well as relationships with external factors. For example, the elasticity of product demand to general GDP for durable goods companies or margin developments as a result of developments in commodity prices for energy companies. Ultimately, the goal was to come up with an earning's forecast and relate that forecast to the stock price to assess whether the company was under- or overvalued. The interesting part of the job was that knowledge on business models was built up over time. The feedback loop, in terms of new corporate financials becoming available every other three or six months, was a learning experience and spreadsheets were modified accordingly.[3] Spreadsheets became more sophisticated as time passed, allowing the user to program its own macros, and statistical packages became available as "add-ins". Parallel to this development, more and better data sources became available, leading to a much higher level of analytical sophistication. In short, technology was on the rise to become an essential part of investment management. Zvi Bodie (1999), one of the greatest thinkers in finance, confirmed this in his article "Investment Management and Technology; Past, Present and Future". He claimed that technological advances had made it possible to put financial theory into practice. But, more importantly, he predicted that investment management would undergo a radical transformation as the result of financial engineering, which he defined as the application of sophisticated mathematical models, computerized information processing, and telecommunications technology. Zvi Bodie was spot on; the investment management sector has seen a lot of new developments since the turn of the century. Data has become a commodity. As a result, the time and efforts spent on finding the right data, cleansing the data, and making it fit for research purposes were reduced significantly, leaving more time for analysis and decision-making. The surge in clean data triggered quant investments, or also called systematic investments, which look to exploit anomalies in the data by applying mathematical models. The significance of having access to clean data became obvious: an anomaly found in dirty data might not be an anomaly at all! Quant investments have gone through different cycles. Exploiting anomalies can lead to appealing uncorrelated[4] returns, but history has also shown that regime changes can bring quant investments in big problems. Perhaps, one of the best examples was the collapse of Long-term Capital Management in 1998 (Lowenstein, 2001). But quant investments never died. Schelling (2021) claims that an investment approach without quants is unthinkable as the human brain is simply not able to follow the sheer growth in data. Experiences such as LTCM only triggered the development of better models and more rigid risk management; a development heavily relying on technology and the surge in better data. An important new quant-driven investment approach is factor investing. It became clear that risk was not the sole driver of investment returns as suggested by the Capital Asset Pricing Model (CAPM), but that a set of several structural factors can do a much better job (Huij & van Gelderen, 2014). The portfolio management systems available nowadays increasingly rely on these factors and do a good job in optimizing and stress testing investment portfolios, especially regarding listed instruments with readily available market prices.[5] One might argue that these systems are making use of simplifying assumptions and therefore do not match reality, but as long as the technology is not replacing human judgment, these systems are of great use.

ADVANCED ANALYTICS ERA

The advanced analytics evolution has been driven by advances in technology. The 1980s and 1990s were the years of statistical analysis (linear and multilinear regression, stochastic process, and Monte Carlo simulation). These analytical techniques were using conventional data, like SEC filings, trading data, macro data, or industry data. After the turn of the century, we witnessed a surge in computing power, cloud computing, and alternative data (satellite picture, web scraping, earning call transcript, Internet of Things with their sensor data or social media sentiment). New technologies such as Machine Learning (with supervised and unsupervised learning), natural language processing (NLP), and even more advanced AI technologies such as deep learning and neural networks became the drivers behind advanced analytics. More recently, quantum computing and synthetic data[6] started to emerge. Although the application of quantum computing is still under review, the gigantic increase in computing power supports the use of AI and will eliminate the need for the use of proxies and other simplifying approaches.

Smart investors continue to use advanced analytics and alternative data sources to become better investors. They want to capture and better understand the dynamics in the capital markets in order to be able to timely adjust portfolios to changing market conditions and to generate excess returns by outsmarting other investors. It's our belief that the increased level of complexity and sophistication will drive a significant gap between smart investors and other investors. This gap is directly linked to the adoption of advanced analytics because the investment environment has become too complex for the human brain to cope with. It is a given that the human brain is powerful and agile, but it also has its limitations. It's not the most powerful processor of data: we get easily lost when the amount of data to deal with starts to pick up. The brain also starts to trick us by trying to impose causality on us while in many cases these causalities are flawed or do not even exist. The literature on behavioral finance has provided many examples of potential biases and flaws in our decision-making. Moreover, we tend to have difficulties to fully understand probabilities. Not so much around the mean or median of a probability distribution but certainly when we move to the tails of a probability distribution. Taleb (2004, 2008) has written extensively about this last topic. Hence, technology helps us to understand the investment environment better, to frame problems, and to make better investment decisions. But is this really true? Did earnings and share price forecasts get any better over time? Most likely not. The problem in the past was that many changes could not be picked up quickly enough by the relatively slow arrival of new data. And due to the limited amount of data, analytical methods did not provide statistically significant outcomes. Technological progress and more data tackles that problem, but the world, including the functioning of capital markets, is constantly changing too. Better still, one could argue that the speed of change has gone up. Hence, many earnings predictions continue to be off, and buy and sell recommendations remain rather unreliable. So, does this mean we're wasting our money on technology? Well, forecasts might still be problematic, but the insights we've gained through technology are significant. We are in a much better position to construct portfolios in line with our objectives. We can use simulations and stress testing to figure out how a portfolio can behave over time and in specific situations. We can back-test new investment strategies and investment ideas. We can create proxies to better differentiate between market and idiosyncratic risks. We can break down investments in specific factors to gain a better understanding of performance drivers. In short, technology has provided us with the tools to have a much better grip on risk[7] and therefore our investment decisions. Put it differently, it helps us to avoid making bad mistakes. Charles Ellis's seminal book *Winning the Loser's Game* (1998) makes perfect sense in this context: as an investor you can win only by exploiting the mistakes of others. By embracing technology, we have become better investors.

CLOUD TECHNOLOGY IS A GAME CHANGER

Another important aspect that we must acknowledge is the fact that the cost of technology has fallen related to storage, operations, and processing power. One of the most important reasons for this is cloud development. Cloud technology has fundamentally changed the way investment management runs its operations nowadays. It is not an exaggeration to say that the public cloud, led by the growth of Google, Microsoft, IBM, and Amazon, is and will be one the biggest game changers in the way technology will impact the investment world. It will also lead to more competition as it allows smaller investment firms to compete directly with larger investment firms. The only thing the investor needs is a browser and an internet connection. So, for investment firms, there is no longer a need to purchase expensive computers with lots of storage and memory. Financial analysts can access programs and storage from any location through an internet connection, which means that data is not confined to an individual's hard drive or to an individual's internal network. The cloud provides investment management firms with a lower cost solution as investment management systems like Order Management System (OMS) or Portfolio Management Systems (PMS) are available in the cloud. External hosting of programs and data eliminates the need for expensive servers. Cloud computing moreover helps to avoid the costs of internal server updates, and there is no need to keep up with the pace of software updates, which can seem constant at times. Maintenance, repair and troubleshooting are the responsibility of the company hosting the systems and therefore reduces IT support costs even more. This development makes it possible to shift a portion of the available technology budget from running the operations to advanced analytics supporting investment activities. In the context of McKinsey's three models, operational efficiency pays for product innovation.

Where newly established investment firms will benefit from the cloud from the start, established investment management companies need to first deal with their legacy systems and IT infrastructure. This implies a transition. In the case of PSP Investments, this involves a structured and deliberate approach to fully eliminate the two main data centers by the end of 2023. During the transition, several PSP Investments' applications already reside in the cloud. The transition of some applications to the cloud will be expensive and time-intensive. The business case supporting the transition was based on four pillars: (1) create more agility to meet the growing demand of investment professionals, (2) to take advantage of the inherent mobility support of cloud-based solutions, (3) to focus the technology department group on creating business value and increased productivity, and (4) to support new use cases for data and analytics.

AI AS A NEW TOOL FOR SMART INVESTORS

At this point, we would like to discuss the role of new technologies such as big data (digitization) and AI. Agrawal et al. (2018) state that the economic significance of AI is that it lowers the price of prediction, which provides more room for human judgment and hence better-informed decision-making. For investors, two important subfields of AI are natural language processing (NLP) and machine learning (ML). In short, NLP means that computers scan documents to look for specific themes, tone of voice/emotions, and drifts in the narrative. The efficiency improvement to scan through multiple documents goes without saying. But the potential benefits go beyond efficiency gains as NLP could lead to better predictions. New technology can detect early indicators we tend to miss by reading documents ourselves. Moreover, with the help of NLP it is possible to cross-validate data and trends without any human intervention. Machine learning is the process whereby computers learn to detect relationships in data and improve as more data points become available without specific instructions. This sounds very much like the financial analyst, who adjusts his/her spreadsheet once new financial data become available. And in essence it is, except that the computer can detect much more complex relationships, and it works with considerably more data. Moreover, the work of the analyst was based on structured data while the computer deals with unstructured data too. The expectation is that ML will lead to many new insights and a better understanding of market dynamics. Every investor is fully aware of the potential of AI, but it doesn't mean that they are fully on top of it; most investors are still experimenting with these new tools. PSP Investments is not different and has started up several AI experiments to determine where the most value addition of these new technologies can be found and how to manage advanced analytics as an integral part of the investment process. Two of these experiments will be discussed.

EXPERIMENT 1: NATURAL LANGUAGE PROCESSING

The first one is an NLP experiment within the private market risk group. To monitor the risk profile of a portfolio company and to determine the risk profile of a new investment, portfolio managers and risk analysts read through multiple articles every day. It is a very labor-intensive process, and the people involved tend to focus on different things. Despite regular meetings and touchpoints to discuss specific holdings and issuers, the process can easily miss early indicators of a weakening credit profile. The idea behind the experiment was that the NLP could help us to analyze global news and ultimately enrich market intelligence related to all investments that we own or could own in the future (not just private loans). The question we were trying to answer was related to emerging risks in the total fund rather than seeking to confirm the existing credit risks within the private loan portfolio. We explored many different types of solutions, as the space is still nascent and evolving. We evaluated technologies offered by established firms, consulting firms, and start-ups and invited eight companies from across the world to pitch their solutions. After four months of demos, we agreed on a partnership with a small fintech firm in Europe. They had developed a tool, which scans more than three million websites a day and applies NLP to filter for specific themes. Together, we spent months defining relevant financial and enterprise risks to train their algorithms. Next, we created a list of the top-1,000 largest PSP Investments' holdings and subsidiaries, further customizing the algorithms to focus only on relevant news associated with PSP Investments' geographies, sectors, and assets. Once the algorithms were in place, unique dashboards were created summarizing the emerging risk trends by industry and geography. Subsequently, we started a four-month pilot program to test the tool. The findings were mixed. The tool certainly improved efficiency and greater productivity, but the real game changer we had hoped for was not there: the early warning signs were simply not meaningful enough. To realize that goal, significantly more time and resources would have been required to train the algorithms even more. We therefore made the decision to pause the project. The project is not considered a failure: after all, the efficiency gains are there, and PSP Investments' data scientists are now better equipped to leverage NLP functionalities in other experiments and projects.

EXPERIMENT 2: MACHINE LEARNING

The second experiment is an application of ML to improve our selection process for external managers. In today's increasingly competitive private equity markets, investment managers will need to look beyond existing relationships and find new ways to evaluate funds, besides previous track record. It is well known that, the performance distribution of private equity funds is rather wide and the difference between top-quartile and average performance determines whether the investment is successful or not. After all, research shows that the average performance in private equity falls short of the average performance in public equity. The research question could be formulated as an ML problem: "What Funds will be part of the top quartile funds environment going forward". The project could rely on a growing amount of private market data. At least seven major providers sell large volumes of historical North American and European PE fund performance data. For example, Cobalt has 40 years of historical data on 21,000 funds, representing 55% global and 80% US coverage. Without ML, it is hard to make sense of the available data and leverage it to support decisions. The project was worked on with four data scientists and PSP Investments' private equity team. Important insights were gained by diving in the academic literature on the topic. For instance, Kaplan and Schoar (2005) showed that private equity returns persist strongly across subsequent funds of the same general partner. Between 2005 and 2019, more than 150 research papers were published on the predictability of private equity returns. Predictive factors largely fall within five categories.

(1) Macroeconomics (e.g., investor sentiment, aggregate private equity fund flows)
(2) Market focus (e.g., country of investments)
(3) Fund structure (e.g., change in fund size, LP investors)
(4) Fund strategy (e.g., GP performance track record)
(5) Team composition (e.g., firm culture, team size)

Armed with the research question, the data, team members, and academic insights, we officially started the project. After a few months, we had created a model which was able to have data for the aforementioned five categories and at the time of writing this chapter, our ML model correctly predicts future performance 70% of the time. We trust that we will improve on this percentage over time when more data is added.

LESSONS LEARNED

We came to realize that to fully benefit from ML, we need even more data than we already had available. Moreover, not all available data is useful, because it is not always clear what the data exactly represents. It emphasizes the role of data scientists: they determine what data is needed to solve specific ML problems. Just having more data as a result of digitization is not the answer; it could very well trigger more confusion than clarity. As said, once we know what data we need, the question is whether we have enough data to use ML successfully. We realized that the substantial amount of required data is not always available for the investment problems we would like to solve; a lesson learned for new experiments.

Any investment firm that has ambitions to improve their data and advanced analytics capabilities will need to focus on the following five elements.

(1) A proper data and advanced analytic strategy; the firm needs to invest significant time in mapping and prioritizing the needs and aspirations of the investment use cases by looking at business impact and technical feasibility;
(2) The technology architecture; the right architecture will help the delivery of what was promised; it must be scalable and support the solutions required by the investment teams;
(3) The data management foundation; cloud based, including internal and external data sources;
(4) An agile delivery operating model; users must be able to tap into data sources and analytical tools to work in a test environment on new ideas;
(5) The right talent or partnership; there is a war of talent in the investment industry and in the data science field.

Organizations will need to modify their remuneration framework to ensure they can attract the right talent that can enable advanced analytics. As importantly, organizations will need to invest to retain and upskill their current talents. As talent will be limited, for more complex or niche advanced analytic use cases, capacity could come from partnering externally in a highly coordinated fashion with internal talent. The behavioral and culture change is critical, often more so than underlying technology, data, and analytics tool changes.

TECHNOLOGY-ENABLED KNOWLEDGE MANAGEMENT

The previous section talked about the continued rise and use of technology in investment management. This section will talk about knowledge management. The two sections are directly linked, when we work on the basis of the following hierarchy between data, information, and knowledge. Data reflects measurements of the world, but by itself it doesn't mean much. As described in the previous section, the sources of data for investment management were limited and relatively simple. And yet, the management of data has always been a challenge because not much attention was paid to data management (i.e., defining, cleansing, structuring, and storage). The challenge was not accounting data but management data. The first is backward looking and used for formal reporting while the latter is any type of data informing the investment decision. Nowadays, the amount of management data is growing exponentially due to the process of digitization. Moreover, measurements of the world are no longer just numbers but can take different formats (sound, voices, pictures, videos, etc.). The role of the data scientist cannot be emphasized enough in this environment. In order to give data more meaning, it's augmented and placed in context; it's what we call information. Information is only more valuable than data when it mitigates uncertainty around specific topics. A random speech (data) doesn't mean much, until we learn it is the chair of the Federal Reserve speaking (information). Or, in the context of digitization, satellite pictures of parking lots are meaningful only when these parking lots are used by visitors to a specific shopping mall. Technology platforms play a crucial role in terms of augmentation and placing data in the right context. Portfolio management systems aggregate data and dice and slice portfolios to provide different perspectives. Yet, that information is still static. It is what we do with that information that matters, which brings us to knowledge management.

UNDERSTANDING KNOWLEDGE

Before we go into more detail of knowledge management, some aspects of knowledge and the role of technology need to be addressed first. First of all, what is the definition of knowledge? Epistemology deals with the theory of knowledge and tries to provide answers on questions such as the definition of knowledge, the sources and structure of knowledge, and the transferability and limits of knowledge. For a long time, the definition of knowledge as "justified true belief" was widely accepted. Beliefs can emanate from psychological factors such as desires and prejudices, as well as from perception (our five senses), introspection (our mental state), memory, reason, and testimony; these are considered true. These beliefs need to be strong and should make sense to fit the definition to be justified. Yet, although this would fit the definition of knowledge, these beliefs are not considered knowledge at all times. After all, a justification based on unreliable and faulty methods cannot lead to knowledge. This suggests that reliability is a necessary fourth condition: the justification for the true beliefs must be infallible and there should be no overriding or defeating truths denying one's belief. In science, knowledge is created by testing ideas in a controlled test environment with probabilification as the driver for justification. Knowledge creation in social sciences faces the problem that most experiments cannot be repeated under similar test conditions while the lack of data stands in the way of proper probabilification. For that reason, justification was often based on reason and triangulation. But technology is changing this approach rapidly. As Zvi Bodie already predicted (see previous section), sophisticated mathematical models and computerized information processing have led to a much better understanding of how economies, markets, and strategies work. The body of knowledge related to finance is growing rapidly and investment beliefs have become more specific. Still, these investment beliefs are modified over time as well. Koedijk and Slager (2011) state that investment theories have undergone several paradigm shifts since 1970. Investment beliefs change as there are no absolute truths and certainties in investment management: knowledge in finance is dynamic.

The second aspect related to knowledge is the distinction between explicit and tacit knowledge. Explicit knowledge is articulated knowledge, that is, expressed and recorded as words, numbers, codes, mathematical and scientific formulae, and musical notations. Explicit knowledge is relatively easy to communicate, store, and distribute and is the knowledge found in books, on the web, and other visual and oral means. New technologies can help to interpret explicit knowledge better by connecting different knowledge sources. Tacit knowledge on the other hand is unwritten, unspoken, difficult to codify, and hidden. Every individual possesses a vast storehouse of valuable tacit knowledge, based on his or her emotions, experiences, insights, intuition, observations, and internalized information. New technologies such as NLP will help us transform tacit knowledge into explicit knowledge. This is hugely powerful, because once the knowledge is explicit, it can be tested on its validity. As a result, the finance industry will become more fact-based and rely less on heuristics.

The third aspect is that knowledge is context dependent. As Nonaka and Takeuchi (1995: 58) pointed out: "First, knowledge, unlike information, is about beliefs and commitment. Knowledge is a function of particular stance, perspective, or intention. Second, knowledge, unlike information, is about action. It is always knowledge 'to some end'". This statement implies an action: knowledge has got value only when acted upon. And for that very same reason, knowledge is context dependent. To solve certain problems, we need to have the appropriate knowledge.

KNOWLEDGE MANAGEMENT WITHIN THE ASSET MANAGEMENT INDUSTRY

Now that we have a better understanding of what knowledge means, we can dive into the interaction between knowledge management and technology. Knowledge management is far from a new management discipline. Already for three to four decades the concept of knowledge management is discussed and improved, triggered by the move from a production-based economy to a knowledge-based economy. Monk and van Gelderen (2016) looked into the status of knowledge management in the investment management industry to conclude that knowledge management was considered of high importance. But at the same time, many investment managers didn't know how to implement such knowledge approach. This was a remarkable finding, given that the investment management industry is a knowledge-intensive industry. Less focus on data and technology in the past is certainly part of the reason. For many years, the C-suite of investment management firms did not include the position of a Chief Technology Officer. The responsibility for data and technology was oftentimes in the hands of someone reporting to the Chief Operating Officer, leading to tactical rather than strategic decisions. Moreover, the budgets allocated to data and technology were oftentimes too low to fully follow technological developments. This led very quickly to the reliance on legacy systems for running the business. The survey in the same study also asked the question who should be responsible for knowledge management. The answers were quite diverse. Of the respondents, 37% stated it should be the Chief Investment Officer as the knowledge activities were primarily investments related. The Chief Executive Officer was mentioned 26% of the time as knowledge management was seen as a competitive edge and of strategic value. The Chief Information and Technology Officer was mentioned in only 11% of responses mainly by respondents who considered knowledge management as an IT project. Perhaps, most remarkable was that 20% of the respondents mentioned that knowledge management was not a C-suite responsibility at all but a line responsibility. We don't support this last view. Given that in this chapter we follow a product innovation strategy aimed at investment activities, we feel that it is a joint responsibility between the Chief Investment Officer and the Chief Data and Information Officer.

KNOWLEDGE MANAGEMENT APPROACH

According to O'Leary (2002a, 2002b), knowledge management is the organizational efforts designed to:

(1) capture knowledge;
(2) convert personal knowledge to group-available knowledge;
(3) create knowledge assets and opportunities for knowledge creation;
(4) introduce measurement systems to understand and follow the added value knowledge delivers.

The very first step is to determine where the knowledge on specific topics sits within and outside the organization. This could be a rather straightforward or challenging activity, depending on the size and complexity of the organization.

The real challenge is to identify the tacit knowledge. Especially, since people with important tacit knowledge might consider this knowledge theirs and are not willing to share it. This is also true with regard to external partners. Very siloed organizations will realize that there is a lot of duplication too. An effective knowledge management system will include a directory with the specific skill set and knowledge areas per employee. A lot of these problems encountered in step 1 are solved when it is emphasized by the C-suite that all knowledge belongs to the company rather than the individual. This is a different way of saying that personal knowledge needs to be converted into group knowledge. Once knowledge is documented, this is not a hard task at all: all documents should be placed on a shared drive and therefore accessible to all employees. Again, the tacit knowledge is harder to share. Yet, a traditional way in many cultures of passing experience on to the next generation is by telling stories. With all the communication technology available, it is very easy to organize learning sessions. Hence, a lot of tacit knowledge will become explicit, simply by talking and debating specific activities.[8] Knowledge assets are oftentimes informal teams with participation from different parts of the firm and external partners. What these participants have in common is experience in a specific field. An obvious example is a sector team with participants from different asset classes. They can share their specific knowledge and views on developments in the sector, compare pricing differences, and determine where the best investment opportunities lie. The external partner could well be a specialist in the field and should therefore be included.[9] New knowledge is created when the participants start to make other investment decisions that differ from the ones they might make in the absence of knowledge assets. The most challenging problem is to measure the value add of knowledge management. Questionnaires are the easiest way to measure the value add. Research methodologies in social science will provide good insights, but advanced analytics will push these insights to the next level. For example, NLP could come of use once we start to link investment recommendations to investment performance. This will lead to a new and more detailed performance attribution approach. Moreover, it provides an opportunity to assess the investment skills of the investment managers. Currently, the performance attribution leaves too much room for interpretation and flawed beliefs on the investment manager's skill set.

TECHNOLOGY-SUPPORTED KNOWLEDGE MANAGEMENT

All organizations with a focus on knowledge management have created a corporate culture in which knowledge sharing is a "must" at all levels of the organization. It's embedded in personal development plans, career path, and compensation. Investment decisions are written up extensively, including assumptions and expectations. At regular intervals, these investment decisions are reviewed and lessons learned are shared with all stakeholders. From a technology perspective, there is no single technology market for knowledge management. Even Gartner, a public company specializing in technology research and consulting company doesn't produce a Magic Quadrant for knowledge management as there are too many solutions supporting knowledge management activities. Knowledge management can be broken up in different activities, each of which can be supported by different technologies to generate, capture, and distribute knowledge; there is no single all-inclusive knowledge management technology. At PSP Investments, we have been leveraging different processes and technologies. For instance, we have launched a Capital Markets' Research Management System to centralize, organize, store, track, and distribute research produced internally, and, to a lesser extent, externally. In terms of requirements, we defined four major categories.

(1) Data search and processing
(2) Content creating
(3) Content consumption
(4) Management oversight

By analyzing the different vendors in the markets, we chose Bipsync as our research management systems because of its knowledge-sharing feature. Bipsync has allowed PSP Investments to build a centralized hub to share curated investment research and insights through thematic pages, intelligent searches, and tags capabilities with all users. Bipsync has allowed PSP Investments to better generate, collectively, new investment ideas to be shared (curated view). The other big technology stack that we are leveraging is Microsoft applications. Microsoft has invested significantly in their knowledge management capabilities. Our approach to general knowledge management from a technology perspective is to make the best use of Microsoft 365. After all, this is the system the users were most familiar with. We are therefore leveraging SharePoint, Teams, Exchange, and OneDrive. Moreover, we started to experiment with Microsoft Viva Topics. Microsoft describes Viva Topics as "a knowledge management system that connects, manages, and protects knowledge and expertise from your organization". Viva Topics uses Microsoft Graph, Search, and ML to identify and connect knowledge across Microsoft 365.

THE SEARCH FOR ESG KNOWLEDGE

An interesting activity to discuss in the context of technology-enabled knowledge management is investments in climate change. Many investors started their ESG activities years ago as part of their stewardship role as an investor. Initially, good governance was the name of the game. In later years, the focus shifted to social and environmental issues too. Earlier on, we emphasized the differences between data, information, and knowledge. If we move to the bottom of the hierarchy, ESG data still primarily consists of qualitative data. Moreover, much of this information is "G" related. More "E" data becomes available, but the data on "S" is still very poor. Thanks to the surge in integrated reporting, these data points are placed in context by issuers to become information. Yet, the information is based on self-reporting and doesn't follow a market standard. ESG knowledge implies that we fully understand the topic and that we can apply this knowledge correctly in our decision-making. And this is exactly where we struggle. Using the definition of knowledge, we firmly belief that ESG is the right thing to do. But is it justified? It is true that more scientific evidence has emerged regarding the benefits of good governance. And is it reliable? Most scientific work is reliable. Still, one of the good governance principles is that the chair and the CEO of a company should not be one and the same person. However, there are many examples of (private) companies with a stellar performance and where the chair is also the CEO of the company. Strictly speaking, this would falsify the theory. The ESG challenge going forward is first and foremost to collect more relevant data points, especially related to the "S" and the "E". For example, we have hardly any workable data on human rights and labor issues. This is also true for "diversity & inclusion", despite the growing attention it receives recently. The second challenge is to transition from this data into true knowledge.

CLIMATE CHANGE IN FOCUS

More recently, climate change has become the ESG focus point. At the time of writing this chapter, COP26 just took place in Glasgow. The reactions in the media are mixed, as there seems to be less willingness by participants than expected to commit to specific climate change targets. From a knowledge perspective, this doesn't come as a huge surprise. We all agree that we should fight climate change, but there is still a lot of uncertainty regarding the right way forward. Yes, we have enough evidence to believe in global warming. Moreover, we have evidence that global warming is directly linked to GHG emissions. But what is the right approach to deal with this problem and what is our knowledge on the topic? Let's follow O'Leary approach and determine what an investment management firm can do to get more grip on its climate change knowledge.[10] The very first step is to make sure that we know who has specific knowledge on the topic. The responsible investment team or ESG team comes directly to mind, but there are multiple other sources too. The investment team focusing on real assets, whether infrastructure, natural resources, or real estate, must have encountered transactions dealing with green assets and/or the transition of brown into green assets.

An obvious investment area in this respect is renewable energy. Studying the investment cases must lead to insights on how renewable energy contributes to a lower carbon footprint. Venture capital could be another source if the investment team invests in new technologies to capture carbon emission and/or make assets more carbon efficient. The listed equities investment team is yet another source: equity analysts should have a good view on how listed companies deal with ESG issues, including climate change. And last, but not least, a thematic research team could assess available external research. For example, the International Energy Agency and other scientific institutions provide valuable insights. This quick and dirty inventory will already lead to an impressive collection of internal knowledge sources. However, the problem is that all these sources have their own specific views and approaches and do not necessarily work together. The available knowledge needs to be organized, which is part of O'Leary's step 2. The different data sets and documents available need to be combined into one centralized depository. This requires a dedicated technology approach as many sources aren't using the same text format, and data/information is often not standardized and/or irrelevant in another context. To a large extent, it is about data cleansing and interpreting documents to assess its external validity. Advanced analytics can help enormously to do the job. Once this is done, step 3 comes into play: the formation of a knowledge asset, being an intra-disciplinary team with a common focus. The purpose is to complement each other, fill knowledge gaps, and to create new knowledge. Step 1 already provided insights who in the organization has relevant knowledge on the topic and therefore should be considered part of the knowledge asset. External sources should be considered too. Especially, when specialized external managers have been selected[11] to form strategic relationships on the topic. External sources could also include universities and memberships of institutions such as the World Economic Forum. The collective knowledge on climate change will grow and new knowledge is created, simply by having discussions and combining different perspectives. Technology plays an important role as data scientists help to select the appropriate new data sets to test new hypotheses and assumptions. Moreover, the knowledge should be embedded in the different systems. For example, ESG data needs to be linked to specific holdings and combined with performance data to be able to assess specific ESG strategies. Moreover, by including only carbon emission data in the portfolio management system, we learn what the impact of our investment decisions is on the portfolio's carbon footprint. And in order to test the impact of climate change scenarios on the total portfolio, we need the right functionalities in our systems. This is all easier said than done; the biggest challenge related to climate change is that it is still a nascent discipline. There are a lot of known unknowns and even unknown unknowns. For example, there is no agreement on the right methodology to measure a carbon footprint. Moreover, sustainability ratings of different suppliers tend to rank companies in complete opposite orders (see Johnson & Swanepoel, 2021), and international policies on climate around the world are not aligned. It could well be the reason why COP26 might not have been as impactful as hoped for, as it relies on O'Leary's step 4. This last step deals with measuring the impact of the knowledge. However, the body of knowledge related to climate change is currently much less sophisticated than the body of knowledge related to other investment themes. Knowledge management related to climate change seems to be between step 3 and step 4; we're still in the process of completing the full body of knowledge and learning to apply what we know on climate change in the best way possible.

SUMMARY

We started the introduction to this chapter with the question on how difficult investing really is. Globalization, free capital flows, and the surge in information technology and computing power have made the world of investing more transparent but also more complex. The efficient market hypothesis makes even more sense now than when it was introduced several decades ago due to the quicker price discovery processes but at the same time more challenging because of the increased complexity. Irrespective of the right answer, the conclusion of this chapter is that in the current day, investing cannot take place without relying on data and technology. We choose to discuss technology as an enabler of the investment process, but technology is equally important for client servicing and investment operations. We touched on the increasing amount of available data, especially due to digitization. But, the abundance of data also triggers the question what to do with it. We can easily claim "more is less" if the data is useless for the decisions we need to make. Data scientists bring in the human judgment in this respect. New technologies such as AI are potential game changers as it will allow us to analyze more data and in a different way than before. The expectation is that these new technologies, or advanced analytics, will provide us with new insights to improve our investment process. Yet, the jury is still out: we do see papers and articles expressing successful implementations, but we don't read about the many failed attempts. In the second section of this chapter, we argued that knowledge management is crucial for investment managers to be successful. It touches on the idea that successful investment strategies and investment decisions should be not only fact based but also tested for validity. A different way of saying the same thing is that we should strive for the highest academic rigor. Given the complexity of today's investment world, we cannot rely on narratives and gut feeling anymore. Building up collective knowledge, instead of relying on the sum of the individual knowledge, is crucial to create new knowledge. This chapter talked about ESG activities specifically because of the nascent nature of these activities. Much of the data is still based on self-reporting, measurement methodologies differ greatly, and national ESG policies have not been synchronized yet. The discussion on the closing statement at COP26 is telling in that respect. So, what does this all mean for a skillful investment manager? In line with Monk and van Gelderen (2016), we would typify a skillful investment manager by the ability to act on changing market conditions by creating new superior knowledge and abandoning obsolete knowledge. The true impact of skills on investment performance, it turns out, is largely dependent on an organization's ability to foster enduring and valuable knowledge and to adjust investment strategies accordingly. To do so, technology should be fully embraced; it's the only way forward to maximize the value add of human decision-making.

NOTES

1 PSP Investments is responsible for the investments of the post-2000 liabilities of the Canadian government's pension plans. All information related to PSP Investments in this chapter is presented solely to support the narrative of the two authors and is not an official positioning of PSP Investments.
2 This title is borrowed from the book by Ashby Monk and Dane Rook (2020), which provides an excellent overview of how technology is shaping the investment world.
3 As Rebonato (2007) points out, this very low-frequency data makes it almost impossible for analysts to determine the true trend in the company's earnings.
4 Here, the assumption is that the anomalies are not correlated with general market movements.
5 One area of further development is related to private assets and the integration of public and private assets in a portfolio management system. Given that the price discovery process and asset pricing models for private assets are very different from public assets, the integration of both is not a trivial task.
6 Data generated by computer simulation as an alternative to real-world data.
7 We use risk in case the outcome is unknown, but the probability distribution governing that outcome is known. In case of uncertainty, both the outcome and the governing probability distribution are unknown.
8 Obviously, this requires a safe environment and corporate culture in which people feel free to speak up and make mistakes.
9 See Monk and van Gelderen (2019) on the role of strategic partnerships.
10 This part is, to a large extent, based on the experience within PSP Investments. The use of technology plays an important role in all steps described.
11 In this respect, PSP Investments works closely with TPG and Brookfield to invest specifically in opportunities related to climate change. These opportunities are asset and benchmark agnostic and therefore fall outside of the mainstream asset mandates.

REFERENCES

Agrawal, A., Gans, J., & Goldfarb, A. (2018). *Prediction Machines; the Simple Economics of Artificial Intelligence*. Cambridge, MA: Harvard Business Review Press.

Bodie, Z. (1999). *Investment Management and Technology: Past, Present, and Future*. Available at: https://ssrn.com/abstract=178629 (Accessed: 6 January 2022).

Ellis, C. D. (1998). *Winning the Loser's Game; Timeless Strategies for Successful Investing*. New York: McGraw-Hill.

Huij, J., & van Gelderen, E. (2014). Academic knowledge dissemination in the mutual fund industry; can mutual funds successfully adopt factor investing strategies? *Journal of Portfolio Management*, 40(4), 157–167.

Johnson, D., & Swanepoel, J. (2021). *ESG: Changing the Landscape of Investing.* Available at: www.aima.org/article/esg-changing-the-landscape-of-investing.html (Accessed: 6 January 2022).

Kaplan, S. N., & Schoar, A. (2005). Private equity performance: Return, persistence, and capital flows. *Journal of Finance*, 60(4), 1791–1823.

Koedijk, K., & Slager, A. (2011). *Investment Beliefs; a Positive Approach to Institutional Investing.* New York: Palgrave Macmillan.

Lo, A. (2004). The adaptive market hypothesis: Market efficiency from an evolutionary perspective. *Journal of Portfolio Management*, 30(5), 15–29.

Lowenstein, R. (2001). *When Genius Failed; the Rise and Fall of Long-Term Capital Management.* New York: Random House.

Monk, A. H. B., & Rook, D. (2020). *The Technologized Investor; Innovation Through Reorientation.* Palo Alto, CA: Stanford Business Books.

Monk, A. H. B., & van Gelderen, E. (2016). Knowledge management in asset management. *The Capco Institute Journal of Financial Transformation*, 43, 93–105.

Monk, A. H. B., & van Gelderen, E. (2019). *Filling Knowledge Gaps via Networking and External Partnerships.* Available at: https://ssrn.com/abstract=3331643 (Accessed: 6 January 2022).

Nonaka, I., & Takeuchi, H. (1995). *The Knowledge Creating Company: How Japanese Companies Create the Dynamics of Innovation.* New York: Oxford University Press.

O'Leary, D. E. (2002a). Knowledge management in accounting and professional services. In V. Arnold & S. G. Stutton (Eds.), *Researching Accounting as an Information Systems Discipline.* Sarasota, FL: American Accounting Association, pp. 273–283.

O'Leary, D. E. (2002b). Knowledge management across the enterprise resource planning systems life cycle. *International Journal of Accounting Information Systems*, 3(2), 99–110.

Rebonato, R. (2007). *Plight of the Fortune Tellers: Why We Need to Manage Financial Risk Differently.* Princeton and Oxford: Princeton University Press.

Schelling, C. M. (2021). *Better Than Alpha; Three Steps to Capturing Excess Returns in a Changing World.* New York: McGraw Hill.

Taleb, N. N. (2004). *Fooled by Randomness: The Hidden Role of Chance in the Markets.* London: Penguin.

Taleb, N. N. (2008). *The Black Swan; the Impact of the Highly Improbable.* London: Penguin.

10

Finance, Sustainability, and Technology

Co-Evolution in Asset Owners' Context

Winston Ma*

SUPER ASSET OWNERS

Who holds power in financial markets? For many, the answer will probably be the large investment banks, big asset managers, and hedge funds that are often in the media's spotlight. But increasingly a new group of long-term investors, which includes some of the world's largest sovereign wealth funds (SWFs), public pension funds, and central bank reserve funds, have emerged to become the very influential capital markets players and investment firms, with more than $30 trillion in assets under management ("super asset owners"), according to the data compiled by Global SWF in 2021.

Decades ago, these super asset owners were few, lightly staffed, and seemingly one step behind their more adventurous institutional fund peers. Today, they have transformed themselves from remote passive allocators to local, direct, active investors fostering the tech unicorns and displacing public markets as the most important sources of capital. The shift in the risk profile of their investments, from safe, real assets to the frontiers of tech innovation suggests that across the board these long-term investors are "grown-up" investors that will play a leading role in the forthcoming digital economy.

* Winston Ma, CFA is Founding Partner of CloudTree Ventures and Adjunct Professor at the NYU School of Law on sovereign wealth fund (SWF) topics. He is former Managing Director and Head of the North America office at China Investment Corporation (CIC) and the author of *The Hunt for Tech Unicorns* (2020).

DOI: 10.4324/9781003262039-12

This chapter will illustrate their two important and directly linked roles in the global digital economy: the new venture capitalists and ESG guardians.

THE NEW VENTURE CAPITALISTS—"UNICORN MAKERS"

Given their typically global mandate and long-term investment horizon, the asset owners increasingly build their portfolios based on major future trends rather than on short-term market movements. Furthermore, they are not just passive actors affected by global megatrends; instead, they actively influence the megatrends by their investments. For example, Temasek of Singapore has identified six structural trends, which collectively define the direction of its investment strategy: "Investing for a Better, Smarter, More Sustainable World" (see Figure 10.1).

Digital transformation of the world economy is arguably the most important global trend today, and that is the new investment frontier for these super asset owners. Their ample resources and long time horizon, as well as their need to diversify globally and by sector, have helped to transform the private markets for digital companies. They have helped create and sustain an environment that has fostered the rise of the likes of Uber, Alibaba, Spotify, and other transformative players in the digital economy, as well as the well-known unicorn-maker, the Softbank Vision Fund.

Because of their large portfolio size, these super asset owners tend to write bigger checks into tech start-ups than typical venture capital (VC) funds in the Silicon Valley. For example, in 2018, Ant Financial, the fintech arm of Chinese e-commerce giant Alibaba, raised around $14 billion in what market watchers called the biggest-ever single fundraising globally by a private company (according to market data firm Crunchbase, $14 billion amounted to the largest confirmed single fundraising round in history). Thanks to the billions of investments from Singapore SWF GIC and Temasek, as well as Canadian pensions like CPPIB, the fundraising valued the company at over $150 billion, making Ant Financial the highest valued unicorn in China (and the world).

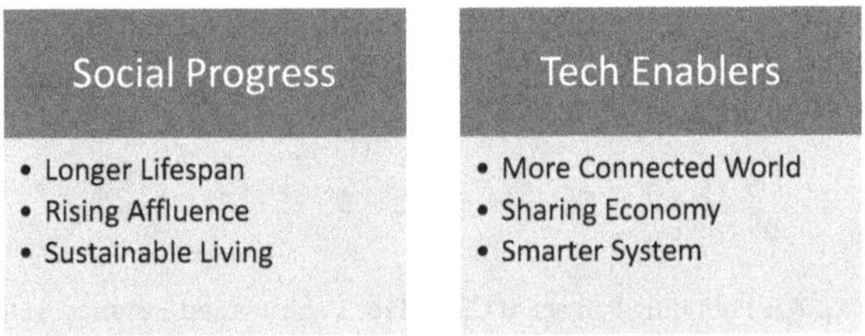

FIGURE 10.1 Temasek Identified Six Structural Trends

But what has fundamentally changed the venture investment landscape is the $100 billion Vision Fund that Saudi SWF fund PIF jointly established with Mubadala (SWF fund of UAE) and Japanese telecommunications giant SoftBank Group in 2017. To put things in perspective, in 2018, the entire VC fund industry was reported to have raised a total of $53.9 billion, slightly over half of Vision Fund's war chest. The scale and speed of Vision Fund investments across the globe is the best example how the super asset owners have altered the VC ecosystem as the powerful "unicorn makers."

ESG GUARDIANS

For decades, many of these long-term funds preferred to remain in the shadows. Little was known about them, and their nature on the long-term helped keep it this way. In recent years, however, the nature of these investors has begun to evolve. Alongside accumulating a large and growing pool of capital, these asset owners have transformed operations in three critical ways: attracting better talent, adding more asset classes, and expanding into active investment strategies.

No longer simply channeling their trillions through Wall Street handlers, these asset owners have instead become active, direct investors. As they get involved in their portfolio companies directly and deeply, the long-term investors are also becoming key arbiters of ESG and SDG principles. As major holders of equities, they have weighed in on sustainability, governance, climate change, and more. In doing so, they have united across continents, giving one voice to their trillions as they speak to the companies with whose management they engage.

For example, on climate change, the most significant movement is the One Planet SWF Working Group formed by six hydrocarbon wealth powers (Norway and five Middle East funds including ADIA, KIA, PIF, QIA, and the more recently joined Mubadala) and the New Zealand Superannuation Fund (NZ Super). Representing several trillions of assets under management, the funds held the One Planet Summit on December 12, 2017, which was followed by the Climate Finance Day (building upon the success of the 2015 Paris Agreement to collectively mitigate the effects of climate change), and the working group was established at the event.

For the asset owners, climate change is both a financial risk for long-term portfolios and an opportunity, as the development of technology and changes in government policy create new avenues for investments. During the transition to a lower-carbon economy, long-term investors have embraced opportunities ranging from solar and wind energy infrastructure in both developed and emerging markets to early stage venture investments in the battery and mobility sectors.

For example, combining big spending on direct investments with promotion of ESG goals, a pair of deep-pocketed asset owners, GIC (Singapore) and ADIA (UAE), have teamed up to back green, sustainable energy in the developing world. Both participated, in 2019, in a nearly $500 million equity round to back a pair of green energy projects totaling $2 billion in India. This brings their aggregate investment to $2.2 billion in the issuer, Greenko Holding. With the latest round, Greenko Holding will be developing the two (2.4 gigawatt total) projects, each with wind and solar generation and hydro energy storage. GIC is the majority shareholder of Greenko, which holds the record for Asia's largest green bond issuance at $1 billion.

Besides being the only non-oil SWF fund in the One Planet working group, NZ Super signed onto a broader grouping launched at the same time which is more favored by pension funds. Characterized by *Bloomberg Business Week* (2019) as "the biggest, richest, and possibly the most benevolent bully the corporate world has ever seen," *Climate Action 100+* has been signed by more than 450 investors from across dozens of countries, who collectively control more than $40 trillion in assets, including prominent pension funds such as ABP, BCI, CDPQ, CalPERS, GPIF, ISIF, and OTPP. They have pledged to work with their investee companies to ensure that they are minimizing (and disclosing) the risks and maximizing the opportunities presented by climate change.

Now the tech revolution is presenting the same mix of opportunities and risks for the asset owners. On the one hand, investing into the high-growth tech sector can diversify their portfolios and generate superior financial returns. Given both their capital power and long-term investment horizons, they are best positioned for financing such digital infrastructure (such as smart cities) that is critical for a sustainable global economy (Kamiya & Ma, 2019). On the other hand, major technological and disruptive innovations are disrupting traditional industries, putting asset owners' existing portfolio companies at risk. They must act to "future-proof" their portfolios, as well as their own operating models. As will be seen in the next section, these long-term investors are all rushing into the digital economy revolution.

Naturally, the asset owners' dual roles of new venture capitalists and ESG guardians met in the emerging digital economy. This chapter will analyze long-term investors' growing impact on the "new economy" ESG topics in three key directions.

FIRST, SETTING ESG STANDARDS IN THE CYBERSPACE

The long-term asset owners' size alone means that their actions, collectively and even individually, can have material impacts even when the intent is simply prudent management. They expect ESG to be an integral part of corporate strategy. That includes making expenditures to address ESG issues, while clearly communicating the rationale and benefits to the business strategy.

For example, Norway's fund NBIM holds, on average, 1.5% of every listed company on Earth, making it an investor that boards around the globe must heed (see Box 10.1). Leveraging its ESG experience from the carbon energy sectors, similar responsible investing actions are being taken by the Norwegian NBIM, and it was not shy about voting against management of Google, Amazon, and Facebook.

Box 10.1 Talk Versus Walk

There are two main approaches that these institutional investors deploy when they seek to influence the strategies of their portfolio companies. To achieve ESG aims, for example, they may remain as shareholders or (co-)owner and engage with the top management and boards of such companies in order to reduce emissions (the "talk" channel). Or, they can "vote with their feet," by divesting polluting companies from their portfolio (the "walk" channel).

NBIM is well positioned for active engagement with public companies' management. By most accounts, its $1 trillion plus portfolio holds, on average, 1.5% of every listed company on Earth. NBIM's report on responsible investing released in March 2020, covering its 2019 voting, engagement with management, and follow-up, runs to over 100 pages. Of the more than 9,000 companies in which it holds voting shares, NBIM cast votes in more than 97%, and it was not shy about voting against management even in its top holdings, such as Google, Amazon, and Facebook.

For climate change, NBIM has exercised both options: on the one hand, engaging with companies developing strong decarbonization strategies; and on the other hand, divesting from heavy polluters like coal and fossil fuel companies. An ongoing and intriguing debate among asset owners is whether it is better to divest or better to engage. In practice, many asset owners use both channels and typically start with "talk."

Another digital economy ESG play was led by NZ Super. A March 15, 2019 shooting massacre at two mosques in Christchurch, New Zealand, left 51 dead, and horrifyingly, it was livestreamed on Facebook and disseminated on Twitter and YouTube. In a swift and focused response, NZ Super took the lead in organizing a campaign, *Christchurch Call*,[1] which set out voluntary commitments for governments, companies, and wider society to work together to eliminate terrorist and violent extremist content online—the world of

Facebook, Google (YouTube), and Twitter. The $40 billion NZ Super has taken the lead in promoting this powerful trend, and *Christchurch Call* is the first global coalition to campaign about social media issues. After launching *Christchurch Call*, NZ Super quickly rallied the major New Zealand institutional investors; within a week most had signed up to support the cause. By the end of 2019, 102 asset managers from around the globe, controlling more than $13 trillion in assets, have signed up.

Their actions reveal a major shift: ESG-conscious asset owners are starting to campaign for a sustainable cyberspace, using tactics developed from "green investments" in sectors relating to fossil fuels and climate change. Until recently, the New Zealand and Norway funds are best known for their decarbonization efforts. Both have integrated climate risks into their investment processes thoroughly and systematically. NZ Super has developed low-carbon portfolio strategy for its whole portfolio, and NBIM divested thermal coal positions from its holdings.

Now they are focusing on the major tech companies, which reflects the increasing sophistication of the SIF investors, because tech companies are often deemed to be greater ESG pioneers than many other sectors. That's most obvious for the E (environmental) aspect. For example, Google and Apple have built green headquarters. The tech industry in general has earned (relatively) high ESG scores because innovations tend to do social and environmental good. For example, a December 2019 report commissioned by the telecom industry estimated that the use of mobile technology enabled people to reduce greenhouse gas emissions by 2,135 million tons in the previous year, the size of Russia's annual emissions.

The asset owners are looking now at the social (S), and more fundamentally, the governance (G) issues of the digital economy. The rapid pace of technological advancement, especially artificial intelligence (AI) and machine learning (ML), is creating disruption and anxiety in the society. At the same time, the institutions that have traditionally had the responsibility of shaping the societal impacts of new technology are struggling to keep up with its rapid change and exponential impact. Through their influence on tech companies, the asset owners can join efforts with government and society stakeholders to usher in a sustainable digital transformation.

As tech giants such as GAFA (Google Amazon, Facebook, and Apple), as well as numerous AI-driven start-ups (some of which may quickly emerge as dominant global players), gather ever more data about their users, they are increasingly shaping people's lives and politics. For new investments, these long-term investors' ESG policies have led to greater scrutiny of the tech companies and impact of their innovation, especially their dealings with data privacy, information security, and their role in enabling government and corporate surveillance, at a time data is viewed by many as the "new oil" of the "new economy," as well as playing a key role in controlling pandemics. For existing portfolio companies, they take on more active governance roles to mitigate and even pre-empt advanced tech's negative externalities on society.

SECOND, USING TECH TO BECOME BETTER ESG/SDG INVESTORS

Amid disruptions from new technologies, the sustainability of the world economy is critical for the asset owners that seek long-term, sustainable returns from their investments. Consequently, most SIFs make global tech investments, either through external funds or directly; at the same time, they are integrating ESG factors into their investment process, leveraging tech capabilities for data analysis.

For example, in July 2018, One Planet published an Investment Framework designed to accelerate efforts to integrate financial risks and opportunities related to climate change in the management of large, long-term asset pools like those of asset owners, including the following aims:

- Foster a shared understanding of the key principles, methodologies, and indicators related to climate change;
- Identify climate-related risks and opportunities in their investments; and
- Enhance their investment decision-making frameworks to better inform their priorities as investors and participants in financial markets.

One Planet hopes that more asset owners and then the general institutional investors' industry will adopt the Investment Framework. Its success, interestingly, is dependent on data and technology. That's because across the industry, high-quality company-level environmental data—for example, those relating to carbon emissions and environmental impact—is still not readily available.

To make informed investment decisions, investors demand timely, relevant, accurate, and complete climate-related data. As such, the Investment Framework encourages long-term investors to adopt agreed standards that promote the disclosure of material climate-related data. With the help of big data technology, the investors collectively would improve the volume, quality, and consistency of financial data to promote ESG investments effectively.

APG, the pension manager for ABP and a few other Dutch pension schemes, is another great example. APG expresses its commitment to responsible investing by codifying such investing within one of its nine headline investment beliefs, and it has used digital tech for implementation.

For instance, relating to the ESG and SDG discussions in the previous section, whereas some asset owners say they are waiting for standardized data or more academic proof to implement ESG strategies, APG has used AI to select companies that contribute sufficiently to the UN SDGs. They use this by ingesting vast amounts of structured and unstructured data. Responsible investing experts have trained the machines to identify potential Sustainable Development Investments (SDIs), including to which SDG they contribute.

Recognizing that this challenge is common across other asset owners, APG decided to spin out this intellectual property (IP) to the SDI Asset Owner Platform. With PGGM (NL), Australian Super, and BCI (Canada) joining the SDI Asset Owner Platform, the ambition is to utilize technology to its fullest and refine and extend the algorithms in a transparent way, thus fulfilling their fiduciary duty in an efficient way. With the end product of SDI classifications and the underlying data being available via regular market data distributors, the SDI Asset Owner Platform aims to set a broad standard used by a broad group of investors. This further creates a lever in the engagement of the long-term asset owners and their asset managers with their holdings and to monitor and steer their portfolio on investing into the SDGs.

Identifying SDI is only a fraction of how technology can and is applied. Alternative data in combination with AI and ML is now starting to get fully embedded in managing the portfolio and portfolio risks. Applications adding climate risk overlays on the global positioning system (GPS) locations of physical assets in the investment portfolios are getting more common. This has now unleashed also in the ESG domain an all-out race on access to alternative data and the talent required to create value out of it (Monk et al., 2019, 2021). Next to the war on tech talent, APG hired a meteorologist to their responsible investing team for interpretation of the climate data. This emphasizes the commitment these long-term asset owners have to become better ESG/SDG investors.

Another example is CIC, China's sovereign wealth fund (CIC, 2020). In 2020, following a review of peer experience and their own practices, CIC formulated an ESG investment policy framework to take sustainability into account throughout the lifecycle of their investments. Take Logicor, a large portfolio of logistics assets in Europe, as an example. After completing its investment in Logicor, which manages an extensive network of over 600 properties across 17 countries in Europe, CIC encouraged Logicor to develop stronger ESG policies, formulate an ESG development strategy, and publish regular ESG reports. These include leveraging new technologies to boost resource utilization efficiency and curb energy use and greenhouse gas emissions.

THIRD, USING TECHNOLOGY TO IMPROVE THE ESG OF THE LONG-TERM ASSET OWNERS THEMSELVES

The use of technology is increasingly prevalent not only on the ESG investment side but also on the operation of the asset owners themselves. For example, the participant side of pension funds. In 2020, four major Dutch pension providers, APG, Blue Sky Group, Nationale-Nederlanden, and PGGM, launched *Mijnwaardeoverdracht.nl* (MyValueTransfer). The joint initiative optimizes value transfers using decentralized technology, which is also known as blockchain. Already about 50 percent of the participants can use the platform. In the near future, more pension providers will join the platform, which will further increase its reach.

A value transfer is the transfer of an accrued pension pot from a previous job to the pension pot of a new job. Until now, arranging a value transfer has been complicated and time-consuming. The site connects the administrations of parties in the pension sector with decentralized technology. In this way, all the information is available at once to compare the various options and to transfer the pension.

The platform is one of the first blockchain-based applications available to the general public. The participating parties jointly designed the platform. Because all parties exchange the necessary information in real time, they reduce the turnaround time of a value transfer from nine months to approximately 30 minutes. In a clear step-by-step plan, the pension saver compares the current and old pension scheme and can thus make a well-considered choice. The decentralized setup also safeguards the privacy of users of the platform, which has been determined by independent auditors. In short, new blockchain technology can speed up and simplify a process for the pension saver while achieving efficiency at the back end.

These asset owners are now investigating where this philosophy can be put to further use. For example, one pension policy requires pensioners abroad to make an expensive and sometimes dangerous annual trip to an embassy. A digital app then makes it possible to provide this proof once before being shared with the required parties, instead of the participant going through the currently lengthy process with each party separately.

CONCLUSION

The world's long-term investors have shaken off their traditional, passive investor roles and stepped into the vanguard of the digital transformation we are all living through. As increasingly active investors, they can increase engagement with the companies in which they hold meaningful stakes—especially in the emerging tech unicorns. They are becoming new "ESG guardians" by applying their expertise from carbon energy sector into the new digital economy. Using new technologies, the asset owners are becoming better ESG investors across the board.

As long-term investors, they can reap higher long-term returns of environmental, social risk-adjusted portfolios, and ESG engagement. And given the funds are some of the world's biggest investors, their ESG positions can affect how quickly corporations put their businesses on a more sustainable footing. As the long-term investment capital of the world, how they respond to ESG matters will have long-term positive impact in the corporate world.

However, there is an acute paucity of ESG data, calling the asset owners working with the tech sectors beyond investment relationship. There is a lack of long-term empirical evidence that links ESG criteria to financial returns and demonstrates outperformance compared to mainstream investments. The good news is that investors are at a unique moment in time when technology has become applicable to real-world and real-time scenarios as they now have access to sufficient computing power, connectivity, and effective algorithms to analyze data.

As seen in many examples of this chapter, the super asset owners are also investing in digital technologies for their own investment capabilities. They reorganize their ESG investment efforts based on the convergence of technological innovation and data, which is altering how investments are not only conceived but also implemented. For example, AI and ML are used to improve and even guide decision-making, and during such a process, long-term, high-quality ESG data may actually emerge from these long-term investors' in-house IT systems.

Moving forward, long-term asset owners will increasingly lead ESG and the SDGs in the digital economy, relying on AI to monitor the conduct of portfolio companies, chiding the management of others, and rebalancing their portfolios to de-risk them for climate change and technological disruption. Where appropriate, they will not hesitate to create platforms as lever for the impact they can and want to have. The future of investing is at an inflection point, and these long-term asset owners are becoming guardians for both global climate change and our digital future. Given their long-term perspective in an increasingly shortsighted world, we should be happy to have them picking up this role.

NOTE

1 www.christchurchcall.com

REFERENCES

Blomberg Businessweek (2019). *Climate Group With $32 Trillion Pushes Companies for Transparency.* Available at: https://twitter.com/BW/status/1116321522778505216 (Accessed: 10 January 2022).

CIC (2020). *2020 Annual Report.* Available at: www.morefay.com/AR2020/EN/mobile/index.html (Accessed: 10 January 2022).

Kamiya, M., & Ma, W. (2019). Sovereign investment funds could be the answer to the SDGs. *World Economic Forum.* Available at: www.weforum.org/agenda/2019/12/sovereign-wealth-funds-sdgs/ (Accessed: 7 January 2022).

Monk, A., Prins, M., & Rook, D. (2019). Rethinking alternative data in institutional investment. *Journal of Financial Data Science*, 1, 14–31.

Monk, A., Prins, M., & Rook, D. (2021). Data defense in sustainable investing. In H. Bril, G. Kell, & A. Rasche (Eds.), *Sustainable Investing.* London: Routledge, pp. 263–284.

11

A Digital Twin for Finance

Artificial Intelligence Supporting the Implementation of Environmental, Social, and Governance Targets

Christof Mascher

INTRODUCTION

With the progress of information technology, the advancing digitalization, and in particular the development of Artificial Intelligence (cognitive and autonomous computing), subsystems of the economy—the markets—are developing digital ecosystems that replicate individual economic and societal segments as referential worlds. These virtual representations are using different layers of digitalization: data, generated from the physical world, are translated into information, describing the real world, which is then transformed into knowledge to form the basis for potential decisions. Such digital ecosystems and their concatenated replications are "based on the idea that a digital informational construct about a physical system could be created as an entity on its own"—according to Grieves and Vickers (2016: 92).

"The idea that the information about a physical object can be separated from the object itself and then mirror or twin that object is a concept referred to as the *Digital Twin*" as described by Grieves (2019: 270). A Digital Twin is a virtual representation of an object or a system, a real-time digital counterpart updated from real-time data, that uses simulation, machine learning, and other Artificial Intelligence to support decision-making. Grieves (2014: 1) has summarized this in the Digital Twin concept model: "It contains three main parts: a) physical products in Real Space, b) virtual products in Virtual Space, and c) the connections of data and information that ties the virtual and real products together."

DOI: 10.4324/9781003262039-13

Solutions like the Digital Twin, and in this context the intensive application of Artificial Intelligence, are paving the way to a new approach of a *fundamental business transformation*. The broad adoption of this new generation of systems and tools supports companies and entire industry sectors alike to achieve substantial productivity gains unlocking efficiency potential to significantly improve their performance level. Ultimately, digital disruption leads to the transformation of the business models of the affected industries, as portrayed by Christensen and Raynor (2003) or Siebel (2019).

Digital ecosystems adopting the Digital Twin concept to financial markets in a first step mirror or replicate the physical "real" market and, in a second, but crucial movement, upended this model: changing the mirror to a digital master platform. This concept of the Digital Twin model—first developed and successfully implemented for the manufacturing industry—will facilitate a sophisticated interplay of information technology, Artificial Intelligence, digitalization, and sustainability. With this approach, there will be the possibility to integrate the *principles of responsible management as drivers of economic transformative disruption* into digital platforms: digital management and *environmental* and social stewardship—a foundation for sustainable finance.

Such an economic disruption in combination with business transformation leads to the option of Schumpeter's creative destruction. A creative destruction that could fundamentally change the financial and consequently the economic system as highlighted by Moloi and Marwala (2020: 91, 110) to unlock implementation of environmental, social, and governance targets.

The Digital Twin concept provides a new view on planning and steering options of physical systems and thus economic markets. This concept offers the possibility not only to replicate the actual markets and their economic events but also to actively influence them and to subsequently generate controlling effects. These active steering and influencing options raise the question of the role of Artificial Intelligence in this context. Searle (1980: 417) introduced the differentiation of "cautious" (or weak) as "very powerful tool" and "strong" Artificial Intelligence as "a mind" with understanding and other "cognitive states". This chapter is using the "cautious" meaning: Artificial Intelligence and the Digital Twin framework are used as powerful tools of creative destruction.

This chapter first demonstrates, based on affinities between financial services and information management, the application of tools of information technology, notably Artificial Intelligence, in various areas of the financial services industry to optimize existing value chains. In addition to optimization, the consequent application of Artificial Intelligence and extrapolation of digitalization *steers the heading* to a fundamental business transformation driven by digital ecosystems. A description of the Digital Twin concept ecosystem presents the basics and the components of the model. The Concept Model describes the importance of architecture and the role of data in combining physical and virtual spheres and in expanding digital ecosystems with novel information streams, with Artificial Intelligence serving as a decisive tool to master the challenge of quantity and quality of data. The model could change the product creation and simulation process fundamentally, thus laying the foundation, forming the basis and framework conditions for incorporating a controlling possibility of intervention, especially in the sense of the principles of a sustainable, socially responsible, and governance economy. This development can help to improve resource consumption and reduce waste, enhancing the management of physical resources, contributing to sustainable and responsible social measures.

DIGITAL INFORMATION MANAGEMENT AND FINANCIAL SERVICES

Value creation in the field of financial services is inextricably linked to the global use of information technology. The financial industry replicates developments from a vast variety of economic sectors. This behavior is characterized by successive technical "revolutions" and business transformations. First, it is based on large-scale harmonization and standardization, without which the great productivity potential of automation could not have been harvested, nor accomplished. Second, the technological development of hardware and software, the development of semiconductors, computers, the Internet, cloud, sensors, and Internet of Things (IoT) that were accompanied following the logic of Moore's law by a dramatic reduction in unit prices has made the ubiquitous use of information management technology possible. This far-reaching standardization in conjunction with extensive automation, achieved through the intensive use of information technology, is now being further developed into a truly digital and fundamental business transformation through the data-based interconnectedness of objects and people, supported by Artificial Intelligence.

This extensive establishment of information technology, supported by an ever-increasing use of Artificial intelligence, can be observed in all sectors of the finance industry (banking, insurance, investment—and asset management) and across the entire chain of value creation—planning, development/design, product (business innovation), marketing and sales, production/operation, customer services, and corporate functions. In addition, driven by the specific nature of products of the financial services segments—predominantly intangible, they represent information about objects of economic life—the combination with digitalization favors a new dimension of flexibility. The data modules of this information describe the characteristics, status, connections, and transactions of the underlying assets. Data elements and the language connecting them are essential tools of information technology. Their application to any subsystem (economic system, social system, ecosystem etc.) is information management. In this sense, financial services management has always been—and still is—information management and thus predestined for the use of the developments in information technology.

This holds true even more regarding data as a digital representation of objective reality. "Sometimes a difference in degree (in other words, more of the same) becomes a difference in kind (in other words, different than anything else)." Brynjolfsson and McAfee (2016: 54) have described this "digitization of just about everything"—the translation of physical objects, products, services, and information into data—as fundamental enabling force. But beyond that, products, services, or transactions keep permanently adding information and producing data on their own, thus "adding value to existing products and services and potentially changing the value proposition to customers by harnessing information in some way" as highlighted by Peppard and Ward (2016: 210). This supplementary information strategy, first coined by Zuboff (1988: 10) as "informating," is a complimentary force driving together with the IoT the emergence of digital ecosystems. IoT data delivered by myriads of sensors, the digitalization of everything, and "informating" from the wrapping of physical objects with a data layer is essential for the formation of digital ecosystems.

APPLICATION OF ARTIFICIAL INTELLIGENCE IN FINANCE—EXAMPLES

Risk Analysis—Digital Platform

Detailed information about risk and its development over time constitute the fundamental basis for the entire finance industry. Financial and economic risk information describe the objects of finance. And these objects of the financial services industry—this applies similarly to banking, investment, and asset management or insurance—can be produced on a large scale, any changes can be closely observed and measured. Information about these objects and respective trends and changes is replicated as data. This lays the foundation for both historic analysis and future prediction.

Historically, information-intensive industries such as the finance industry have collected and stored such data over decades. Now, in the "second machine age," these traditional sources of information are complemented with unprecedented quantities of structured and unstructured data. This explosion of data volumes is described by Brynjolfsson and McAfee (2016: 66): "The digitization of just everything—documents, news, music, photos, videos, maps, personal updates, social networks, requests for information and responses to these requests, data for all kinds of sensors, and so on—is one of the most important phenomena of recent years." And "As more data become available and the economy continues to change, the ability to ask the right questions will become even more vital" (p. 123).

One differentiating technology to cope with both this quantitative and qualitative challenge is Artificial Intelligence. Different types of sensors, covering the entire range from a device to the communication of a person (voice and text), produce this data and make it available to digital business models. These models are used on a large scale in insurance and asset management and support detailed analyses of risk structures and risk profiles. With machine learning or deep learning, they help to identify hidden patterns and complex relations. Lastly, the integration of real-time data adds high complexity to digital platforms and thus opens the door to a new level of product design using Artificial Intelligence. Examples are sophisticated investment products, bundling information of various sources (information or investment objects) in combination with forecast models to potential customer portfolios or, in insurance interactions, of treatment methods and medications or constitutions of patients for health insurance products, health care, and its related services.

As a digital replication of the underlaying business world, a comprehensive digital platform allows for a completely redefined product design process, supported by Artificial Intelligence in a layered approach. First, by identifying the individual (risk) objects and the connected financial prediction (forecast). Second, based on this first layer, by bundling and designing new products. This allows not only to understand the historical development of risks and products but also to prototype new products (strategies) and execute back-testing and simulations of these new offers.

Telematics—Digital Product

Telematics is an interesting example of "informating to add value to services" (Peppard & Ward, 2016: 212) in motor insurance. IoT sensors and smart technologies monitor the movements and activities of the object vehicle (autonomous driving also uses this data) as well as the driving style and behavior of the driver. This connected and almost real-time information about object and person can replace the traditional risk parameters like location, age, driving experience, or history of claims.

Based on the sensors' data, the assessment of the specific risk and a new calculation of the risk price (premium) can be executed. Further, options for risk avoidance (advice and assistance function) as well as behavior change (driving style) are encouraged and linked. Drivers can "learn" via apps and adjust their driving style. Less risk-prone driving is rewarded by correspondingly reduced insurance premiums.

New insurance products such as "Pay as you drive" or "pay how you drive" are offered by insurance companies. Respective collected data are used to enrich services, for instance, in car theft detection or prevention. Further, the evaluation of claims or car damages can be supported, and garage and repair services can use these data to minimize the cost of repair. Telematics is an excellent example of the cross-divisional transformation potential of the use of IoT, data analytics, machine learning, and Artificial Intelligence tools: new product features, adjusted risk measurement and prizing, new customer services, and digitized business processes. The traditional approach to just simply digitizing existing products, services, and business processes is replaced by disruption—finally resulting in new business models using data and information to design new products, customer services, and business processes.

Claims Management—Digital Service

A particularly impressive demonstration of how the use of Artificial Intelligence can increase productivity levels is the area of claims and benefit management in the insurance sector. Damage to houses or apartments but also to cars can be quickly detected and precisely described by using various sensors. Image recognition systems, based on machine learning and deep learning tools, are used to examine, identify, and categorize claims. Preassessment of claims and the damage evaluation process can be automated: a faster, better claims management process with fewer errors (for example, in motor own-damage insurance processing: images of damaged car parts can determine the type and the size of a damage and subsequently accurately calculate the costs of repair). This allows for essential steps in the workflow to be automated and dramatically accelerated.

Fighting claims fraud, insurance companies use predictive analysis supported by Artificial Intelligence tools to identify patterns of irregular or fraudulent behavior. Minimizing fraud is a substantial lever to reduce insurance premium—and waste.

Sensors in cars can detect and predict damage or, for instance, an imminent wear and tear that can result in damage, if not repaired in time (the parallels to the predictive maintenance of a machine park in other industries are obvious). Checks and replacements can be organized on an as-needed basis to avoid damage. In the event of damage occurred, the remedy (on-the-spot repair, pick-up service of the garage, organization of the repair) can be initiated and carried out based on an automated report.

In living spaces, sensors can detect damage caused by the monitored objects themselves (water breakage, fire etc.) as well as damages caused by external events (natural events such as wind, fire, flooding, but also theft and burglary) and initiate necessary damage containment measures, notify emergency and rescue services, and ultimately start claims processing. Data and information of these objects build an image of the object to be protected. This representation of the object (virtualization) forms the basis for action and reaction to protect or minimize damage to the object itself and to the people living in them.

OPERATIONAL RISK MANAGEMENT—IN IT, CYBERSECURITY, DATA PRIVACY, AND COMPLIANCE

The finance world is a business with extraordinary security needs—this is true not only for IT security including cyber threats but also for data compliance and data privacy. The task of protecting the assets of companies and customers in data centers, networks, personal computers, and business software systems has become paramount. The ubiquitous presence of network access points, smart and connected devices and machines and their connection (IoT etc.), and communication to and with multiple exchange points has become a game changer and has created a completely new risk scenario. New vulnerabilities have been added to the existing ones, attacking customer services and products directly. Distributed denial of service (DDOS) or ransomware attacks do not only compromise IT infrastructure, IT systems, or backup services but also block essential customer services and thus bear huge financial risks for corporations.

Artificial Intelligence is redefining the defense mechanisms and cybersecurity walls. Machine learning tools in combination with data analytics can be implemented, continuously monitoring the various activities, status, and behavior of devices, analyzing potential patterns, identifying malicious software like viruses or malware components. "AI-based approaches are able to recognize anomalous patterns as they arise. They do so by calibrating models based on network traffic behavior and scoring anomalies according to the extent to which they deviate from the norm" (Daugherty & Wilson, 2018: 56). According to Daugherty and Wilson (2018: 56), this modelling is "redefining an entire industry." Such a digital model is based on data of existing objects, enriched with analytical insights and design information, and is building a platform that helps better identifying the risks of the physical world and additionally digitally defines actions for protection within the real world.

Digital models and digital modeling are used in a broad context. Customers expect their products, communication, and data to be safe—but not in a restricted IT-understanding. Data protection and data compliance can be supported with digital models using Artificial Intelligence tools, identifying new patterns, and implementing best practice protection measures. Next to addressing IT-only areas like data privacy, digital models can be leveraged for regulatory affairs or even product security.

Anti-money laundering and financial fraud fighting are major concerns for financial companies. With massive use of algorithms, machine learning, speech recognition, or neural networks evaluating huge amounts of structured and unstructured data, Artificial Intelligence enables a totally different level of automation and sophisticated execution to identify potentially fraudulent activities. With the integration of analysis of unstructured data of external sources (i.e., media) new content and quality levels can be targeted: eliminating redundancies, identifying new customer behaviors, or reducing the noise of so-called false positives, thus reducing massive process costs.

Risk models and in particular financial risk models are digital representations of "real" risks: from threats connected to network access points, devices, the overall IT infrastructure, and systems to data protection, data privacy, and compliance to external and internal procedures like anti-money laundering or fraud management, these financial risk models are founded on digital modeling based on real data, managed and reinforced by machine learning and other Artificial Intelligence tools, supporting the design of products and services and guiding remediating measures. These models are based on replicated data of the physical sphere, augmented with analytical insights and design knowledge. They help to create digital platforms that do not only support a better understanding of the real world but furthermore identify design choices and measures for the real world.

INTRODUCING THE DIGITAL TWIN FOR THE DIGITAL PLATFORM FOR FINANCE

The aforementioned examples of applying Artificial Intelligence in the value creation of the financial services industry show similarities to endeavors in the manufacturing industry. As described by Fraunhofer Institute—see Spath et al. (2013)—in Germany, the term "Industry 4.0" was coined. This term describes the comprehensive digitization strategy of the manufacturing economy which led to substantial optimization. Impressive transformation results have been achieved by using the interconnection of IoT and Internet of People (IoP) based on digital data provided by sensors, smart devices and machines, and information from humans.

It is time for information-intensive industries such as finance to start undergoing a similar fundamental digital transformation. Such a fundamental change toward a new digital business model should replace the existing overly hesitant and fragmented approaches, which still largely are optimizing only paper-driven processes. New technology should not just simply be added to the existing landscape—no "lipstick" approach, but as sketched by Guillebaud (2016: 137), a modified platform must be built as "higher purpose," using components like digital modeling, virtual engineering, or a Digital Twin.

What is common to these methods is the digital mirroring—initially coined by Gelernter (1991)—of the physical world, the digital replication of physical objects. In the manufacturing industry, these approaches—especially the Digital Twin—have been successfully implemented. Prominent examples are General Electric with the Predix platform or Siemens with the Mindsphere platform.

Digital Twin Concept Model

"A Digital Twin is a digital representation of a product instance (real device, object, machine, service, or intangible good) or an instance of a product-service system (a system consisting of product and associated service)." This is the definition of the Scientific Society for Product Development, according to Stark et al. (2019: 1).

As mentioned, the concept of the Digital Twin was first developed for the manufacturing industry. The following remarks are based on the work of Michael W. Grieves and John Vickers as outlined in Grieves (2014) and Grieves and Vickers (2016) and aim to transfer the concept of the manufacturing to the financial industry.

In manufacturing, the Digital Twin works as a virtual representation of a physical machine or good. This virtual replication maps the respective states of an object and thus allows predictions about the behavior of the replicated object system. This opens new perspectives for simulation (testing) but also for the timely evaluation of changes (decisions) in the object system (almost at runtime). According to Grieves (2014: 1), the "Real Space," the "Virtual Space" as corresponding counterparts and the "connections of data and information" are the three fundamental pillars of the Digital Twin Concept Model (see Figure 11.1).

The "mere" digital replication of physical systems is extended by the active interaction (communication) between the physical real system and the virtual digital ecosystem. The connections between the physical/real sphere and the digital/virtual sphere are twofold: data flowing from the physical/real sphere to the digital/virtual product and information available from the digital/virtual product to the physical/real environment. The data streams in this figure that flow from physical object to virtual space, forming there a replication of the object system, are called digital shadow. Information and processes that flow from virtual to physical space, taking over control tasks, are called digital triggers. The virtual object taking over the leading role is also described as digital master. Stark et al. (2019: 1) explain the difference: "The digital master contains the product geometry as well as behavioral models of this product or system." A Digital Twin therefore can be started from a digital master or can be generated from a digital shadow.

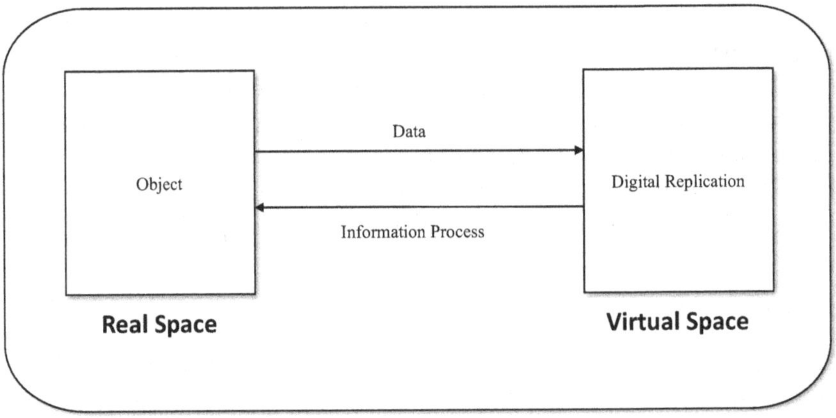

FIGURE 11.1 Information Mirroring Model
(Source: based on Grieves, 2014: 2.)

The Digital Twin contains both subsets or instances—the digital shadow as replication of the real product and the digital master as leading object. The interplay between these different digital subsets and as well as between the physical and virtual worlds is based on the digitization (data) of the physical products on the one hand and the digital information generated by the digitized virtual products about the production process—or generally the information of the respective digital ecosystem—on the other hand. This data collection and the common architectural link ensure the applicability of this multi-way connection between physical and virtual sphere (including the different subsets of the digital twin). Grieves (2014: 3) describes this as Unified Repository of virtual and physical worlds: "Both virtual development tools and physical collection tools would populate the Unified Repository." Replication, real-time simulation, digital prototyping, digital product design, digital engineering, testing, back-testing, and so on are all based on permanent interaction and communication of virtual and physical spheres—all these methods would finally support the transfer of solutions and products, designed at the digital master level, to the real physical system.

Digital Twin for Finance

Considering the nature of the financial industry as an "information copy/replication" of the economic world, it almost comes as a surprise that the Digital

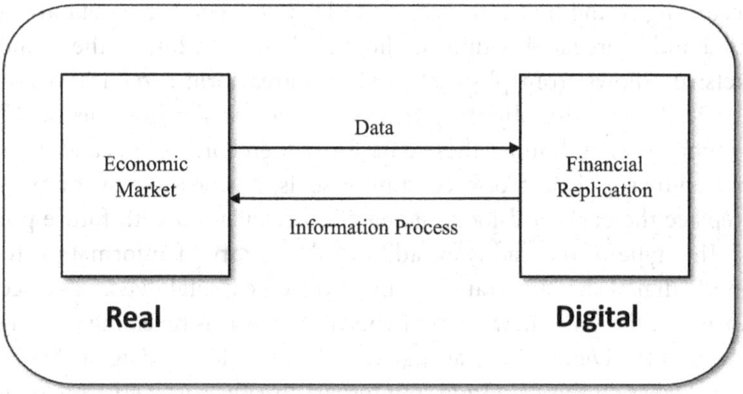

FIGURE 11.2 Financial Digital Twin
(Source: in analogy to Grieves, 2014: 2.)

Twin Concept Model has not been transferred sooner (data rich, intangible products etc.). Introducing and applying the Digital Twin concept via data replication and informating follows a stringent approach.

In a first initial step, the finance Digital Twin will copy the manufacturing Digital Twin: the data describing the "real" economic system of markets are replicated into a "virtual" finance system and these data, in combination with information flows originating from the finance digital ecosystem, are the glue between the real and the virtual finance world (see Figure 11.2).

All sources of information describing the conditions and changes of the economic world are needed and form the basis for the development of the Digital Twin for finance. The amount of data required and the complexity of the data connections pose enormous challenges to management and technology. Technical and scientific breakthroughs like cloud computing, IoT, or machine-readable data (big data) were preconditions to meet this challenge of scale. With these significant achievements, data became for the first time "digital" and thus manageable with the means of Artificial Intelligence, in particular machine learning and natural language processing. Additionally, traditional financial service companies have been categorizing automatically huge amounts of data, as Kai-Fu (2018: 110) has explained: "For instance, insurance companies have been covering accidents and catching fraud, banks have been issuing loans and documenting repayment rates, and hospitals have been keeping records of diagnoses and survival rates. All of these actions generate labeled data points."

According to the first instance of the Digital Twin, these data are accumulated and aggregated within the finance digital shadow of the economic markets: the flows from physical to virtual area form a replication of the economic or business object system. Artificial Intelligence tries to eliminate human bias and mines these data for hidden correlations and patterns. Supported by sophisticated forecasting models, it is possible to complement and replace the backward-looking analytical calculation with future predictions. This type of data adds an additional category of information to the economic digital shadow, transforming it into the digital master as a second instance. The design of new components or products is reversing the original approach of the Digital Twin as digital replication: for the Digital Twin, it is irrelevant whether the economic counterpart already exists. A new product in planning stage—a digital prototype as a third instance of the Digital Twin—can already own its own Digital Twin structure. Grieves and Vickers (2016: 96) defined the Digital Twin Model Lifecycle and stated, "that this conceptual model was and is intended to be a dynamic model that changes over the lifecycle of the system."

The relation between economic or business systems and finance systems needs to be captured as a data-driven "digital" one. This "digital" data must be understood as essential building blocks that do not only reproduce the economic world in a digital shadow or are subsequently created. This would be a reactive approach and insufficient. In contrary, based on bidirectional interfaces, the interactions of the Finance Digital Twin and the economic subsystems—digital shadow and digital triggers—reflect differences and deviations of the real from the virtual system. The "designing" finance system takes over control tasks and starts corresponding correction and regulation requests. This transforms a digital shadow as first instance into a digital master as second instance of the Finance Digital Twin. The thus generated added value not only provides a better exchange of information but also opens the option of a real digitally driven design of the financial services subsystem. In this creation phase, the digital prototype as third instance of the Finance Digital Twin is shaping the design of new developments. Hence with this, the Digital Twin Model for finance enables the integration of advanced simulations into both the "past" (back-testing) and into the future (prediction).

The three digital instances of the Digital Twin—digital shadow, digital master, digital prototype—together with the economic markets form the basis of the virtuous cycle of the Finance Digital Twin (see Figure 11.3). The digital replication of economic systems is extended by the active interaction between the virtual digital ecosystem and the physical real system—the Finance Digital Twin Concept Model.

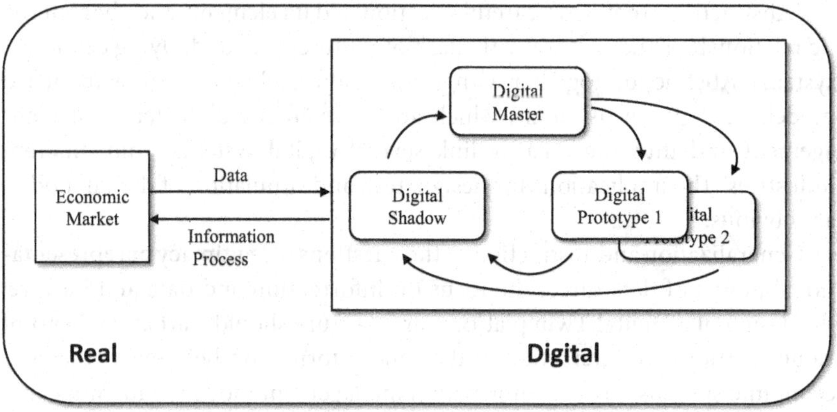

FIGURE 11.3 Interaction Within the Financial Digital Twin

The Digital Twin Concept Model allows to understand and manage better the complexity of real economic movements. But the crucial test of applying the Digital Twin Model to finance is the correct integration and connection between virtual and physical "economic products": the financial generalization of the business activities and products.

Data replication of the physical in the virtual world and vice versa as typical challenge of a Digital Twin in the manufacturing industry does arise in a modified form within finance: it is not about "only" representing a machine or a supply chain through data but about the information world of the economy, which itself represents to a certain extent a description of the underlying real economic systems (and thus uses elements of replication). This leads finally to a semantic question of a correct *generalization*: does the "translation" of the "virtual" finance layer—despite the huge amounts of data that are needed to represent the economic systems—correctly represent the "real" economy?

There is a second question. A Digital Twin, and in particular the digital master of a digital economic ecosystem, does not require all the basic data of the economic system or the economic subsystems. In comparison to the Digital Twin of the manufacturing industry, this is not a disadvantage—on the contrary. It is possible to focus only on data required by the financial digital ecosystem and eliminate unnecessary detailed information. Despite all the power of the cloud computing platform, this "abstraction" of the "focused" concept leads to a helpful significant reduction of data and size of models with positive implications on cost and performance.

"Abstraction" requires a careful selection of data elements and characteristic relationships that take over the task of representing underlying economic systems. Abstraction together with generalization allow to work with virtual models of digital ecosystems, which are more "focused" in terms of management and thus more easily link several digital systems from different industries. The implications for design, test, and simulation of digital models are obvious.

Generalization and abstraction or the questions of legitimacy or representational power of data direct the focus on information and data architecture: the design of a Digital Twin platform architecture should start at the heart of value creation: the interaction of data and information between virtual and economic systems. Precise information management models, data modeling, or the broad usage of knowledge graph concepts to support abstraction and generalization are the prerequisites for the suite of neural language processing, speech and image recognition tools etc. Without Artificial Intelligence the crucial management of interfaces based on uniform information and data architecture would not be possible and thus is of great importance for the connectivity and networking of digital ecosystems like a Digital Twin.

This information and data architecture enables supplementing information and additional basic data: missing or newly identified data needed to complement the Digital Twin can thus be added to the model. This architectural principle ensures a controlled and structured growth and expansion of the digital platform.

Next to this vertical addition or integration of data, there is a horizontal effect: the integration of digital systems of different economic industries. This means that cross-sectoral coupling of subsystems—economic sectors—can be considered, too. Grieves (2019: 178) describes this horizontal integration as aggregation of Digital Twin Instances (DTI): "Digital Twin Aggregates (DTAs) are the aggregation or composite of all the DTIs." The "focused" finance Digital Twin Concept Model offers much potential in this respect for new levels of productivity. More importantly, this horizontal integration of systems, reflecting different markets, is a key success factor for the implementation of principles of sustainable management.

The information and data architecture structures *feedback* loops and controls of the financial Digital Twin. The architectural design defines the formal framework that enables feedback procedures: test, simulation, steering, and control (information trigger), replication of the "real" world of the economy: data that "fills" this structure and connects physical and virtual worlds. This data household, permanently enriched by both the economic and financial (virtual) sides of the Digital Twin, can be used to run tests, simulations, backtests, and to generate improvement proposals, which can be applied to the original economic systems.

Design and Product Development as Decisive Components of the Digital Twin Finance

The potential and power of the financial Digital Twin concept can be aptly demonstrated by its design and product development capabilities. This can be derived from the interaction of the triad of digital master, digital prototype, and digital shadow.

To understand economic and financial trends or future developments of companies (predictions), huge amounts of data, even data of not used so far or new sources, are used as part of a new "experimenting" process to generate and extrapolate answers to these questions. The digital shadow offers the database for developing an understanding of connections and interdependencies of individual trend lines and whatever extrapolations or developments within the digital master might have been unnoticed otherwise. Various analytical output (supported by Artificial Intelligence) of this research will be integrated into the digital master, forming the basis for testing new opportunities for designing products (risk or investment objects), based on options for new and unexpected prototypes and better hypotheses: digital prototypes and digital shadows will enable better tests and based on the data of the shadow will create more accurate insights. The use of Artificial Intelligence in these different stages of the ecosystem of the financial twin—observation, replication, hypotheses generation, back-testing, testing and simulation, and permanent repetition—will drive the identification and combination of new alternatives, better product design, and stimulate steering signals back to economic markets: creating digital prototypes. Combined with the increasing availability of customer data, this will lead to a new level of product customization and delivery.

Continuous observation (data-based analysis replacing intuition) of the behavior of risk or investment objects ("products") of a real economic market, reflected in its Digital Twin, enables recognition of behavioral abnormalities and the initiation of reactive measures. As part of an active flow back of expertise within the framework of the Digital Twin, the acquired knowledge must be actively used in the sense of "feedback to design." Therefore, the Digital Twin will be used in the future for optimizing current products as well as for new developments.

Digital shadows representing the economic markets, digital masters, and multiple digital prototypes form a virtuous cycle, ultimately influencing the "real" economic markets and systems. There are two principal ways how this virtuous cycle of the Finance Digital Twin Concept Model is supporting the implementation of environmental, social, and governance (ESG) principles. With the translation of ESG values in data attributes, it is possible to identify financial objects (investments or risks) and their "ESG dividend" as part of the financial digital replication. In that regard, Artificial Intelligence helps to refocus resources into ESG high-value activities. In a second step, these financial objects can be combined and integrated into financial products—again, designed based on Artificial Intelligence analysis: trying to find best-case scenarios, redirecting investments, bringing better quality to markets faster. The simulation and combination of these components and their potential impact on environmental targets like efficient use of energy and raw materials or social goals such as health, safety, or diversity can be effectively integrated into the planning and steering effects of the Finance Digital Twin model.

The virtuous cycle of the Digital Twin is enforcing the implementation of environmental, social, and governance principles.

CONCLUSION

Peter Drucker has characterized the closing decades of the twentieth century as a period of radical change and disruption and predicted an "age of discontinuity." The explosion of information technology and in its core Artificial Intelligence disrupts both existing business models and entire industries. The forces of discontinuity are twofold: first, digitalization and its tools and methods—like the Digital Twin—is the motor of this fundamental transformation. Second, the shaping of new ways finally dematerializes and discontinues the traditional way of doing business. The transfer of the Digital Twin from manufacturing to finance industry supports this twofold discontinuity.

Digitalization is first virtualization (translating into data) and "informating" (adding data) and second "creative destruction" by applying the disruptive power of information technology. As mentioned, the three components of the Digital Twin: (1) replication of the "real" world, (2) designing and composing the new "ecosystem," and (3) simulation and testing the new artifacts in finance require a consequent and fundamental digitalization. If the working methods of the established approach are maintained and "digital" information is understood as a mere ex-post addition, the gigantic possibilities will remain unused. The conversion to a creative digital approach of the Digital Twin replaces the one-way communication with a bidirectional exchange of digital information, the "passive" replication with an active design possibility, thus inevitably changing the work processes. Also, for the genuine way of working of the Digital Twin, the separation between business and development is outdated and unproductively disturbing. The model of the Digital Twin for Finance does not only map the operational subsystem but, even more important, also intervene in the form of financial design and product decisions.

The implementation of industrial digitalization and the Digital Twin Concept Model is a real chance to radically change and improve economy and society. This opens up vast possibilities to truly progress the implementation of responsible management of resources by linking digital management and environmental stewardship. The virtuous cycle of the Digital Twin, based on Artificial Intelligence with embedded ESG steering, will enable to implement the decarbonization of industry to substantially increase the efficiency of resource consumption (land, water, material, food) and in particular all types of energy production and consumption.

According to Porter and Heppelmann (2015), as they reflect the "broader implications" of the radical digital transformation and the concerned product development, "A revolution is under way in manufacturing. The effects are not confined to manufacturing, however, but are spreading to other industries that use—or could use—smart, connected products, including services." This development will "change the trajectory of society's overall consumption. After decades of ever more, ever cheaper, and ever more disposable everything, businesses and consumers may well need fewer things."

REFERENCES

Brynjolfsson, E., & McAfee, A. (2016). *The Second Machine Age: Work, Progress, and Prosperity in a Time of Brilliant Technologies*. New York: Norton Paperback.

Christensen, C. M., & Raynor, M. E. (2003). *The Innovator's Solution: Creating and Sustaining Successful Growth*. Boston: Harvard Business School Press.

Daugherty, P. R., & Wilson, H. J. (2018). *Human + Machine: Reimagine Work in the Age of AI*. Boston: Harvard Business Review Press.

Gelernter, D. (1991). *Mirror Worlds: Or the Day Software Puts the Universe in a Shoebox—How It Will Happen and What It Will Mean*. Oxford and New York: Oxford University Press.

Grieves, M. (2014). *Digital Twin—Manufacturing Excellence through Virtual Factory Replication*. Available at: www.3ds.com/fileadmin/PRODUCTS-SERVICES/DELMIA/PDF/Whitepaper/DELMIA-APRISO-Digital-Twin-Whitepaper.pdf (Accessed: 31 October 2021).

Grieves, M. (2019). Virtually intelligent product systems: Digital and physical twins. In S. Flumerfelt et al. (Eds.), *Complex Systems Engineering: Theory and Practice*. Reston, VA: American Institute of Aeronautics and Astronautics, pp. 175–200.

Grieves, M., & Vickers, J. (2016). Digital twin: Mitigating unpredictable, undesirable emergent behavior in complex systems. In F.-J. Kahlen, S. Flumerfelt, & A. Alves (Eds.), *Trans-Disciplinary Perspectives on System Complexity*. Dordrecht: Springer, pp. 85–114.

Guillebaud, D. (2016). *Disruption Denial*. London: LID Publishing Limited.

Kai-Fu, L. (2018). *AI Superpowers: China, Silicon Valley, and the New World Order*. Boston and New York: Houghton Mifflin Harcourt.

Moloi, T., & Marwala, T. (2020). *Artificial Intelligence in Economics and Finance Theories*. Dordrecht: Springer.

Peppard, J., & Ward, J. (2016). *The Strategic Management of Information Systems: Building a Digital Strategy* (4th edition). Hoboken: Wiley.

Porter, M. E., & Heppelmann, J. E. (2015). *How Smart, Connected Products Are Transforming Companies*. Harvard Business Review Digital. Available at: https://hbr.org/2015/10/how-smart-connected-products-are-transforming-companies (Accessed: 31 October 2021).

Searle, J. R. (1980). Minds, brains and programs. *Behavioral and Brain Sciences*, 3, 417–457.

Siebel, T. M. (2019). Digital Transformation, Survive and Thrive in an Era of Mass Extinction. New York: Rosetta Books.

Spath, D. et al. (2013). *Fraunhofer Studie IAO: Produktionsarbeit der Zukunft—Industrie 4.0.* Available at: https://www2.iao.fraunhofer.de/images/iao-news/produktionsarbeit-der-zukunft.pdf (Accessed: 31 October 2021).

Stark, R. et al. (2019). *Digital Twin.* Available at: www.wigep.de/fileadmin/Positions-_und_Impulspapiere/Positionspapier_Gesamt_20200401_V11_final.pdf (Accessed: 31 October 2021).

Zuboff, S. (1988). *In the Age of the Smart Machine: The Future of Work and Power.* New York: Basic Books.

12

Efficiently Allocating Capital to Transition to a Sustainable Economy

Madelyn Antoncic

INTRODUCTION

Environmental, social, and governance (ESG) investing has been one of the most important topics in asset management this past decade. Not only have ESG retail funds and ETFs grown significantly over the past several years, but mainstream investors are increasingly incorporating ESG into their investment decisions given the expectation that ESG enhances performance.

Given the broad range of what it means to invest sustainably, including what has come to be known as "greenwashing," it is hard to pin down the precise size of the ESG market. Funds focused on ESG, as of the time of this writing, are reported to have hit $2.3 trillion in Assets Under Management (AUM), up from approximately $750 billion over the past five years, with European sustainable fund continuing to account for the bulk of fund flows according to Morningstar data (Murugaboopathy & Jessop, 2021). More broadly, the Global Sustainable Investment Alliance reported a third of invested AUM in five of the world's biggest markets now include some ESG focus through a less-well defined process known as 'ESG integration' as opposed to investing according to specific sustainability mandates (Jessop, 2021). While the trajectory of ESG points in the right direction, we'll need to triple the amount invested in clean energy by 2030 to contain climate change according to the International Energy Agency (Browning, 2021).

With all of the money being invested in ESG and with significant amounts of capital needed to achieve our collective goals, in this chapter we step back and look at whether all of the capital is being most efficiently allocated or if

DOI: 10.4324/9781003262039-14

the severe data problems and limitations in ESG reporting lead to unintended consequences and capital allocation distortions.

We begin with a brief discussion of the ESG evolution. Next, we turn our attention to the data and how data problems likely cause misallocation of capital. We then discuss where ESG reporting is likely heading over the next 18 months. We then turn to the potential, still evolving role of artificial intelligence (AI) and Natural Language Processing in distilling ESG data to help inform decision-making. We conclude with suggested enhancements and necessary steps needed to better allocate capital to help transition to a net-zero sustainable economy.

THE ESG EVOLUTION

In 2006, the late Kofi Annan, the United Nations Secretary-General, launched the Principles for Responsible Investment (PRI) supported by "leading institutions from 16 countries, representing more than $2 trillion in assets owned" (United Nations, 2006). The PRI provided a framework for institutional investors to take ESG issues into their investment decisions. The fundamental underpinning of the PRI was to encourage investing for long-term sustainable development rather than short-term gains.

Two years later, the tenets of the PRI and the need for taking a long-term view on sustainability took on a greater meaning and sense of urgency with the release of the United Nations Intergovernmental Panel for Climate Change (United Nations, 2007). This report linked human action to global warming and laid bare the need to address sustainability in a more systematic manner. Responding to this report, many national pension funds managing intergenerational assets and already keenly focused on driving long-term performance were interested in finding an investment instrument which could support climate change. This pursuit of an investment instrument led a group of Swedish pension funds to approach the World Bank Treasury and together they co-created the World Bank's first green bond "demonstrating the potential for investors to support climate solutions through safe investments without giving up financial returns" (World Bank, 2018).

At the same time, the advent of the Great Financial Crisis (GFC) brought to life the need for a greater emphasis on governance and protecting an entity's reputation, arguably one of its most valuable intangible assets. Poor governance was shown to have had direct and significant negative financial consequences for companies and their investors such as was seen with Lehman Brothers that suffered the largest bankruptcy in history (Antoncic, 2018).

In other words, so-called nonfinancial risks become financial risks (Antoncic, 2019a). This is more true today than ever before with global intangible assets, the majority of which are unreported on balance sheets due to accounting standards, were estimated to be $74 trillion in 2021, up 1,145% over the past 25 years (Brand Finance, 2021). As of 2020, 90% of the value of the S&P 500 was intangible assets, up from 68% over the past 25 years with the beginning of the wave of society broadly adopting technology and just 17% in 1975 (Ali, 2020).

This new focus on nonfinancial risks entailed a significant "shift from short-termism to focusing on the long-term sustainability of companies" and on the needs of all stakeholders. In other words, companies have to uphold their "contract with society in order to maintain their license to do business" (Antoncic, 2020).

Yet, while more than 3,404 organizations, 18% of which are asset owner signatories, from 135 countries, representing more than $121 trillion in assets as of March 2021, have become signatories to the PRI (PRI, 2021), up from just $20 trillion a decade ago, only a fraction of asset managers is truly "walking the talk."

In its 2021 Responsible Investing Survey of 805 respondents from around the world, RBC Global Asset Management found that while many asset managers and asset owners are signatories, when asked "to what extent are ESG principles used as part of your investment approach and decision making," only 28% responded "significantly" while 28% responded "not at all," and 44% responded "somewhat." Only 31% of the respondents said their investment policy addresses climate risk, with 60% responding No and 9% Not Sure (RBC Global Asset Management, 2021).

So why is this? Part of the answer can be found in the belief by some institutional asset owners and managers that ESG issues, also known as nonfinancial risks and opportunities, are in conflict with their fiduciary duties to act in the best interest of their beneficiaries. In fact, when asked what was the reason for <u>not</u> incorporating ESG factors in their investment approach, 39% responded it was inconsistent with their fiduciary duty while 26% responded it will not impact their investment returns. Fourteen percent cited it was not important to plan members and an additional 14% said they had insufficient resources to integrate ESG (RBC Global Asset Management, 2021).

Part of the answer can be found also in the lack of high-quality ESG data. When asked how satisfied are they with the current quality of ESG-related disclosure provided by issuers, only 23% responded very or somewhat satisfied, and only 20% said they were somewhat or very satisfied with the current amount of ESG-related disclosure provided by issuers (RBC Global Asset Management, 2021).

Yet, part of the answer is in where the rubber hits the road and where the real money talks: AUM fees. In fact, the results of the RBC survey are consistent with academic research which "conclude(s) that only select funds improve ESG while many others use the PRI status to attract capital without notable changes to ESG" (Kim & Yoon, 2020). Academic research has also shown even active managers who sign onto the PRI increase their AUM and increase their fees, yet also show no improvement in ESG issues such as in voting.

There is a growing profit motive on the part of investment managers in calling funds "ESG" or "sustainable." Labeling funds "ESG" adds about 5bps that a manager can charge in fees. Not only have there been recent reports about fund managers overstating their sustainability efforts (Kowsmann & Brown, 2021), but there has been a wider trend or renaming hundreds of funds with the ESG labels. ETFs have also been renamed to incorporate ESG labels and track new indices (Shifflett, 2021). This has all prompted the SEC to revisit the SEC "name rule" prohibiting materially deceptive and misleading names. Maybe that also needs a "new, truth in advertising, label" (Gensler, 2021).

An important implication of "greenwashing" is not only at the corporate reporting level but also at the asset manager level. We need a way to eliminate all "greenwashing" and better measure and assess how corporations are using ESG to drive policies and decision-making and how asset managers incorporate ESG risks and opportunities into their decision-making.

"IN GOD WE TRUST. ALL OTHERS MUST BRING DATA." (W. EDWARDS DEMING)

OECD estimates we will need $6.9 trillion a year to meet the climate and development infrastructure requirements to achieve the Paris Agreement and deliver on the 2030 Agenda for Sustainable Development (OECD, 2021).[1] Funding the European Green Deal is projected to cost $1.1 trillion in investments over the next ten years, on Europe's path to being the first net-zero continent by 2050 (Petrequin, 2020). And the previous UN estimate of a $2.5 trillion annual funding gap developing countries face in order to achieve the UN SDGs by 2030 (UNCTAD, 2014) could be $1.7 trillion higher per year, according to the OECD, due to COVID-19 emergency and response spending (OECD, 2021).

With the significant amounts of capital needed to achieve our collective goals, we need to ensure capital is being allocated efficiently to drive progress toward transitioning to a net-zero economy and delivering on the UN SDGs. The only way we can accomplish this is by having better quality data with which to make informed decisions at every level. The first step toward this goal requires harmonization of standards at the corporate entity-level reporting and better data from ESG raters, rankers, and score providers.

First, at the corporate entity level, there is a lack of generally accepted agreed-upon standards and reporting requirements. Corporations now largely self-report some ESG data, and while we have made significant progress over the past 18 months, there still are no agreed standards, but instead entities use a variety of methodologies, metrics, and approaches. Moreover, the data suffer from self-reporting bias since it is generally unaudited. In addition, ESG metrics are updated infrequently, typically on an annual basis; therefore, there is a lack of real-time data available for investing. Thus, investors "may be fundamentally constrained by a lack of high-quality, firm-level ESG data, to serve as key inputs in assessing, managing, and monitoring the ESG risks and opportunities that a company faces" (Antoncic, 2019b). Lastly, "the practice has been widely criticized for lacking the rigor of traditional financial reporting" (Antoncic, 2019b), which results in significant "green-washing" and data biases. ESG reporting needs to have the same robust processes, controls, and rigor with audit trails as in financial reporting.

There are four key issues which need to be addressed at the entity reporting level to address harmonization. First, there is no agreement across all of the stakeholders on the definition of materiality. This is largely driven by the fact there has not been consistent agreement across jurisdictions concerning the "users" and "use cases" of ESG data. Should the question of materiality be only financial? Should entities report only on how externalities impact the company? This is the narrowest definition of materiality and would not necessarily be helpful in directing capital to the best users of that capital to achieve the transition to a net-zero economy nor would it be useful to achieve societal goals. A broader and more widely accepted approach to materiality is the concept of "double materiality." Double materiality takes the approach to reporting on ESG issues that can impact the company as well as on how the company's actions can impact the environment or society. A less frequently used alternative approach to materiality, yet one which deserves serious study, looks at materiality dynamically. This takes the view that an ESG issue may be immaterial today but can become financially material in the future. This brings up the important concept of the inter-temporal nature of materiality which needs to be studied. Is ESG reporting meant to focus on the short term, the intermediate term, or the long term? Clearly, if ESG reporting is to be useful to determine capital allocation which has long-term implications one cannot just consider today's static view of materiality.

The second key issue which needs to be addressed to come to agreed standards is the question of universality. Is materiality different across different industries? Taking this approach, unless it was empirically statistically significantly proven, makes materiality subjective. A more widely held view is the concept of "universality," meaning materiality is not unique to an industry. Finally, the third issue which need to be addressed at the entity reporting level is the question of scope. This is the question as to which categories and how many categories should be included within each of the three ESG pillars: E, S, and G. The wide variety of categories used as well as the varying definitions of the same category at the reporting level by companies makes comparison of an ESG score difficult (Kotsantonis & Serafeim, 2019). This is a very important topic which doesn't get enough attention to which we will return.

While these issues are definitional with respect to ESG reporting, even if all of these issues were resolved and even if we had a global set of agreed ESG reporting standards and companies produced better ESG reporting data, there are still problems. At the corporate level, companies have inconsistencies in what they discuss in their ESG commentaries and what they include in their financials. According to a recent study by Carbon Tracker Initiative and the Climate Accounting Project (Hodgson, 2021), a review of 107 global companies in the carbon-intensive sectors (including energy, cement, and transport) revealed that more than 70% of the companies did not indicate whether they considered climate when preparing their 2020 financial statements. Moreover, nearly 75% of the companies had commentaries in the front of the report that were either not reflected in the financials or inconsistent using higher oil prices in the valuation of the assets and liabilities of the company. In addition, they found companies' assumptions about future oil prices used by oil and gas companies were sometimes "considerably higher" than IEA's "net-zero map to 2050." Yet, according to the study, the Big 4 Auditors rarely noted the discrepancies (Hodgson, 2021).

Lastly, we need more disclosure from the financial industry. Financial institutions are the enablers. Financial companies are failing to disclose information about their climate risk. The climate impact from almost all financial institutions is driven by their financed activities. Yet, according to Carbon Disclosure Project (CDP) (CDP, 2021), only 25% of financial institutions report on their financed activities. The financed emissions of these financial institutions are over 700 times *larger* than their reported operational emissions. Half of financial institutions did not conduct any analysis of how their portfolios impact climate change. CDP found the credit, and market risks identified as a result of this lack of analyses are up to $1 trillion.

Due to the lack of agreed ESG standards and the lack of consistently reported ESG data, major discrepancies exist across vendors who rate, rank, and provide company ESG scores. This has led to significant noise and a lack of useful ESG data for investment purposes. This is not surprising since ESG ratings can be only as good as the underlying data and the methodologies used.

Raters, rankers, and score providers use different frameworks and methodologies to impute missing data; different categories (scope) within each of the three pillars along with qualitative judgments on weighting the categories and metrics; and they use different key indicators and metrics. In addition, some data providers incorporate controversy data. One study has shown a significant amount of variability in a company's rating depending on the methodology a rater or ranker uses (Kotsantonis & Serafeim, 2019).

The outcome is poor correlation across raters for the same company. Berg et al. (2019) showed the average correlation across data providers for the same company was 54% while the range was 38–71%. They looked at the composition of what drives the differences in the scores and found three main drivers: scope—the number of categories within the three ESG pillars; measurement; and weighting of the categories (Berg et al., 2019). They showed the biggest driver of the difference in correlations is scope. The average difference across all raters was 35% for scope and measurement, respectively, and 4% for weight. However, for MSCI 50% of their difference is explained by scope and 33% for measurement and the rest by weight. While for ASSET-4 (Refinitiv) 25% of the variability is explained by scope while 38% is explained by measurement and the rest by weight. Finally, when the data providers create their indices they re-weight the scores to ensure "best in class" ESG companies in an industry are included in the indices.

While measurement differences are widely cited, there are other, more importantly intentional bias differences introduced into the scoring that really call into question the usefulness of using these ESG scores for capital allocation. OECD's research shows there are significant ESG rating biases built into the ratings and rankings against small and medium size enterprises (SMEs) (Boffo & Patalano, 2020). They show higher market capitalization and higher revenue companies consistently receive better ESG scores than lower market capitalization companies. Moreover, according to the International Organization of Security Commissioners (IOSCO), there is uneven coverage with certain industries and geographic areas benefiting from more coverage over others (IOSCO, 2021). All of these differences likely lead to material capital allocation distortions.

THE ROAD AHEAD

Due to these data problems and the need for better-quality, consistent, and comparable data, there is a growing movement toward ESG reporting standardization. However, the challenge in obtaining universal harmonization and convergence of ESG standards is complicated by different jurisdictions holding different public policy objectives and legal frameworks. In the US, for example, the SEC takes the position that "accounting financial standards do not seek to influence the outcome of investor capital allocation decisions or management activities (but instead) are for better reporting" (Peirce, 2021). On the other hand, sustainability standards evolving in other jurisdictions such as in the EU are designed to achieve specific objectives and economic activities. Disagreement as to the "users" and "use cases" across jurisdictions also contributes to different approaches in the evolving regulations on ESG reporting. Nonetheless, there are significant changes which will be in place over the next 18 months, some mandated by rules and regulations and others bringing convergence of voluntary frameworks.

First, IFRS formally launched the new International Sustainability Standards Board (ISSB) to develop a comprehensive global baseline of high-quality sustainability disclosure standard (IFRS, 2021). The announcement coincided with the UN COP26 climate change conference in Glasgow in November 2021. The ISSB will sit alongside the International Accounting Standards Board (IASB). The baseline disclosure standards will first focus on "E" (Environment) with uncertainties around ISSB's adoption of "S" and "G" given different social norms and different corporate ownership structures across different legal jurisdictions. These baseline standards will build upon standards coming out of various voluntary frameworks as well as on the Financial Stability Board's Task Force on Climate-related Financial Disclosures (TCFD) and work out of the World Economic Forum and apply the concept of "financial materiality," meaning they will focus on the needs of investors, not all stakeholders. However, "double materiality" is a broader definition of materiality and is widely accepted and more fully captures potential ESG risks and opportunities. It is notable that the Global Reporting Initiative (GRI), which is the standards framework covering the full spectrum of ESG issues and used by over 90% of corporations, is not joining in this consolidation. According to a KPMG 2020 survey of sustainability reporting, around three-quarters (73%) of the world's largest 250 companies and two-thirds (67%) of the 5,200 companies comprising the largest 100 firms in 52 countries now use GRI (GRI, 2021).

Separately, the European Commission is on its own very prescriptive path. The EU Taxonomy, which is a classification system, is designed to direct investments toward sustainable projects and economic activities to achieve the European Green Deal. The taxonomy provides a clear definition of what is "environmentally sustainable" and identifies six environmental objectives: climate change mitigation; climate change adaptation; sustainable protection of water and marine resources; transition to a circular economy; pollution prevention and control; and protection and restoration of biodiversity and ecosystems (European Commission, 2021).

Beginning January 2024, large companies based in the EU, EU subsidiaries, and all companies listed on EU-regulated markets in the EU (except micro-enterprises) must adopt the Corporate Sustainability Reporting Directive (CSRD) which amends the Non-Financial Reporting Directive (NFRD) and must provide limited assurance that an economic activity and project for which a company obtains funding makes a substantive contribution to one or more of the six environmental objectives laid out by the EU. In addition, all companies obtaining funding must meet the "Do No Significant Harm" (DNSH) criteria by showing the economic activity and project which is obtaining funding does not do any significant harm to the other environmental objectives of the EU. Moreover, these economic activities and projects must comply with the minimum human rights safeguards[2] and comply with the Technical Screening Criteria (still not formally agreed as of the time of this writing), which are a set of qualitative and quantitative criteria to determine whether an economic activity substantially contributes to the environmental objectives while DNSH to the others.

Parallel to this, asset managers creating funds in, or selling funds into, the EU as well as investors and pension funds are also subject to the Taxonomy. Beginning March 2021, investors were required to comply with the Sustainable Finance Disclosure Regulation (SFDR). Investors are required to take a phased-in approach initially showing compliance with the EU Taxonomy covering activities that substantially contribute to climate change mitigation and climate adaptation on a high-level, principle basis, known as Level 1. Beginning January 2022, investors will have to comply with Level 2, which requires an investor or asset manager to *show evidence of alignment* with the EU Taxonomy starting with those first two objectives. Asset managers must disclose how the ESG product they are creating "promotes" the environmental objective or how it "contributes" to the environmental objectives. Beginning in January 2023, asset managers must disclose how their products align with the other four objectives. For each product, investors have to document how and to what extent they have used the taxonomy to determine the sustainability of the underlying investments, calculated separately for each of the environmental objectives, and have to show the percentage of underlying investments that are taxonomy-aligned. By standardizing disclosure of a financial product, the SFDR aims to eliminate greenwashing.

Globally, many countries are implementing some corporate sustainability reporting requirements with some countries further along than others, but none has requirements as prescriptive as the EU Taxonomy. Some frameworks will be built around multi-stakeholder disclosure while the US rules will be built around investor protection. Many countries are mandating or suggesting compliance with TCFD, which is an overarching framework recommending disclosure across four categories: governance; strategy; risk management; and metrics and targets. However, TCFD does not provide any quantitative metrics or guidance. Some countries and stock exchanges require mandatory corporate sustainability reporting disclosures while others allow for a "comply or explain" provision.

Separately, with respect to the ranking, rating, and score providers, we likely should expect to see regulation and oversight of the data providers at least to the extent around controls and processes in a similar way as the credit rating agencies have been regulated post the GFC. Both IOSCO and the European Securities Market Authority (ESMA) have indicated an interest in examining the prospect of oversight given the significant variation across data providers' ESG rankings as well as due to the potential conflicts of interest arising out of the fee-based services on how to improve their scores that these data providers offer companies they rate and rank.

So, while significant progress has been made on corporate sustainability reporting and while we expect the next 18 months will bring the next generation of further enhanced reporting, there will still be large differences across jurisdictions. While this will all produce more data, for sustainability reporting we likely will still lack truly harmonized standards as we have in financial reporting. Moreover, sustainability reporting largely still lacks a "contextual framework," which we will discuss as one of the missing links to truly meaningful sustainability data. Therefore, the transition to a net-zero sustainable economy and achieving the UN SDGs will be hampered by a lack of comparable and consistent data, the first step toward contextualization, to enable the efficient allocation of capital.

CAN BIG DATA PROVIDE AN ALTERNATIVE TO MEASURING THE SUSTAINABILITY FOOTPRINT OF COMPANIES AND HELP OVERCOME EXISTING DATA SHORTCOMINGS FOR INVESTING?

As we move forward with the energy transition, we clearly need more and better disclosure to help stakeholders make better decisions about the allocation of capital to help drive progress. Clearly, there are consequences to the differences in company ESG ratings and rankings which likely cause capital allocation distortions. Mainstream investors are increasingly incorporating ESG into their investment decisions. Passive money is being invested and benched to ESG indices that are flawed not only due to methodology problems, but there are build-in biases toward large market capitalization companies away from SMEs, and there is uneven coverage of industries and geographic areas. As a result, companies which perhaps should not be included in indices are being included and thus are rewarded with higher stock prices as index trackers include those companies in their portfolios. By definition, given the fixed number of companies typically included in an index, this means that other companies which likely should be included are being displaced. Can technology provide the solution for ESG/SDG reporting, scores, rankings, ratings, and benchmarking?

The question of the impact of incorporating unexpected financial information on stock price adjustments and the profit opportunities that can exist during the adjustment process has long been of interest in academic research and financial markets (Antoncic, 1983). The impact of unexpected, nonfinancial information on stock prices and investing is only now evolving in theory and practice. A review of the literature on the uses of technology in finance shows various use cases across financial markets, banking and lending, internet finance, and credit service company, as well as fraud detection and risk management (Hasan et al., 2020). There are other potential use cases for big data, including for companies to assess their supply chain risks especially by monitoring their suppliers on human rights issues; for insurance companies concerning director and officers insurance both in their due diligence and in monitoring reputational risk issues among senior managers; and for corporate boards to understand how they compare with peers. Boards need to measure and understand their sustainability "reputational footprint" and benchmark themselves against their peers. Using Big Data and AI, a corporate board could integrate sustainability data into its business model and strategic decisions to give it a competitive advantage versus its peers (Antoncic, 2021a).

Drilling down more specifically to sustainability investing, one area Big Data and AI is playing a role is in sentiment analysis, which scores a company on the number of times certain ESG issues are mentioned. A company would have a positive sentiment score when the number of times there is a positive mention about an ESG issue exceeds the number of negative ESG mentions, divided by the total number of mentions. All else equal, this could provide a useful complement to the reported sustainability data. While corporations now largely self-report some sustainability data, due to the lack of standards and metrics along with significant "greenwashing" and self-reporting data biases, ESG scores contain a significant amount of noise and thus are of limited use for investment purposes. Big Data, can enhance reported data with "alternative data" by leveraging AI technologies, Machine Learning (ML), and Natural Language Processing (NLP) to cull through tens of thousands of news items, social media, and other venues in dozens of languages, providing up-to-date information for thousands of firms beyond what is in unaudited annual firm reports or firms' marketing efforts. Moreover, Big Data can make this information available daily for investors and all stakeholders—not just annually when a firm generates an unaudited sustainability report (Antoncic, 2020). A Big Data approach could reduce self-reporting bias and "greenwashing" and can show which firms are effectively having a positive or a negative ESG footprint thus enabling the integration of sustainability factors into the decision-making of global investors. Moreover, the use of large-scale unstructured data can provide more comprehensive and timely insights.

However, there are biases built into using Big Data to extract ESG sentiment through public information found in various news outlets including in social media. For example, Begenau et al. (2018) show the use of Big Data in financial markets has lowered the cost of capital for large firms, relative to small ones, enabling large firms to grow larger because larger firms produce more data providing Big Data technology more financial data to process, attracting more investor interest. That logic can be extended to the use of news reports, blogs, and other social media items Big Data use for ESG sentiment analysis because large firms are covered more broadly given their broad economic activities. All else equal, large firms typically attract greater analysis and media coverage than small firms and have more access to external PR and lobbying firms that can help put a positive spin on even the most negative information.

Second, there are scenarios where technology can go wrong or provide imperfect information relying on publicly available information such as newspaper articles, which may lead to false or biased scores. A perfect example of news which could lead to a positive sentiment score, and a positive sentiment momentum for some energy giants would be the news that they are selling billions of dollars of assets reducing their carbon emissions, while mining companies are exiting coal projects. Off-loading polluting projects as companies map out their future in a lower-carbon economy is seemingly positive news. However, these projects, and their emissions, are not being eliminated. Instead, these mature assets have high operating expenditures and are being sold to smaller and private companies, as well as to private equity firms sensing an opportunity to extract value while the marginal return for larger companies are too low to continue to invest in them. These smaller and private companies typically go under the radar when it comes to environmental scrutiny (Hodari, 2021). Clearly, Big Data sentiment analysis in this case could come to the wrong conclusion.

Going beyond just sentiment analysis and using Big Data to actually read Corporate Sustainability Reports (CSRs) is fraught with error problems. First, as discussed earlier, there are no consistent standards, metrics, or definitions of materiality or even of topics and categories. In addition to these issues, unlike with financial reports, CSRs come in too many varieties with reported numbers and metrics displayed in text, tables, inside images, figures, graphs, pie charts, and links. As with financial reporting, to be most useful whether to analysts and investors reading reports or for machines to scan and scrape reports, sustainability reporting needs to mature to the level of not only consistent standards but also consistent standardized reports. At the end of the day, there is no substitute for consistently reported ESG data and reporting.

A growing area of measurement in the sustainability space is a new approach of using technology to measure the economic cost of a company's activities on externalities. Research by environmental economists, at World Wide Fund for Nature (WWF), UK, has developed models which can calculate how a company's activities may present future risks and opportunities by measuring how its pollution or its water consumption, for example, impacts the environment (Balch, 2021). These models can show investors the monetary impact a company may have on externalities across the four main capitals: natural capital; human capital; social capital; and financial capital which may potentially become internalized through either regulation or reputational risks (GIST, 2020).

Technology and Big Data are providing the tools needed to measure the impact companies are having on the environment and society and to assess a company's impact-adjusted profits. The Impact Weighted Accounts Initiative (IWAI) is an initiative underway at the Harvard Business School that measures the environmental impact of companies on their revenue and shows, for example, a material reduction in reported revenue once the environmental impact is taken into consideration (Serafeim & Trinh, 2020). They are creating a methodology that can measure the financial impacts of various products across a company which goes beyond just measuring impact on the operational level.

The IWAI analyzed companies in their 2018 data set to calculate the true profitability of companies once they take into account the environmental costs the companies create. From their research they found that many companies' environmental costs exceed their total profits. They found,

> [O]f the 1,694 companies which had positive EBITDA in 2018, 252 firms (15%) would see their profit more than wiped out by the environmental damage they caused, while 543 firms (32%) would see their EBITDA reduced by 25% or more.
>
> (Cohen & Serafeim, 2020)

They noted that not all companies have a negative impact with some having a positive impact through their products and employment practices which are not reflected in their stated profitability.

WHERE DO WE GO FROM HERE?

While there has been significant progress on ESG reporting over the last couple of years, we still have far to go toward efficiently enabling a transition to a net-zero, sustainable economy. We have witnessed a bottom-up and a top-down evolution on ESG reporting, evolving from civil society and academics, to activist investors to mainstream investors. Investor engagement with public policy makers has helped influence regulators to become involved. Boards are beginning to adopt an ESG lens through which they drive policies and decision-making largely driven by investor demand for sustainability disclosure. Many boards are showing commitments, adding goals with more quantitative metrics and tying management compensation and even their cost of capital to achieving these goals. We have come a long way although there is more to do. Every board should have a sustainability committee, and boards should include people with ESG skills. The board must be engaged for ESG reporting to have any meaning. They have to set the tone. Nonfinancial metrics are equally as important as financial metrics and need the same robust processes, controls, and rigor as in financial reporting (Antoncic, 2021a).

Yet, all of this as well as harmonizing ESG reporting standards is only a first necessary condition toward truly efficiently allocating capital to help transition to a net-zero sustainable economy. In fact, without completing the puzzle, as a society we may be misallocating capital into the wrong companies and projects since we need scientifically based sustainable development measurement indicators that tie into sustainable "thresholds" or "outer boundaries."

Rarely do companies take into account natural boundaries and answer the question "Relative to What?". ESG reporting is usually measured in absolute terms: X tons of CO_2 emitted, Y volumes of water recycled; or as "intensity indicators," which are relative only to a unit of production or revenue. This approach to ESG reporting which fails to compare indicators to ecological ceilings does not take into account limited resources which have sustainability thresholds and outer boundaries that a company uses. This approach fails to take into account how a company is sharing those limited resources. Moreover, indicating and tracking *how* companies will transform to a sustainable economy is virtually nonexistent. In other words, we need to *contextualize* sustainability reporting in order for it to have real meaning.

Baue builds on prior work of others and lays out a framework based on a "Three-Tiered Typology" for tracking progress toward achieving sustainable development (Baue, 2019). Tier One indicators focus on the absolute or intensity indicators. This is what most companies report today although, as we discussed earlier, they still need to be harmonized and improved. But to have meaning, these indicators need to be contextual and make them relative to something. Contextualized Tier Two indicators take the absolute or intensity indicators and make them relative to sustainability "thresholds" in ecological, social, and economic systems. In other words, making the indicator relative to, and account for, boundaries that exist a company's Tier Two indicators allocate their "fair-share impacts" on common capital resources within the thresholds of their carrying capacities.[3] Tier Three indicators *track transformation* and are more qualitative in nature taking into account policy, process, practice, and perception (Baue, 2019).

Work is already under way at both the UN and multilateral organizations and the Global Thresholds & Allocations Council (GTAC),[4] a multi-stakeholder group established to provide an authoritative approach to reporting ESG performance in relation to generally accepted boundaries and limits. Their mission is to identify and validate thresholds determination and allocation methodologies and disseminate off-the-shelf methodologies which corporations and investors can use.

In other words, in order to truly walk-the-talk to efficiently transition to a net-zero global sustainable economy, we need to recognize there are ecological limits and take into account a company's fair share use of those limits, and we need to measure *how* sustainable development will be achieved from our current unsustainable systems.

REFRAMING THE CONVERSATION: SUSTAINABILITY STANDARDS-SETTING AND MEASUREMENTS ARE ECONOMIC ISSUES

What does this all tell us? Truly allocating capital to the best alternative uses to ensure a smooth and effective transition to a sustainable economy needs "new tools in the toolbox." Sustainability standards-setting and measurements are complex, scarce resource allocation issues that are being addressed by people in various fields who do not have the right skill sets or tools. Developing ESG standards and measurements has thus far been dominated by business management consultants, financial analysts, engineers, accountants, and regulators with input from investors and other stakeholders. It has to move beyond that world and into the world where the people have the right tools and training to address scarce resource allocation issues.

We need a new way of thinking about and determining which companies, projects, and economic activities are contributing to sustainability and which are not. We need to be on a path to sustainability. Right now we still have too many competing frameworks and views about how to get to the end-state. Moreover, none of those frameworks helps answer the key question: how do we allocate scarce natural, human, social, and manufactured capital?

Transitioning from an unsustainable economy to a sustainable economy requires the serious input of economists as well as scientists. Economics is concerned with the allocation of scarce resources and goods across societies. Working with environmental and other scientists, economists should not only have a seat at the table, but they should have the "head-seat." Thus far, economists are not even in the room. Economists have the tool kits, the models, the thought-processes, and the way of thinking to solve complex scarce resource allocation problems. Economists assess the various factors which determine the availability of scarce resources, and their limits, to help determine resource allocation choices.

Nothing is scarcer than the capacity of the environment, yet economists are totally missing in all of the discussions. No allocation of a scarce resource, for example, can be more important than allocating scarce water across international river basins. The World Bank gave the warning shot across the bow over 25 years ago. Economist Ismail Serageldin warned "many of the wars this century were about oil, but wars of the next century will be over water" (Connor, 1995).

Science shows us we do not have long to get on the right path to sustainability. It is time to bring in the professionals who are trained in a way of thinking that can be extended to a wide range of problems. No problem is more important today than figuring out how to transition to a sustainable economy and maximize societies' collective utility, given the ecological and natural resource constraints that we face.

CONCLUSION

Hardly a day goes by that we do not hear some warnings about climate change and its consequences. All of the scientific evidence shows we need to quickly reverse course. Unless we properly manage the use of natural resources including forests, water and marine life, land, minerals, and the atmosphere, the planet and humanity are at great risk. Along the way, there will be many consequences including economic and geopolitical. Economically, according to Swiss Re Institute's stress-test analyses, the global economy could lose up to 18% of GDP, or $23 trillion, by 2050, if no mitigating actions are taken (Swiss Re Institute, 2021).

"Environmental concerns are national security issues of the future" (Annan, 2001). Geopolitically, friction including wars could break out among countries as they compete for scarce resources and for rare earth minerals needed to produce renewable energy technology, and conflicts could arise over the Artic as the ice melts and countries compete for the region and access to opened passageways. We may see economic conflicts between the developing economies and the developed economies over which should pay the transitioning costs as developing economies are hardest hit by climate-change-related catastrophes and developed economies have been the biggest contributors to climate change.

Financial markets—investors and financial institutions—have the opportunity and the responsibility to help reverse course on climate change. Countries and multilateral organizations do not have all of the capital needed to achieve the Paris Agreement, the EU Green Deal, and the UN SDGs. They need the private sector and the financial markets to mobilize capital to where it can be most efficiently deployed to reverse course on our dependencies on technologies harmful to the environment and introduce new clean and alternative sources of energy. One of the biggest challenges is not the lack of capital but instead the lack of data for investment decisions. This severely constrains the ability to make ESG-driven decisions to mobilize the institutional capital to where those investments are most needed at the scale required to close the enormous annual financing gaps.

We need the correct data and the correct scarce resource allocation analyses. The path we are on will most likely lead to misallocations of capital due to all of the data problems and biases we have discussed. We need to direct capital to companies and technologies of the future. And we need economists to help answer the most significant question facing us: how do we best allocate scarce resources to where capital is needed most?

Appendix 1

The UN SDGs are a universal call to action established in 2015 by 193 countries.

- The SDGs encompass ESGs but are broader and address some of our largest macro systemic risks we face.
- There are 17 SDGs, 169 targets, and 231 "unique" indicators.
- The SDGs focus on the elimination of poverty, hunger, life on land, life under water, economic growth, as well as the environment, social, and governance (ESG issues).
- Companies sometimes get overwhelmed—they look at 17 SDGs, 169 targets, and 231 unique indicators and wonder where to begin.
- What they need to keep in mind is that the SDGs were designed for countries, not companies.
- In fact, of the 17 SDGs, only ten directly apply to companies.
- Of the 169 targets, only six directly apply to companies.
- And of the 231 "unique" indicators, only 21 directly apply to companies.
- To facilitate companies reporting on their contribution to the SDG agenda, in 2016, UNCTAD,[5] which is part of the UN Secretariat, whose main function is data collection and analysis to facilitate public policy, launched its work on The Global Core Indicators (GCIs), which are baseline core indicators (UNCTAD, 2019). This work was done with a view to improving comparability of sustainability and SDG reporting and its alignment with the SDG macro indicators (Antoncic, 2020, 2021b).

See Appendix 2 for a discussion of the GCIs.

Appendix 2

UNCTAD-ISAR's created the Global Core Indicators through a multi-year, multi-stakeholder effort by governments, regulators, standard-setting agencies, and investors.

These recommendations were endorsed by the thirty-sixth session of ISAR, with participation of about 400 delegates, representing about 100 members states of UNCTAD, which will encourage the companies in their respective countries to report using these metrics. Reporting under these recommendations will inform global national statistical offices and regulators. Many more countries are supporting the GCIs, independently of the ISAR membership.

The GCIs are a common set of indicators which fulfill all of the quantitative requirements—consistent, comparable, material, universal, and common to all businesses—and also facilitate convergence of financial and nonfinancial reporting, something none of the other measurement systems does, making the GCIs suitable for consolidated, integrated reporting, and legal entity reporting.

UNCTAD's framework and indicators are also consistent with TCFD and can be the implementation tools for TCFD. Moreover, the indicators can link firm-level reporting, into national statistics and reporting and help inform where capital needs to be redirected to achieve the SDGs.

There are only 33 GCIs which provide a road map for reporting on company's contributions to the SDGs. They are the only set of company-level SDG indicators that are common, comparable, and universal to all businesses and focus on quantitative metrics, not narrative disclosures, covering, four main disclosure elements: (1) economic, (2) environmental, (3) social, and (4) institutional and governance. They are limited only to a number of SDG indicators over which companies have control and for which they already gather data as part of their regular reporting cycle or where a company has access to relevant sources of information.

The GCIs create synergies and complementarities across other frameworks and can be used for ESG reporting. They are based on key reporting principles with a view toward enhancing consistency of financial and nonfinancial reporting. These indicators make a business case for companies wanting to contribute to the SDGs. They are directly relevant to a company and tie into the macro SDG indicators.

Lastly, the GCIs cover company microlevel sustainability indicators, which link corporate microlevel data to SDG macro-level indicators and to macro national statistics. The GCIs contextualize with metrics such as GHG emissions (Scope 1 or 2) per unit economic net value added of each company within a country which maps into a country's GDP. The indicators facilitate companies reporting on their contributions and on their share of their respective country's contributions to sustainability and to the SDG agenda.

Source: based on and excerpts from UNCTAD (2019) and Antoncic (2021b).

NOTES

1 The UN Sustainable Development Goals (SDGs) are a much broader set of sustainability issues than traditional ESG issues (see Appendix 1). The SDGs have more factors and address the full spectrum of *global macro systemic issues* that matter to all stakeholders, all businesses, and all countries. The SDGs "are a universal call to action" established in 2015 by 193 countries "to end poverty, protect the planet and ensure that all people enjoy peace and prosperity by the year 2030, leaving no one behind" (United Nations, 2021).
2 The OECD guidelines on multinational enterprises and the UN guiding principles on business and human rights.
3 See: www.r3-0.org
4 See: www.r3-0.org/gtac/
5 United Nations Conference on Trade and Development is part of the UN Secretariat.

REFERENCES

Ali, A. (2020). *The Soaring Value of Intangible Assets in the S&P 500*. Available at: www.visualcapitalist.com/the-soaring-value-of-intangible-assets-in-the-sp-500/ (Accessed: 2 November 2021).

Annan, K. (2001). *Speech of Mr Kofi Annan, General-Secretary of the United Nations, During the 97th Meeting of the Association of American Geographers*. Available at: https://iguwater.wordpress.com/news/speech-of-mr-kofi-annan-general-secretary-of-the-united-nations-during-the-97th-meeting-of-the-association-of-american-geographers/ (Accessed: 3 November 2021).

Antoncic, M. (1983). Shifts in equilibrium stock prices due to information shocks: A problem in the measurement of imperfectly observed time varying parameters. *Federal Reserve Bank of New York Research Paper, Number 8311*.

Antoncic, M. (2018). *Lehman Failed for Good Reasons*. Available at: www.nytimes.com/2018/09/17/opinion/lehman-brothers-financial-crisis.html (Accessed: 2 November 2021).

Antoncic, M. (2019a). Why sustainability? Because risk evolves and risk management should too. *Journal of Risk Management in Financial Institutions*, 12(3), 206–216.

Antoncic, M. (2019b). ESG: A market challenge with a market solution. *Accounting Today*. Available at: www.accountingtoday.com/opinion/esg-a-market-challenge-with-a-market-solution (Accessed: 2 November 2021).

Antoncic, M. (2020). Uncovering hidden signals for sustainable investing using Big Data: Artificial intelligence, machine learning and natural language processing. *Journal of Risk Management in Financial Institutions*, 13(2), 106–113.

Antoncic, M. (2021a). A paradigm shift in the board room: Incorporating sustainability into corporate governance and strategic decision-making using big data and artificial intelligence. *Journal of Risk Management in Financial Institutions*, 13(4), 290–294.

Antoncic, M. (2021b). The global core indicators: A sustainability risk management and reporting framework. *Journal of Risk Management in Financial Institutions*, 14(3), 224–228.

Balch, O. (2021). *Big Data Helps Put Numbers on Sustainability*. Available at: www.ft.com/content/2a405cf6-9592-4de2-960b-4c3e5d0df030 (Accessed: 5 November 2021).

Baue, B. (2019). *Compared to What? A Three-Tiered Typology of Sustainable Development Performance Indicators: From Incremental to Contextual to Transformational.* United Nations Research Institute for Social Development. Available at: www.unrisd.org/UNRISD/website/document.nsf/(httpPapersForProgrammeArea)/CBE444C58139C45A8025848C00547012?OpenDocument (Accessed: 5 November 2021).

Begenau, J., Farboodi, M., & Veldkamp, L. (2018). Big data in finance and the growth of large firms. *NBER Working Paper 24550.* Available at: www.nber.org/system/files/working_papers/w24550/w24550.pdf (Accessed: 5 November 2021).

Berg, F., Koelbel, J. F., & Rigobon, R. (2019). Aggregate confusion: The divergence of ESG ratings. *MIT Sloan School of Management Working Paper 5822-19.* Available at: www.econbiz.de/Record/aggregate-confusion-the-divergence-of-esg-ratings-berg-florian/10012104392 (Accessed: 3 November 2021).

Boffo, R., & Patalano, R. (2020). *ESG Investing: Practices, Progress and Challenges.* Available at: www.oecd.org/finance/ESG-Investing-Practices-Progress-Challenges.pdf (Accessed: 3 November 2021).

Brand Finance (2021). *Global Intangible Finance Tracker (GIFT), Annual Review of the World's Intangible Values.* Available at: https://brandirectory.com/download-report/brand-finance-gift-2021.pdf (Accessed: 2 November 2021).

Browning, N. (2021). *Investment in Clean Energy Must Triple by 2030 to Curb Climate Change -IEA.* Available at: www.reuters.com/business/sustainable-business/world-must-triple-clean-energy-investment-by-2030-curb-climate-change-iea-2021-10-13/ (Accessed: 2 November 2021).

Carbon Disclosure Project (CDP) (2021). *The Time to Green Finance: CDP Financial Services Disclosure Report 2020.* Available at: www.cdp.net/en/research/global-reports/financial-services-disclosure-report-2020 (Accessed: 3 November 2021).

Cohen, R., & Serafeim, G. (2020). How to Measure a Company's Real Impact. *Harvard Business Review Sustainable Business Practices.* Available at: https://hbr.org/2020/09/how-to-measure-a-companys-real-impact (Accessed: 5 November 2021).

Connor, S. (1995). *Water Shortages 'to Be New Cause of Wars'.* Available at: www.independent.co.uk/news/water-shortages-to-be-new-cause-of-wars-1595148.html (Accessed: 3 November 2021).

European Commission (2021). *EU Taxonomy for Sustainable Finance.* Available at: https://ec.europa.eu/info/business-economy-euro/banking-and-finance/sustainable-finance/eu-taxonomy-sustainable-activities_en (Accessed: 3 November 2021).

Gensler, G. (2021). *Prepared Remarks Before the Principles for Responsible Investment "Climate and Global Financial Markets" Webinar.* Available at: www.sec.gov/news/speech/gensler-pri-2021-07-28 (Accessed: 3 November 2021).

GIST (2020). *Quantity the Real Impacts of Companies on People and the Environment.* Available at: www.gistimpact.com/ (Accessed: 5 November 2021).

GRI (2021). *Sustainability Reporting Is Growing, With GRI the Global Common Language.* Available at: www.globalreporting.org/about-gri/news-center/2020-12-01-sustainability-reporting-is-growing-with-gri-the-global-common-language/ (Accessed: 3 November 2021).

Hasan, M., Popp, J., & Oláh, J. (2020). Current landscape and influence of big data on finance. *Journal of Big Data,* 7. Article number: 21(2020).

Hodari, D. (2021). *Energy Giants Ditch Oil and Coal Projects. Smaller Rivals Want Them.* Available at: www.wsj.com/articles/energy-giants-ditch-oil-and-coal-projects-smaller-rivals-want-them-11618997401 (Accessed: 2 November 2021).

Hodgson, C. (2021). *Widespread Lapses in Climate Reporting Found in Company Accounts.* Available at: www.ft.com/content/b3d12f4f-5d23-4378-93b7-06d1e891e547 Accessed: 3 November 2021).

IFRS (2021). *IFRS Foundation Announces International Sustainability Standards Board, Consolidation With CDSB and VRF, and Publication of Prototype Disclosure Requirements.* Available at: www.ifrs.org/news-and-events/news/2021/11/ifrs-foundation-announces-issb-consolidation-with-cdsb-vrf-publication-of-prototypes/ (Accessed: 3 November 2021).

IOSCO (2021). *Environmental, Social and Governance (ESG) Ratings and Data Products Providers Consultation Report*. Available at: www.iosco.org/library/pubdocs/pdf/IOSCOPD681.pdf (Accessed: 3 November 2021).

Jessop, S. (2021). *Sustainable Investments Account for More Than a Third of Global Assets*. Available at: www.reuters.com/business/sustainable-business/sustainable-investments-account-more-than-third-global-assets-2021-07-18/ (Accessed: 2 November 2021).

Kim, S., & Yoon, A. S. (2020). How committed are active-investment managers to ESG? *The Columbia Law School Blue Sky Blog*. Available at: https://clsbluesky.law.columbia.edu/2020/04/21/how-committed-are-active-investment-managers-to-esg/ (Accessed: 2 November 2021).

Kotsantonis, S., & Serafeim, G. (2019). Four things no one will tell you about ESG data. *Journal of Applied Corporate Finance*, 31(2), 50–58.

Kowsmann, P., & Brown, K. (2021). *Fired Executive Says Deutsche Bank's DWS Overstated Sustainable-Investing Efforts*. Available at: www.wsj.com/articles/fired-executive-says-deutsche-banks-dws-overstated-sustainable-investing-efforts-11627810380 (Accessed: 2 November 2021).

Murugaboopathy, P., & Jessop, S. (2021). *Global Sustainable Fund Assets Hit Record $2.3 tln in Q2, Says Morningstar*. Available at: www.reuters.com/business/sustainable-business/global-sustainable-fund-assets-hit-record-23-tln-q2-says-morningstar-2021-07-27/ (Accessed: 2 November 2021).

OECD (2021). *Global Outlook on Financing for Sustainable Development 2021: A New Way to Invest for People and Planet* Available at: www.oecd-ilibrary.org/sites/6ea613f4-en/index.html?itemId=/content/component/6ea613f4-en (Accessed: 3 November 2021).

Peirce, H. (2021). *Letter to the IFRS re: Proposed Targeted Amendments to the IFRS Foundation Constitution to Accommodate an International Sustainability Standards Board to Set IFRS Sustainability Standards*. Available at: www.sec.gov/news/public-statement/peirce-ifrs-2021-07-01 (Accessed: 3 November 2021).

Petrequin, S. (2020). *EU Lays Out 1 Trillion-euro Plan to Support Green Deal*. Available at: https://apnews.com/article/europe-ursula-von-der-leyen-ap-top-news-international-news-environment-5d4db8ffda58f03f090a04c35f0a2dc8 (Accessed: 3 November 2021).

Principles for Responsible Investment (PRI) (2021). *Annual Report 2020*. Available at: www.unpri.org/about-the-pri/annual-report-2020/6811.article (Accessed: 2 November 2021).

RBC Global Asset Management (2021). *Key Findings: 2021 Responsible Investment Survey*. Available at: www.rbcgam.com/en/ca/about-us/responsible-investment/our-latest-independent-research (Accessed: 2 November 2021).

Serafeim, G., & Trinh, K. (2020). A Framework for Product Impact Weighted Accounts. *HBS Working Paper 20–076*. Available at: www.hbs.edu/impact-weighted-accounts/Documents/Preliminary-Framework-for-Product-Impact-Weighted-Accounts.pdf (Accessed: 5 November 2021).

Shifflett, S. (2021). *Funds Go Green, but Sometimes in Name Only*. Available at: www.wsj.com/articles/funds-go-green-but-sometimes-in-name-only-11631179801 (Accessed: 2 November 2021).

Swiss Re Institute (2021). The Economics of Climate Change: No Action Not an Option. *Swiss Re Institute Climate Stress-test Report*. Available at: www.swissre.com/dam/jcr:e73ee7c3-7f83-4c17-a2b8-8ef23a8d3312/swiss-re-institute-expertise-publication-economics-of-climate-change.pdf (Accessed: 2 November 2021).

UNCTAD (2014). *Developing Countries Face $2.5 Trillion Annual Investment Gap in Key Sustainable Development Sectors, UNCTAD Report Estimates*. Available at: https://unctad.org/press-material/developing-countries-face-25-trillion-annual-investment-gap-key-sustainable (Accessed: 3 November 2021).

UNCTAD (2019). *Guidance on Core Indicators for Entity Reporting on Contribution Towards Implementation of the Sustainable Development Goals*. Available at: https://unctad.org/en/pages/PublicationWebflyer.aspx?publicationid=2469 (Accessed: 3 November 2021).

United Nations (2006). *Secretary-General Launches Principles for Responsible Investment' Backed by World's Largest Investors*. Available at: www.un.org/press/en/2006/sg2111.doc.htm (Accessed: 2 November 2021).

United Nations (2007). *UN News Global Perspective Human Stories. Evidence Is Now 'Unequivocal' That Humans Are Causing Global Warming—UN Report*. Available at: https://news.un.org/en/

story/2007/02/207742-evidence-now-unequivocal-humans-are-causing-global-warming-un-report (Accessed: 10 January 2022).

United Nations (2021). *Sustainable Development Goals*. Available at: www.un.org/sustainabledevelopment/ (Accessed: 3 November 2021).

World Bank (2018). *From Evolution to Revolution: 10 Years of Green Bonds*. Available at: www.worldbank.org/en/news/feature/2018/11/27/from-evolution-to-revolution-10-years-of-green-bonds (Accessed: 2 November 2021).

13

Assessing ESG from a Position of Wealth

Elias Ghanem

What's old is new as societal positioning around sustainability is motivated by its potential to meet specific needs. Notably, Environmental, Social, and Corporate Governance (ESG) maturation aligns with psychologist Abraham Maslow's 1943 hierarchy of human motivation. Even now, in the technology-driven 2020s—age, geography, gender, and socioeconomic status all affect reason and needs. In this chapter, we explore the attitudes and impact of high-net-worth individuals (HNWIs) – those with discretionary investable assets of more than USD1 million—in terms of their appetite for sustainable investing (SI) and ESG agendas. Further, we offer technology solutions for financial institutions seeking to support their investment goals. While HNWIs may represent only 1.1% of the world's population, they control 46% of global household wealth, firmly positioning them to affect ESG growth, according to Visual Capitalist (2021), which extrapolated Credit Suisse data.

Typically, HNWIs seek to safeguard and grow generational wealth with long-term horizons. They represent a narrow social stratum uniquely positioned to balance *personal values* with *financial value* thanks to the capacity to quickly leverage significant amounts of funds over long periods—a capability many retail investors do not command. Increasingly, more and more affluent individuals are weaving a range of sustainability initiatives into their investment decisions.

A Maslovian-like pyramid illustrates how potential sustainability topics relate to physiological needs (see Figure 13.1)—shelter and survivability, financial security, belonging, esteem/accomplishment, and finally,

DOI: 10.4324/9781003262039-15

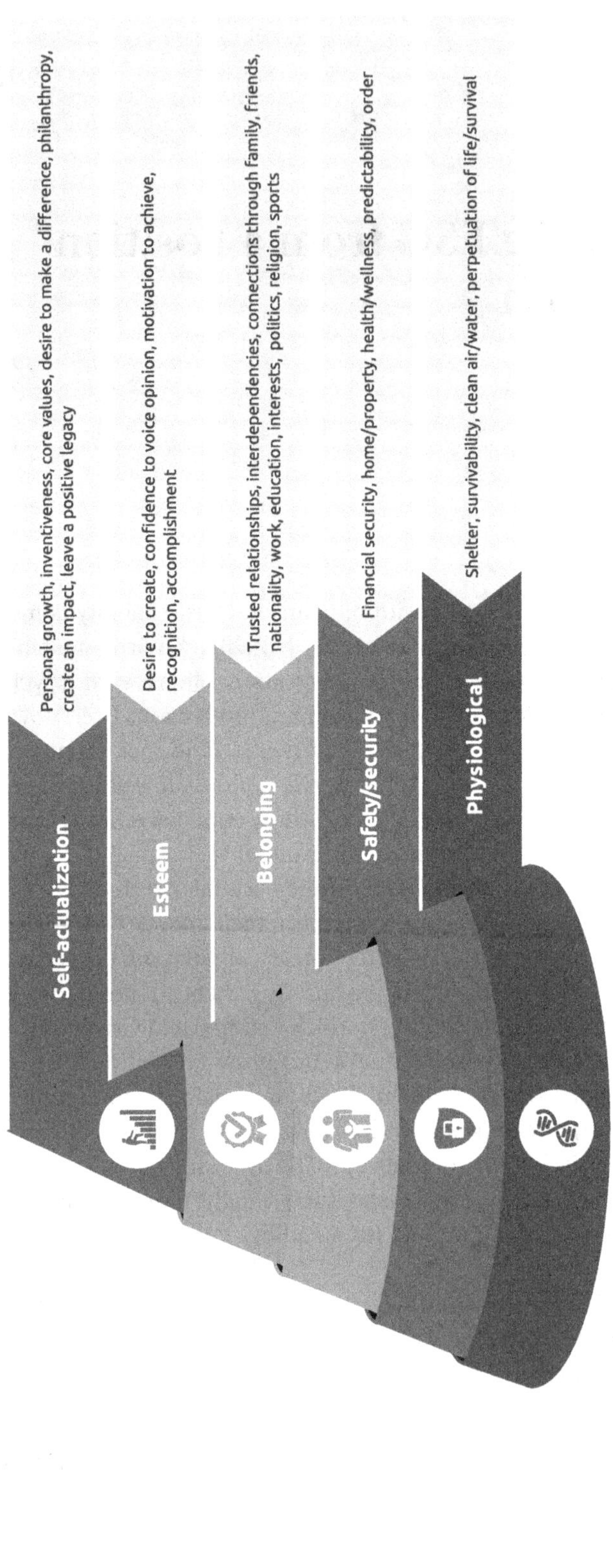

FIGURE 13.1 Sustainability through Maslow's Hierarchical Lens

(Source: Capgemini Financial Services Analysis, 2022.)

self-actualization/creating an impact, according to analysis from Capgemini's Financial Services.

Essentials such as access to food, clean air/water, and financial security anchor Maslow's pyramid (see Figure 13.1). As individuals meet those necessities, their needs expand to include belonging and respect within a family, community, profession, or corporate environment, including compliance with governance principles. Finally, feel-good self-actualization tops the hierarchy, including the desire to live one's core values and leave a positive legacy for coming generations. Maslow said self-actualization is "*becoming everything one is capable of becoming*" (Maslow et al., 1970).

He contended that humans drive to satisfy their basic physiological needs before progressing to higher-level belonging, social acceptance, and self-actualization (Maslow et al., 1970). Thus, affluent investors with access to life's necessities are poised to fulfill broad personal and societal growth functions. However, in real-world terms, self-actualization for a Norwegian school teacher probably looks different from that of a Ugandan coffee farmer. Similarly, for a millennial call center employee in Chicago, ideas about giving back may be starkly unlike those of a soon-to-retire HNWI in Singapore.

The pandemic catalyzed corporate stakes in sustainability. As COVID-19 upended daily life and global economies—turning skies blue over New Delhi and unclogging choked highways for the first time in years—attitudes about sustainability seemed to change overnight. From HNWIs to high school students, the worldwide rallying cry was for individuals, corporations, and governments to play a more significant and transparent role in endorsing ESG activity. However, corporates and sectors that made only a halfhearted pre-pandemic commitment to ESG initiatives found themselves on the losing end of opportunity as notions dissipated that sustainability funds are not yet capable of robust returns (Banking Exchange, 2021).

ESG fund managers now say their focus on nontraditional risks led them to build portfolios filled with companies that—so far—have been COVID-19 resilient. For example, during the height of the pandemic in 2020, large funds with ESG criteria outperformed the broader market, according to a report published in April 2021. ESG fund managers say their focus on so-called nontraditional risks led to their building portfolios of companies that were resilient to the worst of COVID-19's adverse effects on the overall economy (American Veterans Group, 2021).

According to Capgemini (2020), more than a quarter (27%) of HNWIs are interested in sustainable investment products. For example, in early 2021, major HSBC shareholders filed a climate resolution urging the bank to shape definitive measures to reduce lending to fossil fuel-intensive companies (Banking Exchange, 2021).

In a letter to CEOs during the pandemic, Larry Fink, CEO of the world's largest asset manager, BlackRock, said, "*Climate change has become a defining factor in companies' long-term prospects . . . but awareness is rapidly changing, and I believe we are on the edge of a fundamental reshaping of finance*" (BlackRock, 2020). BlackRock, which manages USD9 trillion in assets, has pressed for more disclosure in recent years. Before the 2021 proxy season, the company initiated more concerted actions around disclosing adherence to ESG principles (BlackRock, 2021).

ESG INVESTING HAS LONG PASSED THE NICHE *TREND* PHASE

Shareholders are exerting pressure. Forty percent of ultra-high net worth individuals (UHNWIs) – those with USD30 million or more to invest—say they want sustainable investment products from their wealth managers, according to the 2020 Capgemini World Wealth report (Capgemini, 2020). Is their interest an illustration of their Maslovian desire for reputational respect and self-actualization—or even a feeling of responsibility or give-back?

In the United States, sustainable funds outperformed traditional funds by 4.3% in turbulent 2020—the most significant performance difference recorded since 2004, according to a report by Morgan Stanley's Institute for Sustainable Investing. The Institute moreover found that the median total return for US sustainable taxable bond funds was 0.9% higher than traditional taxable bond funds (BusinessWire, 2021).

Using a green revenue data set of globally listed firms covering approximately 98% of global market capitalization (2009–2016), the Grantham Research Institute on Climate Change and the Environment found that revenues from environmental goods and services were quickly proliferating and totaled USD1.6 trillion in 2016, representing around 4% of turnover (Grantham Research Institute on Climate Change and the Environment, 2020).

In December 2021, FTSE Russell CEO Arne Stall said,

> There is so much that needs to happen through finance to support sustainability and climate goals in particular. Financial markets have a huge role because this is all about reallocating capital to transition to a much lower carbon economy globally. . . . The answer is transparency and standardization of data and methodologies, so people speak a common language. I think of it as a base of truth. Because currently, people are saying similar things but might mean entirely different things because they're working with different data sets, definitions, and methodologies. So yes, there will need to be much more standardization.
>
> (FTSE RUSSELL CONVENES SERIES, 2021)

Multigenerational HNWIs are joining youthful ESG and SI proponents. Generationally, millennials (up and coming corporate leaders) and their younger counterparts, Generation Z, are leading the environmental charge—no matter their position on the wealth spectrum. Researchers at Hiroshima University found that millennials and Gen Z are more sustainability-orientated—even when it comes to money. In a study questioning commitments to sustainable behaviors and willingness to earn less to work for a more sustainably minded company, Japanese survey participants (ages 18–30) were far more likely to value and practice sustainable behaviors, such as paying more for sustainably developed products, than their older counterparts. The results, published in the *Journal of Cleaner Production*, focused on achieving the United Nations Sustainable Development Goals (SDGs). Researchers said that by 2030 when today's younger generations dominate the workforce, they are likely to make genuine efforts to create a sustainable future and play a substantial role in achieving SDGs (Hiroshima University, 2021).

Compared with their older counterparts, Gen Z and millennials worldwide talk more about the need for climate change action; and are doing more to get involved through volunteering, rallies, and protests. They are at the forefront of the climate debate, with high-visibility Swedish activist Greta Thunberg and youth groups such as the Sunrise Movement urging increased attention to climate change (Sunrise Movement, 2022).

With a nod to the Maslovian hierarchy, anxiety about the future is an emotional reaction to climate change among those most engaged with the issue on social platforms. Hence, as millennials surpass baby boomers to become the largest adult generation, they will likely adopt investment strategies that significantly impact the economy and the planet's well-being. ESG investing appears to have come of age in 2021, as sustainability interests filter to mainstream markets.

ESG PRIORITIZATION OFTEN DEPENDS ON INVESTOR AGE, WEALTH, AND GEOGRAPHIC PARAMETERS

In Asia, where society drives innovation and climate change affects Asian business, societal unrest is evident. The region is vulnerable to high-impact weather events, particularly China. Close to 150 million people live in coastal areas threatened by rising sea levels as polar ice caps melt faster than previously forecast. Again, a throwback to Maslow's prioritization of physiological well-being and safety.

Sustainability is not a Western construct; COVID-19 fueled a shift toward *inconspicuous consumption* for China's millennials. In Q-1 2021, China's National People's Congress (NPC) formalized its 14th Five-Year Plan, which vigorously promotes green consumption (Jing Daily, 2021). The central bank of the People's Republic of China – People's Bank of China (PBoC) – defines green finance as a series of policy and institutional arrangements to attract private capital investments into green industries such as environmental protection, energy conservation, and clean energy, through financial services. China has expanded its green finance sector to become the world's second-largest green bond market after the United States. According to official PBoC data, China had 12 trillion yuan (USD1.8 trillion) in outstanding green loans—the highest in the world—by the end of 2020. With support from the financial community, China seeks to reach peak carbon emissions by 2030, and carbon neutrality by 2060 (South China Morning Post, 2021).

China's first green taxonomy, China Green Bond Endorsed Catalogue, was released in 2015 and updated in 2019. The regulating authorities across the country have also issued climate risk management guidelines, green prudential policies, and mandated sustainability-related disclosures. Additionally, the People's Bank of China leads biodiversity and financial stability initiatives within the Network for Greening the Financial System (NGFS), a group of central banks aiming to scale up green finance and develop climate change recommendations for central banks (Official Monetary and Financial Institutions Forum, 2022).

The pandemic elevated consumers' focus on sustainability and willingness to devote their resources directly toward a sustainable future, according to a 2021 IBM survey of more than 14,000 consumers in nine countries. Nine in ten consumers surveyed reported that the pandemic affected their views on environmental sustainability, and COVID-19 was the top factor in influencing their opinion—more than wildfires/brushfires, weather events, and news coverage (IBM, 2021). The same study also reveals differences in consumer opinion across geographies, with *super-sizing* predisposed US citizens being somewhat nonchalant about sustainability. For example, only 51% of US consumers said addressing climate change was *very* or *extremely important* to them, compared with 73% of respondents from all other markets (IBM, 2021).

US policy on sustainability took on more definition in 2021. The Federal Government announced a net-zero target for 2050. Additionally, the New York Stock Exchange published corporate guidance on ESG disclosures; and the Federal Reserve joined the Network for Greening the Financial System (NGFS). However, the US State Department takes a long view on innovation and relies on the American private sector for cutting-edge technology and its wide adoption. Moreover, American policymakers defer to US tech company perspectives to craft strategies to advance US technology when conducting diplomatic negotiations, including those around sustainability (US Department of State, 2022).

Although science and innovation are central to human progress and national economic success, the United States invests just 2.8% of its GDP in research and development to support a range of public policies (Aspen Economic Strategy Group, 2021). In contrast, the EU supports numerous policies and regulations to promote a green economy, notably several climate risk management guidelines, mandatory climate-related financial disclosures, and a stress test. In addition, other countries often use the EU's sustainable taxonomy and green-bond standard as benchmarks.

Throughout Europe, governmental regulations drive innovation—the EU Action Plan of Sustainable Growth (March 2018), the Green Deal (December 2019), the Proposal for a European Climate Law (March 2019), the Circular Economy Action Plan (March 2020), the Farm to Fork Strategy (May 2020), the Climate Pact (December 2020), and the EU Regulation on Sustainability-Related Disclosures (March 2021) (Crowell, 2021).

Furthermore, in line with the UN SDGs (2015) and the Paris Climate Change Agreement (2015), Europe set an ambitious target to reduce its emissions by at least 50% by 2030 and achieve climate neutrality by 2050. Therefore, it's no surprise that Europeans are keen on ESG and SI.

Sustainable investing is becoming increasingly mainstream. And, as millennials benefit from the new tech-economy wealth and the impending *great wealth transfer* (when Silent Generation individuals and baby boomers bequeath an estimated USD30 trillion to USD68 trillion to adult children), institutional investors, such as pension funds, likely will embrace ESG initiatives. In addition, we expect similar behavior as millennials assume more corporate leadership roles and adopt ESG strategies that look beyond immediate financial profit.

A Capgemini Financial Services survey and analysis of high-net-worth individuals found that different HNWI segments respond differently to sustainable investing, with 41% of those under age 40 indicating interest (see Figure 13.2). Therefore, this segment can be expected to engage more enthusiastically than its predecessors and represents robust future revenue potential for wealth management firms.

A March 2021 Capgemini Research Institute report included a survey of 11,000+ consumers and found that those who prefer to invest in assets with a positive societal impact despite lesser returns increased from 31% before the COVID-19 outbreak to 46% by November 2020 (Capgemini, 2021a).

TECHNOLOGY WILL ENABLE ESG DECISIONS (EDUCATING, VIEWING, TRACKING, MEASURING)

As the global economy bounces back from pandemic aftershocks and braces for ongoing climate change impact, HNWIs are scrutinizing their investment

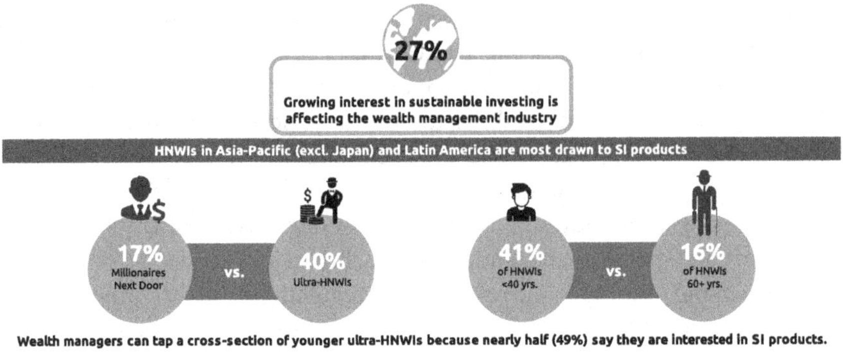

FIGURE 13.2 Youthful HNWIs Demonstrate Interest in Sustainable Investing (Source: Capgemini Financial Services Analysis, 2021; World Wealth Report, 2020.)

portfolios from a big picture, call-to-action perspective, and seeking sound ESG investment opportunities.

As HNWIs' interest in sustainable investing matures (to include demand for information about SI opportunities and customized sustainable investing solutions), financial institutions will require technical support to meet client needs and measure the impact and returns from ESG investing. Calculated investment decision-making is challenging with complex data and no single standard for measuring ESG credentials. AI and machine learning tools can offer credible analysis and truthful results, giving wealth management firms and investors a more accurate view of a fund's actual ESG merits.

- A top challenge for 41% of wealth management firms and 36% of wealth managers is finding accurate ESG impact data, according to Capgemini's World Wealth Report 2021. In addition, the lack of clarity regarding sustainable investment returns also is problematic (Capgemini, 2021b).
- The report found that 38% of wealth management firm executives believe sustainable investing might deliver less competitive returns. What's more, nearly half (47%) of wealth managers said they needed more sustainable investing information to convince clients of ESG benefits and returns.
- Capgemini's 2021 Wealth Report went on to find that 43% of UHNWIs (those with ≥USD30 million in disposable income) and 39% of HNWIs aged 40 or younger are likely to ask their firm for an ESG score for products offered. Not surprisingly, industry executives noted a growing demand for sustainable investing education, which underscores the need to build informational resources for clients and advisors.

HNWI clients favor SI products focused on environmental risks and climate change, followed by ethical and effective corporate governance systems. However, there is a slight mismatch in firms' perception of HNWI priorities	HNWI' focus-area priority	Firms' perception of HNWI focus-area priority
Effectively managing environmental risks	55%	43%
Addressing climate change, reducing carbon footprint	55%	45%
Effective and ethical corporate government systems	54%	63%
Socially conscious business policies and practices	52%	55%

FIGURE 13.3 As HNWIs Demand SI Products Devoted to Environmental Risks, Wealth Firms Play Catch Up

(Source: Capgemini Financial Services Analysis, 2021; World Wealth Report, 2021.)

More than half of HNWI seek sustainable investments focused on environmental risks and climate change, followed by ethical and effective corporate governance systems. However, a gap exists between what HNWIs want and what wealth management firms believe they want (see Figure 13.3)

Tech giants appear to be omnipresent in ESG funds because of their reputation for having small carbon footprints. Indeed, tech companies that unlink computing, power consumption, and greenhouse gas emissions from fossil fuels will continue to be attractive SI candidates. Still, other less high-profile yet worthy opportunities exist.

For example, B2B FinTech Loanwell emphasizes the *social* component of ESG by modernizing community lending to enable equitable access by making the loan origination process more efficient. The minority-owned Durham, North Carolina firm offers lenders an end-to-end platform with intake, origination, underwriting, closing, servicing, and reporting (Hypepotamus, 2022).

Wealth managers responding to a 2021 Capgemini survey said their high-net-worth clients ask them to embed ESG scoring into their investment portfolios. Only 15% of HNWI respondents had no ESG score preference, and 22% said they wanted to invest in companies with the highest ESG score (see Figure 13.4).

ESG-related conversations require a deep understanding of client preferences, backed by extensive research to generate highly personalized responses that enable advisors to shape meaningful portfolio discussions. Advisors must construct portfolios that fully align with client aspirations and make potential decisions around ESG choices and impact.

Several technology firms develop interactive reports that allow clients to view complex portfolios on multiple devices through a digital reporting platform. Investors and wealth managers will create, manage, configure, and evaluate reports in near real-time.

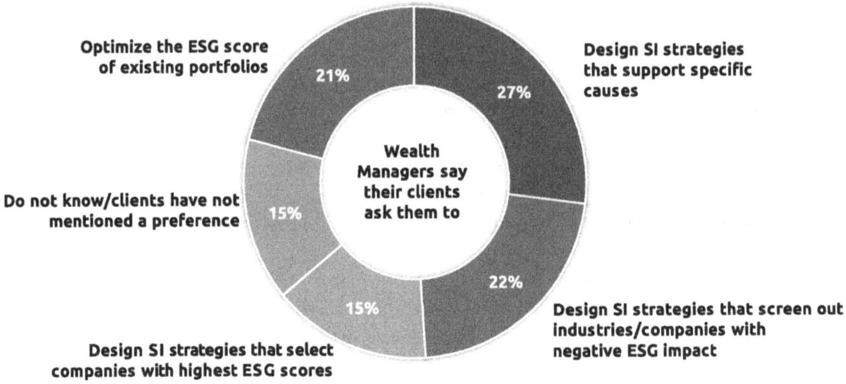

FIGURE 13.4 HNWIs Seeking Sustainable Investing Want ESG Scoring Embedded into Their Portfolios (%), Q1 2021 (Global)

(Source: Capgemini Financial Services Analysis, 2021; WWR, 2021 Wealth Manager Survey, Mar–Apr 2021.)

BNP Paribas Securities Services ESG marketplace, *Manaos*, an open servicing platform designed for institutional investors to manage post-trade investment data, aims to become a source for ESG data and sustainability monitoring and reporting. As part of its Open ESG strategy, Manaos partners with leading sustainability FinTechs to give users ready access to a wide range of ESG data and analytics tools (BNP Paribas Securities, 2021).

The unfolding context pushes WealthTechs and technology specialists into a pivotal enabling role. Because without appropriate technology solutions, the labor intensity of getting ESG right could be prohibitive.

The lack of global reporting standards and agreement on what is pertinent for each sector has led ESG data and rating providers to adopt unique methodologies and processes, making it difficult for companies to manage their narratives on sustainability and determine standard criteria. Further complicating the landscape for corporates is the growing number of investors developing personal ESG ratings by leveraging multiple data sources.

The most innovative wealth firms build synergistic relationships with technology specialists to meet HNWI demand for easy-to-access personalized information and individualize clients' ESG investment strategies.

Data analytics and behavior analysis fueled by AI and machine learning will enable financial institutions to combine fiscal and ESG data and take a granular look at the ESG impact of specific companies and assets. The result? More actionable investment decision-making.

Box 13.1 Wealth Management Firms Are Not Well Positioned to Lead the Charge for ESG Rating Standardization and Improvement

Why? They are paying off 25 years of tech debt. Investors began expressing interest in mobile/online interaction in 1997, but FS firms were worried about Y2K. Then, overnight dot.com success stories flaunted the power of e-commerce. But everything went bust with the 2008 financial crisis.

During recovery, tech debt grew, and by the time FIs began to notice, the post-2008 crisis forced budgets to prioritize regulatory compliance. In addition, digital debt continued to climb as consumers embraced Amazon and Google.

Now, fast track to 2012–2021, tech innovation and digitalization are at the top of the wealth management agenda to meet HNWI demand for new virtual services and sustainability products. Can banks deliver accurate ESG scores to meet all client expectations across all channels?

Artificial intelligence (AI) is a transformational technology that can constructively influence sustainable development. With an almost 80% positive impact on SDGs, AI can be critical in implementing climate strategies to reduce organizations' greenhouse gas emissions by an average of 13% (Capgemini, 2021c).

In the not-too-distant future, open-source tools that automate consumption and impact measurement reports will be available.

London-based start-up Sylvera uses machine learning technology to analyze visual data such as satellite imagery and lidar (remote sensing) to boost accountability and credibility around carbon offsetting projects. In Q2 2022, Sylvera closed USD32.6 million in funding to help it scale up. Current customers include Delta Air Lines, grain trader Cargill, and US management consultants Bain & Co (Sylvera, 2022).

New York-based MSCI (a provider of portfolio analysis tools and ESG and climate products) and Refinitiv (a US/UK financial market data and infrastructure specialist) help firms reduce emissions and develop solutions that rate, track, and measure ESG targets (Refinitiv, 2020).

Beyond expanding core wealth management competencies, future-proofing requires wealth management firms to push legacy mindset boundaries. Successful new-age wealth management firms will be expertise-driven but also data-driven, exclusive, and broad-ranged (see Figure 13.5). As a result, they will provide measurable high performance and value, and sustainability.

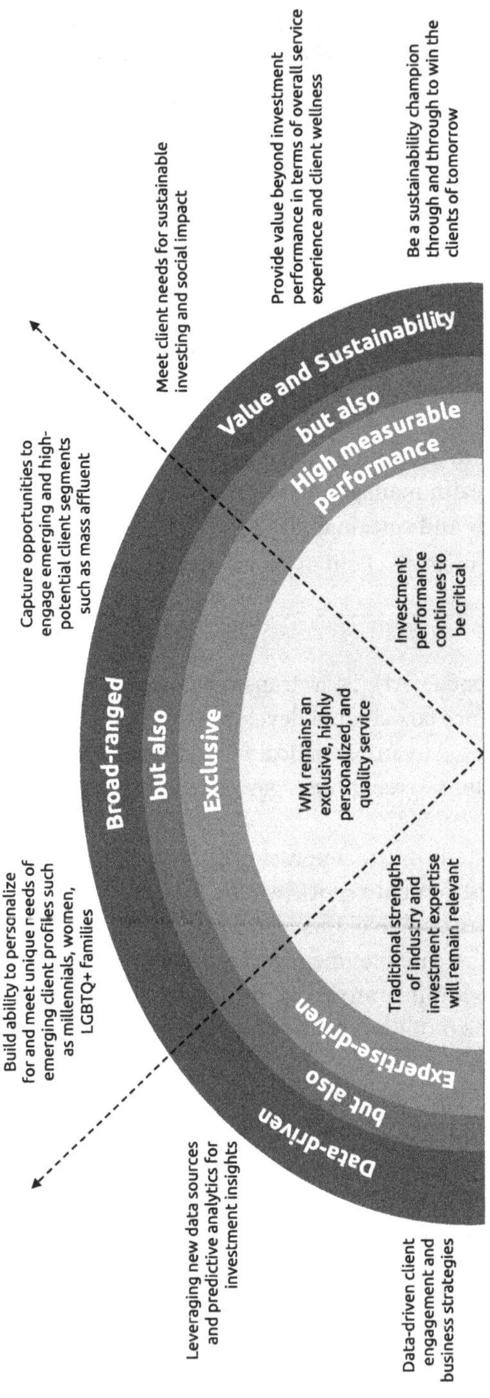

FIGURE 13.5 A Wealth Management Firm's Cultural Mindset Can Open Doors to New Opportunity

(Source: Capgemini Financial Services Analysis, 2021; Capgemini World Wealth Report, 2021.)

Future-focused wealth management firms are adopting new business strategies such as ecosystem collaboration, comprehensive digital and data solutions, and diversity hiring to meet the unique needs of new customer segments, including women, millennials, and LGBTQ+. All approaches are essential to capture growth opportunities, address client needs, and bolster client loyalty.

THE EVOLUTION FROM WEALTH CREATION TO WEALTH-BACK

As digitalization offers more people the opportunity to invest and potentially become rich, a transition from *wealth creation* to *wealth-back* may emerge. As a result, wealth management firms can position themselves to offer valuable advisory support to the mass-affluent segment (those with USD1 million to USD5 million in investable wealth).

Theoretically, the democratization of wealth gives ordinary folks the same opportunity for income generation and savings as HNWIs—it levels the playing field and may motivate investors to give back through a portfolio skewed toward sustainable investments. However, in today's pivotal era in which the consequences of inaction around sustainability are unavoidable, inherent Maslovian safety needs may influence investor ESG decisions.

With the help of technology and ecosystem tech partners, financial institutions can transform how clients consume ESG investment and fund-related information by moving away from static offline interaction toward personalized interactive, multichannel engagement.

Aligning values with value—today, HNW investors firmly believe (and they express it) that wealth and responsibility go hand in hand. As such, they want to ensure every part of their strategy for financial management aligns with their ethics—from advisor selection to transparent investment credentials.

Therefore, tomorrow's financial institutions must build responsibility into the heart of their business and make it resonate throughout clients' life stages while complementing their lifestyle. The most successful wealth advisors will personalize their clients' sustainable investing experience through enablement, education, and transparent tracking, rating, and measurement.

The growing interest in sustainable investing offers wealth firms a high-potential engagement opportunity. Among the ultra-HNWI segment—those with more than USD30million in investable assets—SI is building considerable momentum. While 27% of HNWIs overall are interested in SI products, 40% of ultra-HNWIs are willing to put cash into sustainability (see Figure 13.6).

Industry experts and executives maintain that as the global transition to a net-zero economy accelerates, commitment to sustainable investing is

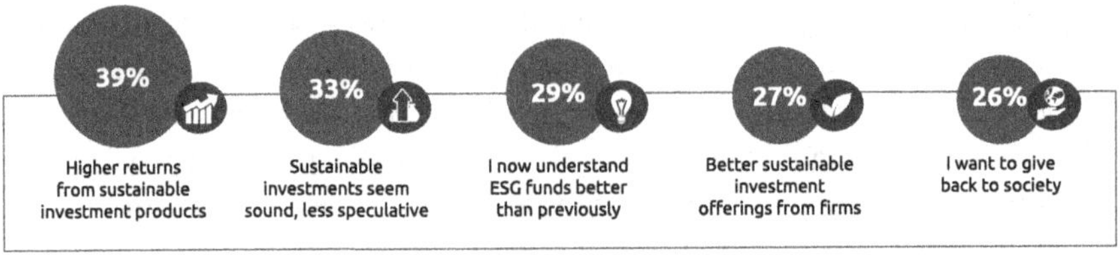

FIGURE 13.6 High Returns, Low-Risk Spark HNWI Interest
(Source: Capgemini Financial Services Analysis, 2021; Capgemini World Wealth Report, 2021.)

irreversible and here to stay. And as performance continues to improve, the profound impact of ESG investing will endure.

Now more than ever, HNWIs are positioned for self-actualization. They are bringing their core values to life by making a sustainable difference, earmarking philanthropic resources, and leaving a positive legacy. Maslow would approve.

DISCLAIMER

The information contained herein is general in nature and is not intended and should not be construed as professional or legal advice or opinion provided by Capgemini to the user. While effort has been made to offer current and accurate information, errors can occur. Therefore, this information is provided as-is, with no guarantee of completeness, accuracy, or timeliness, and without warranty of any kind, express or implied, including any warranty of performance, merchantability, or fitness for a particular purpose. In addition, changes may be made in this information from time to time without notice to the user. The user is cautioned that this material may not be applicable to or suitable for the user's specific circumstances or needs and may require consideration of additional factors if any action is to be contemplated. Capgemini assumes no liability for errors or omissions or use of this material. This material is not intended as an offer or solicitation for the purchase or sale of any financial instrument.

REFERENCES

American Veterans Group (2021). *Investors Are Aligning Their Investments With Their Values: Can Companies With Strong ESG Records Outperform Their Peers?* Available at: www.americanvetsgroup.com/investors-are-aligning-their-investments-with-their-values-can-companies-with-strong-esg-records-outperform-their-peers (Accessed: 21 February 2022).

Aspen Economic Strategy Group (2021). *Science and Innovation: The Under-Fueled Engine of Prosperity.* Available at: www.kellogg.northwestern.edu/faculty/jones-ben/htm/Science%20and%20Innovation%20_%20Underfueled%20Engine%20of%20Prosperity.pdf (Accessed: 8 February 2022).

Banking Exchange (2021). *Climate Leads Investors' Post-Pandemic ESG Priorities.* Available at: https://m.bankingexchange.com/recent-articles/item/8585-climate-leads-investors-post-pandemic-esg-priorities (Accessed: 10 February 2022).

BlackRock (2020). *Larry Fink's 2020 Letter to CEIs: A Fundamental Reshaping of Finance.* Available at: www.blackrock.com/uk/individual/larry-fink-ceo-letter (Accessed: 15 February 2022).

BlackRock (2021). *Investment Stewardship Q3 2021 Global Quarterly Report.* Available at: www.blackrock.com/corporate/literature/publication/blk-qrtly-stewardship-report-q3-2021.pdf (Accessed: 20 February 2022).

BNP Paribas Securities (2021). *BNP Paribas Securities Services' ESG Marketplace, Manaos, Strengthens Its Sustainability Offering with Util and V.E Partnerships.* Available at: https://securities.cib.bnpparibas/bnp-paribas-securities-services-esg-marketplace-manaos-strengthens-its-sustainability-offering-with-util-and-v-e-partnerships (Accessed: 10 February 2022).

BusinessWire (2021). *Morgan Stanley Sustainable Reality Report Reveals U.S. Sustainable Funds Outperformed Traditional Funds by 4.3% in 2020.* Available at: www.businesswire.com/news/home/20210224005399/en/Morgan-Stanley-Sustainable-Reality-Report-Reveals-U.S.-Sustainable-Funds-Outperformed-Traditional-Funds-by-4.3-in-2020 (Accessed: 20 February 2022).

Capgemini (2020). *World Wealth Report 2020.* Available at: www.capgemini.com/nl-nl/wp-content/uploads/sites/7/2020/07/World-Wealth-Report-WWR-2020.pdf. (Accessed: 10 February 2022).

Capgemini (2021a). *After the COVID-19 Vaccine . . . What Will Define Success in the Financial Services New Normal?* Available at: www.capgemini.com/be-en/after-the-covid-19-vaccine-what-will-define-success-in-the-financial-services-new-normal (Accessed: 10 February 2022).

Capgemini (2021b). *World Wealth Report 2021.* Available at: https://worldwealthreport.com (Accessed: 10 February 2022).

Capgemini (2021c). *Conversations for Tomorrow: Why Sustainability Means Collective Action, Bolder Leadership, and Smarter Technologies.* Available at: www.capgemini.com/us-en/research/conversations-for-tomorrow/edition-1 (Accessed: 10 February 2022).

Crowell (2021). *ESG From a European Perspective.* Available at: www.crowell.com/NewsEvents/Events/PastEvents/Environment-Social-and-Governance-ESG-from-a-European-Perspective (Accessed: 10 February 2022).

FTSE Russell Convenes Series (2021). *FTSE Russell CEO on Climate and Sustainable Investing: 'Time Is Running Out'.* Available at: www.ftserussell.com/blogs/ftse-russell-ceo-climate-and-sustainable-investing-time-running-out (Accessed: 20 February 2022).

Grantham Research Institute on Climate Change and the Environment Working Paper 331/Centre for Climate Change Economics and Policy Working Paper 263 (2020). "Green revenues, profitability and market valuation: Evidence from a global firm-level dataset." Available at: www.lse.ac.uk/GranthamInstitute/wp-content/uploads/2020/01/working-paper-331-Kruse-et-al.pdf (Accessed: 21 February 2022).

Hiroshima University. (2021). Millennials and generation Z are more sustainability-orientated—even when it comes to money, researchers find. *ScienceDaily.* Available at: www.sciencedaily.com/releases/2021/03/210331103635.htm (Accessed: 22 February 2022).

Hypepotamus (2022). *Durham-based Loanwell Has a Better Fintech Solution to Help Small Businesses Access Capital.* Available at: https://hypepotamus.com/feature/loanwell-durham (Accessed: 20 February 2022).

IBM (2021). *COVID-19 Pandemic Impacted 9 in 10 Surveyed Consumers' Views on Sustainability.* Available at: https://newsroom.ibm.com/2021-04-22-IBM-Study-COVID-19-Pandemic-Impacted-9-in-10-Surveyed-Consumers-Views-on-Sustainability (Accessed: 10 February 2022).

Jing Daily (2021). *Why Sustainability Is Trending With China's Millennials.* Available at: https://jingdaily.com/sustainability-trend-china-millennials-oqliq (Accessed: 10 February 2022).

Maslow, A. H., Frager, R., Fadiman, J., McReynolds, C., & Cox, R. (Eds.). (1970). *Motivation and Personality* (2nd edition). New York: Harper and Row.

Official Monetary and Financial Institutions Forum (OMFIF) (2022). *Sustainable Policy Tracker: China.* Available at: www.omfif.org/sfpt-china (Accessed: 10 February 2022).

Refinitiv (2020). *Refinitiv Builds Out ESG Research Offering.* Available at: www.refinitiv.com/en/media-center/press-releases/2020/december/msci-esg-research (Accessed: 15 January 2022).

South China Morning Post (2021). *Explainer | What Is Green Finance, and Why Is It Important to China's Carbon-neutral Goal?* Available at: www.scmp.com/news/china/politics/article/3128167/what-green-finance-and-why-it-important-chinas-carbon-neutral (Accessed: 22 February 2022).

Sunrise Movement (2022). *About the Sunrise Movement.* Available at: www.sunrisemovement.org/about (Accessed: 25 January 2022).

Sylvera (2022). *We've Raised $32M in Series A Funding to Become a Source of Truth for Carbon Markets.* Available at: www.sylvera.com/blog/series-a-announcement (Accessed: 21 February 2022).

US Department of State (2022). *Innovation Policy.* Available at: www.state.gov/innovation-policy (Accessed: 25 January 2022).

Visual Capitalist (2021). *This Simple Chart Reveals the Distribution of Global Wealth.* Available at: www.visualcapitalist.com/distribution-of-global-wealth-chart/ (Accessed: 15 February 2022).

14

The Rise of ESG Data

A Tectonic Transparency Shift

Inna Amesheva

INTRODUCTION

In May 2017, *the Economist* pronounced data to be "the new oil" (The Economist, 2017). In a similar vein, *ESG* ("Environmental, Social and Governance") data promises to be "the new gold'. This is an apt analogy because ESG data can be as difficult to find, it also requires a robust set of quality checks before it is fit for end-use and is just as prone to controversies as the precious metal. The uptake of sustainable investing over recent years, powered by growing demand for more conscious investment choices, as well as the top-down requirements of regulators, has turned ESG data into a highly sought-after commodity. Companies can no longer get away with purely financial disclosures as part of their annual reporting cycles. Indeed, as the demand for extra-financial information grows, sustainability reports have become an indelible part of regular corporate disclosures, and not only for major global blue-chip companies, and they are projected to become as important and ubiquitous as financial reporting in the next three to five years.

Markets are increasingly beginning to accept that a failure to successfully shift to a lower-carbon and more equitable future poses significant risks to investors, to economies, and to environmental ecosystems alike. Policy makers, central banks, regulators, corporations, and investors have become increasingly aware that sustainability matters and that the non-financial data required to measure it is critical to the core institutions of the modern financial system. Yet, we currently face a global collective action problem—across

DOI: 10.4324/9781003262039-16

political boundaries, legal regimes, and capital markets—that can only be solved by collective solutions.

In this chapter, the author presents an overview of the systemic developments regarding sustainability data, as well as the need for regulators, standards bodies, data providers, and technology service providers to collaborate to create a well-functioning ecosystem for ESG data. The chapter is structured as follows: (i) an overview of the rising tidal wave of policy initiatives, drawing parallels with the evolution of the global financial reporting regime; (ii) description of the key national and regional initiatives that have the aim of strengthening the quality and credibility of ESG information; (iii) analysis of the major challenges that have so far afflicted the world of sustainable finance and corporate sustainability disclosures more broadly; and (iv) the technology imperative: given the intractable complications of ESG data, technology-enabled solutions will play a pivotal role in resolving the most persistent challenges of sustainability measurement and integration.

MACRO TRENDS IN RESPONSIBLE INVESTING

This growing focus on sustainability has extended far beyond early adopters such as the European Union to include regional policies, national and state laws, and stock exchange guidelines. Across the world's 50 largest economies, the Principles for Responsible Investment (PRI, 2021) has documented over 750 hard and soft law policy revisions, across some 500+ policy instruments, which support, encourage, or require the consideration of long-term

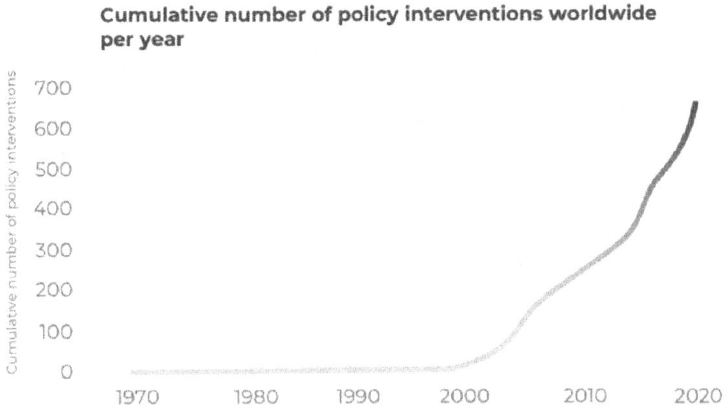

FIGURE 14.1 The Global ESG Regulatory Tsunami
(Source: Copyright ESG Book © 2022.)

sustainability information—environmental, social, and governance (ESG) factors, drivers, and data disclosures. Of the top 50 economies, 48 have some form of policy designed to help investors consider sustainability risks, opportunities, and/or outcomes. Furthermore, a second key observation in these new hard and soft law policy revisions is the fact that sustainable finance policy is a twenty-first-century phenomenon. Of the provisions identified, 97% were developed after the year 2000 (see Figure 14.1). The pace has continued to increase exponentially over the last 12 months—with over 160 new or revised policy instruments issued in 2021 alone or 30% more than the year before (PRI, 2022).

As demonstrated by PRI, nearly half of policy instruments are currently aimed at corporate sustainability disclosure, with investor disclosures and stewardship code instruments following closely behind (PRI, 2021).

While stakeholders approach sustainability from varying perspectives and target different objectives, there is growing consensus that capturing high-quality non-financial or ESG data is critical. Integrating ESG data has become indispensable in:

- Designing new national carbon reduction and sustainability disclosure targets;
- Building better risk management systems;
- Calibrating future scenario analyses and financial institution stress testing;
- Informing corporate strategy focused on long-term sustainable growth;
- Building investment strategies with the objective of ensuring better risk-adjusted returns.

Additionally, while there is no one universal definition of "fiduciary duty" across countries and jurisdictions, the incorporation of material non-financial data has driven many institutional investors to recognize their "duty" to provide the highest standard of care to their beneficiaries and participants of investment plans by explicitly integrating ESG data into the investment process (UNEP FI, 2021).

This growing demand and consensus around the importance of sustainability data has resulted in attention on the infrastructure needed to create sustainable capital markets and scale high-quality standardized data, sustainable products, and sustainable investing strategies. These solutions need to align core financial market infrastructure and top-down national and mandatory regulations with bottom-up market-driven products and platforms. The building blocks for a twenty-first-century information economy focused on sustainable capital markets and democratizing sustainable investing is within reach, but collective solutions must be built to facilitate this process.

Framework: Global Sustainable Action Plan for Non-Financial Data

The growing demand for reliable and comparable sustainability data cannot be solved independently by any single nation, regulator, sustainability standard, investor, or service provider. A global sustainable action plan for non-financial data is required. In this section, the author proposes that a global sustainable action plan for ESG data consists of four building blocks—all of which are required to achieve high-quality data for market participants.

- The first building block consists of extending the core infrastructure of capital markets by including sustainability objectives—advancing financial accounting standards to include non-financial or sustainability accounting standards and sustainability frameworks.
- The second building block consists of national regulations building in sustainability or non-financial information into the growing mandatory requirements needed by investors, consumer protection, and to align with larger global policies or planetary boundaries.
- The third building block consists of leading data and research providers developing new products that are directly aligned with the sustainability standards, frameworks, and regulations.
- The final building block consists of leveraging platform technologies to scale sustainable or non-financial data disclosure across thousands of companies and distribute that non-financial data across global capital markets.

CORE INFRASTRUCTURE FOR FINANCIAL AND NON-FINANCIAL DATA

The twentieth century demonstrated that high-quality financial information is essential to create capital markets that are transparent, accountable, and efficient. Financial accounting standards were critical to the development of capital markets and evolved across different regions to establish a set of principles that companies can follow when they prepare and publish their financial statements. Financial accounting standards provide a standardized way of describing a company's financial performance—in an understandable data-driven language that regulators enforce, auditors assure, and investors implement to make better-informed decisions in capital markets. Publicly listed companies on stock exchanges and financial institutions are legally required to publish their financial reports and data in accordance with now well-established accounting standards. These standards for financial data foster trust, growth, and long-term financial stability in the global economy.

As a starting point, it is necessary to understand that frameworks generally provide principles-based guidance on how information is structured, how it is prepared, and what broad topics are covered. Meanwhile, standards provide specific, detailed, and replicable requirements for what should be reported for each topic, including detailed reporting metrics. In other words, frameworks and standards are complementary tools, and each has a critical function to play in ensuring a comprehensive reporting landscape. The following are some of the major financial and non-financial data frameworks and standard-setting bodies for both financial and non-financial data (Table 14.1).

GRI and SASB (now via the Value Reporting Foundation, VRF and its integration with IFRS) provide compatible standards for sustainability reporting, which are designed to fulfill different purposes and are based on different approaches to materiality: (1) SASB's industry-specific standards identify the subset of sustainability-related risks and opportunities most likely to affect a company's financial condition (e.g., its balance sheet), operating performance (e.g., its income statement), or risk profile (e.g., its market valuation and cost of capital); (2) GRI Standards focus on the economic, environmental, and social impacts of a company, and hence its contributions—positive or negative—toward sustainable development. Users of the GRI Standards identify issues that are of primary importance to their stakeholders (i.e., material issues). Importantly, the concept of materiality should be seen as a dynamic one since if not already financially material at the time of reporting, these impacts may become financially material over time.

Collaboration Across Frameworks and Standard-Setters

Significant progress has been made to work in partnership across both financial and non-financial standards and reporting frameworks. Major standard-setting bodies have announced and started implementing initiatives designed to streamline sustainability reporting and ultimately introduce a more coherent and manageable reporting landscape for corporations and their stakeholders alike.

Tracing the evolution of the harmonization wave of sustainability ratings and standard-setting bodies, the Global Initiative for Sustainability Ratings (GISR) was co-founded in 2011, by the non-profit Ceres and Tellus Institute, the two organizations that co-founded the GRI more than a decade earlier. The missions of the two initiatives were complementary from the outset, each focused on different stages of the information value chain. While GRI pioneered the concept of standardized sustainability reporting, GISR sought to bring the same rigor and comparability to sustainability ratings. GRI brought order to disparate disclosure frameworks emerging in the late 1990s and early 2000s, while GISR sought to bring order to the increasingly chaotic field of sustainability ratings, ranking, and indices. Together, the two played vital roles in elevating the practice of ESG and sustainable investing worldwide.

TABLE 14.1
The Frameworks and Standards for Financial and Non-Financial Data

The Frameworks and Standard Setters for Financial Data	
• Financial Accounting Standards Board (FASB)	The independent, private-sector, not-for-profit organization that establishes financial accounting and reporting standards for public and private companies and not-for-profit organizations that follow Generally Accepted Accounting Principles (GAAP).
• International Accounting Standards Board (IASB)	Not-for-profit international organization responsible for developing a single set of high-quality, global accounting standards, known as IFRS Standards. IFRS Standards are now required in over 140 jurisdictions, with many others permitting their use.
The Frameworks and Standard Setters for Non-Financial Data	
• Global Reporting Initiative (GRI)	An international independent organization that has pioneered corporate sustainability reporting since 1997. GRI helps businesses, governments, and other organizations understand and communicate the impact of business on critical sustainability issues such as climate change, human rights, corruption, and many others.
• Sustainability Accounting Standards Board (SASB)	An independent standard-setting organization that develops and maintains robust reporting standards that enable businesses around the world to identify, manage, and communicate financially material sustainability information to their investors. SASB standards are evidence based, developed with broad market participation, and are designed to be cost-effective for companies and decision-useful for investors.
• Value Reporting Foundation	In November 2020, the International Integrated Reporting Council (IIRC) and the SASB announced their intention to merge into the Value Reporting Foundation, which was officially formed in June 2021. The Value Reporting Foundation is a global nonprofit organization that offers a suite of resources designed to help businesses and investors develop a shared understanding of enterprise value—how it is created, preserved, and eroded.
• International Sustainability Standards Board	ISSB was formed on 3 November 2021 at COP26 in Glasgow with the mission to develop—in the public interest—standards that result in a high-quality, comprehensive global baseline of sustainability disclosures focused on the needs of investors and the financial markets. The intention is for the ISSB's standards to cover important sustainability topics on which investors want information. It will begin with climate, due to the urgent need for information on climate-related matters. It is also the intention that the ISSB will develop both thematic and industry-based requirements.
• Task Force for Climate-Related Financial Disclosure (TCFD)	Designed to solicit consistent, decision-useful, forward-looking information on the material financial impacts of climate-related risks and opportunities, including those related to the global transition to a lower-carbon economy. The TCFD recommendations are adoptable by all organizations with public debt or equity in G20 jurisdictions for use in mainstream financial filings.

Such initiatives paved the way for further collaboration discussions between the dominant ESG standards bodies GRI and SASB in July 2020. The partnership aims at helping stakeholders streamline reporting along both regimes, with the goal of providing greater clarity on how the two regimes can be used concurrently (SASB, 2020). Moreover, in September 2020, the

IFRS Foundation launched a consultation regarding the need for a global sustainability reporting standard and the role IFRS can play in the process (IFRS, 2021b). At COP26 in Glasgow, IFRS reaffirmed this coalition-based approach, announcing the establishment of the "International Sustainability Standards Board"(ISSB) comprising existing standard-setters and frameworks, including TCFD, CDSB, VRF, and WEF, the initiative also garnering support by IOSCO (NGFS, 2021).

Indeed, we can trace back calls for consistency in climate-related reporting to 2015 (CDSB, 2015). The formation of the ISSB marks a momentous shift in how sustainability data is perceived across capital markets. Sitting alongside the International Accounting Standards Board (IASB), ISSB is poised to become the global sustainability disclosure baseline, similar to the evolution of the financial reporting ecosystem in the last century.

According to the IFRS Foundation's revised constitution (IFRS, 2021a), the ISSB will be in charge of all ESG-related technical matters of the IFRS Foundation, including:

(1) Developing and pursuing the IFRS Foundation's technical agenda, subject to consultation requirements with the IFRS Trustees and the public; and
(2) Preparing and issuing Sustainability Disclosure Standards and exposure drafts, following the due process stipulated in the constitution.

To furnish the ISSB with a solid foundation on which to build this technical work, the IFRS Foundation also established the Technical Readiness Working Group (TRWG), which includes representatives from the VRF, CDSB, TCFD, IASB, and World Economic Forum. The disclosure standards developed by ISSB will ultimately build on the TCFD Recommendations and the SASB Standards. Starting with a focus on climate-related disclosures, the ISSB aims to facilitate compatibility with numerous jurisdiction-specific reporting requirements, such as the EU's proposed Corporate Sustainability Reporting Directive, thereby streamlining a currently fragmented sustainability disclosure landscape.

Such projects signal a commendable and well overdue shift toward a better coordinated and significantly improved sustainability data landscape. Once these alignment efforts are successfully implemented, both the issuers and the end users of ESG information stand to benefit from a significantly enhanced sustainability data environment.

ESG REGULATIONS AND POLICY INITIATIVES: A RISING TIDE

The second building block within the framework for a global sustainable action plan on non-financial data is national and regional regulation. In the following section, the chapter explores the most significant global and EU-focused developments in the field of ESG regulation and policy initiatives.

One of the dominant high-level sustainable finance initiatives is the Network for Greening the Financial System (NGFS). It consists of leading global central banks and supervisors who acknowledge that climate-related and environmental risks also represent a source of financial risks and that central banks and supervisors should ensure that the financial system builds up resilience to these material risks. As of June 14th 2022, the NGFS comprised 116 members and 19 observers. Members include the European Central Bank, European Banking Authority, Bank of England, De Nederlandsche Bank, Banque de France, Deutsche Bundesbank, Norges Bank, Hong Kong Monetary Authority, Monetary Authority of Singapore, and Bank of Japan. Observers include the International Monetary Fund, Organisation for Economic Cooperation and Development, and World Bank and the International Finance Corporation.

Building on such global efforts, the last years have seen an emergence of regional ESG regulatory developments, among which the European Commission's 2018 Action Plan on Sustainable Finance. EU policy makers set out a comprehensive strategy to connect finance with sustainability throughout the European Union—with policies targeting reorienting capital flows toward a more sustainable economy, mainstreaming sustainability information into risk management, and fostering transparency and long-termism through sustainability disclosure. In addition to the European regulatory regime, there are a number of regional or national legislators that are beginning to adopt better defined and more standardized sustainability reporting duties for companies within their jurisdictional remits.

These include the Hong Kong Exchange ESG listing rules, the Singapore Exchange sustainability reporting guidance (implemented on a comply or explain basis), the revised UK Stewardship Code covering the reporting of material ESG issues in disclosure obligations (Financial Reporting Council, 2020), as well as the recent US Securities and Exchange Commission ESG reporting recommendations draft (Securities and Exchange Commission, 2020). In jurisdictions like India, the pace of ESG regulatory developments has increased rapidly in the last decade, with some recent notable changes including the Stewardship Code for Mutual Fund and AIF companies and applicability of revised "Business Responsibility and Sustainability Reporting" framework for the country's top 1,000 listed entities. These developments come in addition to various country-level commitments to reach carbon neutrality and streamline sustainability disclosures (Asian Investor, 2021). In light of recent political developments in the United States, the Biden administration has likewise focused efforts on climate change risk management, as well as on introducing an enhanced level of corporate disclosure and due diligence regarding business sustainability practices and investors' integration of ESG risks into the investment process.

EU Spotlight: The EU Action Plan on Sustainable Finance

In March 2018, the European Commission released an Action Plan for Financing Sustainable Growth. The plan is a response to recommendations from the High-Level Expert Group (HLEG) on Sustainable Finance, which were submitted to the Commission on 31 January 2018. The European Union Action Plan (also called the EU Green Deal) has paved the way for other jurisdictions around the globe as an example of policy-driven sustainability integration into market practices. The EU's sustainable finance and data strategy is also emerging as one of the key building blocks that underpin the depth and extent of sustainability data disclosures by market participants in Europe and beyond. The EU Green Deal has thus emerged as perhaps the most ambitious package of measures introduced so far by a regulatory body, having the core objective of reallocating capital toward a more sustainable, long-term direction. The Plan outlines reforms in three main areas, segmented along ten core strategic objectives (see Figure 14.2).

It is designed to ensure the successful integration of sustainability considerations into economic decisions by requesting streamlined information disclosures from the entire spectrum of market participants, including financial markets, investment firms, pensions, and insurance providers, as well as corporate issuers.

In the following, the author outlines some of the main legal instruments that underpin the EU sustainable finance disclosure framework, so as to shed light on the core building blocks of the European data disclosure regime. Figure 14.3 presents a summary of the major regulatory initiatives that underpin the Action Plan's strategic objectives.

Sustainable Finance Disclosure Regulation (SFDR)

Of particular importance and relevance to financial market participants is the Regulation on Sustainability-related Disclosures in the Financial Services Sector ("SFDR" or "Disclosure Regulation")—a regulatory framework that became mandatory for financial market participants that have a European footprint, as of 10 March 2021. Under the Regulation, asset managers and other entities offering financial products in the EU will need to implement a due diligence policy with respect to the principal adverse impacts of investment decisions on the sustainability factors covered in the framework. Notably, the Regulation is applicable to *all* financial market participants, regardless of whether they purport to be offering sustainability-related

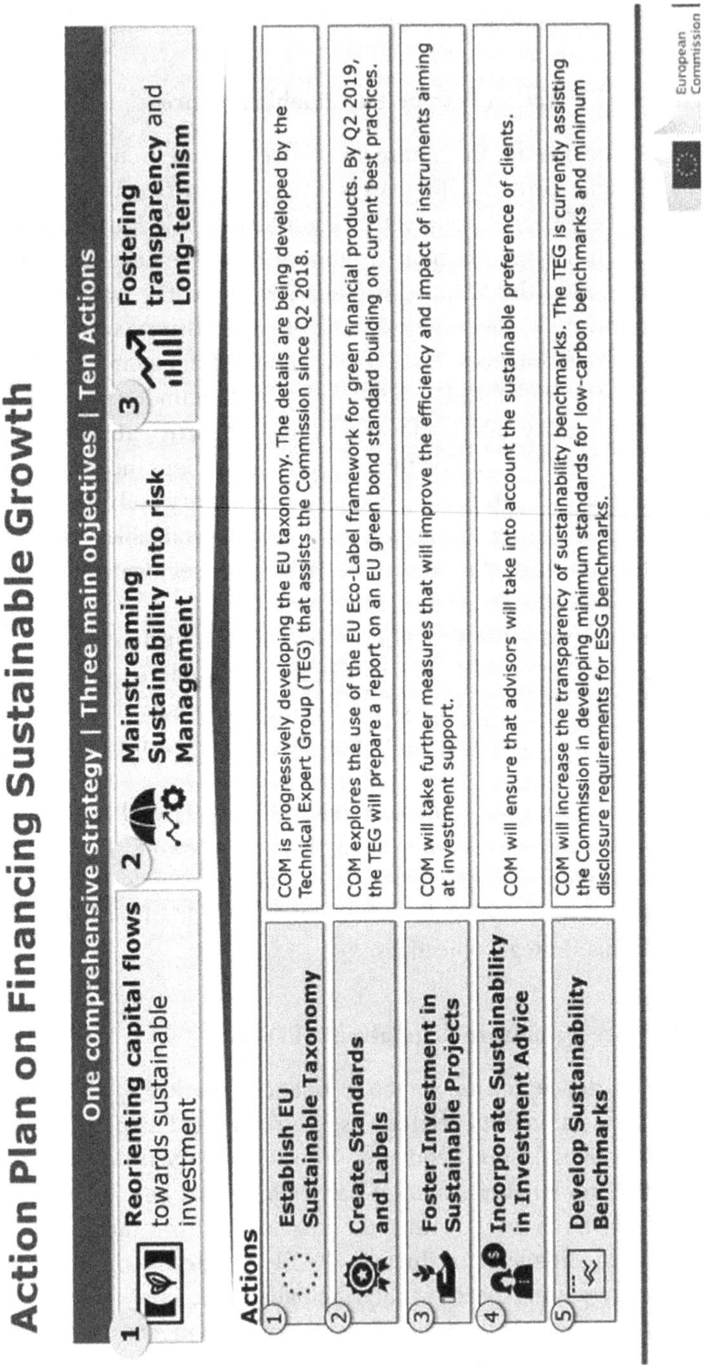

FIGURE 14.2 EU Sustainable Finance Action Plan Objectives

(Source: EU Commission Action Plan on Financing Sustainable Growth, 2018.)

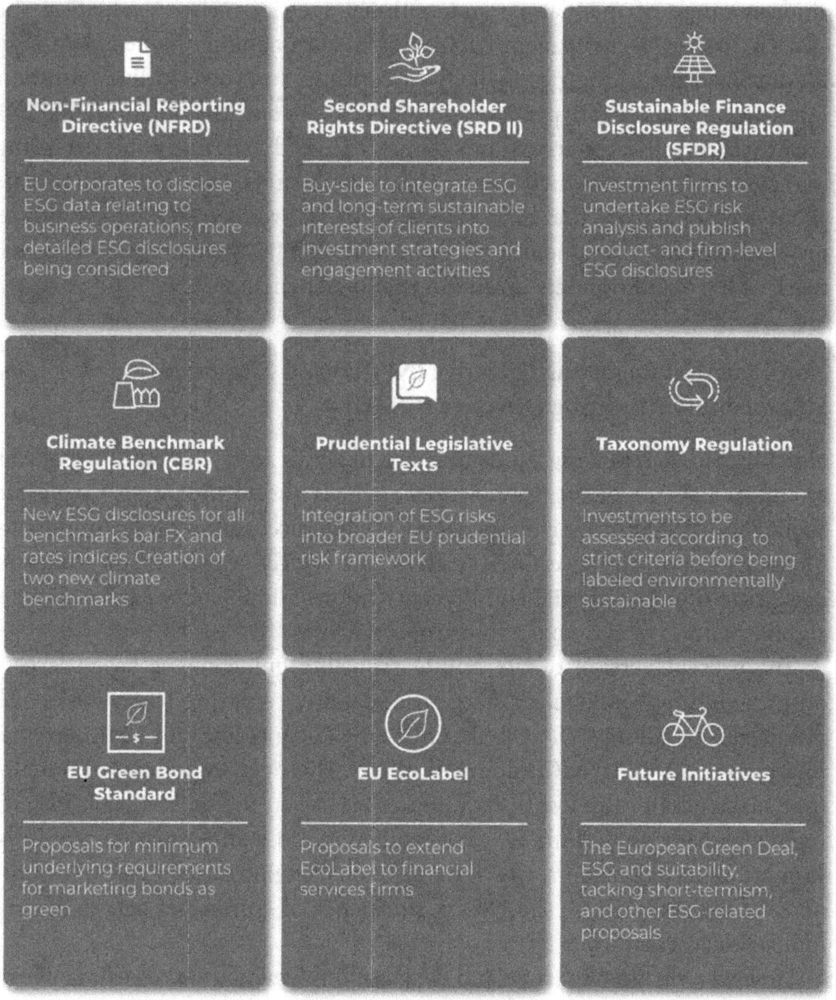

FIGURE 14.3 Overview of the Main ESG Regulatory Initiatives in the EU
(Source: copyright: ESG Book © 2022.)

products or not. The SFDR is hence an important part of the EU's ambitious legislative program to make ESG concerns a central plank of regulation in the financial services industry.

The SFDR has so far proved to be among the better-defined ESG regulatory instruments, designed to establish clear reporting boundaries and metrics for regulated entities. In particular, as the current version of the Regulation stands, entities should be prepared to report along a defined set of quantitative sustainability indicators, or principal adverse impacts (PAI), segmented along a range of mandatory and optional metrics—when evaluating the adverse impact of investment decisions on sustainability themes. Although the finalized list of metrics is likely to continue to evolve in line with best reporting and disclosure practices, it is indeed welcome that financial markets are provided with a concrete frame of reference and a starting point regarding the scope and extent of their sustainability disclosures. The SFDR will impact all international firms that market their financial products in the EEA and/or provide relevant investment services to EEA clients. The extra-jurisdictional reach of EU legislation sets up an international benchmark.

Non-Financial Reporting Directive (NFRD) and Corporate Sustainability Reporting Directive (CSRD)

Notably, SFDR reporting guidelines are likely to form the building blocks of future ESG reporting frameworks such as the forthcoming Corporate Sustainability Reporting Directive (CSRD), the successor to the current Non-Financial Reporting Directive (NFRD). The NFRD lays down the rules on disclosure of non-financial and diversity information by companies above a certain size and of systemic public importance.

The present version of the NFRD reporting guidelines is based largely on the building blocks of existing sustainability reporting frameworks and standards, including CDP, CDSB, GRI, OECD Guidelines for Multinational Enterprises, SASB, UNGC, and many others. This open-endedness of the current sustainability disclosure requirements in even the most advanced ESG regime globally, that of the EU, has resulted in too many disparate reporting formats, units and extents, which makes it challenging to aggregate and compare trends and analyze the ESG performance of companies across diverse industries and sectors.

However, the precise scope and extent of implementation regarding which of the aforementioned frameworks to integrate and reference is largely left to the discretion of the reporting company. The objectives of the NFRD revision are therefore twofold: first, to improve disclosure of climate and environmental data by companies to better inform investors about the sustainability of their investments and, second, to give effect to changes required by the new Disclosure Regulation and the forthcoming Taxonomy Regulation.

Following the April 2021 EU Sustainable Finance Package, there is now greater clarity regarding the direction of travel of sustainability reporting in the EU. The EU introduced a proposal for overhauling the NFRD, to be superseded by a new CSRD. According to the proposal, nearly 50,000 companies in the EU will become subject to detailed EU sustainability reporting standards, an increase from the 11,000 companies that fall under the current requirements. Moreover, the EU Commission proposed the development of standards for large companies and separate, proportionate standards for SMEs, which non-listed SMEs can use voluntarily. Another notable feature of the new proposal means that the CSRD would most likely require all companies within scope of the Directive to seek assurance for reported non-financial information. The new legislation aims to ensure alignment with other EU initiatives on sustainable finance, in particular the SFDR and the Taxonomy Regulation. The objective of regulators is hence to reduce complexity and the potential for duplicative reporting requirements, which is commendable. While the CSRD update still needs to pass through the EU's cumbersome legislative process, it is expected that companies would need to apply the standards for the first time to reports published in 2024, covering financial year 2023.

EU Sustainable Finance Taxonomy

These developments mean that policy makers are now moving in the direction of a more clearly defined set of metrics and indicators that would need to be commonly reported by corporate entities, in line with the disclosures required by SFDR and other well-defined regulatory instruments such as the EU Sustainable Finance Taxonomy.

The Taxonomy is intended to function as a unifying framework that defines what constitutes a sustainable economic activity in European capital markets. The EU regulators are thereby creating a detailed classification system of (mainly environmental) factors that financial participants who purport to pursue certain sustainability objectives need to meet before they can market their products and services as sustainable on European markets. The goal of the Taxonomy is hence to avoid greenwashing and introduce a common foundation upon which to align definitions and ensure greater comparability of sustainability disclosures.

To qualify as green, an investment needs to contribute to at least one of the following six objectives, while not significantly harming any of the other five.

(1) Climate Change Mitigation—the activity contributes to greenhouse gas stabilization consistent with the goals of the Paris Agreement, through certain prescribed means including, for example, the generation of renewable energy.
(2) Climate Change Adaptation—the activity includes adaptation solutions that substantially reduce the adverse impact (or risk) of the current and expected future climate on (i) other people, nature, or assets; or (ii) the economic activity itself, in each case without increasing the risk of an adverse impact on other people, nature, and assets.
(3) Sustainable Use and Protection of Water and Marine Resources—the activity substantially contributes to achieving the good status of water

bodies or marine resources, or to preventing their deterioration when they are already in good status, through certain prescribed means (including, for example, through wastewater management).

(4) Transition to a Circular Economy—the economic activity contributes substantially to waste prevention, reuse and recycling, through certain prescribed means (including, for example, by improving the recyclability of certain products).

(5) Pollution Prevention and Control—the activity contributes substantially to pollution prevention and control through certain prescribed means (including, for example, by preventing or, where that is not practicable, reducing pollutant emissions into air, water, or land (other than greenhouse gasses)); and

(6) Protection and Restoration—the activity contributes substantially to protecting, conserving, or restoring biodiversity and to achieving the good condition of ecosystems, or to protecting ecosystems that are already in good condition, through certain prescribed means (including, for example, sustainable land use and management).

In addition to contributing to one of these six objectives, for an activity to qualify as an environmentally sustainable activity under the Taxonomy Regulation, the activity must also comply with the following criteria.

- No Significant Harm—the activity must not significantly harm any of the environmental objectives mentioned earlier.
- Minimum Social and Governance Safeguards—the activity must be carried out in compliance with a number of minimum social and governance safeguards as referred to in the Taxonomy Regulation.
- Compliance with Technical Screening Criteria—the activity must comply with technical screening criteria for each of the six objectives that will be specified by the European Commission.

The EU Green Taxonomy has emerged as one of the most detailed and granular ESG disclosure requirements issued till date by any regulatory body globally. While introducing such comprehensive reporting obligations leaves a lower degree of discretion and flexibility to companies in terms of the expected scope of reporting, this also ensures that disclosures follow a more streamlined structure that makes reported data easier to analyze, compare, and integrate into investment decisions. As these various legislative measures come into force, it will be more important than ever to ensure that corporate-level sustainability disclosures are comparable and actionable, given they form the foundation of disclosures required by investors and financial markets.

Application Beyond EU Borders

Despite the fact that the chapter has so far discussed legislation that applies in the European context, the EU sustainable finance framework is likely to produce a significant ripple effect across jurisdictions. Indeed, its applicability will certainly extend beyond the remit of the EU itself. This applies both in terms of setting an example of best reporting practices but also in light of the fact that instruments such as the SFDR will impact all international firms that market their financial products in the EEA and/or provide relevant investment services to EEA clients. The extra-jurisdictional reach of EU legislation sets up an international benchmark for regulated entities and establishes a frame of reference for other regulators that are looking to set up their own ESG disclosure frameworks in place.

In summary, one of the key building blocks of a global sustainable finance action plan is a consistent, effective, and scalable regulatory framework. The EU has already provided a good starting point, but its successful implementation will be key. Moreover, the extra-jurisdictional nature of the EU Green Deal means that a large-scale mobilization effort is needed and robust ESG data disclosure capacity building needs to be ensured to allow for meaningful sustainability integration in practice. In this regard, identifying and effectively addressing the prevailing ESG data challenges that exist today will be a prerequisite.

MAIN ESG DATA CHALLENGES TODAY

Mainstreaming sustainability will remain a challenge as long as publicly available ESG data is not easily accessible at scale. Today, sustainability is being integrated into the financial system through hundreds of sustainability ratings and ranking organizations. Over 72% of corporations use ESG ratings to inform their decision-making (Euronext Corporate Services, 2020). Yet, the majority of sustainability ratings and rankings are still underpinned by unreliable third-party data, whose sources are not transparent and carry significant errors and costs, unrelated to the company being rated. This affects a corporation's cost of capital and long-term profitability in ways that the company is prevented from impacting directly. Additionally, more than $100 trillion of assets under management are committed to the PRI, while many of the world's largest public companies have pledged to meet net-zero targets, as sustainability shapes global markets in the twenty-first century. However, a lack of disclosure, limited accessibility, and inconsistency of ESG data are limiting the acceleration of capital allocation toward low-carbon and sustainable business activities, just when it is most urgently needed. The commitments made following the conclusion of the Paris Agreement in 2015 amplify a critical market need for accessible, comparable, and transparent ESG data to build trust and alignment among companies, investors, and standard-setters and to reliably measure progress on sustainable development.

These are also the reasons why policy makers are increasingly exploring the possibility of regulating ESG data and ratings agencies, given their growing impact on financial stability. For instance, in November 2021, the International Organization of Securities Commissions (IOSCO) issued a report pointing out the current ecosystem challenges that exist within ESG ratings and data products and calling for enhanced regulatory scrutiny of such products (IOSCO, "Environmental, Social and Governance (ESG) Ratings and Data Products Providers," Nov. 2021). In response, the Indian securities regulator Securities and Exchange Board of India (SEBI) published a set of draft rules in January 2022, according to which providers of ESG ratings and commentary would have to obtain accreditation from SEBI, on a two-yearly basis. The initiative focuses on scrutinizing the processes and policies each data provider follows regarding transparency, methodology, and conflict of interest. It is likely that other regulators around the world, such as the UK's Financial Conduct Authority, the European Securities and Markets Authority, and the European Commission might soon follow suit toward introducing more stringent regulations governing the conduct of the ESG data market.

Poor data coverage, the unknown scope of errors, and limited transparency over the data origination process create a lack of trust in sustainability data. Combined with substantial costs from third-party data vendors, this limits the use of raw ESG data at scale. The prevalent status quo results in a disconnected system where neither the issuer nor the end user of sustainability data benefits from this process. The following are some of the leading ESG data challenges today.

- Proliferation of ESG standards and reporting frameworks: given there is no agreement currently on the content and scope of data to report on, there exist a multitude of reporting types and various formats of presenting sustainability information (open text descriptions, tables and charts, images, or web versions of data infographics). This makes it challenging for data to be extracted and analyzed at scale, with a high confidence interval regarding data accuracy.
- Cherry-picking of material topics and incomplete reporting: naturally, companies report data on different topics based on their industry, sector, size, geography, etc. They are invited to self-select their material topics, leaving a lot of room for interpretation as to what is material for a particular company, and hence—what specific data points to report on.
- Data coverage: data errors are common when sustainability data is integrated by third-party raw data providers. Moreover, sustainability data

coverage remains inadequate in emerging and private markets (WRI, 2016). This is problematic, given that the credibility of data sources is seen as the most important factor in determining ESG data quality (Sustainability Institute, 2019).

- Data access and ownership: ESG data access is currently limited, given that the costs for sustainability data can range widely, depending on the specific use case. Moreover, once the data is reported, companies forfeit ownership of their data and have little control over how stakeholders use and integrate their data (Berg et al., 2019).
- Reporting burden: Companies suffer from ESG survey fatigue: for example, large-cap companies receive in excess of 200 sustainability questionnaires per year (Governance and Accountability Institute, 2018), taking them an average of 18 workdays to submit a response to a single data request (Conference Board, 2018). This is compounded by the restrictions imposed by inadequate annual data reporting cycles in terms of data timeliness.

These are just but a few of the prevalent sustainability data problems that afflict global markets at the dawn of the global ESG movement. In view of the complex nature of these ESG data challenges, involving numerous stakeholders, technical implementation issues around the intricacies of systematizing sustainability information, and the urgency of taking action to successfully implement the global sustainable development agenda, powerful tools will be needed to facilitate the ESG data collection and analytics process. In essence, what is needed is effectively harnessing the role of technology and data-sharing protocols for the public good.

THE TECHNOLOGY SOLUTION IMPERATIVE

The earlier observation that growing regulatory requirements put a premium on proactive ESG data management and an emphasis on raw sustainability information has significant ramifications to how sustainability information is being managed today. The days of relying on high-level third-party ESG ratings and rankings, while disregarding the underlying drivers and raw data indicators, are soon coming to an end. This is motivated by both bottom-up investor demand and top-down regulatory action. This also means that emerging ESG data infrastructure and technology solutions that are flexible, yet proactively measure the most relevant sustainability issues (for example, decarbonization and human rights due diligence), are more critical than ever.

Creating a scalable technology data infrastructure that supports diverse use cases and reporting requirements (see Figure 14.4) is fundamental to achieving the mission of truly mainstreaming sustainable finance. This can be achieved only through next-generation sustainable intelligence capabilities.

FIGURE 14.4 Technology Aligned to the Building Blocks for a Global Sustainable Action Plan

(Source: copyright: ESG Book © 2022.)

The proliferation of non-financial reporting standards and disclosure regimes, while welcome and necessary, can also result in a considerable reporting burden for corporates that leads to the inconsistent application of ESG data into investment decisions in financial markets. What is needed is the effective harmonization between what are now wildly diverging approaches to data disclosure, a clear mapping between reporting frameworks and indicators, as well as a growing consistency of sustainability disclosures over time. Achieving this is of vital importance for the successful functioning of sustainable markets. The successful alignment between ESG reporting practices across diverse standards and metrics will be key in reducing reporting fatigue while at the same time streamlining information disclosure and the decision-usefulness of data.

The good news is that market-driven technology solutions already exist. Platforms like ESG Book (www.esgbook.com)[1] present a unique opportunity to transform the world of business. Indeed, ESG Book makes an effort at systematizing the world's predominant reporting provisions and integrates a mapping between overlapping metrics, which is designed to align the reporting indicators of various frameworks and as a result—reduce the disclosure requirements that companies have to comply with. This approach also forms the backbone of the ethos adopted in developing ESG Book's research and data solutions. Transparency and a framework-agnostic approach to sustainability data sit at the heart of technology infrastructure that can be free of systemic bias and adopted at scale. Such an approach focuses on creating an integrated technology ecosystem that serves as both the data collection engine for reporting entities, but also as the analytics and delivery infrastructure for end users of reported ESG data.

Harnessing the potential of advanced technology tools to support data disclosure along well-established and custom-built reporting frameworks, including the numerous ESG regulatory developments that are entering into force, provides significant added value to platform users that need help in navigating the increasingly complex sustainability reporting landscape. Based on the amount of reported data on the platform, a suite of analytics and added-value functionalities will gradually be integrated into the tool, in turn allowing for sustainability integration into strategy, risk management, and investment decisions.

If we want to mainstream sustainable finance, we need to democratize the ownership and use of ESG data. This requires a fundamental change in the way data is provided, interpreted, and applied. Currently, companies and investors do not have the opportunity to act on their own to change the data system they operate in. ESG Book brings together an ecosystem of partners around a technology infrastructure platform to provide a company-centric digital solution, empowering corporations to report their sustainability data digitally, streamlining the data collection process, and easing the current reporting burden.

The following is an excerpt of the guiding principles the platform has committed to.

(1) Companies are custodians of their own data and leverage the platform's digital infrastructure: With ESG Book, corporates gain back control over their sustainability data by being in charge of submitting, updating, editing, and maintaining their data in real time, unrestricted by the annual reporting data cycle. This improves transparency as well as market-driven oversight from investors, banks, and business partners and reduces errors common within the existing ESG data ecosystem.
(2) Transparency on data usage and interactions brings more meaningful reporting: Once directly connected to their stakeholders, companies are empowered to report on what is most valuable or requested by stakeholders, reducing the noise in reporting and identifying data gaps more clearly.
(3) Accessibility and non-discrimination: Reported raw data on ESG Book is made available to all users and displayed in a non-discriminatory manner, independent of judgment in the form of opaque ratings and rankings.
(4) Easing the reporting burden: ESG Book cross-populates multiple reporting questionnaires, standards, and frameworks simultaneously. For

instance, after disclosing CO_2 emissions once, other related questionnaires will also be populated with the same applicable data point. This frees up internal company resources to go beyond reporting, toward action-driven insights.

(5) Framework-agnostic: ESG Book provides a level-playing-field to all stakeholders, allowing parties to collect and report data based on sustainability questions from multiple reporting frameworks (e.g., SFDR, EU Taxonomy, GRI, SASB, TCFD,) at the same time.

ESG Book is built on the foundation that it is the very interaction between companies, investors, and consumers that creates the virtuous circle that encourages the former to make a continuous disclosure of their metrics and to improve them, and the latter—to use them to make more conscious consumer choices and to be consistent with them over time. In other words, this creates a self-sustaining ecosystem that does not deviate abruptly from the path of market freedom that we have travelled over the last two centuries (the results of which need not be recalled) but which is implemented with a new awareness that allows market agents to rebalance priorities, prices, and production in real time.

CONCLUSION

The disclosure of non-financial information by companies and their investors is only going to grow across the globe, a phenomenon that will not leave developing and emerging markets unaffected. The resulting improved level of ESG data availability and data quality is in turn going to result in better-informed financial decisions. The objective is a more robust and resilient market infrastructure that is better prepared to integrate and digest sustainability information, as well as improved longer-term economic performance. This chapter has outlined the evolution of ESG data over time, stressing the need for greater coherence in sustainability reporting, rationalized and coherent frameworks, built on what is ideally effective and replicable regulation. In turn, this enables stakeholders to generate and better systematize ESG data, empowered by the technology infrastructure that helps them to transparently access and interpret it. The author has sought to demonstrate that technology tools can empower a mature entrepreneurial fabric made up of "socialized" (to borrow Schumpeter's term) entrepreneurs, responsible for a society which is aware of the impact of each stakeholder on the social fabric and responds accordingly. In other words, this helps shape a world made up of responsible individuals who are less and less dependent on being bureaucratically regulated, as they are able to freely identify the most efficient solutions for a better and more sustainable future.

NOTE

1 The author is an employee of ESG Book GmbH.

REFERENCES

Asian Investor (2021). *Fund Houses Struggle With New HK ESG Disclosure Rules.* Available at: www.asianinvestor.net/article/fund-houses-to-struggle-with-new-hk-esg-disclosure-rules/469494 (Accessed: 24 February 2022).

Berg, F., Kölbel, J. F., & Rigobon, R. (2019). *Aggregate Confusion: The Divergence of ESG Ratings.* Available at: https://papers.ssrn.com/sol3/papers.cfm?abstract_id=3438533 (Accessed: 24 February 2022).

Climate Disclosure Standards Board (CDSB) (2015). *The Consistency Project.* Available at: https://live-cdsb.pantheonsite.io/consistency-project (Accessed: 24 February 2022).

Conference Board (2018). *ESG Rating and Ranking Initiatives—a Necessary Evil?* Available at: www.conference-board.org/blog/postdetail.cfm?post=6756 (Accessed: 24 February 2022).

Euronext Corporate Services (2020). *Why Your Organisation's ESG Rating Is (Increasingly) Important.* Available at: https://blog.corporateservices.euronext.com/en/esg-rating (Accessed: 24 February 2022).

Financial Reporting Council. *The UK Stewardship Code 2020.* Available at: www.frc.org.uk/getattachment/5aae591d-d9d3-4cf4-814a-d14e156a1d87/Stewardship-Code_Final2.pdf (Accessed: 24 February 2022).

Governance and Accountability Institute (2018). *Annual ESG Survey & Query.* Available at: www.ga-institute.com/newsletter/press-release/article/post-its-annual-esg-survey-query-time-public-companies-are-in-response-mode.html (Accessed: 24 February 2022).

International Financial Reporting Standards (IFRS) (2021a). *IFRS Constitution.* Available at: www.ifrs.org/content/dam/ifrs/about-us/legal-and-governance/constitution-docs/ifrs-foundation-constitution-2021.pdf (Accessed: 24 February 2022).

International Financial Reporting Standards (IFRS) (2021b). *IFRS Foundation Trustees Consult on Global Approach to Sustainability Reporting and on Possible Foundation Role.* Available at: www.ifrs.org/projects/work-plan/sustainability-reporting/ (Accessed: 24 February 2022).

Network for Greening the Financial System (NGFS) (2021). *Progress Report on Bridging Data Gaps.* Available at: www.ngfs.net/sites/default/files/medias/documents/progress_report_on_bridging_data_gaps.pdf (Accessed: 24 February 2022).

Principles for Responsible Investment (PRI) (2022). *Regulation Database.* Available at: www.unpri.org/policy/regulation-database (Accessed: 24 February 2022).

Principles for Responsible Investment (PRI) (2021). *88 New Policies Added to PRI's Regulation Database.* Available at: www.unpri.org/pri-blog/88-new-policies-added-to-pris-regulation-database/8532.article (Accessed: 24 February 2022).

Sustainability Institute (2019). *Rate the Raters 2019: Expert Views on ESG Ratings.* Available at: https://sustainability.com/wp-content/uploads/2019/02/SA-RateTheRaters-2019-1.pdf#page=11 (Accessed: 24 February 2022).

Sustainability Accounting Standards Board (SASB) (2020). *Promoting Clarity and Compatibility in the Sustainability Landscape.* Available at: www.sasb.org/blog/gri-and-sasb-announce-collaboration-sustainability-reporting (Accessed: 24 February 2022).

Securities and Exchange Commission (2020). *Response to Climate and ESG Risks and Opportunities.* Available at: www.sec.gov/sec-response-climate-and-esg-risks-and-opportunities (Accessed: 24 February 2022).

The Economist (2017). *The World's Most Valuable Resource Is No Longer Oil, but Data.* Available at: www.economist.com/leaders/2017/05/06/the-worlds-most-valuable-resource-is-no-longer-oil-but-data (Accessed: 24 February 2022).

United Nations Environment Program Finance Initiative (UNEP FI) (2021). *Fiduciary Duty in the 21st Century*. Available at: www.unepfi.org/investment/fiduciary-duty (Accessed: 24 February 2022).

World Resources Institute (WRI) (2016). *Navigating the Sustainable Investment Landscape*. Available at: https://wriorg.s3.amazonaws.com/s3fs-public/Navigating_the_Sustainable_Investment_Landscape_0.pdf?_ga=2.241964098.1759491928.1539090645-1190900029.1493379393 (Accessed: 24 February 2022).

15

ESGT—Exponential Technology Requires Exponential Responsibility

Andrea Bonime-Blanc and Dante A. Disparte

INTRODUCTION

In an era of exponential technological change and disruption leaders everywhere must up their game and engage in exponential responsibility. How do they do that? By embracing a holistic environmental, social, governance, *and technological* (ESGT) approach to intangible risk and opportunity management, by incorporating such considerations into strategic planning and product and service R&D and by exponentially turning up the volume on technology governance in all its nuances and incarnations.

The digital transformation agenda preoccupying corporate boards and senior executives has become an all-consuming pillar of leading large, global enterprises. This is as true in the private sector as it is in the government domain and, although less so, also in civil society. Pressure to keep up with the proverbial technological Jones's has led companies to digitize (and digitalize) all facets of their business models. Partly motivated by a quest for efficiency, partly (albeit insufficiently) motivated by an unyielding quest to improve cyber resilience, all, in the private sector at least, motivated by a drive to improve the bottom line.

On top of all that, digital natives are entering the workplace in force, populating the large tech companies, or creating exciting new business models and innovations that outpace and defy many of the old business ways. This new workforce is also demanding, among other things, that far greater attention be paid to all things environmental, social, and governance (ESG). Indeed, many are going further, throwing down the gauntlet and leaving companies

DOI: 10.4324/9781003262039-17

perceived to be "green washers" or what we like to call "ESG or ESGT-washers" to go to greener pastures: purpose-driven established businesses, starting their own businesses from scratch or joining civil society or governmental agencies.

The challenge, however, as is revealed by many teachable lessons in the perils of making digital transformation an outcome as opposed to a journey, is that responsibly harnessing technology requires an evolved governance framework akin to the ESG frameworks that have become, albeit mostly recently, *de rigueur* in corporate management circles. In short, the T of technology is missing in today's ESG frameworks, however fleeting they may be in enterprise governance and management practice.

This chapter addresses how the "T" in ESGT needs to be folded into the overall ESG governance conversation and implementation at all kinds of businesses—from the most established, traditional multinationals and small-to-medium size enterprises (SMEs) to the newest start-ups including pure tech plays. T is not a separate, siloed endeavor that is narrowly related to risk management or digital transformation as it often is in bigger, more established businesses. Nor should T be the be all, end all of a newer, pure tech company or start-up. Indeed, the T is an essential and intricate part of the management and governance of all things intangible or ESGT, whether in the context of an established multinational, an SME, or a start-up. In fact, T is part of every organization's reality regardless of purpose—for profit, non-profit, educational, governmental, intergovernmental, among others. Akin to established companies' "discovery" of all things digital and the sudden need for tech governance within their virtual walls, many of the purely digital or technology-focused new businesses popping up everywhere must also open their lens to incorporate relevant ESG considerations into their tech-heavy focus.

In other words, both the traditional digitizing businesses and the newer purely digital businesses need to integrate and interconnect their particular ESGT issues, risks, and opportunities though they may come at it from different angles—the former from a place where ESG is becoming necessary or is already established and T has been operating in a separate silo; the latter from a place where ESG is nowhere to be found and T dominates everything. Both must develop and achieve a similar outcome: a leadership (management and board) that gets ESGT—that is, an understanding of how their business' specific E, S, G, and T issues, risks, and opportunities affect, interact with, and integrate into their particular business model, mission, vision, purpose, people, strategy, products, and services. Think about what future technological governance challenges await us and get ready now. See Table 15.1 from the Imperial College of London for a sneak preview of the

TABLE 15.1
Future Most Disruptive Technologies

Higher ↑	El Space Elevators	Vr Fully Immersive Virtual Reality	Co Artificial Consciousness	Qt *"We Can't Talk About This One"*
	Is Invisibility Shields	Ph Factory Photosynthesis	Th Transhuman Technologies	Te Telepathy
Socio Economic Disruption	Qs Quantum Safe Crypto-Graphy	Cp Cognitive Prosthetics	Ud Data Uploading to the Brain	Rd Reactionless Drive
↓ ***Lower***	Me Internet of DNA	Tc Thought Control Machine Interfaces	Dr Dream Reading and Recording	Wh Whole Earth Virtualization
	Sooner ←	Time		→ Later

Source: Assembled From The Imperial College of London Table of 100 Disruptive Technologies

(Source: Andrea Bonime-Blanc & GEC Risk Advisory. Table first appeared in A. Bonime-Blanc. *Gloom to Boom*. Routledge 2020. Based on Imperial College of London data.)

most far-out exponential, and as yet uninvented, technologies that could develop and how you as a person, citizen, worker, student, leader are or are not prepared to deal with it.

The following first section of this chapter discusses the very unique context of our times that makes this ESGT discussion not only possible but necessary. In the second section, we discuss what ESGT actually is and how to embed it into strategy. The third section shares several examples of ESGT use cases and, in the fourth section, we provide our thoughts for future-proofing ESGT governance by providing leaders—both management and board—with resilience and sustainability guidance.

CONTEXT, CONTEXT, CONTEXT

Framing the ESGT Approach

The COVID-19 pandemic has exacerbated the tension to responsibly harness technology as a cornerstone of the digital transformation agenda while at the same time accelerating the world's technological adoption and dependency by more than a decade in a single year, raising the stakes. From ensuring household, business, and government continuity, the reliance on technology during the pandemic has been one of the few global differentiators as few global systems did not strain under the weight of a global "work from home experiment". This, of course, has been true mostly for those fortunate enough to have reliable internet connectivity along with the flexibility implied by nomadic work, but it has happened at an unprecedented scale. In this transition, which can be likened to nothing short of a *Great Correction* in terms of the world's political, economic, and commercial systems, how technology is deployed, governed, and made available to the world has emerged as one of the most important questions of our times.

From keeping pace with rampant cyber threats such as the Colonial gas pipeline ransomware attack that hobbled critical gas supplies to the US east coast in 2021, and the exponential rise in health-care facility cyberattacks during the pandemic, to the crippling vulnerabilities and lessons learned from not having an "air gap" between vital industries and the Internet, cyber threat abatement is no longer "nice to have". Rather, it has become a governance must have—a cornerstone for boards, as much as for cabinets and war rooms. At the same time, even so-called fortress nations and companies endowed with fortress balance sheets were enfeebled by arcane approaches to business productivity, for which employees' physical presence in an office was construed as a measure of productivity rather than as a measure of vulnerability and old-fashioned modes of production as economic output shifted from industrial production to services.

The inherently distributed nature of professional nomadic knowledge workers, who were once told that working outside of corporate firewalls would produce cyber vulnerabilities, were the most adaptive people when COVID-19 shifted the world to an unending virtual reality. This virtual reality has not only blown apart the physical construct of center city offices, but it has also emboldened an itinerant knowledge worker class to never return to a 9 to 5 office job again. Some companies are responding favorably (if begrudgingly) by accommodating this shift while others are clinging to the office as the means of production, if nothing else, in recognition of the balance sheet liability represented by empty commercial real estate. Many sectors have no such luxury, raising important questions about how equity and employee rights become universalized, when the means of physical production and economic output still require an actual presence. Indeed, the world's supply chain challenges, in which global supply chains resemble a Stradivarius violin that is at once priceless, fragile, and tightly strung, evidence the need for people as the principal nodes of production and demand.

A more foundational vulnerability was also exposed, which is that the provision of even basic services, whether in the public or private sphere, was also revealed to be nearly impossible without technology at the core.

From the false choice of asking a global electorate to stand in physical lines despite quarantines and social distancing directives, to the inability to carry out even a range of basic services over distances such as teaching, learning, executing real-time payments, among others, drove home one fundamental point—the Internet and all the goods, services, and connectivity it carries is foundational to the modern world. So much so that it needs to be reframed not as the source of company or country competitive advantage or a part of a proprietary technology array but rather as purveyor of digital public goods and common critical infrastructure. How this is governed, including many points of tension such as privacy versus security, censorship resistance, digital copyright protections, among so many others, is a critical governance frontier.

Despite this essential nature of technological connectivity, many of the world's leading institutions are being caught flat-footed by digital transformation and technological risk. There is a governance turpitude on display in how the topmost leaders respond to harnessing technology when it works and, critically, when it fails. It would be wise to remember that a digital space race is afoot in the world, but that just because a process or system can be digitized and made more efficient does not mean that it should.

Some of the governance challenges that will be highlighted in this chapter include managing and responding to cyber risk, addressing broader technological equity challenges such as ubiquitous access to the Internet (along with its affordability), questions relating to algorithmic biases from how people are hired, to how they are granted credit, as well as the perils of autonomous systems, business model automation, and decentralization. All these technological forces are conspiring to challenge governance guardrails and the very corpus of the modern enterprise itself as the world adapts to an always-on, internet-native modus operandi.

The Megatrends of Our Turbulent Times

To understand the crux of our times described earlier, it is important to pan out to a higher distance (the proverbial 60,000-ft view) to understand the convergence of several key existential, strategic, and material megatrends at this specific moment in history. The following is a summary of the multi-year megatrends that are now present which have been developing variously for several years and will continue to change and mutate into the foreseeable future with different and new incarnations over time (see Box 15.1). The point is that all leaders everywhere must be cognizant of and gain situational awareness about these megatrends as they chart their ESGT strategy while developing responsible ESGT governance.

Box 15.1 The Five Megatrends of Our Turbulent Times (2021–2022)

(1) Technological Disruption at the Speed of Light

This is what happens when the pace, depth, and breadth of technological innovation across the world in every sector—business, government, and society—happen at breakneck speed in practically all walks of life—whether in biology, ecology, AI, quantum, or nanotech. This gives rise to both the potential for highly constructive developments or hugely destructive ones depending on whether the tech capabilities are in good or bad, knowledgeable or ignorant, ethical or unethical hands.

(2) Leadership and Institutional Trust Recalibrating

Leadership and Institutional Trust Recalibrating is a multiyear megatrend (first developed in 2021–2022 as "*Leadership and Institutional Trust Plummeting*") based on the fact that, unfortunately, the mediocre-to-bad leadership behaviors we have witnessed for years, even decades, at every level—government, society, business—continue to be deeply concerning. However, in the *ESGT Megatrends Manual 2022–2023*, this megatrend morphed from "Plummeting" to "Recalibrating" to reflect some possible green shoots of better leadership both in the corporate and political spaces, best exemplified in the latter space by Ukrainian President Zelenskyy's stalwart pro-democracy leadership in the face of Putin's aggression in 2022.

(3) Complex Interconnected Risk Intensifying

By definition, this megatrend states that risk is more complex, systemic, large-scale, and interconnected than ever. We call it *Complex Interconnected Risk Intensifying* because what was already a megatrend for a few years—the deep interconnection between different kinds of risk both affecting and morphing—continues to accelerate as our pandemic year has dramatically illustrated.

(4) Geopolitical Tectonics Shifting

This megatrend has been years in the making at both the domestic/national level and the international level and encompasses both the deterioration of democracy in established and emerging democracies (as proven in numerous studies) and the attack on and/or organic weakening of several key international governance institutions, with some interesting twists and turns recently emerging with the election of the Biden/Harris Administration in the United States.

(5) Stakeholder Capitalism Rising

Milton Friedman's "shareholder primacy" form of capitalism has been taking "incoming" for more than a decade but with the pandemic forcing business to think more broadly about its other key stakeholders—namely employees and customers—the rise of stakeholder capitalism has advanced substantially in the past few years. The pandemic has put in stark relief certain needs and expectations of key stakeholders (safety, health, WFH, equity, inclusion, and diversity) that were ignored for too long, adding rocket fuel to the rise of ESG investing. Indeed, 2021 may be an intensifying turning point for this megatrend. This megatrend is mostly about stakeholders—all kinds but the key is to know which ones are the most important for your organization. This megatrend is mostly dominated by the S in ESGT, but as with the other megatrends there are aspects of this megatrend that touch on all the other categories as well.

(Source: Adapted from A. Bonime-Blanc. The ESGT Megatrends Manual 2021–2022 Edition. Diplomatic Courier 2021 and A. Bonime-Blanc. The ESGT Megatrends Manual 2022–2023 Edition. Diplomatic Courier 2022.)

Tangled in Webs—From Web 1.0 to Web 3.0

As technology and software clash with all facets of society and the global economy, the need for enduring approaches to governance anchored in first principles is crucial. The creative destruction cycle that drives the global economy forward has little respect for incumbency—especially not for too long. In the same way as the Internet dethroned the traditional print media stalwarts, other industries are now under wholesale reinvention and assault from emerging technologies—including the very form of the corporation.

The first generation of the Internet looks decidedly analog and even benign compared to today's emerging third generation of the web. The world's response to each of these transitions is marked by the same blend of anxious ambivalence, fear, and eventual embrace as technology fades to the background and outcomes come to the foreground. This process of change is normal at the individual, household, community, societal, and even the global level, as technology and how it is ultimately utilized is a manifestation of our uniquely human attributes and desires. But what if the *Deus ex Machina* continues to replace the people behind the global Profit and Loss (P&L) that moves the economy forward relegating humanity, like so many automata, to merely existing in an always-on metaverse where we are alone together?

When the world was tangled in web 1.0 the democratization of information and the reduction of friction in communication and knowledge sharing trumped the risk of misinformation and disinformation emerging as threats to truth and democracy. Yet, despite loud and credible voices signaling that web 1.0 was a threat to global order, it mostly bent the arc of Moore's law in favor of a more inclusive and distributed information web. While the emergence of web 1.0 was a net gain to the world, its benefits have certainly accrued disproportionately to a few postal codes within Silicon Valley.

The next generation of the Internet tangled the world into a web 2.0 of online commerce, which over the course of several decades posed challenges to traditional industries, from retail to global supply chains. It allowed anyone armed with an internet-connected device to participate in a global marketplace, discover global pricing, albeit at the mercy of business models that insidiously monetized data, eroded privacy, and were just as rent seeking as the very analog business models they were meant to transform.

Nonetheless, here too, the second generation of the web unlocked trillions of dollars (or some other currency) in global output as category-creating firms ravenously consumed traditional sectors and created entirely new ones. A market correction was born from the detritus of the Great Deleveraging caused by the 2008 financial crisis. This global crisis exacerbated the decline in institutional and leadership trust through the dislocation of trillions in public value in what many would say was a generational privatization of gain and socialization of losses as taxpayer-funded bailouts propped up moribund banks and other industries. Alongside this decline, the void in privacy protection in internet commerce—both licit and illicit—gave rise to early prototypes and internet architecture that are the seeds of web 3.0 and mark how software may very well begin to consume the last bastions of power—namely the world's banks, its corporate structure, and seats of power.

The emergence of web 3.0, an internet where the exchange of value undergoes the same reduction in friction and instantaneity in banking, is first consuming financial services, but the art of what is now possible is much bigger—and scarier to its opponents. In the third entanglement of the web, in which we are only in the opening innings, privacy and security are not trade-offs. Anonymity or pseudonymity are said to be guaranteed courtesy of public key cryptography and the emergence of distributed systems such as public blockchains. All actors in the system armed with little more than a basic internet-connected device are unitary, operating *pari passu* with even the largest most powerful interests on the planet. Their votes, voice, and value creation (or capture) can now accrue to them individually courtesy of an emerging internet of value—one that breaks the back of rent-seeking business, economic, and political models.

The building blocks of this internet of value are no longer an abstraction because of the maiden decade of public blockchains, which are proving to be a foundational layer of technology, rivaled only by the Internet itself. A more than $3 trillion-dollar cryptographic asset class now stands on the shoulders of this breakthrough innovation, in which more than 200 million people worldwide are early adopters, proving that digitally native financial services may not yet be too big to fail but are certainly too big to ignore. So much so that more than 90% of the world's central banks are contemplating some form of digitization of their national thrift or fiat currencies in the form of central bank digital currencies (or CBDCs in the industry's parlance). This proves that imitation is in fact the sincerest form of flattery. How these innovations are governed, however, whether privately or publicly, is critical not only to monetary and economic policy but also to how money moves and how power shifts around the world.

Blockchain is not only challenging the bastions of Wall Street and global financial services with the reinvention of the very form factor of money—where the words on US bank notes *In God We Trust* are being replaced by *In Code We Trust*—it is also challenging the form factor of the corporation and complex financial services. Decentralized autonomous organizations or DAOs and decentralized finance or DeFi are doing to companies and capital markets what web 1.0 did to media and web 2.0 did to commerce. These changes are underway, and the proverbial genie is out of the bottle, much to the consternation of financial markets regulators, central banks, and political power structures. Despite all the breakthroughs in technological innovation, even when the code or the technology array becomes obsolete—because it always does—the most enduring activity is governance.

ADDING THE T TO ESG—*ESGT*

Now let's turn our attention to some of the more practical aspects of what confronts us. We believe that business leaders who seek to identify and integrate their specific technology issues, risks, and opportunities into a larger ESG/ESGT strategy framework need to approach this process both deliberately and systematically.

To begin with, it is critically important to do a deliberate and systematic audit of the key ESGT issues, risks, and opportunities that relate to *your* specific business, footprint, employee/third-party population, assets, business plan, and strategic objectives, to achieve your own typology or taxonomy of relevant issues. While it is always advisable to use existing frameworks to help with such a review process (like the Sustainability Accounting Standards Board (SASB), e.g.), none of the existing frameworks does justice to the identification of technology issues, risks, and opportunities that we think should be integrated into such an exercise. Hence our advocacy of an ESG+T approach.

Before continuing, a clarification is necessary: we are not advocating ESGT as a new framework designed to compete with the existing alphabet soup of ratings or frameworks. Far from it. What we are advocating is that businesses conceptualize a holistic approach to ESGT governance and strategy because these issues are all interconnected and can be bucketed into a portfolio of the most important "intangibles" of our times deeply related to reputation, resilience, sustainability, and value. Not doing so in today's turbocharged world guarantees missing a slew of important, critical, material, and maybe even organizationally existential issues, risks, and opportunities for your business that could mean the difference between mediocre survival or demise and long-term sustainability and value creation.

A good place to start thinking about the big picture technology issues that are part of your organization's footprint is to check on which UN Sustainable Development Goals (SDGs) are most relevant to your business. In her book *Gloom to Boom: How Leaders Transform Risk into Resilience and Value* (Routledge 2020), Andrea has made the case that all SDGs have a potential technological component or intersection. See Table 15.2.

TABLE 15.2
United Nations Sustainable Development Goals—Technology-Related Issues

SDG—Technology Related	E	S	G	T
1. No Poverty		X	X	X
2. Zero Hunger	X	X	X	X
3. Good Health and Well-being		X	X	X
4. Quality Education		X	X	X
5. Gender Equality		X	X	X
6. Clean Water and Sanitation	X	X	X	X
7. Affordable and Clean Energy	X	X	X	X
8. Decent Work and Economic Growth		X	X	X
9. Industry, Innovation, and Infrastructure	X	X	X	X
10. Reduced Inequalities		X	X	X
11. Sustainable Cities and Communities	X	X	X	X
12. Responsible Consumption and Production	X	X	X	X
13. Climate Action	X	X	X	X
14. Life Below Water	X		X	X
15. Life on Land	X		X	X
16. Peace and Justice—Strong Institutions		X	X	X
17. Partnerships for the Goals		X	X	X

(Source: Andrea Bonime-Blanc & GEC Risk Advisory. Table first appeared in: A. Bonime-Blanc. Gloom to Boom. Routledge 2020.)

Table 15.3 illustrates how big data/digital products and services can be created that relate directly to one or more of the 17 SDGs. These are examples of what the UN—together with its other public, private, and non-profit partners around the world are doing—to harness big data, and data science and analytics to support and further the 17 SDGs.

TABLE 15.3
UN SDG Data for Good Examples

SDG # 1—No Poverty.
Spending patterns on mobile phone services can provide proxy indicators of income levels.
SDG #2—Zero Hunger.
Crowdsourcing or tracking of food prices listed online can help monitor food security in near real time.
SDG #3—Good Health and Well-Being.
Mapping the movement of mobile phone users can help predict the spread of infectious diseases.
SDG #4—Quality Education.
Citizen reporting can reveal reasons for student dropout rates.
SDG #5—Gender Equality.
Analysis of financial transactions can reveal the spending patterns and different impacts of economic shocks on men and women.
SDG #6—Clean Water and Sanitation.
Sensors connected to water pumps can track access to clean water.
SDG #7—Affordable and Clean Energy.
Smart metering allows utility companies to increase or restrict the flow of electricity, gas, or water to reduce waste and ensure adequate supply at peak periods.
SDG #8—Decent Work and Economic Growth.
Patterns in global postal traffic can provide indicators such as economic growth, remittances, trade, and GDP.
SDG #9—Industry, Innovation, and Infrastructure.
Data from GPS devices can be used for traffic control and to improve public transport.
SDG #10—Reduced Inequality.
Speech to text analytics on local radio content can reveal discrimination concerns and support policy response.
SDG #11—Sustainable Cities and Communities.
Satellite remote sensing can track encroachment on public land or spaces such as parks and forests.
SDG #12—Responsible Consumption and Production.
Online search patterns or e-commerce transactions can reveal the pace of transition to energy-efficient products.
SDG #13—Climate Action.
Combining satellite imagery, crowd-sourced witness accounts, and open data can help track deforestation.
SDG #14—Life Below Water.
Maritime vessel tracking data can reveal illegal, unregulated, and unreported fishing activities.
SDG #15—Life on Land.
Social media monitoring can support disaster management with real-time information on victim location, effects, and strength of forest fires or haze.
SDG #16—Peace, Justice, and Strong Institutions.
Sentiment analysis of social media can reveal public opinion on effective governance, public service delivery, or human rights.
SDG #17—Partnerships for the Goals.
Partnerships to enable the combining of statistics, mobile, and internet data can provide a better and real-time understanding of today's hyper-connected world.

(Source: United Nations Global Pulse.)

TABLE 15.4
A Sampling of ESGT Issues

Environmental	Social	Governance	Technology
• Climate Change • Sustainability • Water • Air • Earth • Carbon Emissions • Energy Efficiency • Natural Resources • Hazardous Waste • Recycled Material Use • Clean Technology • Green Buildings • Biodiversity • Animal Rights • Pandemics	• Human Rights • Labor Rights • Child Labor • Human Trafficking • Human Slavery • Health & Safety • Workplace Conditions • Workplace Violence • Product Safety • Fair Trade • Data Privacy • Discrimination • Harassment • Bullying/Mobbing • Diversity & Inclusion	• Corporate Governance • Leadership • Culture • Business Ethics • Geopolitics • Corruption/ Bribery • Fraud • Money Laundering • Anti-Competition/ Anti-Trust • Regulatory Compliance • Conflicts Of Interest • Compensation Disclosure	• Cybersecurity • AI Geopolitics • Data Mining • Internet of Things • Artificial Intelligence • Machine Learning • Deep Learning • Robotics • Automated Robotic Processing • Military Robotics • Surveillance • Dark Web • Fake News • Deep Fakes—Visual • Deep Fakes—Audio • Biometrics • Wearables • Nanotechnology • Bioengineering • CRISPR

(Source: Andrea Bonime-Blanc & GEC Risk Advisory. Table first appeared in: A. Bonime-Blanc. *Gloom to Boom*. Routledge 2020.)

Next comes the creation of your own typology or taxonomy of relevant E, S, G, and T issues, risks, and opportunities that become part of the planning, risk management, crisis scenarios, research and development, and value creation or protection of your organization. Table 15.4 gives a sampling of ESGT issues, risks, and opportunities that can serve as a jumping-off point for the creation of a customized taxonomy or typology for a company.

And to get this done properly and comprehensively, it is essential that the right leaders and experts sit around the ESGT issues brainstorming table. Figure 15.1 suggests an approach that combines an interdisciplinary team within a company (including outside experts as needed) that is specifically focused on the identification of key:

(1) Emerging ESGT issues
(2) ESGT stakeholders
(3) ESGT risks and reputation risks
(4) ESGT opportunities
(5) ESGT crisis preparedness

All in furtherance of either avoiding value destruction or achieving value protection, creation, or even innovation, as further visualized in Figure 15.2.

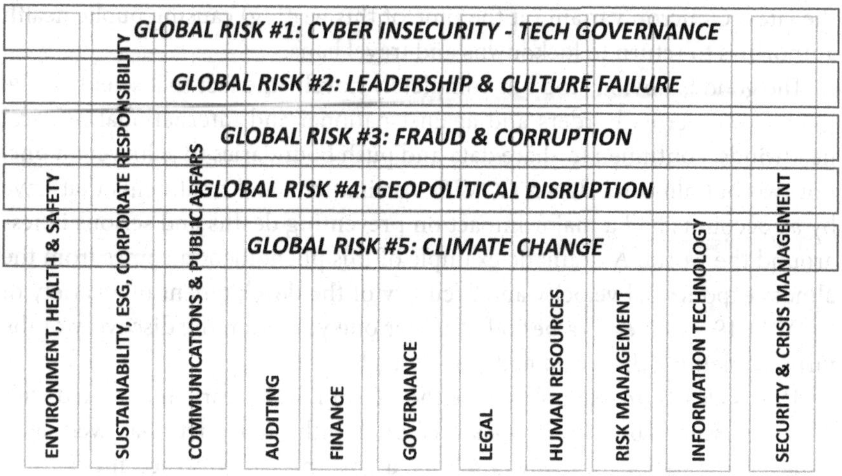

FIGURE 15.1 The Risk Management Cross-Functional Imperative

(Source: Andrea Bonime-Blanc & GEC Risk Advisory. Figure first appeared in: A. Bonime-Blanc. *Gloom to Boom*. Routledge 2020.)

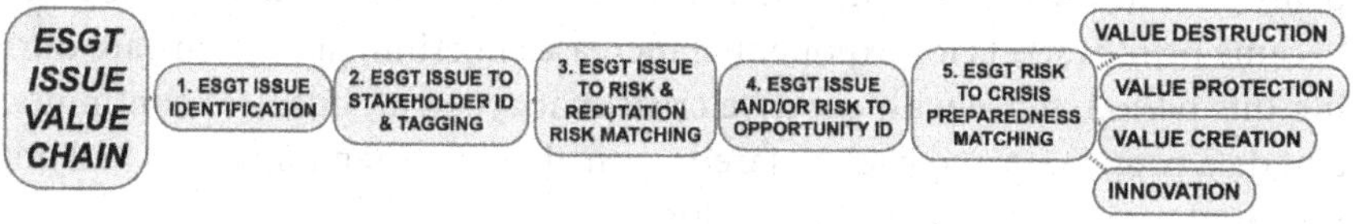

FIGURE 15.2 ESGT Issue Value Chain

(Source: Andrea Bonime-Blanc & GEC Risk Advisory. Figure first appeared in: A. Bonime-Blanc. *Gloom to Boom*. Routledge 2020.)

THE RISK AND THE REWARD OF ESGT: USE CASES

In this section, we provide several examples and/or use cases of ESG + technology including the good, the bad, and the ugly.

COVID-19 and COVID-19 Vaccinations in Record Time

What has happened over the past two years since the COVID-19 pandemic erupted is certainly unprecedented in modern times in terms of both the bad and the good. The bad is obvious—COVID-19 and its variants have caused, at this writing, more than five million deaths officially (many more unofficially), and new variants are still popping up regularly around the world, with the latest Omicron variant (at the time of this writing) causing public health authorities to return to lockdowns and travel bans.

The good is obvious too but completely novel—the fact that scientists the world over, across borders and against national and international political headwinds, continued to share data and push boundaries to achieve not one, not two but almost a dozen COVID vaccinations and treatments that have by all accounts had a major impact on preventing deaths and serious illness around the world. A dramatic example of this phenomenon comes from the almost exponential velocity and accuracy of the development of a variety of COVID-19 vaccines in a period of under one year from the discovery of the virus, something the world had never seen before.

This is clearly an example where the "T" in ESGT clearly intersected with E and S issues—biological, social, labor, health, and safety—as well as G issues—how well a company, a school, a government governed the issue of pandemic management and prevention.

Companies that paid attention to the science and data were able to take better care of their people, processes, products, and services by doing such things as protecting their frontline workers from a health and safety standpoint, enabling remote work where possible, deploying supply chain backup plans and, in the case of many health-care facilities and municipalities that became prime targets for exponential increases in criminal ransomware during this period, those with effective crisis management, business continuity, and data protection and backup fared so much better than those who had not prepared properly for such eventualities.

What can be said about the difference between the entities that succeeded (survived and maybe even thrived) through this period and those that suffered personnel, financial, and/or reputational damage? The former knew what their key ESGT issues, risks, and opportunities were prior to the pandemic—their management and boards were either prepared or able to pivot quickly to a deeply changed world around March 2020. They had the governance, strategy, and tactical blueprint to manage through the crisis and be resilient. Some even managed to get ahead of the specter of government defense production powers (typically used during times of war to redirect private supply chains) to proactively shift their output to focus on lifesaving, but scarce, public health supplies.

McKinsey has done a variety of studies on the difference in performance between a resilient, sustainable, and innovative company to one that is not. The innovators are not only better prepared for the crisis, but they also survive better through the crisis and beyond—financially, reputationally, and otherwise. For example, in one such study, McKinsey found that in normalizing for market capitalization from 2007 (right before the global financial crisis) through 2014, not only did the innovators outperform the non-innovators by 10% during the crisis, the pre-crisis innovators (and thus more resilient companies) also outperformed the S&P 500 market itself by more than 30% in the post-crisis years.

COP26, Climate Crisis, Climate Tech

At the time of this writing, the Glasgow, Scotland, COP26 had just closed with mixed reviews from a broad spectrum of stakeholders. Some of the feedback included:

- *"History has been made here in Glasgow"*
- *"We've kept 1.5 alive though on life support"*
- *"There's real progress and it's not enough"*
- *"Blah, blah, blah"*

A full spectrum of actors was present at the COP26 Glasgow meeting—from the most devoted global climate activists (Greta Thunberg, Vanessa Nakate, and others) and the most vulnerable island nations (Tuvalu and Maldives) to the still climate-denying/obfuscating industries (and their service providers) and "developing" countries still bent on using coal (India and China).

In total, 197 parties to the UN Framework Convention on Climate Change (UNFCCC) showed up, haggled, took several steps forward and sideways, and then a couple backwards, and at the eleventh hour of an extra workday approved the shape of a new climate agreement. So, was it a lot of "blah blah blah" or actual, tangible progress? A little bit of both and a lot of muddling through. It certainly was policy "sausage-making" on a grand, global scale. Whether you think it was progress, atrophy, or worse, a key accomplishment of COP26 is that it represents a true inflection point in shutting down the international climate change denial machine.

There has been enough written by true experts in climate change and the environmental and resilience challenges the world and all of its components are facing over the coming decades than for us to repeat anything of additional value here; so, what we will do instead is provide a lens into the "boom" part of the "gloom to boom" equation, as it were.

Despite the serious and severe obstacles to maintaining a 1.5°C warming above that of the Industrial Revolution through 2050, the silver lining to much of the concern is that it is rattling cages across the world in business, government, and society, releasing good animal spirits in the financial and technological innovation markets.

Indeed, in the business world we are seeing an unprecedented explosion of climate invention and pent-up demand for financing and growth in climate technology. Trends in global climate tech investment show that they have nearly quintupled over the past five years[1] and investment is probably still a fraction of what will happen over the next decades.

There is hope in this confluence of global crisis with business opportunity—specifically an environmental and social global crisis with enormous technological innovation opportunity. What needs to happen as these trends continue to evolve is that leaders and the companies they create and operate in this space understand the critical need for a holistic ESGT governance and strategic approach within their own organizations. This will provide them with greater reputational upside—because they will be practicing what they preach—as well as resilience, sustainability, and value creation.

Congolese Cobalt: Where the E, the S, the G, and the T Meet

The *New York Times* produced an alarming investigative report on "A Power Struggle Over Cobalt Rattles the Clean Energy Revolution" on November 20, 2021. In essence, it is the story of the rich mineral land and mining operations, specifically for cobalt, that exist within Congo, specifically for lithium battery production. Cobalt is a critical ingredient in the green revolution because it is essential for lithium battery production which in turn is a key component of the electrical car revolution, specifically for the likes of Tesla and the exponentially growing competition in the electrical vehicle market worldwide. The paradox of this story is that there is geopolitical big power competition with serious social and economic consequences locally over a key ingredient in the green technology revolution involving the environmentally destructive mining of local lands.

This story has all manner of ESGT issues, risks, and even opportunities intersecting within the storyline, illustrating the deep interconnection between the environmental, social, governance, and technological issues, risks, and opportunities of our times.

- Environmental: the ravaging of land, biodiversity, and homes in a cobalt-mining-rich zone of Congo by both private/public and national/international interests;
- Social: the exploitation and maltreatment of poor local populations—of their homes, health, safety, work opportunity;
- Governance: governance issues exist at several key levels in this story:
    - local, national, international, and geopolitical governmental levels, especially the fierce China–US rivalry to secure rare earth minerals worldwide in which the Chinese are way ahead (see chart in the article);
    - company level—corporate governance level for the Chinese, American, and other companies competing locally to access/control the rights;

- supply chain level to secure reliable, resilient cobalt supply for the likes of Tesla and other auto manufacturers worldwide.
- Technology: In its insatiable and exponentially growing demand for cobalt (among other minerals) to create batteries for electric vehicles (which are supposed to help with carbon reduction), companies like Tesla contribute to the aforementioned concerns and issues and in turn have a responsibility to develop not only responsible tech governance but also responsible ESGT governance for their products and services.

Once again, we see the inextricable interconnection of environmental, social, governance, and technology issues in a serious global climate story, which will require all actors—whether at the governmental, business, or social levels—to think holistically about ESGT strategies, governance, and resilience for the benefit of their key respective stakeholders.

Digital Chatter—How AI and Human Intelligence Uncover Early Actor Risk Intelligence

As the startling data in Table 15.5 show, what happens on the Internet in one minute does not just stay on the Internet. The astounding and exponentially growing volume and velocity of information on the surface, deep and dark webs permeate our daily lives in ways known and unknown, real and perceived, true and false, harmless and weaponized.

So, what is "digital chatter?" Digital chatter is the summation of conversations happening online that takes place across the surface and deep web. It includes open or indexed and closed or dark social media channels as well as forums and messaging apps. And it is growing exponentially in volume, variety, and velocity.

Table 15.6 shows the wide variety of risks and crises that can materialize from digital chatter—many of which did not exist before the age of social

TABLE 15.5
What Happens on the Surface Web Every 60 Seconds

Facebook	150,000 messages shared
Facebook	147,000 photos uploaded
WhatsApp	41,666,667 messages shared
Instagram	347,222 shares posted
Twitter	319 new users joined
YouTube	500 hours of video uploaded
Reddit	479,452 people engaging with content
TikTok	2,704 new users gained

(Source: Statista and Domo, 2021.)

TABLE 15.6
Risks and Crises Materializing From Digital Chatter

• Disinformation, misinformation, fake news, misrepresentation, misleading content • Content that creates an illusion of association between extremist views and a brand of individual associated with the brand • Missed adverse events and compliance failures • Misinterpreted, inauthentic, or polarizing statements by a brand regarding social issues • Violence and threats against employees, leaders, brand VIPs, brand ambassadors, customers, or physical sites and assets • Coordinated physical or digital events and campaigns	• Claims of systematic organizational issues • Scandals or hate speech involving employees, leaders, brand ambassadors, and beyond • Political and social polarization, activism, and campaigns • Negative customer experiences, product complaints, and questions • Leaks, breaches, and other cybersecurity incidents • Large, repetitive volumes of undesirable, hurtful, or irrelevant content • Antagonistic, harmful, illegal, or otherwise unpleasant content posted by users that does not align with brand values or terms of use

(Source: The Total Economic Impact of Crisp Early Warning Risk Intelligence, Forrester Consulting on behalf of Crisp, April 2021.)

TABLE 15.7
Intentional and Unintentional Amplifiers of Harmful Digital Chatter

- Dissatisfied customers or employees
- Celebrities, influencers
- Competitive brands
- Social media users who've done poor research
- Bad actors with malicious intent, trolls who intentionally antagonize
- Conspiracy theorists
- Individual activists, ideological objectors, politicians, activist, or political organizations
- Sensationalist, partisan, activist, or biased media
- Nation states and hostile government organizations
- Bot networks
- Spammers, hackers, or others with financial, political, competitive, or social ill-intent

(Source: The Total Economic Impact of Crisp Early Warning Risk Intelligence, Forrester Consulting on behalf of Crisp, April 2021.)

media—certainly not susceptible to the amplification and velocity they are subject to today. Table 15.7 provides a sense of the actors involved in amplifying some of these examples of digital chatter—all of us have examples of our own where we have seen, for example, a dissatisfied customer berating a brand on Twitter or celebrity/influencer amplifying exponentially fake information because of their celebrity status.

The ESGT lesson learned from this specific use case is that every brand, every company, needs to consider that digital chatter—something mostly at the intersection of social and technological elements of ESGT—must be managed at the organizational level. For example, from a leadership and governance standpoint, think about the questions in Table 15.8 and whether they have ever been properly addressed in your organization.

TABLE 15.8
Questions Leadership and the Board Should Consider About Digital Chatter Affecting Their Brand/Company

- Is the risk management function adjusting forward, scanning the horizon for new risks (like those highlighted by digital chatter) not just identifying what's traditionally been in their risk register?
- Has digital chatter monitoring been properly integrated with enterprise risk management?
- What is the company doing to understand digital chatter as it pertains to their brand—anything? If so, what? Is it simple social media listening (which may be good for marketing but not risk management)? Or are they doing something more sophisticated that picks up early embers of potential brand reputational damage from the darkest corners of the Deep Web and social media?
- If digital chatter is being monitored, what are the resources being used—AI, human intelligence, or both? Preferably both.
- Is there an interdisciplinary team that is capable of analyzing and addressing the results of such monitoring including the CCO, CRO, and other key players like legal, HR, and operations?
- How are the issues surfacing through digital chatter being escalated internally, including to the board if necessary?
- Are there board members who are equipped to understand these issues? Boards should reflect the diverse expertise needed to oversee risk and strategy in these rapidly changing times.
- Are risks accelerated by digital chatter incorporated into the company's resilience program (crisis, business continuity, data protection)?

(Source: A. Bonime-Blanc and V. Sharma. Digital Chatter: What Boards Need to Know. Ethical Boardroom. May 2021.)

FUTURE-PROOFING BUSINESS: BUILDING STRATEGIC AND RESILIENT ESGT LEADERSHIP AND GOVERNANCE

As we have tried to present in this chapter, there is no business model that does not include an array of technological and digital transformation issues, risks, and opportunities. Indeed, we believe everything is interconnected—one way or another—by technology—existing, developing, yet to be developed. Also, we believe deeply that almost all (if not all) of the new technologies that are being developed at the speed of light have the opportunity to be great, good, bad, or deeply ugly and dangerous.

What is the x-factor that explains the difference between the various potential impacts of technology? Human intelligence, ethical leadership, and thoughtful governance. Indeed, how early and how often moral, ethical, judicious, socially conscious filters and governors are applied on technological exploration, invention, discovery, development, or application is the critical determinant of whether such tech will be neutral, beneficial, or dangerous to humanity and even life on Earth.

Take drones—an amazing new invention of the past decade or so which is constantly evolving, miniaturizing, and becoming more precise. One of us loves the aerial travel footage in remote locations that travel drone film companies have developed, for example. But the use of drones—their neutral, beneficial, or detrimental—impacts always revolve around the people creating and/or using such innovations. They can be used, on the one hand, by the likes of the World Food Programme to precision deliver desperately needed food supplies to remote and/or dangerous locations to starving populations beset by civil strife. On the other hand, drones can also be used—even by rank amateurs—to deliver destruction and lethality—as seen in an unsuccessful but very close call drone attack against the Iraqi Prime Minister in late 2021.

Thus, it is incumbent on leaders everywhere to exercise responsible leadership at the intersection of ESG and technology. To be able to do so, leaders must integrate all relevant technology issues, risks, and opportunities into the earliest part of any discovery, invention, or research and development effort and throughout its development, operationalization, and sale of products and services relating to such technologies. It also means developing an overarching strategic and business planning effort that takes into account all ESGT issues, risks, and opportunities relevant to the particular business and which includes all of the right people sitting at the strategy formulation table—not just the financial leaders but the ethicists, the risk, the legal and the governance experts and others as needed by the particular business (chief medical officers in a pharma company, aviation safety experts in an aircraft manufacturing company, AI ethicists in a software company, and so on). Figure 15.3 provides a big picture illustration of how leaders must develop organizational strategy to include not only the traditional financial and operational details that always go into strategy formulation but also the ESGT ones we have been talking about in this chapter.

Of course, it also means understanding who is selling you software and/or the tech that has gone into certain products or services in your supply chains. Witness the SolarWinds case where Russian state actors were able to breach the security software company's loose security to implant malicious software into their software system. As a reminder, SolarWinds had/has a who's who of Fortune 500 companies as well as a multitude of the most sensitive US government agencies as clients. The nation state actors in this case knew exactly what they were doing exploiting the loose security posture of a company that was supposed to provide cybersecurity to some of the most valuable companies in the world and the most nationally sensitive agencies in the US.

Also witness the emerging NSO Group scandal in late 2021—the Israeli company selling stealth surveillance capabilities to any taker (often authoritarian governments and a full spectrum of "bad actors") that circumvented, among other supposed privacy protective software, Apple iOS on iPhones allowing the purchaser of the NSO software to surreptitiously hear and see everything in and through a particular person's iPhone. Upon the exposure of the NSO story, several serious consequences have followed including an almost unprecedented US Government action banning the company from

FIGURE 15.3 An ESGT-Integrated Organizational Strategy
(Source: Andrea Bonime-Blanc & GEC Risk Advisory. Figure first appeared in: A. Bonime-Blanc. *Gloom to Boom*. Routledge 2020.)

selling in the US and Apple lodging a major lawsuit against NSO. These two actions alone may bankrupt the company.

So how do companies and other organizations start their ESGT governance and strategic journey? In this final section of our chapter, we leave you with some food for thought on what resilient leadership (both management and oversight) looks like (adapted from the "10 Commandments of Resilient Leaders" in *Gloom to Boom*).

(1) Resilient leaders—in business, in society, and in government—integrate ESGT issues, risks, and opportunities into their organization's strategy.
(2) Resilient leaders empower and support a cross-functional team of ESGT experts to run an ESGT value chain approach to spotting,

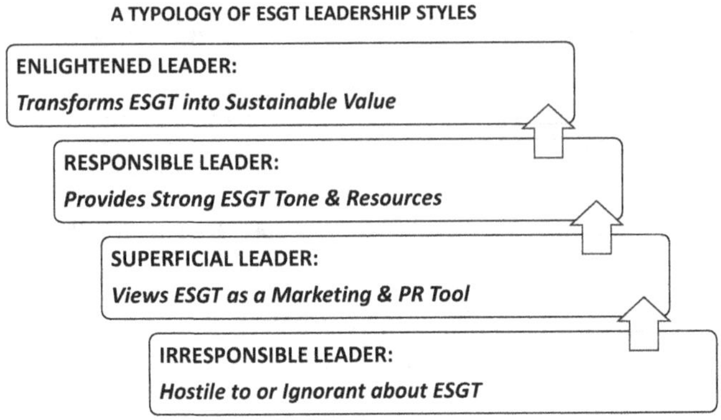

FIGURE 15.4 The ESGT Leadership Typology

(Source: Andrea Bonime-Blanc & GEC Risk Advisory. Figure first appeared in: A. Bonime-Blanc. *Gloom to Boom*. Routledge 2020.)

analyzing, mitigating, and/or deploying all relevant ESGT issues, risks, and opportunities.

(3) Resilient leaders "walk the talk" supporting ESGT matters not only verbally but substantively—by setting the tone from the top as well as specifying concrete resources and budgets.
(4) Resilient leaders aspire to become at least "Responsible Leaders" and at best "Enlightened Leaders" (as these concepts are developed in *Gloom to Boom* and briefly explained in Figure 15.4).
(5) Resilient leaders focus on building and institutionalizing a culture of integrity where stakeholders including employees speak up without fear of retaliation, managers "listen up," and executives and the board "act" accordingly.
(6) Resilient leaders are attuned to and savvy about the world around them and how it affects their organization's existing and future planned footprint—they understand and can translate how the "Megatrends of our Turbulent Times" (see earlier).
(7) Resilient leaders understand and cater to their most important stakeholders—not just their perceived top stakeholder (shareholders for business, e.g.).
(8) Resilient leaders allow for mistakes to be made and through their speak up/listen up culture they learn lessons and undertake continuous improvement, innovation, and sustainability.
(9) Resilient leaders look at the long-term horizon while minding the short-term as well.
(10) Resilient leaders welcome ESGT oversight—whether from a board of directors, governors or trustees, or other governmental entity.

Thus, the topic of responsible ESGT leadership and governance in an age of exponential, rapid-fire technological change is complicated, multifaceted, fraught, and potentially a losing battle. But this does not mean leaders in business, government, and society should not do their utmost to protect people, assets, and planet—early and often. Indeed, we should all double and triple down on building strategic ESGT governance and strategic resilience and sustainability including focusing on technological solutions to some of the exponential technological challenges of our time.

John Le Carre's hero Smiley is told in "Smiley's People" by a colleague as he is in hot pursuit of an evil enemy to: "Go home, George. Get yourself a bit of love and wait for Armageddon". We do not think it is time to go home yet but we are in an eleventh-hour situation to rein in the cowboy wild west culture that has dominated technology governance (or the lack thereof) for the past few decades.

We cannot afford to wait for a technological Armageddon. We still have time to defuse the potential out-of-control exponential technology bombs by developing responsible, deeply knowledgeable, and canny, ESGT-savvy, and resilient leaders. Doing so can continue to harness technological innovation as a force for good. As the net gains from web 1.0 and 2.0 have shown, the gains of an emerging web 3.0, which is a correction of where (and how) past technological disruption fell short, can now enshrine good conduct and true participation in coding. We should embrace these developments and acknowledge that throughout time and into the future, when all else fails, governance is the real breakthrough.

NOTE

1 https://dealroom.co/uploaded/2021/10/Dealroom-London-and-Partners-Climate-Tech.pdf

16

Mastering Sustainability Requires Technology, Finance, and the Powers of Homo Deus

Herman Bril, Georg Kell, and Andreas Rasche

INTRODUCTION—MASTERING SUSTAINABILITY IS A MUST

The world is in a pickle, as always. Homo sapiens, or wise man in Latin, faced insurmountable challenges and is the only one not extinct from several species grouped into the genus Homo. Michael Bhaskar (2021: 27) explains in *Human Frontiers* that

> understanding history means understanding both ideas and the conditions that give rise to ideas. They are not the decorative flowers gilding human civilisation, outgrowths of everything else; they are the soil, the atmosphere, the supporting superstructure itself. Big ideas matter. Having an account of how ideas form, mutate, spread, combine, recombine and grow, and what they are in the first place matters.

Currently, the world population is estimated at 7.87 billion and is still growing (Statistic Times, 2021), contrary to Malthus's belief in the eighteenth century that population growth would result in disease, famine, war, and calamity. The reason for Malthus's misjudgement is that for 200 years, technological developments born of human creativity have been providing more and more food resources (Jaeger, 2021). But the concept of unlimited growth leading to disaster never disappeared. The Club of Rome published the *Limits to Growth* in 1972, stating that the limits to growth on this planet will be reached sometime within the next 100 years (Meadows et al., 1972). Will they be right this time?

DOI: 10.4324/9781003262039-18

The possible existential risk of a self-inflicted hothouse planet is staring us in the face. The IPCC (2022) reported that

> [C]limate change impacts and risks are becoming increasingly complex and more difficult to manage. Multiple climate hazards will co-occur, and multiple climatic and non-climatic risks will interact, resulting in compounding overall risk and risks cascading across sectors and regions. Some responses to climate change result in new impacts and risks.

The big question is whether technological progress driven by human imagination can find a solution quickly enough to cope. But humanity is trapped in a systemic technology paradox. According to Bhaskar (202: 162),

> layers accrete in any system over time. Various exceptions and edge cases are factored in, whether legal code or software use, piling on more complexity. No one can get the total view or understand all the elements and how they interact. And every increase in complexity, even on subcomponents, whether of urban infrastructure, a market, a technology, or a legal system, necessitates more specialisation, more distance to the frontier.

Put simply, every solution creates more complexity and new problems, like Sisyphus, who was punished by the god Zeus, who forces him to roll a boulder up a hill for eternity. Carey King (2021: 413) explains in *The Economic Superorganism* that we are caught in a conundrum:

> On the one hand, the individualistic and profit-seeking structure of capitalism drives innovation, creativity, and the ability to both create and solve energy and environmental problems. On the other hand, the biophysical nature of superorganism means that physical limits and natural laws constrain its space of solutions such that we might not be able to solve all social and environmental problems simultaneously.

As Vaclav Smil (2021: xi) points out in *Grand Transitions*, "our evolutionary experience does not justify any claims about unstoppable progress to ever-greater capabilities. Our fortunes remain circumscribed by many natural imperatives, and civilisation remains vulnerable to catastrophic events". The transition towards a Net-Zero economy by 2050 is the biggest challenge we have ever faced.

So, we face a daunting prospect but without a choice. We must muddle through harder and master sustainability. We must embrace the spirit of imagination, invention, and of being prosocial. The principles of Enlightenment—the ideals of reason, science, humanism, and progress—lifted us out of the Dark Ages and brought us tremendous prosperity (Pinker,

2018). Nowhere is the demand to step up and deliver big new ideas more urgently needed than in planetary survival (Bhaskar, 2021).

FROM PHYSICAL TO DIGITAL IS A CRITICAL GAME CHANGER

Humanity's appetite for energy has grown steadily and exponentially since the Industrial Revolution. Conserving energy will be necessary but is not the solution to achieve the Paris Climate goals, because efficiency often leads to greater usage; this is known as the Jevons Paradox. Jevons (1865/1906) stated:

> Now, if the quantity of coal used in a blast-furnace, for instance, be diminished in comparison with the yield, the profits of the trade will increase, the new capital will be attracted, the price of pig-iron will fall, but the demand for it increases; and eventually the greater number of furnaces will more than make up for the diminished consumption of each. And if such is not always the result within a single branch, it must be remembered that the progress of any branch of manufacture excites a new activity in most other branches.
>
> (Jevons, 1865/1906: 141)

Nevertheless, a general reduction in primary energy consumption is needed, particularly a significant improvement in energy efficiency in heating energy (Jaeger, 2021).

Digital technologies are already changing how energy is used and consumed across the economy. As digitalisation expands, it creates new opportunities to optimise energy use and decrease greenhouse gas emissions. The Center for Climate and Energy Solutions' *Climate Innovation 2050* initiative has engaged closely with leading companies across diverse sectors to examine challenges and solutions to decarbonising the US economy by 2050. The initiative identified the following digitalisation opportunities to decarbonise in the following sectors (see Box 16.1).

Box 16.1 Digitalisation Opportunities to Decarbonise Sectors

- Power: Digitalisation can improve the grid's ability to integrate more variable renewable energy, create an interconnected grid with multi-directional power flow, and expand the use of demand–response strategies (including smart charging of electric vehicles).
- Transportation: In addition to enabling electric vehicles to provide flexible load and storage resources for the power grid, digitalisation of transportation can improve fuel efficiency (e.g., through route optimisation) and enable autonomous driving systems.

- Buildings: Digitalisation of buildings—such as through energy management systems, innovative heating and cooling systems, and connected appliances and equipment—can improve the comfort of occupants while reducing energy use.
- Industry: "Smart manufacturing" approaches can optimise energy and resource use, improve supply chain management, and allow for differentiation of products based on environmental attributes.
- Oil and gas: Digitalisation in the oil and gas sector can help with preventive maintenance, detect, and reduce emission leaks and improve the sector's environmental footprint.
- Agriculture: "Smart farming" approaches can reduce emissions-producing inputs (e.g., fertilisers) and water use, better manage livestock production and animal health, enable urban and vertical farming, and improve accounting of carbon sequestration.

Source: Ye, 2021: 1.

FROM GLOBAL TO LOCAL, DEMATERIALISATION AND SHARING LEAD US CLOSER TO A CIRCULAR ECONOMY

The global supply chain underlying the manufacturing of many products results in massive shipping and transportation activities, producing a significant carbon footprint. Integrating information technology with innovative manufacturing processes and materials science will reverse part of the globalisation of supply chains. The comprehensive implementation of three-dimensional printing (3DP) technology has developed significantly and can now perform crucial roles in many applications, with the most critical being manufacturing. As with all new technology, 3DP initially was highly expensive but got cheaper relatively quickly as the market for 3DP has shown some of the quickest growth within the manufacturing industry in recent years. Integrating the Internet of Things (IoT), AI, and cloud manufacturing, 3DP allows for the digitalisation and localisation of more manufacturing (Singh et al., 2021).

Also, these technological developments drive dematerialisation, the absolute or relative reduction in the quantity of materials required to serve economic functions in society. In common terms, dematerialisation means doing more from less. This also fits in with the sharing economy concept, a socioeconomic system based on the sharing of resources. It includes the shared creation, production, distribution, trade, and consumption of goods and services by people and organisations. These systems take various forms, often leveraging information technology (mainly digital platforms like Uber or Airbnb) to empower consumers and corporations with information that enables distribution, sharing, and reuse of excess capacity in goods and services. Ultimately, the objective is to create a circular economy, defined by the Ellen MacArthur Foundation (2022) as

> a systemic approach to economic development designed to benefit businesses, society, and the environment. In contrast to the 'take-make-waste' linear model, a circular economy is regenerative by design and aims to decouple growth from the consumption of finite resources gradually.

It is often underestimated the extent to which these trends are exponential instead of linear. Interaction between technology, the economy, and the broader social and political system feeds on each other like coevolution. Innovation and diffusion depend on developments in other social "subsystems" or spheres and on the extent to which the changes in these different spheres of society are congruent, supporting (instead of counteracting) each other (Fagerberg et al., 2020).

FROM DIGITAL TO THE GREEN ELECTRIFICATION OF EVERYTHING

Decarbonising globally requires massive electrification of our energy use. This means a significant increase in the share of renewable energies in electricity generation and a massive expansion of energy capacities to increase the percentage of electricity in primary energy consumption. We need to solve the problem of baseload capacity to manage supply and demand, which requires, according to Jaeger (2021: 253):

- A massive expansion of the possibilities for storing electricity,
- Further technological improvements and efficiency gains, and
- A gigantic decentralisation of the energy supply makes the energy supply more secure and ultimately much cheaper since transport and large-scale distribution of the centralised energy system are no longer necessary.

The International Energy Agency's (IEA) Electricity Market Report showed that global electricity demand grew by 6% in 2021, the largest percentage rise since 2010 (IEA, 2022). Sadly, coal met more than half of the increase in global demand, resulting in CO_2 emissions from electricity rising by almost 7%, a record high. The IEA's short-term outlook to 2024 expects rapidly growing renewables almost to match moderate demand growth, with fossil fuel generation set to stagnate over the next three years. The IEA concludes that today's policy settings are insufficient to cut emissions. We still have a long way to go.

FINANCE POWERS INNOVATION AND THIS TRANSFORMS FINANCE

We live in a Schumpeterian world of creative destruction. As we wrote in *Sustainable Investing—A Path to a New Horizon* (Bril et al., 2021), new situations require novel responses, development requires experiments and innovation. The only constant in life is change. Non-equilibrium is the natural state of the economy, and therefore it is always open to change due to fundamental uncertainty and technical innovation (Arthur, 2014). Aghion (2021: 15) describes creative destruction as

> the process by which new innovations continually emerge and render existing technologies obsolete, new firms constantly arrive to compete with existing firms, and new jobs and activities arise and replace existing jobs and activities. It is the driving force of capitalism, ensuring its perpetual renewal and reproduction, but at the same time generating risks and upheaval that must be managed and regulated.

The fuel of creative destruction, besides human imagination, is finance, as mentioned in Chapter 1. Given radical uncertainty about future economic returns, as proven by history many times: two modes of financing have prevailed to fund new technology. Both are decoupled from the textbook calculation of net present value from the project over its economic life. One has been government investment in pursuit of national development or national security, like the US Defense Advanced Research Projects Agency (DARPA). DARPA is an agency within the Department of Defense responsible for catalysing the development of technologies that maintain and advance the capabilities and technical superiority of the military. The other is financial speculation like, for example, the dotcom bubble in the late 1990s, as explained by Bill Janeway (2018) in *Doing Capitalism*.

Technology is also transforming finance. Fintech companies are new players that are applying technology to improve financial services and provide an end-to-end internet application. Financial technologies, including AI, big data, NLP, robotic process automation, and APIs, are used to automate investments, insurance, trading, banking services, and risk management. Finance is seen as one of the industries most vulnerable to disruption by technology because its core business is information and data.

A new dawn for asset managers is now emerging and pushing for the next frontier—Autonomous Asset Management. Today, financial technology makes it possible to capture hidden information, analyse large data sets, identify complex, non-linear relationships, and reduce human biases and errors. AI can automatically adapt to dynamically changing markets. And, as a result, active sustainable investing becomes scalable, hyper-customisable, and cost-effective, like, for example, the autoCIO platform (Arabesque, 2021). The technologized investor uses big data, SaaS, cloud, NLP, AI, and APIs to drive down the marginal costs of an additional investment strategy to almost zero based on platform economics. Robo-advisors are digital platforms that already provide automated, algorithmic investment services with minimal supervision. The industry has experienced explosive growth; robo-advisors reached nearly $1 trillion in 2020 and are expected to reach $2.9 trillion globally in 2025 (Áelex, 2021).

Prasad (2021) explains in his book *The Future of Money* how the digital revolution is transforming currencies and finance. The emergence of new institutions and platforms will improve competition, service, and transparency, as well as promote innovation and reduce costs. But they will also create challenges for regulators and financial stability. Although not without challenges, cryptocurrencies are an excellent example of a significant conceptual and technical advance in financial markets. China's central bank is experimenting with a Central Bank Digital Currency (CBDC), the e-CNY, to ensure the central bank's role in controlling digital payments at a time when two fintech players, Alipay and WeChat Pay, are striving to dominate the payment landscape. Also, the fintech revolution provides an opportunity for developing countries to leapfrog developed economies by rapidly adopting new, cost-effective, and more efficient ways of conducting banking and financial transactions, and notably, enabling financial inclusion. Large portions of the population lack access to the banking system, leaving them bereft of saving, credit, and insurance products. The fintech revolution carries the prospect of democratising finance by providing the economically underprivileged with access to the financial system.

The Organisation for Economic Co-operation and Development (OECD) (2020) has published a comprehensive report explaining the tokenisation of assets and exploring its implications for both the financial markets and the regulators. Distributed ledger technologies (DLTs), such as blockchain, will transform financial markets. Tokenisation of assets involves the digital representation of real (physical or financial) assets on distributed ledgers or the issuance of traditional asset classes in tokenised form. The OECD (2020: 7) report stated that

> The application of DLTs and smart contracts in asset tokenisation has the potential to deliver many benefits, including efficiency gains driven by automation and disintermediation; transparency; improved liquidity potential and tradability of assets with near-absent liquidity by adding liquidity to currently illiquid assets; faster and potentially more efficient clearing and settlement. It allows for fractional ownership of assets which, in turn, could lower barriers to investment and promote more inclusive access by retail investors to previously unaffordable or insufficiently divisive asset classes, allowing global pools

> of capital to reach parts of the financial markets previously reserved to large investors. The flow of private financing from capital owners to SMEs could be eased and facilitated, enhancing access to financing for SMEs.

Crypto-asset market capitalisation grew by 3.5 times in 2021 to $2.6 trillion, yet crypto-assets remain a small portion of overall global financial system assets (FSB, 2022). But, as history would predict, it comes with financial speculation. The crypto-mania resulted in venture capital firms investing $33 billion in crypto start-ups in 2021, more money than all previous years collectively (Blockworks, 2022). This resulted in 64 crypto unicorns globally; more than half of the global crypto unicorns reached the $1 billion threshold this year alone. This fresh high return-seeking risk capital catalyses trial-and-error innovation in digital finance, producing winners and losers. The concept of digital finance also led to responses from regulators. For example, the Federal Council in Switzerland (2022) published *Digital Finance: Areas of Action 2022+*. It identified 12 areas of action to provide the best possible regulatory framework and to work on cross-cutting issues regarding competitiveness, financial stability risks, client protections, and the reputation of the Swiss financial centre, specifically relating to the use of data, clouds, DLTs, cybersecurity, AI, green fintech, teaching, and research. Furthermore, in the US, the Federal Reserve Bank of Boston is preparing jointly with MIT for the Digital Currency Initiative. In February 2022, they jointly published a study called: *Project Hamilton Phase 1—A High-Performance Payment Processing System Designed for Central Bank Digital Currencies* (Federal Reserve Bank of Boston, 2022). COVID-19 accelerated contactless payment, and it is not hard to imagine a cashless society sooner rather than later.

WILL GREENWASHING BE WASHED OUT, AND WILL ESG VANISH AS A TRANSITIONARY PHENOMENON?

ESG has rapidly become a household term over recent years, leading to confusion about what it means and creating unrealistic expectations about its effects (Serafeim, 2021). Concerns about greenwashing are rising, as is criticism around whether green investing is even working. Some of this criticism may be due to a lack of understanding of the essential nature of ESG, which has remained unchanged ever since the concept was first coined in 2004 (IFC et al., 2005). It is a transient phenomenon that tries to come to grips with the massive transformation societies and markets are currently undergoing. ESG investing will remain relevant so long as current price signals and regulations do not fully capture the true costs and benefits of what is yet to come. Technologies like AI and NLP create healthy transparency by scanning millions of news articles 24/7 globally, tracking companies' behaviour. The machines are becoming better and better in determining if the green business emperors are wearing no clothes. Blockchain technology could solve the challenge of managing greenhouse gas emissions along complex supply chains. The Rocky Mountain Institute (RMI, 2022) is developing "Horizon Zero", a system to create digital twins, as explained in Chapter 11, of emissions and track them via a blockchain architecture that creates transparency around the emissions associated with a product at every stage of its life cycle. Blockchain architecture's enhanced traceability features will allow insights that create accountability where it was previously impossible—improving climate disclosures and GHG markets. Datafication of a company's societal and environmental footprint therefore enables greater transparency, measurement, and the calling out of greenwashing.

New ESG technology platforms, like ESG Book (www.esgbook.com), connect corporates directly to investors for accessible and digital corporate sustainability information. Additionally, regulatory developments, such as the EU Sustainable Finance Disclosure Regulation (SFDR), will further reduce the risk of greenwashing and improve disclosure. SFDR, which aims at financial markets participants, is backed by further regulation of European companies' ESG disclosures. From 2023 onwards, corporate ESG disclosures are regulated through the EU Corporate Sustainability Reporting Directive (CSRD). Bruno Le Maire, Minister for Economic Affairs, Finance and Recovery discussed CSRD by saying that:

> Companies with more than 250 employees or listed companies will now have to translate their environmental, social and governance policy into standardised, justified and certified information documents. This means greater transparency for citizens, consumers, and investors so that businesses can play their full part in society. This is the end of greenwashing. Today, Europe is setting the rigorous non-financial reference standards of tomorrow, in line with our environmental and social ambitions.
>
> (European Council, 2022)

A key outcome of COP26 was the establishment of a new International Sustainability Standards Board (ISSB) to develop a global baseline for disclosure standards on climate and other ESG matters. This will be a necessary step to mainstream sustainable investing. Ultimately, we need to internalise externalities and bring back ethics and values. We have forgotten about *The Theory of Moral Sentiments* written in 1759, by Adam Smith and have become carried away with Milton Friedman's dogma *The Social Responsibility of Business is to Increase its Profits*, so long as it stays within the rules of the game (Friedman, 1970/2007). However, the rules of the game are changing, and it is time to let go of Milton Friedman (Ruggie, 2021). Mark Carney (2021) explained that markets don't exist in a vacuum, and effectiveness is determined partly by the rules of the state and partly by society's values. If left unattended, the markets will corrode those values. We are learning the hard way that ignoring planetary boundaries creates transition and physical risk, in turn impacting returns and, more importantly, our planet and society as a whole.

ESG is not a panacea that will solve "the tragedy of the commons" or the horizon (Carney, 2015) by itself. ESG investing requires coordinated global efforts from policymakers, regulators, corporates, investors, and consumers.

ESG, TECHNOLOGY, AND GEOPOLITICAL HAVOC

In the final days of completing this book, Russia started an unjustified war against Ukraine. In a barbarian attack against the citizens of Ukraine and a gross breach of human rights, we are thrown back into the Cold War again. Already, over two million citizens of Ukraine are fleeing into the EU and the UK, while their cities are being shelled by Russian rockets. Our hearts go out to the people of Ukraine. The 193-member United Nations General Assembly voted, with only five countries against, to isolate Russia for deploying its "aggression against Ukraine" and demanding Russian troops stop fighting and withdraw (see UN A/ES-11/L1).

The US, the UK, and the EU issued unprecedented harsh sanctions against Russia. Even Switzerland, usually remaining neutral, decided to freeze Russian assets. BP and Shell announced extensive divestments in Russia, writing off tens of billions of dollars. Many global companies halted their activities in Russia, and institutional investors announced divestments of Russian investments. Thomas Friedman wrote in *the New York Times*: *The Cancellation of Mother Russia Is Underway*: "The sanctions imposed on Russia that are crippling its economy, critically threatening companies and shattering the savings of millions of Russians at an unprecedented speed and scope" (Friedman, 2022).

Businesses and investors globally are impacted and need to come to grips with a new reality. Energy and commodity prices are spiking in a period where inflation was already high. The sanctions will result in a deep economic recession in Russia, but the West will also feel the pain. If ESG means anything, doing business with or investing in a country led by warmongers is not an option, from both a moral and risk perspective.

The war in Ukraine will also create new and unexpected discussions at the intersection of ESG and technology. For instance, it is likely that we will see increased pressure for defense technology (e.g., weapons) to be classified as being socially sustainable. Only four days after Russia's invasion into Ukraine, Bloomberg reported that defense lobbyists are using the window of opportunity to lobby for inclusion of relevant technology into the upcoming EU social taxonomy (Ainger & Arons, 2022). Discussions about the role of such technology in the context of ESG can therefore be expected to intensify over the months to come. This will also require more discussions about the precise ESG effects of different types of weapons (e.g., offensive versus defensive).

The war has also put another issue centre stage: cybersecurity. As the conflict further unfolds, cyberattacks on private and public targets are turning into a real threat that needs to be taken seriously by corporations and governments alike (see also Chapter 15). Even before the Russian invasion of Ukraine, cybersecurity failure was an escalating problem with nearly 20% of respondents ranking it as a short-term business risk according to *The Global Risks Report 2022* (World Economic Forum, 2022). It can be expected that Russia's cyber forces will launch attacks against Western and Ukrainian targets to weaken the communications, energy, and financial infrastructure. It is therefore important that teams looking at firms' cybersecurity are working closely with corporate functions assessing geopolitical risks and physical security (Kolbe et al., 2022).

The war has many more consequences for managing ESG, as one of us recently argued (Kell, 2022). For instance, it will impact the fight against climate change, as countries and companies are rethinking their energy mix in the light of increased uncertainty and vulnerability. While we will see short-term market turbulence (e.g., with rising energy prices), there is also a potential upside. As countries are becoming more aware of their fossil fuel dependency and the associated risks that such dependency creates, decarbonisation and the creation of an energy infrastructure based on renewable sources will get an unexpected further boost.

It is too early to predict what will happen, but one thing is for sure, the ESG community needs to rethink how to deal with geopolitical risk. Especially how such risk intersects with the impacts of climate change which are being inflicted on a world already stressed in various other ways.

IT IS US WHO NEED TO MASTER SUSTAINABILITY AND LEAD FROM THE FRONT

The organisational psychologist Adam Grant said in February 2022 on Twitter:

> Too many people spend their lives being dutiful descendants instead of good ancestors. The responsibility of each generation is not to please their predecessors. It is to improve things for their offspring. It is more important to make your children proud than your parents proud.

Sustainability, technology, and finance are leading to a profound transformation for corporations and investors. It is time to rethink how markets integrate ESG and how we can drive necessary changes in the real economy towards decarbonisation, a healthy planet, and a prosocial society that makes our children proud.

REFERENCES

Áelex (2021). *Examining the Impact of the Rules on Robo-Advisory Services in Nigeria.* Available at: www.aelex.com/examining-the-impact-of-the-rules-on-robo-advisory-services-in-nigeria/ (Accessed: 10 March 2022).

Aghion, P., Antonin, C., & Bunel, S. (2021). *The Power of Creative Destruction.* Cambridge, MA: Harvard University Press.

Ainger, J., & Arons, S. (2022). *Weapons Group Points to Ukraine to Shape ESG Rulebook.* Available at: www.bloomberg.com/news/articles/2022-02-28/weapons-group-points-to-ukraine-in-bid-to-shape-eu-s-esg-rules (Accessed: 10 March 2022).

Arabesque (2021). *Arabesque Introduces Autonomous Asset Management.* Available at: www.arabesque.com/2021/09/20/arabesque-introduces-autonomous-asset-management/ (Accessed: 10 March 2022).

Arthur, B. W. (2014). *Complexity and the Economy.* Oxford and New York: Oxford University Press.

Bhaskar, M. (2021). *Human Frontiers—The Future of Big Ideas in an Age of Small Thinking.* Cambridge, MA: MIT Press.

Blockworks (2022). *VCs Invested $33b in Crypto and Blockchain Startups in 2021.* Available at: https://blockworks.co/report-vcs-invested-33b-in-crypto-and-blockchain-startups-in-2021/ (Accessed: 10 March 2022).

Bril, H., Kell, G., & Rasche, A. (2021). *Sustainable Investing: A Path to a New Horizon.* London: Routledge.

Carney, M. (2015). *Breaking the Tragedy of the Horizon: Climate Change and Financial Stability.* Available at: www.bankofengland.co.uk/-/media/boe/files/speech/2015/breaking-the-tragedy-of-the-horizon-climate-change-and-financial-stability.pdf?la=en&hash=7C67E785651862457D99511147C7424FF5EA0C1A (Accessed: 10 March 2022).

Carney, M. (2021). *Value(s): Building a Better for All.* London: William Collins.

Ellen Macarthur Foundation (2022). *The Circular Economy in Detail.* Available at: https://archive.ellenmacarthurfoundation.org/explore/the-circular-economy-in-detail#:~:text=A%20circular%20economy%20is%20a,the%20consumption%20of%20finite%20resources (Accessed: 10 March 2022).

European Council (2022). *Council Adopts Its Position on the Corporate Sustainability Reporting Directive (CSRD).* Available at: www.consilium.europa.eu/en/press/press-releases/2022/02/24/council-adopts-position-on-the-corporate-sustainability-reporting-directive-csrd/?utm_source=LinkedIn.com&utm_campaign=2022-02-24-Corporate-Sustainability-Reporting-Directive&utm_content=carousel (Accessed: 10 March 2022).

Fagerberg, J., & Verspagen, B. (2020). Innovation—diffusion, the economy and contemporary challenges: A comment. *Industrial and Corporate Change*, 29(4), 1067–1073,

Federal Council Switzerland (2022). *Digital Finance: Areas of Action 2022+.* Available at: www.newsd.admin.ch/newsd/message/attachments/70126.pdf (Accessed: 10 March 2022).

Federal Reserve Bank of Boston (2022). *Project Hamilton Phase 1—A High-Performance Payment Processing System Designed for Central Bank Digital Currencies.* Available at: www.bostonfed.org/publications/one-time-pubs/project-hamilton-phase-1-executive-summary.aspx (Accessed: 10 March 2022).

Financial Stability Board (FSB) (2022). *Assessment of Risks to Financial Stability from Crypto-assets.* Available at: www.fsb.org/2022/02/assessment-of-risks-to-financial-stability-from-crypto-assets/ (Accessed: 10 March 2022).

Friedman, M. (1970/2007). The social responsibility of business is to increase its profits. In W. C. Zimmerli, M. Holzinger, & K. Richter (Eds.), *Corporate Ethics and Corporate Governance.* Berlin and Heidelberg: Springer, pp. 173–178.

Friedman, T. (2022). *The Cancellation of Mother Russia Is Underway.* Available at: www.nytimes.com/2022/03/06/opinion/putin-ukraine-china.html (Accessed: 10 March 2022).

Intergovernmental Panel on Climate Change (IPCC) (2022). *Sixth Assessment Report—Climate Change 2022: Impacts, Adaptation and Vulnerability.* Available at: www.ipcc.ch/report/ar6/wg2/ (Accessed: 10 March 2022).

International Energy Agency (2022). *Electricity Market Report: January 2022*. Available at: www.iea.org/events/electricity-market-report-january-2022 (Accessed: 10 March 2022).

International Finance Corporation (IFC), UN Global Compact, & Federal Department of Foreign Affairs Switzerland (2005). *Investing for Long-Term Value*. Available at: www.ifc.org/wps/wcm/connect/9d9bb80d-625d-49d5-baad-8e46a0445b12/WhoCaresWins_2005ConferenceReport.pdf?MOD=AJPERES&CVID=jkD172p (Accessed: 10 March 2022).

Jaeger, L. (2021). *Ways Out of the Climate Catastrophe: Ingredients for a Sustainable Energy and Climate Policy*. Heidelberg: Springer.

Janeway, W. H. (2018). *Doing Capitalism in the Innovation Economy*. Cambridge: Cambridge University Press.

Jevons, W. S. (1865/1906). *The Coal Question* (reprint of the third edition). New York, NY: Augustus, M. Kelley.

Kell, G. (2022). *War in Europe and Corporate Responsibility*. Available at: www.forbes.com/sites/georgkell/2022/03/08/war-in-europe-and-corporate-responsibility/?sh=41480a3920c2 (Accessed: 16 March 2022).

King, C. W. (2021). *The Economic Superorganism—Beyond the Competing Narratives on Energy, Growth, and Policy*. Cham: Springer.

Kolbe, P. R., Morrow, M. R., & Zabierek, L. (2022). *The Cybersecurity Risks of an Escalating Russia-Ukraine Conflict*. Available at: https://hbr.org/2022/02/the-cybersecurity-risks-of-an-escalating-russia-ukraine-conflict (Accessed: 16 March 2022).

Meadows, D. H., Meadows, D. L., Randers, J., & Behrens III, W. (1972). *The Limits to Growth*. Washington, DC: Potomac Associates.

Organization for Economic Co-operation and Development (OECD) (2020). *The Tokenisation of Assets and Potential Implications for Financial Markets*. Available at: www.oecd.org/finance/The-Tokenisation-of-Assets-and-Potential-Implications-for-Financial-Markets.htm (Accessed: 10 March 2022).

Pinker, S. (2018). *Enlightenment Now: The Case for Reason, Science, Humanism, and Progress*. London: Penguin.

Prasad, E. S. (2021). *The Future of Money—How the Digital Revolution Is Transforming Currencies and Finance*. Cambridge, MA: Harvard University Press.

Rocky Mountain Institute (RMI) (2022). *Biden's Executive Order on Blockchain for Climate Transparency: Here's How It Could Work*. https://rmi.org/bidens-executive-order-on-blockchain-for-climate-transparency/ (Accessed: 21 March 2022).

Ruggie, J. G. (2021). Corporate purpose in play: The role of ESG investing. In H. Bril, G. Kell, & A. Rasche (Eds.), *Sustainable Investing: A Path to a New Horizon*. London: Routledge, pp. 173–190.

Serafeim, G. (2021). ESG: Hyperboles and reality. *Harvard Business School Working Paper, No. 22-031*. Available at: www.hbs.edu/ris/Publication%20Files/22-031_b9b34057-062a-48a8-8950-61e0cf37559a.pdf (Accessed: 10 March 2022).

Singh, R., Gehlot, A., Akram, S. V., Gupta, L. R., Jena, M. K., Prakash, C., Singh, S., & Kumar, R. (2021). Cloud manufacturing, internet of things-assisted manufacturing, and 3D printing technology: Reliable tools for sustainable Construction. *Sustainability*, 13(13), Article: 7327.

Smil, V. (2021). *Grand Transitions—How the Modern World Was Made*. Oxford and New York: Oxford University Press.

Statistic Times (2021). *World Population*. Available at: https://statisticstimes.com/demographics/world-population.php (Accessed: 10 March 2022).

World Economic Forum (2022). *The Global Risks Report 2022* (17th edition). Available at: www.weforum.org/reports/global-risks-report-2022 (Accessed: 16 March 2022).

Ye, J. (2021). *Using Digitalization to Achieve Decarbonization Goals*. Available at: www.c2es.org/document/using-digitalization-to-achieve-decarbonization-goals/ (Accessed: 10 March 2022).

Index

Printed in the United States
by Baker & Taylor Publisher Services